The Collected Courses of the Academy of European Law

Series Editors: Professor Loïc Azoulai,
Professor Nehal Bhuta,
Professor Marise Cremona
European University Institute, Florence
Assistant Editor: Anny Bremner
European University Institute, Florence

VOLUME XXV/1
The Internal
Market as a
Legal Concept

The Collected Courses of the Academy of European Law
Edited by Professor Loïc Azoulai,
Professor Nehal Bhuta, and Professor Marise Cremona
Assistant Editor: Anny Bremner

Each year the Academy of European Law in Florence, Italy, invites
a group of outstanding lecturers to teach at its summer courses on
Human Rights law and the European Union law.
A 'general course' is given in each of the two fields by a
distinguished scholar or practitioner, who examines the field as a
whole through a particular thematic, conceptual, or philosophical
lens, or looks at a theme in the context of the overall body of law.
In addition, a series of 'specialized courses' brings together a group
of highly qualified scholars to explore and analyse a specific theme
in relation to Human Rights law and EU law.
The Academy's mission, to produce scholarly analyses which are
at the cutting edge of the two fields, is achieved through the
publication of this series, the Collected Courses of the
Academy of European Law.

The Internal Market as a Legal Concept

STEPHEN WEATHERILL

Jacques Delors Professor of European Law at the University of Oxford, and Fellow of Somerville College

OXFORD
UNIVERSITY PRESS

OXFORD

UNIVERSITY PRESS

Great Clarendon Street, Oxford, OX2 6DP,
United Kingdom

Oxford University Press is a department of the University of Oxford.
It furthers the University's objective of excellence in research, scholarship,
and education by publishing worldwide. Oxford is a registered trade mark of
Oxford University Press in the UK and in certain other countries

Published in the United States of America by Oxford University Press
198 Madison Avenue, New York, NY 10016, United States of America

British Library Cataloguing in Publication Data
Data available

Library of Congress Control Number: 2016953027

ISBN 978-0-19-879480-6 (Hbk.)
978-0-19-879481-3 (Pbk.)

Printed and bound by
CPI Group (UK) Ltd, Croydon, CR0 4YY

Preface

The origins of this book lie in the classes that I taught at the European University Institute in Florence on the summer course on EU law in late June 2014. I am immensely grateful to all the students who participated on the course for their input and feedback, which helped me to clarify in my own mind the shape of the story I wanted to tell in this book about the EU's internal market.

The thematic insight that animates this book is that the EU's internal market is a legal concept that has important implications for the shaping of both the vertical relationship between the competences of the EU and those of its Member States and the horizontal relationship between the powers of the EU's judicial institution, its Court and the EU's political/legislative institutions. But crucially the internal market as a legal concept is an ambiguous legal concept. The Treaty leaves open vitally important questions about its proper shape and development – the Treaty does not define with any precision how deep shall be the cut of EU law into national regulatory autonomy nor does it set out clearly the precise distribution of powers between the judicial and the legislative routes to market-making. Quite how intensely regulated shall be the internal market is similarly left open by the Treaty. This ambiguity generates dynamism – the meaning in practice of the EU's internal market depends heavily on the expression of political preferences through Treaty revision and legislative activity and on the Court's interpretative choices. These have not remained static over time. Moreover, there is space for comparative reflection. The EU has an internal market, but so does Germany and the UK and Australia and the USA. None is exactly the same – they vary because of different choices made over time about the balance between deregulation and re-regulation.

In short the EU's internal market does not possess a precise economic or legal definition or design – rather, it is a political construct that has evolved incrementally over time, and which continues to do so. It is the purpose of this book to trace how and why guiding choices about the interpretation and application of legal rules have contributed to that process of evolution.

The law is as stated at 15 March 2016.

That cut-off date means that this book does not consider 'Brexit', the process unleashed by the UK's referendum held on 23 June 2016. This book is not about 'Brexit' – and at this stage there is in any event little that could usefully be said about Brexit, so calculatedly obscure are its contours. However, the book's treatment of the law governing the EU's internal market shows that one of the claims commonly made by Brexiteers, that the internal market can be confined merely to a deregulatory exercise in free market economics, has no support whatsoever in either EU constitutional law or in EU legislative and judicial practice. The internal market is a contested legal concept, but although deregulation is certainly part of its DNA – reducing 28 diverse patterns of legal regulation is a necessary process of deregulation – so too is re-regulation, in the sense that the space cleared by suppressing 28 diverse rules is typically (though not inevitably) then occupied by the EU's own chosen rule. The internal market is a process, rather than an event.

Contents

Table of Cases   xi
Table of Legislation   xxiii

1. **The Internal Market as a Legal Concept**   1
   A. The 'Internal Market' as an Ambiguous Legal Concept   1

2. **Finding the Internal Market in the Treaty**   3
   A. The Concept of the 'Internal Market' Empowers the
      EU – but Not Without Limits   3
   B. Control and Testing – Negative Law   5
   C. EU Legislative Action – Positive Law   10
   D. The Decorative   13

3. **The Law, Politics and Economics of the Internal Market**   15
   A. The Treaty of Rome   15
   B. The Single European Act and the Political Bargain   16
   C. The Treaty of Lisbon and the Political Bargain   19
   D. The Economics of the Internal Market   21
   E. The Internal Market beyond Economics Alone   24

4. **Principal Themes and Structure**   27

5. **The Internal *Market***   33
   A. The Breadth of the Market as a Legal Concept   33
   B. The Limits of the 'Market'   39
   C. The Internal Market as a Concept Which Takes the Scope of
      Negative Law beyond That of Positive Law   43

6. **The *Internal* Market**   49
   A. Limits, What Limits?   49
      1. Early Years, Easy Years   50
      2. *Dassonville*   51
      3. *Cassis de Dijon*   53
      4. Competition Law   57
   B. Where Do the Limits Lie?   60
   C. Mis-steps and Re-sets   65
      1. *Sunday Trading*   66
      2. The Readjustments   68
      3. Services   70
      4. Adjusting the Readjustment   71
      5. Restrictions on Use   74
      6. Concluding Comments   76

D. People and Citizens   76
    1. Remoteness   76
    2. People and Families   78
    3. Citizenship Too   81
E. State Aid   84
    1. Aid Must Be Granted 'Granted Directly or Indirectly
        Through State Resources'   86
    2. Selectivity   88
    3. Making Connections and Re-Shaping Lines   89
F. Conclusion: The Limits of the *Internal* Market   90

7. **The Personal Scope**   95

8. **Justification**   99
    A. Structure   99
    B. Principles   100
    C. Breadth   103
        1. Breadth – Free Movement Law   103
        2. Breadth – Competition Law   106
    D. Public Health   109
    E. Environmental Protection   112
    F. Protection of the Economic Interests of Consumers   115

9. **Creativity in the Gap between Negative and Positive Law:**
    The Principle of Conferral Unleashed   123
    A. Sport as a Case Study   124
    B. Collective Labour Action as a Case Study   125
    C. Justification and Sensitivity   128

10. **Abuse**   131

11. **Fundamental Rights and National Identity in the Internal Market**   135
    A. Early Years, Early Cases   136
    B. *Schmidberger* and *Omega*   137
    C. National Identity   139

12. **The Internal Market as a Site of Diversity**   143

13. **The Legislative Dimension: Harmonization**   151
    A. The Nature and Purpose of Harmonization   151
    B. Article 114 – an Instrument of Re-regulation   153
    C. Constitutional Commitments to Re-regulation   155
    D. Judicial Review and Re-regulation   156
        1. Judicial Review of Inadequate Standards   156
        2. Judicial Review of Over-regulation   157
        3. Judicial Interpretation of the Harmonized Legislative Acquis   160
    E. The Permissibility of Prohibition   162
    F. Legislative Practice and Re-regulation   163

G. The Limits of Harmonization   •   166
   1. The Slow Road to Emergence of 'Competence Sensitivity'   166
   2. The Single European Act and *Tobacco Advertising I*   168
   3. The Subsequent Case Law   170
   4. Limits, What Limits?   173
H. Subsidiarity and Proportionality   175
   1. Subsidiarity   176
   2. Proportionality   178
   3. Political Controls   179

14. **Legislative Competence More Broadly**   **187**
A. The Wide Sweep   187
B. Labour Market Regulation and Social Policy   189
   1. *Defrenne*   190
   2. Policy Choices   191
   3. From the Treaty of Rome to the Single European Act   194
   4. From the Single European Act via Maastricht to the Treaty of Amsterdam   196
   5. The Lisbon Strategy and Europe 2020   198
C. EU Social Policy Today   200
   1. Spontaneous Alignment   201
   2. Legislation on Social Policy   201
   3. Approximation/Harmonization   203
D. Social Policy – the Current Debate   204
E. Social Policy – the Continuing Debate   207

15. **Pre-emption**   **209**
A. The Directions Contained in the Treaty   209
B. Legislative Practice   211
C. The Sources of Pressure on the Model of Minimum
   Harmonization   212
   1. The Court of Justice   212
   2. The Commission's Attack on 'Minimum Harmonization'   215
D. Normative Perspectives on the Choice between Models
   of Harmonization   219

16. **Conclusion**   **223**
A. Ambiguity and Limits   223
B. Limits and Lines   225
C. Lines and Choices   227
D. Choices and Empowerment   229
E. Empowerment and Ambiguity   232

Index   235

Table of Cases

Adoui and Cornuaille (Cases 115/81 and 116/81) [1982] ECR 1665
(ECLI:EU:C:1982:183) 101
Adria-Wien Pipeline GmbH (Case C-143/99) [2001] ECR I-8365
(ECLI:EU:C:2001:598) 85, 88
AG2R Prévoyance (Case C-437/09) [2011] ECR I-973 (ECLI:EU:C:2011:112) 37
Ahokainen and Leppik (Case C-434/04) [2006] ECR I-9171
(ECLI:EU:C:2006:609) 102, 110
Air Liquide Industries Belgium SA (Joined Cases C-393/04 and C-41/05)
[2006] ECR I-5293 (ECLI:EU:C:2006:403) 88
Aklagaren v. Mickelsson, Roos (Case C-142/05) [2009] ECR I-4273
(ECLI:EU:C:2009:336) 74, 174
Ålands Vinkraft AB (Case C-573/12) judgment of 1 July 2014, not yet
reported (ECLI:EU:C:2014:2037) 97, 113
Albany International (Case C-67/96) [1999] ECR I-5751
(ECLI:EU:C:1999:430) 42, 43, 108, 128
Alemo-Herron (Case C-426/11) judgment of 18 July 2013, not yet reported
(ECLI:EU:C:2013:521) 205, 206, 207,
214, 215
Alfa Vita (Cases C-158/04 and C-159/04) [2006] ECR I-8135
(ECLI:EU:C:2006:562) 92
Alliance for Natural Health (Cases C-154/04 and C-155/04) [2005] ECR I-6451
(ECLI:EU:C:2005:449) 158, 162,
172, 178–9
Alokpa (Case C-86/12) judgment of 10 October 2013, not yet reported
(ECLI:EU:C:2013:645) 83
Alpine Investments (Case C-384/93) [1995] ECR I-1141
(ECLI:EU:C:1995:126) 61
Alsthom Atlantique (Case C-339/89) [1991] ECR I-107 (ECLI:EU:C:1991:28) 68
Andrea Raccanelli (Case C-94/07) [2008] ECR I-5939 (ECLI:EU:C:2008:425). 96
ANETT (Case C-456/10) judgment of 26 April 2012, not yet reported
(ECLI:EU:C:2012:241) 54, 103
Angonese (Case C-281/98) [2000] ECR I-4139 (ECLI:EU:C:2000:296) 96
Anton Las (Case C-202/11) judgment of 16 April 2013, not yet reported
(ECLI:EU:C:2013:239) 140
Antonissen (Case C-292/89) [1991] ECR 745 (ECLI:EU:C:1991:80) 41
AOK-Bundesverband and Others (Joined Cases C-264/01, C-306/01,
C-354/01 and C-355/01) [2004] ECR I-2493 (ECLI:EU:C:2004:150) 36
A-Punkt Schmuckhandels GmbH v. Claudia Schmidt (Case C-441/04)
[2006] ECR I-2093 (ECLI:EU:C:2006:141) 73, 119, 120, 213
Aragonesa de Publicidad Exterior (Joined Cases C-1 and 176/90) [1991]
ECR I-4151 (ECLI:EU:C:1991:327) 114, 158
Árpád Kásler (Case C-26/13) judgment of 30 April 2014, not yet reported
(ECLI:EU:C:2014:282) 160, 161
Ascafor (Case C-484/10) judgment of 1 March 2012, not yet reported
(ECLI:EU:C:2012:113) 54
Association de médiation sociale (Case C-176/12) judgment of 15 January 2014,
not yet reported (ECLI:EU:C:2014:2) 203

Association des Centres distributeurs Édouard Leclerc et al. v. SARL 'Au Blé Vert' et al.
(Case 229/83) [1985] ECR 1 (ECLI:EU:C:1985:1) 131, 132
Association Vent de Colere! (Case C-262/12) judgment of 19 December 2013,
not yet reported (ECLI:EU:C:2013:851) 87
ATRAL SA (Case C-14/02) [2003] ECR I-4431 (ECLI:EU:C:2003:265) 100
Aziz (Case C-415/11) judgment of 14 March 2013, not yet reported
(ECLI:EU:C:2013:164) 160

Bacardi v. TF1 (Case C-429/02) [2004] ECR I-6613 (ECLI:EU:C:2004:432) 111
Banco Español de Crédito v. Joaquín Calderón Camino (Case C-618/10)
judgment of 14 June 2012, not yet reported (ECLI:EU:C:2012:349) 160
Banif Plus Bank (C-472/11) judgment of 21 February 2013, not yet reported
(ECLI:EU:C:2013:88) 160
Baumbast (Case C-413/99) [2002] ECR I-7091 (ECLI:EU:C:2002:493) 7
Berlington Hungary and Others (Case C-98/14) judgment of 11 June 2015,
not yet reported (ECLI:EU:C:2015:386) 61, 71, 73, 105,
106, 135
Bickel and Franz (Case C-274/96) [1998] ECR I-7637 (ECLI:EU:C:1998:563).............. 35
Birute Ŝiba (Case C-537/13) judgment of 15 January 2015, not yet reported
(ECLI:EU:C:2015:14) 160
Blanco, Fabretti (Joined Cases C-344/13, C-367/13) judgment of 22 October 2014,
not yet reported (ECLI:EU:C:2014:2311) 114
Blanco Perez and Chao Gomez (Joined Cases C-570/07 and C-571/07) [2010]
ECR I-4629 (ECLI:EU:C:2010:300) 62
Blesgen v. Belgium (Case 75/81) [1982] ECR 1211 (ECLI:EU:C:1982:117) 68
Bonnarde (Case C-443/10) [2011] ECR I-9327 (ECLI:EU:C:2011:641).................... 91
Bosman (Case C-415/93) [1995] ECR I-4921 (ECLI:EU:C:1995:463) 45, 47, 61, 92,
104, 124, 125, 147
Buet (Case 382/87) [1989] ECR 1235 (ECLI:EU:C:1989:198) 118, 120, 211, 213
Burmanjer et al., (Case C-20/03) [2005] ECR I-4133 (ECLI:EU:C:2005:307)................ 73

Cadbury Schweppes plc, Cadbury Schweppes Overseas Ltd v. Commissioners of
Inland Revenue (Case C-196/04) [2006] ECR I-7995 (ECLI:EU:C:2006:544) 133
CaixaBank France (C-442/02) [2004] ECR I-8961 (ECLI:EU:C:2004:586); Opinion
(ECLI:EU:C:2004:187) 64, 78, 90
Calfa (Case C-348/96) [1999] ECR I-11 (ECLI:EU:C:1999:6) 35
Camar Srl (Case C-102/09) [2010] ECR I-4045 (ECLI:EU:C:2010:236)................... 25
Campus Oil (Case 72/83) [1984] ECR 2727 (ECLI:EU:C:1984:256) 101
Canal Satelite Digital (Case C-390/99) [2002] ECR I-607 (ECLI:EU:C:2002:34) 63, 72
Cassis de Dijon *see* Rewe-Zentrale AG v. Bundesmonopolverwaltung für Branntwein (Case 120/78)
Centros (Case C-212/97) [1999] ECR I-1459 (ECLI:EU:C:1999:126) 132, 144, 152, 192
CGT (Case C-385/05) [2007] ECR I-611 (ECLI:EU:C:2007:37) 196
CHS Tour Services (Case C-435/11) judgment of 19 September 2013, not yet reported
(ECLI:EU:C:2013:574) 161
CIA Security International v. Signalson & Securitel (Case C-194/94) [1996] ECR I-2201
(ECLI:EU:C:1996:172) 6, 147
Citroën Belux (Case C-265/12) judgment of 18 July 2013, not yet reported
(ECLI:EU:C:2013:498) 120, 121
CMC Motorradcenter (Case C-93/92) [1993] ECR I-5009 (ECLI:EU:C:1993:838) 68
Commercial Solvents (Joined Cases 6/73 and 7/73) [1974] ECR 223 59
Commission v. Austria (Case C-28/09) judgment of 21 December 2011,
not yet reported (ECLI:EU:C:2011:854) 106, 113–14
Commission v. Belgium (Case C-2/90) [1992] ECR I-4431
(ECLI:EU:C:1992:310) 34, 112, 114, 188

Commission v. Council (Case 45/86) [1987] ECR 1493 (ECLI:EU:C:1987:163)..............13
Commission v. Denmark (Case 302/86) [1988] ECR 4607
    (ECLI:EU:C:1988:421)....................................104, 112, 188
Commission v. Denmark (Case C-192/01) [2003] ECR I-9693
    (ECLI:EU:C:2003:492)...111
Commission v. France (Case 168/78) [1980] ECR 347 (ECLI:EU:C:1980:51)................6
Commission v. France (Case 188/84) [1986] ECR I-419 (ECLI:EU:C:1986:43) 111
Commission v. France (Case C-154/89) [1991] ECR I-659
    (ECLI:EU:C:1991:76).. 22–3, 55,
    57, 116
Commission v. France (Case C-265/95) [1997] ECR I-6959 (ECLI:EU:C:1997:595) 44, 138
Commission v. France (Case C-184/96) [1998] ECR I-6197 (ECLI:EU:C:1998:495) 61, 147
Commission v. France (Case C-24/00) [2004] ECR I-1277 (ECLI:EU:C:2004:70) 147
Commission v. France (Case C-262/02) [2004] ECR I-6569 (ECLI:EU:C:2004:431) 111, 158
Commission v. France (Case C-333/08) [2010] ECR I-757 (ECLI:EU:C:2010:44) 111
Commission v. Germany (Case 178/84) [1987] ECR 1227
    (ECLI:EU:C:1987:126).. 23, 56, 57,
    115, 118
Commission v. Germany (Case C-103/01) [2003] ECR I-5369 (ECLI:EU:C:2003:301) 178
Commission v. Germany (Case C-271/08) Opinion (ECLI:EU:C:2010:183)................128
Commission v. Greece (Case 192/84) [1985] ECR 3967 (ECLI:EU:C:1985:497)..............51
Commission v. Ireland (Case 249/81) [1982] ECR 4005 (ECLI:EU:C:1982:402) 97
Commission v. Ireland (Case C-272/12 P) judgment of 10 December 2013,
    not yet reported (ECLI:EU:C:2013:812) 85, 193
Commission v. Italy (Case 7/61) [1961] ECR 317 (ECLI:EU:C:1961:31) 33, 50, 104
Commission v. Italy (Case 7/68) [1968] ECR 423 (ECLI:EU:C:1968:51) 5
Commission v. Italy (Case 91/79) [1980] ECR 1099 (ECLI:EU:C:1980:85) 167, 189
Commission v. Italy (Case C-113/80) [1981] ECR 1625 (ECLI:EU:C:1981:139) 114
Commission v. Italy (Case C-110/05) [2009] ECR I-519 (ECLI:EU:C:2009:66) 54, 74
Commission v. Italy (Case C-561/07) [2009] ECR I-4959 (ECLI:EU:C:2009:363) 196
Commission v. Italy (Case C-565/08) [2011] ECR I-2101 (ECLI:EU:C:2011:188) 65
Commission v. MOL Magyar (Case C-15/14 P) judgment of 4 June 2015,
    not yet reported (ECLI:EU:C:2015:362) 88
Commission v. Portugal (Case C-55/02) [2004] ECR I-9387 (ECLI:EU:C:2004:605) 196
Commission v. Portugal (Case C-265/06) [2008] ECR I-2245 (ECLI:EU:C:2008:210) 109
Commission v. Portugal (Case C-255/09) [2011] ECR I-10547 (ECLI:EU:C:2011:695) 44
Commission v. Spain (Case C-358/01) [2003] ECR I-13145 (ECLI:EU:C:2003:599) 116
Commission v. Spain (Case C-211/08) [2010] ECR I-5267 (ECLI:EU:C:2010:340) 77
Commission v. United Kingdom (Case 170/78) [1980] ECR 417 (ECLI:EU:C:1980:53)........23
Commission v. United Kingdom (Case 40/82) [1982] ECR 2793 (ECLI:EU:C:1982:285)......109
Commission v. United Kingdom (Case 170/78) [1983] ECR 2265 (ECLI:EU:C:1983:202).......6
Commission v. United Kingdom (Case 60/86) [1988] ECR 3921 (ECLI:EU:C:1988:382)......211
Commission v. United Kingdom (Case C-382/92) [1994] ECR I-2435
    (ECLI:EU:C:1994:233)...195
Commission and Spain v. Government of Gibraltar and United Kingdom (Cases C-106/09
    P and C-107/09 P) [2011] ECR I-11113 (ECLI:EU:C:2011:732) 85, 88
Competition Authority v. Beef Industry Development Society Ltd
    (Case C-209/07) [2008] ECR I-8637 (ECLI:EU:C:2008:643).......................24
Conegate (Case 121/85) [1986] ECR 1007 (ECLI:EU:C:1986:114) 101
Consiglio nazionale dei geologi (Case C-136/12) judgment of 18 July 2013,
    not yet reported (ECLI:EU:C:2013:489) 108
Consten and Grundig (Joined Cases 56/64 and 58/64) [1966] ECR 429
    (ECLI:EU:C:1966:41)..58, 59, 60
Continental Can v. Commission (Case 6/72) [1973] ECR 215 (ECLI:EU:C:1973:22)...........7

Cooperative Stremsel-en Kleurselfabriek v. Commission (Case 61/80) [1981] ECR 851
 (ECLI:EU:C:1981:75) 58, 59
Corporación Dermoestética SA (Case C-500/06) [2008] ECR I-5785
 (ECLI:EU:C:2008:421) 116
Costa v. ENEL (Case 6/64) [1964] ECR 585 (ECLI:EU:C:1964:66) 31, 52
Cowan v. Le Tresor Public (Case 186/87) [1989] ECR 195 (ECLI:EU:C:1989:47) 35

Danner (Case C-136/00) [2002] ECR I-8147 (ECLI:EU:C:2002:558) 114
Dassonville (Case 8/74) [1974] ECR 837 (ECLI:EU:C:1974:82) 52, 53, 54, 55, 58, 59, 60,
 61, 63, 64, 65, 67, 69, 70, 85, 97, 104, 113, 114,
 144, 225, 226
de Groot (Case C-147/04) [2006] ECR I-245 (ECLI:EU:C:2006:7). 116
Defrenne v. SABENA (Case C-43/75) [1976] ECR 455 (ECLI:EU:C:1976:56) 25, 190, 191,
 192, 193, 194, 195, 197, 200, 204
Demirkan (Case C-221/11) judgment of 24 September 2013, not yet reported
 (ECLI:EU:C:2013:583). 24, 25
Denise McDonough v. Ryanair Ltd (Case C-12/11) judgment of 31 January 2013,
 not yet reported (ECLI:EU:C:2013:43) 159
Dereci (Case C-256/11) [2011] ECR I-11315 (ECLI:EU:C:2011:734) 83, 131, 227, 229
Deserbais (Case 286/86) [1988] ECR 4907 (ECLI:EU:C:1988:434) 116
Deutsche Grammophon v. Metro (Case 78/70) [1971] ECR 487 (ECLI:EU:C:1971:59) 22, 28
Deutsche Paracelsus Schulen (Case C-294/00) [2002] ECR I-6515 (ECLI:EU:C:2002:442) 102
Deutsche Post AG v. Sievers, Schrage (Cases C-270/97 and 271/97) [2000] ECR I-929
 (ECLI:EU:C:2000:76) 191
Deutsche Telekom AG v. Schröder (Case C-50/96) [2000] ECR I-743
 (ECLI:EU:C:2000:72) 191
Deutsches Weintor eG v. Land Rheinland-Pfalz (Case C-544/10) judgment of
 6 September 2012, not yet reported (ECLI:EU:C:2012:526) 158, 159, 206, 215
Digibet (Case C-156/13) judgment of 12 June 2014, not yet reported
 (ECLI:EU:C:2014:1756) 141
Digital Rights Ireland et al., (Joined Cases C-293/12 and C-594/12) judgment of
 8 April 2014, not yet reported (ECLI:EU:C:2014:238). 159
Ditlev Bluhme (Case C-67/97) [1998] ECR I-8033 (ECLI:EU:C:1998:584) 34, 72, 104
DKV Belgium (Case C-577/11) judgment of 7 March 2013, not yet reported
 (ECLI:EU:C:2013:146) 63, 120
DocMorris (Case C-322/01) [2003] ECR I-14887 (ECLI:EU:C:2003:664) 213
Douwe Egberts (Case C-239/02) [2004] ECR I-7007 (ECLI:EU:C:2004:445). 73
Drei Glocken v. USL Centro-Sud (Case 407/85) [1988] ECR 4233
 (ECLI:EU:C:1988:401) 118, 146
Dynamic Medien (Case C-244/06) [2008] ECR I-505 (ECLI:EU:C:2008:85) 72, 102,
 104, 106

Eco Swiss China Time Ltd v. Benetton International NV (Case C-126/97) [1999]
 ECR I-3055 (ECLI:EU:C:1999:269) 7
Einberger v. Hauptzollamt Freiburg (Case 294/82) [1984] ECR 1177 (ECLI:EU:C:1984:81). 40
Eind (Case C-291/05) [2007] ECR I-10719 (ECLI:EU:C:2007:771). 79
Elenca Srl (Case C-385/10) judgment of 18 October 2012, not yet reported
 (ECLI:EU:C:2012:634) 54
Elisabeta Dano (Case C-333/13) judgment of 11 November 2014, not yet reported
 (ECLI:EU:C:2014:2358) 41, 42
Enirisorse SpA (Case C-237/04) [2006] ECR I-2843 (ECLI:EU:C:2006:197), Opinion
 (ECLI:EU:C:2006:21) 89, 90
Eric Libert (Joined Cases C-197/11 and C-203/11) judgment of 8 May 2013,
 not yet reported (ECLI:EU:C:2013:288) 61, 117

ERT v. Dimotiki (Case C-260/89) [1991] ECR I-2925 (ECLI:EU:C:1991:254) 136
Essent (Joined Cases C-105/12 to C-107/12) judgment of 22 October 2013, not yet reported
    (ECLI:EU:C:2013:677) 47, 121
Essent Belgium (Joined Cases C-204/12 to C-208/12) judgment of 11 September 2014,
    not yet reported (ECLI:EU:C:2014:2192) 113, 114
Estee Lauder Cosmetics (Case C-220/98) [2000] ECR I-117 (ECLI:EU:C:2000:8) 119
European Air Transport SA (Case C-120/10) judgment of 8 September 2011,
    not yet reported (ECLI:EU:C:2011:556) 221
Eventech (Case C-518/13) judgment of 14 January 2015, not yet reported
    (ECLI:EU:C:2015:9) 88
Eyssen (Case 53/80) [1981] ECR 409 (ECLI:EU:C:1981:35) 110, 118, 139

FA Premier League et al. v. QC Leisure et al., Karen Murphy v. Media Protection
    Services Ltd (Joined Cases C-403/08 and C-429/08) [2011] ECR I-9083
    (ECLI:EU:C:2011:631) 21–2, 24, 101
Fachverband/ LIBRO (Case C-531/07) [2009] ECRI-3717 (ECLI:EU:C:2009:276) 104
FENIN v. Commission (Case C-205/03 P) [2006] ECR I-6295 (ECLI:EU:C:2006:453) 36
Festersen (Case C-370/05) [2007] ECR I-1129 (ECLI:EU:C:2007:59) .117
Firma Ambulanz Glöckner v. Landkreis Sudwestpfalz (Case C-475/99) [2001]
    ECR I-8089 (ECLI:EU:C:2001:577) 36, 107
FNV Kunsten Informatie en Media v. Staat der Nederlanden (Case C-413/13)
    judgment of 4 December 2014, not yet reported (ECLI:EU:C:2014:2411) 43
Fra.bo SpA (Case C-171/11) judgment of 12 July 2012, not yet reported
    (ECLI:EU:C:2012:453) 97
Fransson (Case C-617/10) judgment of 26 February 2013, not yet reported
    (ECLI:EU:C:2013:280) 105, 135, 156
Friedrich Barth (Case C-542/08) [2010] ECR I-3189 (ECLI:EU:C:2010:193) 77
Froujke Faber (Case C-497/13) judgment of 4 June 2015, not yet reported
    (ECLI:EU:C:2015:357) 161

Gambelli and Others (Case C-243/01) [2003] ECR I-13031 (ECLI:EU:C:2003:597) 105
Garcia Avello (Case C-148/02) [2003] ECR I-11613 (ECLI:EU:C:2003:539) 80, 81
Garkalns (Case C-470/11) judgment of 19 July 2012, not yet reported
    (ECLI:EU:C:2012:505) 61
Gaston Schul (Case 15/81) [1982] ECR 1409 (ECLI:EU:C:1982:135) 28
Gauweiler (Case C-62/14) judgment of 16 June 2015, not yet reported (ECLI:EU:C:2015:7) 141
Gebhard (Case C-55/94) [1995] ECR I-4165 (ECLI:EU:C:1995:411). 62, 64
Geddo v. Ente (Case 2/73) [1973] ECR 865 (ECLI:EU:C:1973:89) 52
Germany v. Parliament and Council (Case C-233/94) [1997] ECR I-2405
    (ECLI:EU:C:1997:231) 157
Germany v. Parliament and Council (Tobacco Advertising I) (Case C-376/98)
    [2000] ECR I-8419 (ECLI:EU:C:2000:544) 168–70, 171, 174, 175, 212, 213,
                                                                                                        214, 226, 228, 232
Germany v. Parliament and Council (Tobacco Advertising II)
    (Case C-380/03) [2006] ECR I-11573 (ECLI:EU:C:2006:772) 170, 193, 212
Gianni Bettati v. Safety Hi-Tech (Case C-341/95) [1998] ECR I-4355
    (ECLI:EU:C:1998:353) 157
GintecInternational (Case C-374/05) [2007] ECRI-9517 (ECLI:EU:C:2007:654) 211
Grunkin, Paul (Case C-353/06) [2008] ECR I-7639 (ECLI:EU:C:2008:559) 81
Grupo Itelevelesa (Case C-168/14) judgment of 15 October 2015, not yet reported
    (ECLI:EU:C:2015:685) 61
Guarnieri (Case C-291/09) [2011] ECR 2685 (ECLI:EU:C:2011:217) 68
Günter Fuß v. Stadt Halle (Case C-429/09) [2010] ECR I-12167
    (ECLI:EU:C:2010:717) 197

Halifax plc, Leeds Permanent Development Services Ltd, County Wide Property
    Investments Ltd v. Commissioners of Customs & Excise (Case C-255/02) [2006]
    ECR I-1609 (ECLI:EU:C:2006:121)..133
Hans Moser v. Land Baden-Württemberg (Case 180/83) [1984] ECR 2539
    (ECLI:EU:C:1984:233).. 50, 60, 76,
                                                                          78, 81
Harry Franzén (Case C-189/95) [1997] ECR I-2471 (ECLI:EU:C:1997:504)..............101
Henn and Darby (Case 34/79) [1979] ECR 3795 (ECLI:EU:C:1979:295)............51, 62, 92
Herbert Karner GmbH v. Troostwijk GmbH (Case C-71/02) [2004] ECR I-3025
    (ECLI:EU:C:2004:181)..137, 213
Herbert Schaible (Case C-101/12) judgment of 17 October 2013, not yet reported
    (ECLI:EU:C:2013:661)..159
Herbert Schwarz (Case C-76/05) [2007] ECR I-6849 (ECLI:EU:C:2007:492)................35
Höfner and Elser (Case C-41/90) [1991] ECR I-1979 (ECLI:EU:C:1991:161)...........36, 116
Horvath (Case 50/80) [1981] ECR 385 (ECLI:EU:C:1981:34)..........................40
Humanplasma GmbH v. Austria (Case C-421/09) judgment of 9 December 2010,
    not yet reported (ECLI:EU:C:2010:760).......................................110
Humbel (Case 263/86) [1988] ECR 5365 (ECLI:EU:C:1988:451).......................35

Iida (Case C-40/11) judgment of 8 November 2012, not yet reported
    (ECLI:EU:C:2012:691)..77, 83
Ilonka Sayn-Wittgenstein v. Landeshauptmann von Wien (Case C-208/09)
    [2010] ECR I-13693 (ECLI:EU:C:2010:806)......................... 80, 139, 140,
                                                                      141, 174
International Fruit Company (Cases 51-54/71) [1971] ECR 1107
    (ECLI:EU:C:1971:128)..51
International Stem Cell Corporation (Case C-364/13) judgment of 18 December 2014,
    not yet reported (ECLI:EU:C:2014:2451).......................................165
International Transport Workers' Federation v. Viking Line ABP (Case C-438/05)
    [2007] ECR I-10779 (ECLI:EU:C:2007:772)..............25, 47, 96, 104, 125, 126, 127,
                                                          128, 129, 147, 148, 190, 192,
                                                          202, 205, 206, 229
Inuit Tapiriit Kanatami et al. v. Commission (Case T-526/10) judgment of
    25 April 2013, not yet reported (ECLI:EU:T:2013:215)..........................162
Ireland v. Commission (Case T-50/06) judgment of 21 March 2012, not yet reported
    (ECLI:EU:T:2012:134)..85, 193
Ireland v. Parliament and Council (Case C-301/06) [2009] ECR I-593
    (ECLI:EU:C:2009:68)..159

J E J Blankaert (Case C-512/03) [2005] ECR I-7685 (ECLI:EU:C:2005:516)................44
Jean-Claude Van Hove (Case C-96/14) judgment of 23 April 2015, not yet reported
    (ECLI:EU:C:2015:262)..160
Jobcenter Berlin Neukölln v. Alimanovic (Case C-67/14) Opinion of 26 March 2015
    (ECLI:EU:C:2015:210)..41
John Greenham (Case C-95/01) [2004] ECR I-1333 (ECLI:EU:C:2004:71)...............111
Jundt (Case C-281/06) [2007] ECR I-12231 (ECLI:EU:C:2007:816).....................34
Jyske Bank (Case C-212/11) judgment of 25 April 2013, not yet reported
    (ECLI:EU:C:2013:270)..213

Katia Beckmann (Case C-164/00) [2002] ECR I-4893 (ECLI:EU:C:2002:330)..............196
Keck and Mithouard (Cases C-267/91 and C-268/91) [1993] ECR I-6097
    (ECLI:EU:C:1993:905)............ 68, 69, 70, 71, 72, 73, 75, 77, 78, 86, 90, 92, 100, 119,
                                                                      226, 227, 232
Kempf (Case C-139/85) [1986] ECR 1741 (ECLI:EU:C:1986:223)........................34

Kernkraftwerke Lippe-Ems GmbH (Case C-5/14) judgment of 4 June 2015,
    not yet reported (ECLI:EU:C:2015:354) 85
Ker-Optika (Case C-108/09) [2010] ECR I-12213 (ECLI:EU:C:2010:725) 54, 91
Kirsammer-Hack v. Hurhan Sidal (Case C-189/91) [1993] ECR I-6185
    (ECLI:EU:C:1993:907)...86
Klas Rosengren (Case C-170/04) [2007] ECR I-4071 (ECLI:EU:C:2007:313)........102, 109, 110
Kohll (Case 158/96) [1998] ECR I-1931 (ECLI:EU:C:1998:171) 105
Konsumentombudsmannen v. De Agostini Forlag AB and TV-Shop i Sverige AB (Joined
    Cases C-34/95, C-35/95 and C-36/95) [1997] ECR I-3843 (ECLI:EU:C:1997:344).......72
Konsumentombudsmannen v. Gourmet International Products (Case C-405/98)
    [2001] ECR I-1795 (ECLI:EU:C:2001:135) 71–2
Krantz v. Ontvanger der Directe Belastingen (Case C-69/88) [1990] ECR I-583
    (ECLI:EU:C:1990:97)...77
Kraus (Case C-19/92) [1993] ECR I-1663 (ECLI:EU:C:1993:125)....................62, 64
Kremzow (Case C-299/95) [1997] ECR I-2629 (ECLI:EU:C:1997:254)...................77

Land Nordrhein Westfalen v. Uecker, Jacquet (Case C-64/96
    and C-65/96) [1997] ECR I-3171 (ECLI:EU:C:1997:285) 49, 79, 81
Land Oberösterreich and Austria v. Commission (Joined Cases C-439/05 P
    and C-454/05 P) [2007] ECR I-7141 (ECLI:EU:C:2007:510).......................209
Laval (Case C-341/05) [2007] ECR I-11767 (ECLI:EU:C:2007:809) 47, 96, 104, 125,
                                                        126, 127, 128, 129, 190, 205
Lawrie-Blum (Case 66/85) [1986] ECR 2121 (ECLI:EU:C:1986:284).....................34
Leclerc-Siplec (Case C-412/93) [1995] ECR I-179 (ECLI:EU:C:1995:26)..................64
Levin (Case C-53/81) [1982] ECR 1035 (ECLI:EU:C:1982:105) 34
Luisi and Carbone v. Ministero del Tesoro (Joined Cases 286/82 and 26/83) [1984]
    ECR 377 (ECLI:EU:C:1984:35) 25, 35

Manfred Sager v. Dennemeyer & Co. Ltd (Case C-76/90) [1991] ECR I-4221
    (ECLI:EU:C:1991:331)...55
Mangold (Case C-144/04) [2005] ECR I-9981 (ECLI:EU:C:2005:709) 203
Marc Michel Josemans v. Burgemeester van Maastricht (Case C-137/09) [2010]
    ECR I-3019 (ECLI:EU:C:2010:774)..40, 41
Margarethe Ospelt and Schlössle Weissenberg Familienstiftung (Case C-452/01) [2003]
    ECR I-9743 (ECLI:EU:C:2003:493)..117
Maria Geurts (Case C-464/05) [2007] ECR I-9325 (ECLI:EU:C:2007:631) 104
Marks and Spencer v. Halsey (Case C-446/03) [2005] ECR I-10837
    (ECLI:EU:C:2005:763)...44
Mary Carpenter (Case C-60/00) [2002] ECR I-6279 (ECLI:EU:C:2002:434) 60, 78, 79,
                                                        81, 92, 131, 227, 229
Massimiliano Placanica (Joined Cases C-338/04, C-359/04 and C-360/04)
    [2007] ECR I-1891 (ECLI:EU:C:2007:133) 105
Maurits Casteels v. British Airways (C-379/09) judgment of 10 March 2011,
    not yet reported (ECLI:EU:C:2011:131) 96
Meca-Medina and Majcen v. Commission (Case C-519/04 P) [2006] ECR I-6991
    (ECLI:EU:C:2006:492)......................... 38, 45–6, 61, 77, 107, 108, 125
Metronome Musik GmbH (Case C-200/96) [1998] ECR I-1953
    (ECLI:EU:C:1998:172)..104, 158
Michaniki (Case C-213/07) [2008] ECR I-9999 (ECLI:EU:C:2008:731) 141
Michel Cognet (Case 355/85) [1986] ECR 3231 (ECLI:EU:C:1986:410) 49
Ministero dello Sviluppo economico v. SOA Nazionale Costruttori (Case C-327/12)
    judgment of 12 December 2013, not yet reported (ECLI:EU:C:2013:827).............38, 61
Mobistar and Belgacom Mobile (Joined Cases C-544/03 and C-545/03) [2005]
    ECR I-7723 (ECLI:EU:C:2005:518)......................................70, 71, 73

Mostaza Claro v. Centro Móvil Milenium (Case C-168/05) [2006] ECR I-10421
(ECLI:EU:C:2006:675) 160
Motosykletistiki Omospondia Ellados NPID (MOTOE) v. Dimosio (Case C-49/07)
[2008] ECR I-4863 (ECLI:EU:C:2008:376) 38, 58

Nationale Raad van Dierenkwekers en Liefhebbers (Case C-219/07) [2008] ECR I-4475
(ECLI:EU:C:2008:353) 104
Nemzeti Fogyasztóvédelmi Hatóság (Case C-388/13) judgment of 16 April 2015,
not yet reported (ECLI:EU:C:2015:225) 161
Netherlands v. Parliament and Council (Case C-377/98) [2001] ECR I-7079
(ECLI:EU:C:2001:523) 172
Nicolas Bressol (Case C-73/08) [2010] ECR I-2735 (ECLI:EU:C:2010:181) 105
Ninni-Orasche (Case C-413/01) [2003] ECR I-13187 (ECLI:EU:C:2003:600) 34

O. and B., (Case C-456/12) judgment of 12 March 2014, not yet reported
(ECLI:EU:C:2014:135) 79
Oberkreisdirektor v. Moormann (Case 190/87) [1988] ECR 4689
(ECLI:EU:C:1988:424) 211
Octapharma France (Case C-512/12) judgment of 13 March 2014, not yet reported
(ECLI:EU:C:2014:149) 210
Oebel (Case 155/80) [1981] ECR 1993 (ECLI:EU:C:1981:177) 68
Omega Spielhallen (Case C-36/02) [2004] ECR I-9609
(ECLI:EU:C:2004:614) 104, 138, 139, 140, 141
Opinion 1/91, [1991] ECR I-6079 (ECLI:EU:C:1991:490). 24

Parliament v. Council (Case C-436/03) [2006] ECR I-3733 (ECLI:EU:C:2006:277) 154
Pavlov and Others (Joined Cases C-180/98 to C-184/98) [2000] ECR I-6451
(ECLI:EU:C:2000:428) 38
Pelckmans Turnhout NV (Case C-483/12) judgment of 8 May 2014, not yet reported
(ECLI:EU:C:2014:304) 78
Pfeiffer and others v. Deutsches Rotes Kreuz (Joined Cases C-397/01 to C-403/01) [2004]
ECR I-8835 (ECLI:EU:C:2004:584) 197
Pfleger (Case C-390/12) judgment of 30 April 2014, not yet reported
(ECLI:EU:C:2014:281) 102, 105, 106, 135
Pfotenhilfe-Ungarn e.V., (Case C-301/14) judgment of 3 December 2015,
not yet reported (ECLI:EU:C:2015:793) 34
Philip Morris (Case C-547/14) pending 214
Pillbox 38 (Case C-477/14) pending. 214
Pohotovost' (Case C-470/12) judgment of 27 February 2014, not yet reported
(ECLI:EU:C:2014:101) 160
Poland v. Council and Parliament (C-358/14) pending. 214
Polisseni (Case C-217/09) [2010] ECR I-175 (ECLI:EU:C:2010:796). 62
Poucet and Pistre (Joined Cases C-159/91, C-160/91) [1993] ECR I-637
(ECLI:EU:C:1993:63) 36
PreussenElektra AG v. Schleswag AG (Case C-379/98) [2001] ECR I-2099
(ECLI:EU:C:2001:160) 87, 104, 113, 188
Prezes Urzędu Komunikacji Elektronicznej, Telefonia Dialog sp. z o.o. v. T-Mobile Polska SA
(Case C-3/14) judgment of 16 April 2015, not yet reported (ECLI:EU:C:2015:232) 58
Procureur de la République v. Association de défense des brûleurs d'huiles usages
(Case 240/83) [1985] ECR 531 (ECLI:EU:C:1985:59) 112
Promusicae (Case C-275/06) [2008] ECR I-271 (ECLI:EU:C:2008:54). 159
Punto Casa and PPV (Joined Cases C-69/93 and C-258/93) [1994] ECR I-2355
(ECLI:EU:C:1994:226) 72

Purely Creative Ltd. and others v. OFT (Case C-428/11) judgment of 18 October 2012,
    not yet reported (ECLI:EU:C:2012:651) 161

Quietlynn Ltd v. Southend on Sea BC (Case C-23/89) [1990] ECR I-3059
    (ECLI:EU:C:1990:300)..68

R v. Birmingham City Council ex p Wesson [1992] 3 CMLR 377 67
R v. IAT and Singh, ex parte Secretary of State (Case C-370/90) [1992] ECR I-4265
    (ECLI:EU:C:1992:296)...79, 131
R v. Secretary of State ex parte BAT and Imperial Tobacco (Case C-491/01) [2002]
    ECR I-11543 (ECLI:EU:C:2002:741)..................... 158, 171, 172, 177, 184, 212
Ratti (Case 148/78) [1979] ECR 1629 (ECLI:EU:C:1979:110).............................211
Rechnungshof v. Österreichischer Rundfunk (Joined Cases C-465/00, C-138/01
    and C-139/01) [2003] ECR I-4989 (ECLI:EU:C:2003:294) 173
Reisebüro Broede v. Gerd Sanker (Case C-3/95) [1996] ECR I-6511
    (ECLI:EU:C:1996:487)...102
Rewe-Zentrale AG v. Bundesmonopolverwaltung für Branntwein (Case 120/78)
    [1979] ECR 649 (ECLI:EU:C:1979:42)............. 6, 18, 53–7, 61, 62, 63, 65, 66, 67, 69,
                        72, 74, 80, 99, 103, 104, 105, 108, 109, 112, 114, 115, 117, 120, 132,
                        135, 144, 145, 146, 147, 152, 191, 226, 228, 229
Reyners (Case 2/74) [1974] ECR 631 (ECLI:EU:C:1974:68)............................144
Rina Services (Case C-593/13) judgment of 16 June 2015, not yet reported
    (ECLI:EU:C:2015:399)...214
Rosanna Laezza (Case C-375/14) judgment of 28 January 2016, not yet reported
    (ECLI:EU:C:2016:60)...114
Rudy Grzelczyk (Case C-184/99) [2001] ECR I-6193 (ECLI:EU:C:2001:458) 7
Ruiz Zambrano (Case C-34/09) [2011] ECR I-1177 (ECLI:EU:C:2011:124) 81, 82, 83, 92,
                        131, 227, 229
Runevic-Vardyn (Case C-391/09) [2011] ECR I-3787 (ECLI:EU:C:2011:291)...........81, 140
Ruth Hunermund and Others v. Landesapothekerkammer Baden-Württemberg
    (Case C-292/92) [1993] ECR I-6787 (ECLI:EU:C:1993:932)..................63, 64, 68

S. and G. (Case C-457/12) judgment of 12 March 2014, not yet reported
    (ECLI:EU:C:2014:136)...79
Sacchi (Case 155/73) [1974] ECR 409 (ECLI:EU:C:1974:40)............................37
Safe Interenvios (Case C-235/14) judgment of 10 March 2016, not yet reported
    (ECLI:EU:C:2016:154)...213
Safety Hi-Tech v. S & T (Case C-284/95) [1998] ECR I-4301 (ECLI:EU:C:1998:352) 157
Saint Prix (Case C-507/12) judgment of 19 June 2014, not yet reported
    (ECLI:EU:C:2014:2007)...34
Santos Palhota and Others (Case C-515/08) Opinion (ECLI:EU:C:2010:245)...............128
Sapod Audic (Case C-159/00) [2002] ECR I-5031 (ECLI:EU:C:2002:343)..................97
SAT v. Eurocontrol (Case C-364/92) [1994] ECR I-43 (ECLI:EU:C:1994:7).................36
Saunders (Case 175/78) [1979] ECR 1129 (ECLI:EU:C:1979:88)...................49, 50, 80
SC Volksbank Romania (Case C-602/10) judgment of 12 July 2012, not yet reported
    (ECLI:EU:C:2012:443)...68
Schindler (Case C-275/92) [1994] ECR I-1039 (ECLI:EU:C:1994:119) 35, 39
Schmidberger v. Austria (Case C-112/00) [2003] ECR I-5659
    (ECLI:EU:C:2003:333)...44, 96–7, 137–9
Scotch Whisky Association (Case C-333/14) judgment of 23 December 2015,
    not yet reported (ECLI:EU:C:2015:845) 110
Seda Kücükdeveci v. Swedex GmbH & Co. KG (Case C-555/07) [2010] ECR I-365
    (ECLI:EU:C:2010:21)...203

SELEX Sistemi (Case C-113/07 P) [2009] ECR I-2207 (ECLI:EU:C:2009:191) 36
SFEI v. La Poste (Case 39/94) [1996] ECR I-3547 (ECLI:EU:C:1996:285) 85
Sheptonhurst v. Newham BC (Case C-350/89) [1991] ECR I-2387
      (ECLI:EU:C:1991:194) 68
Shirley McCarthy (Case C-434/09)[2011] ECR I-3375 (ECLI:EU:C:2011:277) 82
SICES and Others (Case C-155/13) judgment of 13 March 2014 (ECLI:EU:C:2014:145) 133
Simmenthal (Case 35/76) [1976] ECR 1871 (ECLI:EU:C:1976:180) 211
Sky Italia (Case C-234/12) judgment of 18 July 2013, not yet reported
      (ECLI:EU:C:2013:496) 164
Sky Österreich GmbH (Case C-283/11) judgment of 22 January 2013, not yet reported
      (ECLI:EU:C:2013:28) 159, 206
Sloman Neptun (Joined Cases C-72/91 and C-73/91) [1993] ECR I-887
      (ECLI:EU:C:1993:97) 86, 89
Smits and Peerbooms (Case C-157/99) [2001] ECR 5473 (ECLI:EU:C:2001:404) 35
Society for the Protection of Unborn Children Ireland v. Grogan (Case C-159/90)
      [1991] ECR I-4685 (ECLI:EU:C:1991:378) 39, 40, 41
Sokoll-Seebacher (Case C-367/12) judgment of 13 February 2014, not yet reported
      (ECLI:EU:C:2014:68) 109
Spain and Italy v. Council (Joined Cases C-274/11 and C-295/11) judgment of
      16 April 2013, not yet reported (ECLI:EU:C:2013:240). 10, 178
Steinike and Weinlig v. Germany (Case 78/76) [1977] ECR 595 (ECLI:EU:C:1977:52). 85
Steymann (Case 196/87) [1988] ECR 6159 (ECLI:EU:C:1988:475) 34
STM v. Maschinenbau Ulm (Case 56/65) [1966] ECR 235 (ECLI:EU:C:1966:38) 58
Stoke on Trent and Norwich City Councils v. B&Q plc (Case C-169/91) [1992]
      ECR I-6635 (ECLI:EU:C:1992:519) 66, 67, 68, 69, 70, 72, 227
Susanne Sokoll-Seebacher (Case C-367/12) judgment of 13 February 2014,
      not yet reported (ECLI:EU:C:2014:68) 61, 135
Swedish Match (Case C-210/03) [2004] ECR I-11893 (ECLI:EU:C:2004:802). 162

Tankstation 't Heukste & JBE Boermans (Cases C-401 and C-402/92) [1994]
      ECR I-2199 (ECLI:EU:C:1994:220) 72
Terrapin v. Terranova (Case 119/75) [1976] ECR 1039 (ECLI:EU:C:1976:94). 46
Tobacco Advertising I *See* Germany v. Parliament and Council (Tobacco Advertising I) (Case C-376/98)
Tobacco Advertising II *See* Germany v. Parliament and Council (Tobacco Advertising II)
      (Case C-380/03)
Torfaen BC v. B&Q plc (Case 145/88) [1989] ECR 765 (ECLI:EU:C:1989:593 . . . . 58, 66, 67,
                                                                                  68, 69, 70, 72, 227
Torresi and Torresi (Cases C-58/13 and C-59/13) judgment of 17 July 2014,
      not yet reported (ECLI:EU:C:2014:2088) 133
Tourists Guides case *See* Commission v. France (Case C-154/89)

United Kingdom v. Council (Case C-84/94) [1996] ECR I-5755 (ECLI:EU:C:1996:431) 196
United Kingdom v. Council and Parliament (Case C-270/12) judgment of 22 January 2014,
      not yet reported (ECLI:EU:C:2014:18) 157
United Kingdom v. Parliament and Council (Case C-66/04) [2005] ECR I-10553
      (ECLI:EU:C:2005:743) 157
United Pan-Europe Communications Belgium SA (Case C-250/06) [2007] ECR I-11135
      (ECLI:EU:C:2007:783) 104

Van Bennekom (Case 227/82) [1983] ECR 3883 (ECLI:EU:C:1983:354) 100
Van Binsbergen (Case 33/74) [1974] ECR 1299 (ECLI:EU:C:1974:131). 36, 55
Van Gend en Loos (Case 26/62) [1963] ECR 1 (ECLI:EU:C:1963:1). 31, 34, 50, 52
Verein gegen Unwesen in Handel und Gewerbe Koln v. Mars GmbH (Case C-470/93)
      [1995] ECR I-1923 (ECLI:EU:C:1995:224) 72, 117

Vereinigte Familiapress Zeitungsverlags- und vertriebs GmbH v. Heinrich Bauer Verlag
(Case C-368/95) [1997] ECR I-3689 (ECLI:EU:C:1997:325) 104, 136
Viking Line *See* International Transport Workers' Federation v. Viking Line ABP (Case C-438/05)
Vincenzo Manfredi and Others (Joined Cases C-295/04–C-298/04) [2006]
ECR I-6619 (ECLI:EU:C:2006:461) 58
Ving Sverige AB (Case C-122/10) [2011] ECR I-3903 (ECLI:EU:C:2011:299) 161, 216
Vodafone, O2 et al. v. Secretary of State (Case C-58/08) [2010] ECR I-4999
(ECLI:EU:C:2010:321) 157, 172, 173, 175, 178, 179
Volker Graf v. Filzmoser Maschinenbau (Case C-190/98) [2000] ECR I-493
(ECLI:EU:C:2000:49) 77, 78, 92
VTB-VAB NV (Case C-261/07) [2009] ECR I-2949 (ECLI:EU:C:2009:244) 216

Walrave and Koch v. Union Cycliste Internationale (Case 36/74) [1974]
ECR 1405 (ECLI:EU:C:1974:140) 45, 46, 95–6, 97
Walter Rau v. de Smedt (Case 261/81) [1982] ECR 3961
(ECLI:EU:C:1982:382) 22, 56, 57, 101, 116, 138
Watts (Case C-372/04) [2006] ECR I-4325 (ECLI:EU:C:2006:325) 43, 44, 46, 123, 147
Webb (Case 279/80) [1981] ECR 3305 (ECLI:EU:C:1981:314) 36
Wirth (Case C-109/92) [1993] ECR I-6447 (ECLI:EU:C:1993:916) 35
Wouters (Case C-309/99) [2002] ECR I-1577 (ECLI:EU:C:2002:98) 38, 39, 107, 108,
125, 229

X (Case C-686/13) judgment of 10 June 2015, not yet reported (ECLI:EU:C:2015:375) 62

Ymeraga, judgment of 8 May 2013, not yet reported (ECLI:EU:C:2013:291). 83

Zhu and Chen (Case C-200/02) [2004] ECR I-9925 (ECLI:EU:C:2004:639) 79, 82, 92

Table of Legislation

DIRECTIVES

70/50 Commission Directive on the abolition of measures that have an effect equivalent to quantitative restrictions on imports, OJ Sp Ed L 13/29 51

73/404 Directive on the bio-degradability of detergents, OJ 1973 L 347/51 . . . . .153, 167

75/117 Directive on equal pay for equal work, OJ 1975 L 45/19 153

75/129 Directive on collective redundancies, OJ 1975 L 48/29 194

76/207 Directive on equal treatment for men and women, OJ 1976 L 39/40. . . 194

77/187 Directive on safeguarding of employees' rights in the event of transfers of undertakings, OJ 1977 L 61/26 . . . . 153, 194, 195, 205

80/987 Directive on the protection of employees in the event of the insolvency of their employer, OJ 1980 L 283/23 194

85/374 Directive on product liability, OJ 1985 L 210/29 153

85/577 Directive to protect the consumer in respect of contracts negotiated away from business premises ('Doorstep Selling'), OJ 1985 L 372/31, now replaced by Directive 2011/83, OJ 2011 L 304/64 . . . . . . 118, 153, 195, 211, 217, 218
 Preamble 153
 Art 8. 211

90/314 Directive on package travel, OJ 1990 L 158/59 217

92/85 Directive on the protection of pregnant workers, OJ 1992 L 348/1 . . . 198

93/13 Directive on unfair terms in consumer contracts, OJ 1993 L 95/29 . . . . 160, 161, 164, 211, 217, 218
 Art 4(2) 160, 161
 Art 6(1) 160

93/104 Directive on working time, OJ 1993 L 307/18 . . . . .196, 198

94/33 Directive on young people at work, OJ 1993 L 216/12 198

94/45 Directive on European Works Councils, OJ 1994 L 254/64 . . . .197, 198

94/47 Directive on timeshare, OJ 1994 L 280/83 217

96/34 Directive on Parental leave, OJ 1996 L 145/4 197

96/71 Directive on posted workers, OJ 1997 L 18/1 198
 Recital 13. 198

97/7 Directive on distance contracts, OJ 1997 L144/19. . . . . .217, 218

97/74 Directive on the establishment of a European Works Council, OJ 1998 L 10/22 198

97/80 Directive on burden of proof in sex discrimination cases, OJ 1997 L 14/16 197

97/81 Directive on part-time work, OJ 1998 L 14/9 197

98/6 Directive on price indications, OJ 1998 L 80/27 217

98/27 Directive on injunctions for the protection of consumers' interests, OJ 1998 L 166/51 217

98/34 Directive laying down a procedure for the provision of information in the field of technical standards and regulations, OJ 1998 L 204/37 as amended. 147

98/43 Directive on the advertising of tobacco products 168, 170, 212

98/44 Directive on biotechnology, OJ 1998 L 213/13 165

98/59 Directive on collective redundancies, OJ 1998 L 225/16 . . . . .194, 196

99/44 Directive on consumer sales and associated guarantees, OJ 1999 L 171/12 . . . . 161, 164, 211, 217, 218

2000/43 Directive on equal treatment between persons irrespective of racial or ethnic origin, OJ 2000 L 180/22. . . 203

2000/78 Directive establishing a general framework for equal treatment in employment and occupation, OJ 2000 L 303/16 203

2001/23 Directive on transfers of
undertakings, OJ 2001
L 82/16 . . . . .194, 195, 205–6
Art 8. 214
2001/37 Directive on the manufacture,
presentation and sale of tobacco
products, OJ 2001 L 194/26. 165,
171, 214
2001/85 Directive on special provisions
for vehicles used for the carrying of
passengers comprising more than
eight seats, OJ 2002 L 42/1 165
2001/95 Directive on general product safety, OJ
2002 L 11/4 162
2002/14 Directive establishing a general
framework for informing and consulting
employees, OJ 2000 L 80/29 202
2002/30 Directive on the establishment of rules
and procedures with regard to the
introduction of noise-related operating
restrictions at Community airports, OJ
2002 L 85/40 221
2003/33 Directive on the harmonization of
laws relating to advertising and
sponsorship of tobacco products,
OJ 2003 L 152/16 . . . . 165, 170,
171, 175, 212, 213
2003/88 Directive on Working Time,
OJ 2003 L 299/9 . . . . .196, 202
2004/38 Directive on the right of citizens of
the Union and their family members
to move and reside freely within the
territory of the Member States,
OJ 2004 L 158/77 . . . . .41, 42
Art 24. 41
2005/29 Directive concerning unfair
business-to-consumer practices in the
internal market, OJ 2005
L 149/22 . . . . .72, 119, 120,
162–3, 164, 216
Art 3(9) 120
Annex 216
2006/24 Directive on data retention, OJ 2006
L 105/54. . .159
recital 5 159
recital 6 159
2006/54 Directive on the implementation
of the principle of equal opportunities
and equal treatment of men and women
in matters of employment and occupation,
OJ 2006 L 204/23 194
2006/114 Directive concerning misleading
and comparative advertising, OJ 2006
L 376/21 164

2006/123 Services Directive,
OJ 2006 L 376/36 . . . . .214, 218, 219
Art 2 218
Art 15(2) 214
Art 16(3) 214
Art 39. 147
2007/64 Directive on payment services in the
internal market, OJ 2007 L 319/1. . . . 216
2008/48 Directive on credit agreements for
consumers, OJ 2008 L 133/66 216
2008/94 Directive on the protection of
employees in the event of the
insolvency of their employer,
OJ 2008 L 283/36 194
2009/38 Directive on the European Works
Council, OJ 2009 L 122/28 198
2009/73 Directive on common rules for
the internal market in natural gas,
OJ 2009 L 211/94 164
2010/13 Directive on audiovisual media
services, OJ 2011 L 95/1. 164
2011/24 Directive on the application of
patients' rights in cross-border health
care, OJ 2011 L 88/45 35
2011/83 Directive on consumer rights,
OJ 2011 L 304/64 . . . . 118, 211,
216, 218, 220
2014/40 Directive on the manufacture,
presentation and sale of tobacco
products, OJ 2014 L 127/1. . . . . .165, 214
Art 24(2) 214
Art 24(3) 214
2015/1535 Directive laying down a procedure
for the provision of information in the
field of technical standards and regulations,
OJ 2015 L 241/1 147

REGULATION

261/2004 on common rules on compensation
and assistance to passengers,
OJ 2004 L 46/1 159
1924/2006 on nutrition and health claims,
OJ 2006 L 404/9 . . . . .158, 176
Recital 34. 176
717/2007 Regulation (Roaming Regulation),
OJ 2007 L 171/32 . . . . .172, 175, 179
Recital 3. 175
Recital 4. 175
Recital 11. 175
Recital 39. 175
764/2008 Regulation laying down procedures
relating to the application of certain

national technical rules to products lawfully marketed in another Member State, OJ 2008 L 218/21 147

1024/2012 Regulation on administrative co-operation ('the IMI Regulation'), OJ 2012 L 316/1 147

COUNCIL DECISIONS

2010/320 Council Decision, OJ 2010 L 145/6, adopted pursuant to Arts 126(9) and 136 TFEU 193

2010/405 Council Decision of 12 July 2010, OJ 2010 L 189/12 9

2010/707 Decision, OJ 2010 L 308/46 . . . 199

2011/167 Council Decision of 10 March 2011, OJ 2011 L 76/53 9

TABLE OF EUROPEAN UNION AND INTERNATIONAL INSTRUMENTS

Charter of the Fundamental Social Rights of Workers 1989 195
Art 7 195
Convention on the Future of Europe . . . 180, 181
EU Charter of Fundamental Rights 2000 . . . . 20, 100, 105,
106, 113, 114, 129, 135,
139, 140, 156, 157, 170,
193, 203, 204, 205, 229, 232
Chap IV Solidarity 203, 204, 205
Art 1 139
Art 7 159
Art 8 159
Arts 15–17 106
Art 15 . . . . 135, 157
Art 15(1) 158
Art 16 . . . . 135, 157, 158, 159, 205, 214, 215
Art 17 . . . . 135, 157, 159
Art 20 140
Art 21 203
Art 22 105
Art 27 203
Art 28 128
Art 35 . . . . 105, 114, 156, 158, 162
Art 37 . . . . 105, 112, 113, 114, 156, 189
Art 38 . . . . 105, 156, 159, 161, 162, 221
European Convention on Human Rights (ECHR) 50, 82, 92
Art 10 136
General Agreement on Tariffs and Trade (GATT) 1948 52

Art XI 52
Laeken Declaration 2001 180
Single European Act 1987 . . . . . 16–18, 19, 112,
153, 155, 168–70,
188, 189, 196, 197, 233
Art 1 24
Treaty establishing a Constitution 2005 . . . . 20, 180
Treaty establishing the European Community (TEC)
Art 2 EC 114
Art 3 EC 114
Art 3(1)(b) 169
Art 3(1)(g) EC 20
Art 6 EC 114
Art 18 EC 80
Art 43 EC 96, 126
Art 48 EC 96
Art 49 EC 70
Art 57(2) EC 168, 198
Art 66 EC 168, 198
Art 81 EC 7
Art 82 EC 59
Art 85(1) EC 42
Art 94 EC 194
Art 95 EC 172, 217
Art 95(3) EC 177
Art 100 EC 189, 194, 195, 205
Art 118a EC 196, 198
Art 137 EC 202
Art 137(2) EC 194, 196, 202
Art 141(3) EC 194
Art 152 EC 169
Art 152(1) EC 114
Art 235 EC 189
Treaty establishing the European Economic Community (Treaty of Rome (TEEC)) 6, 15, 46, 167,
190, 194
Art 2 . . . . .15, 20
Art 7 95
Art 48 . . . . .50, 62, 95
Art 52 62
Art 57 153
Art 59 95
Art 66 153
Art 100 . . . . 18, 153, 167, 194,
195, 196, 205
Art 100a 18, 153, 168
Art 100a(1) 169
Art 117 . . . . .195, 201
Art 118 202
Art 119 190
Art 235 194

Treaty of Amsterdam 9, 198, 199
  Art 94. 18
  Art 95. 18
Treaty of Lisbon 2009. . . . . 13, 19, 20, 27,
              29, 45, 124, 129, 139,
          154, 159, 180, 181, 185, 224
  Protocol on the application of the Principles
  of Subsidiarity and Proportionality 181
    Art 6. 181
    Art 7. 181
    Art 7(3) 181
  Protocol on the role of National Parliaments
  in the European Union 181
Treaty of Maastricht 1992. . . . . .7, 197
Treaty of Nice. 198
Treaty on the European
    Union 2007 (TEU) 4, 20
  Title IV 9
  Art 2. . . . . .20, 140
  Art 2(3) 189
  Art 3. . . . . .20, 205
  Art 3(1) 20
  Art 3(3) 1, 3, 20, 100, 128,
         155–6, 174, 191, 204, 225
  Art 3(5) 189
  Art 4. 225
  Art 4(1) .4, 48, 68
  Art 4(2) 100, 139, 140, 141
  Art 5. . . . . 2, 8, 12, 33, 39, 43,
            47, 60, 65, 75, 87,90,
           93, 153, 166, 168, 169,
         170, 174, 175, 225, 231
  Art 5(1) 3, 4, 49, 50
  Art 5(2) 3, 4, 48, 68
  Art 5(3) 176
  Art 5(4) 178
  Art 6(3) 139
  Art 20. 9
  Art 21(2)(d) 189
  Art 21(2)(f) 189
Treaty on the Functioning of the
    European Union 2007 (TFEU). 4, 5,
            12, 13, 17, 20, 21,
          33, 45, 95, 100, 103,
         105, 106, 109, 123, 135,
         143, 147, 151, 152, 154,
         155, 157, 166, 170, 174,
         187, 188, 202, 209, 232
  Pt 3 3
  Pt 3, Title I 3
  Pt 3, Title X 200
  Pt 3, Title XVIII 187
  Pt 6, Title III. 9
  Title V, Chap 4 9

Title V, Chap 5 9
Art 1–358. 4
Arts 2–6 . . . . 4, 48, 180,
              229, 230, 231
Art 3(1)(b) 4, 176
Art 4(2)(a) 4, 228
Art 4(2)(b) 204
Art 9. 204
Art 11. . . . . .112, 113, 156, 189
Art 12. . . . . .156, 161, 221
Art 13. 13
Art 18. . . . . .41, 95
Art 19. 202
Art 20. . . . . .82, 227
Art 21. . . . . 6, 7, 8, 79, 80,
           81, 140, 174, 225
Art 26. . . . . 10, 11, 15, 19,
        27, 28, 29–30, 31, 68,
         75, 76, 154, 174,
        201, 205, 225, 233
Art 26(1) 11
Art 26(2) 1, 3
Art 27. 11
Art 28. . . . . .5, 34
Art 30. 5
Arts 34–36 6
Art 34. . . . . 31, 49, 51, 52, 53, 55,
       56, 61, 62, 67, 68, 69, 70,
     72, 73, 74, 75, 78, 90, 91, 92,
      96, 97, 103, 108, 112, 144,
     145, 158, 174, 211, 225, 226
Art 36. . . . . 39, 100, 103, 104,
        108, 109, 112, 114,
       115, 209, 211, 228
Art 36, 2nd sentence. 101
Art 38. 33
Arts 39–44 33
Art 39. . . . . .95, 96
Art 43. 34
Arts 45–48 6
Art 45. . . . . 34, 41, 50, 62,
         79, 96, 103
Art 45(3) 101
Art 45(4) 101
Arts 49–55 6
Art 49. . . . . .62, 96, 126, 135
Art 52. . . . . .39, 56, 103, 108
Art 52(1) 101
Art 53. 153
Art 53(2) .168, 198
Arts 56–62 6
Art 56. . . . . 25, 34, 35, 56, 70,
        71, 73, 78, 79, 81, 95,
      96, 108, 135, 140, 174

Art 57. 35
Art 62. . . . . 56, 101, 103, 108,
153, 168, 198
Arts 63–66 6
Art 65(4) 8
Art 81. . . . . 12, 187, 188
Art 100. 5
Art 101. . . . . 7, 36, 50, 57, 58,
91, 107, 108, 225
Art 101(1) 42, 107, 108
Art 101(3) .57, 108
Art 102. . . . . 7, 36, 38, 50,
57, 59, 107, 225
Art 106(2) 38, 39, 107
Art 107. . . . . .7, 85, 86, 87, 88
Art 107(1) 57–8, 84
Art 107(2) 84
Art 107(3) 84
Art 108. 7
Art 113. . . . . .12, 154, 187, 188
Art 114. . . . . 11, 18, 19, 85, 153, 154,
155, 159, 162, 163, 165,
166, 168, 169, 170, 171,
172, 173, 174, 175, 177,
178, 180, 185, 187, 188,
196, 203, 205, 209, 210,
212, 215, 217, 225, 230
Art 114(2) 154, 203
Art 114(3) 162, 177
Art 114(4)–(10) 209
Art 114(4) 12
Art 114(4) et seq. 210, 212, 213
Art 114(5) 12
Art 114(6) .12, 91
Art 115. . . . . 18, 19, 153, 154,
167, 189, 194, 195, 203, 205
Art 116. 12
Art 118. . . . . .12, 187
Art 144. 8
Art 148. 199
Arts 151–161 200
Art 151. . . . . .13, 201, 202, 203
Art 151(1) 195
Art 153. . . . . 12, 127, 194, 198, 202
Art 153(1) 201
Art 153(1)(a)–(i) 202
Art 153(1)(a) 201
Art 153(1)(b) 201
Art 153(1)(c) 201, 202
Art 153(1)(d) 201, 202

Art 153(1)(e) 201
Art 153(1)(f) 201, 202
Art 153(1)(g) 201, 202
Art 153(1)(h) 201
Art 153(1)(i). 201
Art 153(1)(j). 201–2
Art 153(1)(k) 202
Art 153(2) 196
Art 153(2)(a) 202
Art 153(2)(b) 202
Art 153(4) 209
Art 153(5) 47, 126, 127, 202
Arts 154–155 197
Art 156. 202
Art 157. . . . . .190, 191, 200
Art 157(3) 194, 202
Art 162. 13
Art 165. . . . . .45, 124
Art 166. 201
Art 167. 171
Art 168. . . . . .169, 171, 187, 210
Art 168(1) 156, 162
Art 169. . . . . .171, 187, 188
Art 169(2)(b) 12, 212
Art 169(4) 209, 212
Arts 174–178 187
Art 174. 13
Art 175. 13
Art 179. 13
Arts 191–193 189
Art 191. 188
Art 191(2) 110, 112
Art 192. . . . . .12, 188
Art 192(2) 188
Art 192(2)(a) 154
Art 193. 209
Art 194. 187
Art 194(3) 154
Art 258. 33
Art 263(4) 167
Art 263(6) 167
Art 294. 11
Art 309. 13
Arts 326–334 9
Art 326. . . . . .9, 91
Art 345. . . . . .46, 47
Arts 346–348 8
Art 352. . . . . 13, 127, 154,
171, 180, 185, 189, 194
Vienna Convention 1969 24

1

The Internal Market as a Legal Concept

A. The 'Internal Market' as an Ambiguous Legal Concept

Article 3(3) TEU directs that 'The Union shall establish an internal market'. The internal market is defined by Article 26(2) TFEU as 'an area without internal frontiers in which the free movement of goods, persons, services and capital is ensured in accordance with the provisions of the Treaties'. But this falls far short of a complete explanation of what is intended by an 'internal market'.

The account and analysis of the law provided in this volume is built on the claim that the 'internal market' is an *ambiguous* legal concept. One may readily suppose that the United Kingdom possesses an internal market. So does Germany, so does France, so do Australia and Canada and the United States of America, and so on. And the EU aspires to an internal market. But the detailed patterns governing these several internal markets are not uniform. They vary.

They vary according to the extent to which the constituent units are permitted to pursue different regulatory policies. They vary according to the scope of lawmaking competence and powers allocated to the central authority. They vary too according to the governing institutional (judicial and political) arrangements. The quality and intensity of the regulated environment varies according to the choices made. There is a broad band of possible internal markets, ranging from one which is radically decentralized as a result of a choice in favour of unrestricted inter-jurisdictional competition to, at the other extreme, one which is radically centralized in the sense that lawmaking competence has been completely stripped away from the constituent units in favour of the central authority. Within that spectrum there is a huge range of options.

Given the plurality of models of an internal market, the question arises which is the one chosen by the EU – and, further, why, and with what economic, political and constitutional consequences? The driving concern of this inquiry, then, is with *the internal market as a legal concept*. And the point is that although the EU Treaties broadly foresee the construction of an internal market through a combination of judicially applied prohibitions against obstructive national practices and supplementary legislative activity at EU level, they leave much of the detail open. There is a constitutional ambiguity at the heart of the law of the internal market. The view of the Court of Justice of the European Union ('the Court') on the scope of free movement and competition law has an inevitable impact on the degree of autonomy permitted by EU law to public and private actors at state level (call this the vertical issue: the division of responsibility between the EU and Member States) and also on what is expected of the EU legislature in completing the internal market where the Court's application of free movement and competition law runs out (call this the horizontal issue: the division of responsibility between the EU's judicial and political institutions). But different choices have been made at different times about the proper scope and limits of deregulation and re-regulation driven by law, most of all (but not only) by the Court. So the 'internal market' is an ambiguous concept but also a moving target too.

The aim of this analysis is to use the notion that the internal market is a contested and dynamic legal concept as a thematic background to an exploration of the tormented choices regarding the vertical distribution of competences between the EU and its Member States and the horizontal distribution of powers between the Court and the legislative institutions of the EU. The internal market as a legal concept involves a constitutionally sensitive inquiry which operates on several levels.

In this vein, the inquiry is necessarily into the *limits* of the internal market as a legal concept. Limits there must be. This flows from the foundationally important principle of conferral set out in Article 5 TEU, but ambiguity about the precise location of those limits is endemic to the system created by the Treaties. Thus, inquiry into the nature of the internal market is important in itself as an exploration of a contested legal concept which has real practical significance as a means to *empower* the EU, but it also reveals much about the constitutional character of the EU itself as a system based on a limited mandate, the governing rules of which are troublingly slippery.

2

Finding the Internal Market in the Treaty

The internal market is defined in Article 26(2) TFEU as an 'area without internal frontiers in which the free movement of goods, persons, services and capital is ensured in accordance with the provisions of this Treaty'. The aim, then, is a single trading area stretching across the territory of all 28 Member States. In economic terms, the EU is intended to be a single space, unfragmented by national frontiers – which is a bold vision given the centuries of regulatory diversity, political division and cultural heterogeneity that has shaped the European continent.

A. The Concept of the 'Internal Market' Empowers the EU – but Not Without Limits

Article 5(1) TEU declares that '[t]he limits of Union competences are governed by the principle of conferral'. Article 5(2) TEU explains that '[u]nder the principle of conferral, the Union shall act only within the limits of the competences conferred upon it by the Member States in the Treaties to attain the objectives set out therein'.

There is nothing trivial or technical about this. It is constitutionally foundational that the EU may do no more than its Member States have authorized it to do under its governing Treaties. This is central to the EU's claim to exercise legitimate authority. Where it acts, it does so because its Member States have authorized it do so, having given approval at times of Treaty revision or accession according to the domestic constitutional arrangements that pertain to the ratification of international Treaties. By way of corollary, the EU must not act *beyond* the mandate conferred by its Treaty, because that would be to operate in an illegitimate manner, for the required authorization granted by the Member States as Masters of the Treaties would be missing.

Accordingly the EU's commitment made by Article 3(3) TEU to the establishment of an internal market carries *constitutional* significance. So too does Part Three of the TFEU, 'Union Policies and Internal Actions', which takes as its Title I 'The Internal Market', and Article 26(2) TFEU, which defines the internal market as an 'area without internal frontiers in which the free movement of goods, persons, services and capital is ensured in accordance with the provisions of this Treaty'. These provisions locate the pursuit of the internal market as a matter within the EU's conferred competence.

The Internal Market as a Legal Concept. First Edition. Stephen Weatherill.
© Stephen Weatherill 2017. Published 2017 by Oxford University Press.

Examination of the scope of the law of the internal market is, then, a case study in the nature, purpose and practical application of the principle of conferral asserted in Article 5(1) TEU. But it is not simply *a* case study: in fact it has a compelling claim to serve as the best and most revealing of all possible case studies. The internal market as a legal concept does more than anything else in the EU's foundational Treaties to throw into doubt the vitality and reliability of the principle of conferral as a means to defend the autonomy of Member States. That autonomy seems to be guaranteed by the principle of conferral, the corollary of which logically holds that where the EU is not competent to act, the Member States may act unhindered by their obligations under EU law and, indeed, it is spelled out explicitly by both Articles 4(1) and 5(2) that competences not conferred upon the EU in the Treaties remain with the Member States. However, the challenge and the interest of the internal market as a legal concept lies in its broad, ambiguous, malleable and dynamic character. The use of the internal market as a legal concept grants a functionally driven reach to EU law which does much to weaken in *practice* the reliability of the *principle* of conferral. In short, the scope and influence of the internal market is remarkably broad and in consequence the areas of Member State autonomy that are wholly untouched by it are few. This is at the very heart of the inquiry conducted in this volume.

The extraordinary sweep of the internal market as a legal concept is already hinted at by the 'competence catalogue' which is contained in Articles 2–6 TFEU. Article 3(1)(b) TFEU lists 'the establishing of the competition rules necessary for the functioning of the internal market' as an exclusive EU competence. However, this is exceptional. The norm for the internal market is that competence is shared between the EU and the Member States, and this is stipulated in Article 4(2)(a) TFEU. The law of free movement envisages EU control over national restrictions on inter-state trade but, as will be explained, there is scope for national autonomy. Harmonization of laws too, and common policy-making more generally, do not involve the EU alone, and are accordingly a matter of shared competence. So the character of the internal market as a legal concept embraces action taken at both EU and Member State level.

The principle of conferral is put into operation by the Treaties themselves. It is the TFEU (i.e., the Treaty on the Functioning of the European Union), rather than the TEU (i.e., the Treaty on the European Union), which is of principal relevance to the definition and operation of the internal market. The rough shape of the competences conferred on the EU may be grasped from inspection of Articles 2–6 TFEU, but a comprehensive and detailed understanding depends on a trek across the wide and often dry terrain of the whole document, stretching from Article 1 to Article 358. This is where one finds the exact uses made of the internal market as a legal concept, on the basis of which relevant competences are conferred on the EU. A search against 'internal market' throws up a bewildering and unsystematic list of Treaty provisions, but in this chapter order will be placed on the collection by arranging the gathered field among three distinct categories. The first is characterized by use of the 'internal market' as a legal concept in a negative sense: that means practices are forbidden because of their detrimental effect on the internal market. The second category uses the 'internal market' as a legal concept in a positive sense: that means action by the EU is authorized in order to promote the achievement of the internal market. The third category, which is certainly the least important, uses the 'internal market' as a legal concept in a decorative sense: it is conveyed that the internal market is in some way significant and deserving of explicit embrace, but in circumstances where concrete legal consequences are elusive.

The EU's internal market is built on the combination of these negative and positive legal rules. This is, however, deceptively simple. The relationship between the rules is not spelled out by the Treaties and it has proved dynamic, both as a result of periodic and sometimes opportunistic Treaty revision and also because of the interpretative choices, sometimes fluctuating, made by the Court of Justice of the European Union ('the Court'). Moreover, although the objectives of the creation of an internal market are economic in nature, the objectives behind placing economic integration at the heart of the EU's activities are much deeper than merely economic.

B. Control and Testing – Negative Law

The aim of creating and maintaining the internal market requires legal rules that exercise control over measures adopted at national level that are apt to jeopardize that aim. Much of what is at stake here is the subject of elaboration in provisions of the Treaty that do not necessarily explicitly embrace the 'internal market', but are plainly anchored to its pursuit. This covers most obviously, but not only, the provisions on free movement and on competition found in the TFEU.

The EU comprises a customs union. This is made explicit in Article 28 TFEU. This means that, externally, the EU has a common customs tariff applicable to its dealings with third countries. Internally, customs duties on imports and exports between Member States and charges having equivalent effect are prohibited between Member States by Articles 28 and 30 TFEU. A flurry of early case law established that a broad interpretation of this prohibition is required. The Court focuses on the restrictive effect of a national measure, rather than its form or purpose.[1] This interpretative approach has proved of general significant and importance in the development of the law of the internal market, but the particular matter of defining the scope of the prohibition against customs duties is well settled and generates very little case law nowadays. Article 100 TFEU forbids discriminatory systems of internal taxation. State A cannot tax wine produced on its own territory at a lower rate than it applies to wine imported from State B. Litigation in the 1970s, largely initiated by the European Commission ('the Commission') against several Member States, established the scope of the control exercised by this provision over taxation which indirectly protects domestic products. The issue was usually the preference of states to tax the alcoholic drinks typically produced locally at a more generous rate than the products typical of other countries: the question was usually whether the nature of the competitive relationship between the products dictated that discrimination in

---

[1] E.g., Case 7/68, *Commission v. Italy*, [1968] ECR 423 (ECLI:EU:C:1968:51).

WTO

favour of the local product was truly established. So, for example, it was found that France was in violation of EU law because it taxed whisky more heavily than cognac.[2] Moreover, in a demonstration of the saliency of the prohibition against discrimination even in application to products that are in some respects clearly quite different, the Court agreed with the Commission that consumers are prepared to switch between beer and wine, at least where lighter wines are concerned, and consequently the products are in a competitive relationship with each other. This meant that tax rates for beer must be set in such a way as to ensure they do not discriminate against wine.[3] Mixing grape and grain is unwise, but it happens in EU tax law. However, here too litigation is, today, very infrequent. The principles are relatively well-established and they are relatively straightforward.

This is less true of the core Treaty provisions on free movement, conventionally described as the 'four freedoms': freedom of movement of goods, persons, services and capital. The basic aim is to secure free movement of these factors of production between the Member States, which is plainly intimately tied to the pursuit of an internal market for the EU characterized by an absence of internal frontiers. The key provisions are: Articles 34–36 TFEU, which govern goods; Articles 45–48 TFEU on the free movement of workers; Articles 49–55 TFEU setting out the right of establishment and applicable to both self-employed natural persons and to companies as legal persons; Articles 56–62 TFEU on the free movement of services; and Articles 63–66 TFEU concerning capital and payments. These are provisions of immense importance in curtailing practices that are antagonistic to the achievement of an internal market, and the Court has been ready to attribute high significance to them. So, for example, it has declared that the free movement of goods 'constitutes one of the fundamental rules of the Community'[4] and is 'one of the foundations of the Community'.[5] However, although the structural core of these provisions is easily understood – a basic prohibition on barriers to inter-state trade coupled to limited room for the expression of national regulatory autonomy where it is shown to be justified as serving an interest greater than trade integration – much of the detail is complicated and contested and, moreover, some of it has changed over time. And, in stark contrast to the state of the law governing customs duties and discriminatory internal taxation, litigation concerning the Treaty's free movement provisions is frequent and the case law abundant.

Article 21 TFEU provides that '[e]very citizen of the Union shall have the right to move and reside freely within the territory of the Member States, subject to the limitations and conditions laid down in the Treaties and by the measures adopted to give them effect'. This supplies an extra dimension to free movement which, unlike the core provisions dealing with goods, persons, services and capital, was not to be found in the original Treaty of Rome. The status of citizenship of the Union was

---

[2] Case 168/78, *Commission* v. *France*, [1980] ECR 347 (ECLI:EU:C:1980:51).

[3] Case 170/78, *Commission* v. *UK*, [1983] ECR 2265 (ECLI:EU:C:1983:202).

[4] Case 120/78, *Rewe-Zentrale AG* v. *Bundesmonopolverwaltung für Branntwein*, [1979] ECR 649 (ECLI:EU:C:1979:42), at para. 14.

[5] Case C-194/94, *CIA Security International* v. *Signalson & Securitel*, [1996] ECR I-2201 (ECLI:EU:C:1996:172), at para. 40.

added to the system only by the Treaty of Maastricht with effect from 1993. In *Rudy Grzelczyk* the Court hailed EU citizenship as 'destined to be the fundamental status of nationals of the Member States', although this was more rhetorically forceful highlighting of the status than of itself transformative in any profound sense.[6] A high significance is attached to the free movement right, and citizenship as a status suggests a transcending of economic activity and, instead, commitment to the rights of the individual as a person rather than simply as a factor of production. Here too, however, the basic structural questions must be addressed: what is a restriction on the right to move and reside, and to what extent are limitations on the exercise of such rights which are imposed by authorities within the Member States to be accepted as justified? It is clear that the rights of free movement and residence created by Article 21 TFEU are not dependent on economic activity,[7] but the extent to which the status of citizenship expands the legal protection of free movers is not yet fully explored, neither in the legislative domain nor in the Court's case law. In fact, citizenship shares with the internal market itself the quality of an ambiguous legal concept.

The free movement rules control measures adopted by public authorities and, in a less systematic way, acts of private parties too. The competition rules are principally aimed at private practices though they also have some overlap with the public sector. The competition rules in the Treaty are explicitly tied to the internal market. Article 101 TFEU targets bilateral and multilateral restrictive practices and agreements which are 'prohibited as incompatible with the internal market', and Article 102 TFEU forbids abuse of a dominant position 'as incompatible with the internal market in so far as it may affect trade between Member States'. In *Continental Can* v. *Commission* the Court declared that the two provisions 'seek to achieve the same aim on different levels' – and that aim is the 'maintenance of effective competition' within the internal market.[8] They too have been adorned with the Court's discourse of fundamental economic rights. In *Eco Swiss China Time Ltd* v. *Benetton International NV* Article 81 EC (now Article 101 TFEU), was hailed as 'a fundamental provision which is essential for the accomplishment of the tasks entrusted to the Community and, in particular, for the functioning of the internal market'.[9]

Article 107 TFEU uses the phrase 'incompatible with the internal market' in asserting a control over aid granted by a Member State, and then distinguishes between types of aid that 'shall be compatible with the internal market' and aid that 'may be compatible with the internal market'. Article 108 TFEU uses compatibility with the development or the functioning of the internal market as the basis for Commission supervision of aid, while also allowing for the European Council ('the Council'), acting unanimously, to decide exceptionally that aid which that state is granting or intends to grant is considered to be 'compatible with the internal market'.

---

[6] Case C-184/99, *Rudy Grzelczyk*, [2001] ECR I-6193 (ECLI:EU:C:2001:458).
[7] E.g., Case C-413/99, *Baumbast*, [2002] ECR I-7091 (ECLI:EU:C:2002:493), especially para. 83.
[8] Case 6/72, *Continental Can* v. *Commission*, [1973] ECR 215 (ECLI:EU:C:1973:22).
[9] Case C-126/97, *Eco Swiss China Time Ltd* v. *Benetton International NV*, [1999] ECR I-3055 (ECLI:EU:C:1999:269).

Aside from the addition of what is now Article 21 TFEU in 1993, these Treaty provisions have survived essentially unscathed in their substantive form and meaning since the 1950s. The numbering has changed and cosmetic adjustment has been made to the language, but otherwise the narrative is remarkably consistent. The (negative) law of the internal market has deep roots and, unlike so many of the detailed institutional and legislative rules governing the EU's expanding activities, it has not been tinkered with at times of periodic Treaty revision.

So practices are controlled where they threaten the internal market. The concept of the internal market has legal significance: it defines the grip exerted by EU law over autonomy at national level. If a national measure lacks sufficient connection to the internal market, then the point is that the competence rests with the regulating Member State. This is the principle of conferral found in Article 5 TEU in its practical application. The key questions, of course, surround exactly what this entails: when is the legal significance of the internal market exhausted, with the consequence that Member State autonomy prevails? The several definitional questions which concern exactly the question when the internal market as a legal concept empowers, and when it limits, the EU are the subject of detailed exploration below. Once a matter is found to fall within the scope of EU law because of its attachment to the internal market project, the examination turns to whether it is justified. Practices that cause obstructions to cross-border trade are not automatically forbidden. All this is true of both free movement and competition (including state aid) law, albeit that important differences of detail arise in the way that the several provisions fall to be interpreted and applied.

To complete the picture, there are some sector-specific controls on Member State action which are driven by the concept of the 'internal market'. Some also involve the intervention of and/or supervision by the EU's institutions. These take different forms and most, relatively detailed and technical, are not important enough to deserve further attention here. So, for example, Article 65(4) TFEU authorizes legislative action by the Commission or the Council to declare that restrictive tax measures adopted by a Member State concerning one or more third countries are to be considered compatible with the Treaty 'in so far as they are justified by one of the objectives of the Union and compatible with the proper functioning of the internal market'. Article 144 TFEU provides that where a sudden crisis in the balance of payments occurs, a Member State with a derogation may take the necessary protective measures, which 'must cause the least possible disturbance in the functioning of the internal market'. Articles 346–348 TFEU deal with security interests and the maintenance of law and order and include explicit directions to take account of the impact of national action on the functioning of the internal market. Each of these instances is doubtless of relevance in its own particular context, but none reveals anything of broader significance about the nature and purpose of the internal market, save only that it is something that requires defending. The internal market in this sense serves as a benchmark, but an ambiguous one.

The most interesting of this rather ill-sorted collection of provisions that draw on the internal market as a concept requiring protection concerns *enhanced co-operation*, not least because the Court has had the opportunity to deal explicitly with what is at stake. Enhanced co-operation, in short, lies in between unilateral Member State action and EU legislation. Member States wishing to establish enhanced co-operation between themselves are permitted to make use of the EU's institutions and lawmaking processes. The provisions were introduced by the Treaty of Amsterdam with effect from 1999, and have been lightly amended since. Rigorous criteria must be satisfied before enhanced co-operation is permitted. The governing provisions, which concern controls rooted in both substantive criteria that must be satisfied by enhanced co-operators as well as carefully drawn procedural requirements, are contained in Title IV TEU, *Provisions on Enhanced Co-Operation*, which is Article 20 TEU, and in Title III of Part Six TFEU, *Enhanced Co-Operation*, which contains Articles 326–334 TFEU. Of current relevance, according to Article 326 TFEU enhanced co-operation must not undermine the internal market or economic, social and territorial cohesion, nor may it constitute a barrier to or discrimination in trade between Member States, nor may it distort competition between them. The procedural aspects seek to manage the application of these controlling criteria, by providing for a Commission proposal pursuant to a request by Member States and Council authorization with the consent of the Parliament. At least nine participating Member States are required at the outset.[10]

The direction that enhanced co-operation must not undermine the internal market or distort competition between Member States appears especially forbidding, given how broadly these notions are typically understood in substantive EU law. This reveals both the abiding concern to preserve the integrity of the internal market and the deep suspicion that attends enhanced co-operation as a break from the orthodox discourse of uniformity in the EU. The tension here lies between allowing acceleration beyond the speed of the slowest members and controlling the consequent damage done by fragmentation of the EU's integrity. In practice, the provisions on enhanced co-operation have been activated only infrequently. It was as late as 2010, over a decade after their insertion into the Treaties, before they were first formally invoked. This involved authorization to pursue enhanced co-operation in the law applicable to divorce.[11] In 2011 enhanced co-operation in the creation of unitary patent protection was authorized.[12] This provides the most useful insight into what is at stake, since the authorization Decision was the subject of a challenge before the Court. One might assume that the creation of unitary patent protection by some, but not all, Member States would inevitably destabilize existing patterns of, and demand for, patent protection in the EU, and so contradict the requirement to protect the internal market. The relevant Decision offered only brief explanation. It simply asserted that the Treaty pre-conditions were satisfied, offering the frankly superficial observation that the creation of unitary patent protection on the territories of the participating Member States did not affect the availability or the conditions

---

[10] Special rules apply to enhanced co-operation in judicial co-operation in criminal matters and in police co-operation, pursuant to Chapters 4 and 5 of Title V of the TFEU, and to common foreign and security policy.

[11] Council Decision 2010/405 of 12 July 2010, OJ 2010 L 189/12.

[12] Council Decision 2011/167 of 10 March 2011, OJ 2011 L 76/53.

of patent protection on the territories of non-participants.[13] Spain and Italy, the only two Member States which had not requested the Commission to put forward the proposal for this exercise in enhanced co-operation, brought a challenge to the authorization Decision before the Court. The application failed.[14] The Court decided that there was no damage to uniformity, to the internal market, or to cohesion in the EU. If the Decision was superficial, then so too is the Court's ruling: what was planned was to occur within the bloc of participating states only and the Court treated this as the very nature of enhanced co-operation – in other words, it does not involve all Member States. The Court chose not to address the – rather plausible – argument that the impact of enhanced co-operation is inevitably felt, at least indirectly, by non-participants, most of all because of the likely alteration in the attractiveness of the legal regime available in the participating states relative to that which exists in the non-participating jurisdictions. This, one might suppose, is likely to cause a disruption in the operation of the internal market. The Court, disdaining such objections, preferred a generous approach which is apt to allow the concept of enhanced co-operation to enjoy a useful role and, plainly, it means that the political decision to pursue enhanced co-operation will rarely, if ever, be vulnerable to judicial intervention on the basis that it violates the Treaty pre-conditions which seek to preserve the integrity of the internal market. The judgment shows a judicial concern to push the minority to find political, not legal, protection for any anxieties. But it means that the internal market is a strikingly less constitutionally durable control than might have been expected. It is malleable.

C. EU Legislative Action – Positive Law

Stopping public and private actors from impeding cross-border trade is a necessary, but not sufficient, means to realize the EU's internal market. More is needed. In part, more is needed because the prohibition against maintaining barriers to trade is in any event not absolute under free movement or competition law, but rather allows scope to justify such practices. In addition, more is – arguably – needed because, more broadly and more controversially, there is fluctuating political commitment to ensuring the internal market is not merely an exercise in deregulation but rather also a site of regulation. The orthodox understanding is therefore that where negative law gives up, so begins the legislative impetus to creating an internal market – 'positive' rule-making.

Article 26 TFEU itself, home to the definition of the internal market as an area without internal frontiers, contains a loose direction to legislative action in its first paragraph. It provides that the EU 'shall adopt measures with the aim of establishing or ensuring the functioning of the internal market, in accordance with the relevant provisions of the Treaties'. Its third paragraph directs that the Council, on a proposal

---

[13] Recitals 13, 14.
[14] Joined Cases C-274/11 and C-295/11, *Spain and Italy* v. *Council*, judgment of 16 April 2013, not yet reported (ECLI:EU:C:2013:240).

from the Commission, shall determine the guidelines and conditions necessary to ensure balanced progress in all the sectors concerned, subject to the control of Article 27, which requires the Commission to take into account the extent of the effort that certain economies showing differences in development will have to sustain for the establishment of the internal market, and allows the Commission to propose appropriate provisions which, if taking the form of derogations, 'must cause the least possible disturbance to the functioning of the internal market'. This has, however, been of negligible significance in practice.[15]

Overwhelmingly the most important of 'the relevant provisions of the Treaties' to which Article 26(1) TFEU refers as available to the EU as the basis for ensuring the functioning of the internal market is Article 114 TFEU.

Article 114 TFEU concerns harmonization. Its first paragraph provides that it 'shall apply for the achievement of the objectives set out in Article 26'. This, then, is the tie to the internal market. It empowers legislative action 'for the approximation of the provisions laid down by law, regulation or administrative action in Member States which have as their object the establishment and functioning of the internal market'. Approximation and harmonization are conventionally treated as synonyms in this context, and it is the latter word that predominates. The designated procedure is the EU's ordinary legislative procedure, as set out in Article 294 TFEU, and so it rests on a proposal made by the Commission and adoption jointly by the Council, able to decide by qualified majority, and the Parliament.

The internal market as a legal concept creates the legislative competence. There is no competence conferred on the EU to harmonize diverse national rules. There is only a competence to harmonize diverse national rules where that diversity exerts a damaging effect on the internal market. However, once that internal market lever is pulled, anything that is the subject of diverse regulatory treatment at national level may be the subject of legislative harmonization pursuant to Article 114, excepting only the matters excluded by its second paragraph, which are fiscal provisions, provisions relating to the free movement of persons, and those relating to the rights and interests of employed persons.

Article 114 therefore possesses an immense functional breadth. Its purpose is market-making: it is not tied to any particular sector of the economy. Legislative practice confirms this, as Article 114 has been used in a wide range of fields, in all circumstances under a logic that asserts that diversity in regulatory approaches among the Member States impedes the smooth functioning of the internal market and should be replaced by a common EU-wide standard. All this will be examined in depth in Chapter 13: again, it is an exercise in using the internal market as an *empowering* legal concept, but where the *limiting* side of the coin, which the EU's principle of conferral demands must exist, is elusive.

The adoption of harmonized rules at EU level does not entirely exclude the possibility that Member States may apply stricter rules, but this falls to be managed by the Commission on terms which prioritize the need to protect the internal market. So a

---

[15] See P. Oliver (ed.), *Oliver on Free Movement of Goods in the European Union* (5th ed., 2010), at paras 13.89–13.90.

Member State may apply to the Commission to maintain existing or introduce new rules that go beyond the harmonized norm in accordance with Article 114(4) and Article 114(5) respectively, but Article 114(6) cautions that such derogation will be approved only after the Commission has 'verified whether or not they are a means of arbitrary discrimination or a disguised restriction on trade between Member States and whether or not they shall constitute an obstacle to the functioning of the internal market'. The internal market as a legal concept serves as a control on release of national regulatory autonomy.

There are other legal bases scattered across the TFEU which rely on the internal market as a legal concept. Some are worth deeper examination and will be examined closely in Chapter 14, because they tend to reveal once again that the internal market is an ambiguous concept, and that its empowering dynamic tends to be rather more prominent and significant than its limiting potential. The point, then, is the thematically *deceptive* character of the principle of conferral expressed by Article 5 TEU.

Among this collection of legal bases for legislative action which are expressly tied to the internal market are:

- Article 81 TFEU, which provides for measures adopted pursuant to the ordinary legislative procedure for the approximation of the laws and regulations of the Member States in the field of judicial co-operation in civil matters having cross-border implications, 'particularly when necessary for the proper functioning of the internal market';

- Article 113 TFEU, which allows for harmonization of legislation concerning turnover taxes, excise duties and other forms of indirect taxation 'to the extent that such harmonisation is necessary to ensure the establishment and the functioning of the internal market and to avoid distortion of competition' (little used, largely because of the controlling requirement of unanimity in Council);

- Article 116, which envisages the possibility of legislative action pursuant to the ordinary legislative procedure in circumstances where the Commission finds a need to eliminate a difference between the provisions laid down by law, regulation or administrative action in Member States which results in distortion of the conditions of competition in the internal market, where consultation of the Member States concerned has not remedied the situation; and

- Article 118, which directs that in the context of the establishment and functioning of the internal market action pursuant to the ordinary legislative procedure may lead to the adoption of measures for the creation of European intellectual property rights to provide uniform protection of intellectual property rights throughout the EU.

There is an assortment of other legal bases which are not explicitly tied to the internal market, but which on some accounts are or at least should be intimately connected to it. This agenda includes matters such as social policy (Article 153 TFEU), consumer protection (Article 169(2)(b) TFEU) and environmental protection (Article 192 TFEU). Their relationship to the internal market project is contested: are they an integral part of it, or are they supplements to it, or are they corruptions of its economic purposes? These are politically sensitive and contested questions associated with the proper intensity of regulation within the internal market, to which neither the Treaty in general not the internal market as a legal concept in particular provide *constitutionally* unambiguous answers. This debate will be addressed further in Chapter 14.

In the background stands the broadest of all legal bases in the TFEU, Article 352, which provides for legislation to attain one of the objectives of the EU where the Treaty has failed to lay down the necessary powers. The main constitutional constraint placed on reliance on Article 352 TFEU is that it can be relied upon only where no other Treaty Article provides the necessary powers,[16] so it is of a scope that is not only limited in principle but also one that has been narrowed each time the Treaty has been revised to add new sector-specific legislative competences. The main political constraint placed on Article 352 TFEU is that it requires unanimous support in Council. Before the entry into force of the Lisbon Treaty in 2009, this Treaty provision was confined to legislative action associated with the 'common market'. That restriction has been deleted, but was anyway of little practical restraining influence.[17] In truth, however, Article 352 TFEU is of relatively little significance today in the particular context of the internal market.

D. The Decorative

There are provisions in the TFEU which may charitably be read as orienting particular common policies to the objectives at stake in the building of an internal market. One might, however, see them as no more than merely decorative or even random, suggesting that the internal market is sometimes used carelessly as a concept lacking precision.

So, for example, Article 174 TFEU states that 'the Union shall develop and pursue its actions leading to the strengthening of its economic, social and territorial cohesion' and Article 175 TFEU adds that '[t]he formulation and implementation of the Union's policies and actions and the implementation of the internal market shall take into account the objectives set out in Article 174 and shall contribute to their achievement'. But there is no further elaboration of what this might mean. Articles 13, 151, 162, 179 and 309 TFEU suggest a similar self-consciousness about the importance of the internal market but an absence of detail addressing what this should entail. The quest to grasp the meaning of the internal market as a legal concept needs to be detained only briefly here.

---

[16] E.g., Case 45/86, *Commission* v. *Council*, [1987] ECR 1493 (ECLI:EU:C:1987:163).

[17] On past practice, see Schütze, 'Organized Change towards an Ever Closer Union: Article 308 EC and the Limits to the Community's Legislative Competence', 22 *Yearbook of European Law* (2003) 79; Konstadinides, 'Drawing the Line between Circumvention and Gap-Filling: An Exploration of the Conceptual Limits of the Treaty's Flexibility Clause', 31 *Yearbook of European Law* (2012) 227.

3

The Law, Politics and Economics
of the Internal Market

The EU's internal market is built on the combination of these negative and positive legal rules. And it is, as already encountered, defined by Article 26 TFEU as 'an area without internal frontiers in which the free movement of goods, persons, services and capital is ensured in accordance with the provisions of the Treaties'. As has already been introduced and will be elaborated as the core of this volume, this leaves open a number of key issues, most of all those associated with the vertical distribution of competences in the internal market (Member State/EU) and the horizontal distribution of powers at EU level (judicial/political institutions). However, the very concept of the internal market has an erratic, even accidental, history in the development of the EU. This is a brief historical excursion which deserves to be undertaken, even though much of it relates to a state of EU law that is now gone forever, because it offers further confirmation of the ambiguous character of the internal market and insight into how and why this matters.

A. The Treaty of Rome

The Treaty of Rome created the original European Economic Community (EEC) with effect from the beginning of 1958. The concept of an 'internal market' was completely missing from the original text. That Treaty instead focused on the 'common market' as the driving economic and legal concept. The common market was, however, left undefined by the Treaty. The original Treaty of Rome declared in Article 2 EEC that the Community (as it then was) would use the *means* of establishing a common market and progressive approximation of economic policies to achieve wider *ends*, including an increase in stability, an accelerated raising of the standard of living and close relations between the Member States. So economic integration in general, and the common market in particular, was identified in the 1950s as the means to prevent repetition of the wars that had scarred Europe for generations, but it was not an end in itself. What we know today as the EU emerged as a scheme for making conflict between the participating states, most of all France and Germany, not only improbable but even impossible. This is why the first of the Communities established in the 1950s focused on the common functioning of the coal and steel industries – the engines of war. The project of integration (through law) initiated in

The Internal Market as a Legal Concept. First Edition. Stephen Weatherill.
© Stephen Weatherill 2017. Published 2017 by Oxford University Press.

the 1950s was inspired by the political ambition to ensure a more stable system for promoting and managing the interdependence of states in Europe.

It is of course quite wrong to imagine that there was any general intent to write the nation state out of the future development of the European continent.[1] Exactly how to achieve a workable balance between centralized rule-making and institutional depth, on the one hand, and the preservation of the state as a source of political authority and allegiance, on the other, was and remains the most absorbing tension within the EU. Plainly, too, the motivations of those actors, institutions and states involved in the shaping of the project over time reveal fluctuating emphasis between the political and the economic. But from the very beginning the pursuit of economic integration in general, and the common market in particular, lay at the heart of the activities undertaken by what we today call the 'European Union'.

B. The Single European Act and the Political Bargain

The 'internal market' made its debut in the EU legal order only on the entry into force of the Single European Act, with effect from 1987.

In the 1980s, as European economies groaned sluggishly in search of new momentum, it was economic integration that came to the rescue. The plan unveiled by the European Commission ('the Commission') in its 1985 White Paper *Completing the Internal Market* and eagerly accepted by political leaders in the Member States was to re-energize the original economic vision and to complete the EU's single or internal market by the end of 1992.[2] The economic gains on offer were loudly proclaimed by the Commission,[3] have been vigorously doubted both at the time[4] and since[5] and are, in any event, very hard to measure, given the noisy amalgamation of factors influencing the economic record among which disaggregation is impossible. But the '1992 project' was never properly understood as an exclusively technical exercise in making markets in Europe more competitive. Economic aims had been placed at the forefront of a deeper political agenda: the '1992 project' to complete the internal market was strongly motivated by an attempt to wrench not simply the EU's economy but the EU itself out of the sclerotic condition into which it had sunk by the early 1980s. There was in this sense an echo – a conscious if concealed mimicry – of the 1950s. A programme of economic renovation would sustain deeper, though certainly contested and often strategically concealed, political ambitions.[6]

---

[1] See A. Milward, *The European Rescue of the Nation State* (1992).

[2] Commission of the European Communities, COM (85) 310, 14 June 1985.

[3] P. Cecchini, *The Costs of Non-Europe* (1988): the book's title was widely used by the Commission to make its case for pursuit of the '1992 project'. See also A. Jacquemin and A. Sapir (eds), *The European Internal Market: Trade and Competition* (1989); D. Swann (ed.), *The Single European Market and Beyond: A Study of the Wider Implications of the Single European Act* (1992).

[4] E.g., J. Kay (ed.), *1992: Myths and Realities* (1989).

[5] See, e.g., A. El-Agraa, *The European Union: Economics and Politics* (9th ed., 2011), especially Chs 7 and 9.

[6] See R. Bieber, R. Dehousse and J. Pinder (eds), *1992: One European Market? A Critical Analysis of the Commission's Internal Market Strategy* (1988). For an insider's view written by the responsible Commissioner, see Lord Cockfield, *The European Union: Creating the Single Market* (1994).

The Commission, under the inspired and inspirational leadership of Jacques Delors, assembled strong political support for the programme of reform that would lead to the completion of the EU's single or internal market. But more was needed. Law reform was needed. In particular, the prescriptions contained in the Commission's 1985 White Paper made plain the need for a cascade of legislative action to make real the political commitments undertaken. This in turn generated a *constitutional* momentum that led to Treaty revision achieved by the Single European Act (SEA), which came into force in 1987. The instrumental understanding of economic integration within the EU was not altered by the SEA, but the very fact that the SEA, the first major revision of the original Treaties, was required to support the 1992 project serves in itself as a demonstration of the need for conscious and concrete political steps to adjust the lifecycle of the EU.

The most obvious *problem* to which the SEA was a *solution* was blockage to legislative action in the EU. Key decisions required the unanimous support of the Member States in the Council of Ministers ('the Council') – to some extent because this was written into the Treaties, and to some extent because a political practice of unanimous voting had taken hold despite contrary provision in the Treaties. Difficult decisions were rarely taken. How could they be, when just one Member State could exercise a veto? And the expansion of the EU, from six original Member States to 10 by 1981 and 12 by 1986, was at one level a successful demonstration of the system's magnetic attraction, but at the same time it caused ever sterner blockages to legislative momentum by adding yet more veto players in Council. The SEA was the legal means designed to secure the goal of a border-free single internal market by the end of 1992. To this end, its single most important constitutional reform was to provide for the possibility that proposals to harmonize national laws in order to improve the functioning of the internal market could be adopted in Council by a species of majority voting: qualified majority voting (QMV). The veto was lifted.

The logic of 'QMV' in Council rests on the facilitation of decision-making, and periodic Treaty revision has extended the areas in which the Council is able to act by QMV, to the point where today a requirement of unanimity in Council is exceptional in the Treaty on the Functioning of the European Union (TFEU). But it was the SEA that initiated that dynamism, and it did so expressly in order to promote the creation of the internal market. The SEA made some other significant adaptations too, including a notable increase in the influence of the Parliament in the legislative process, which has also emerged as a dynamic and transformative trend in the incremental pattern of Treaty revision over time.

The Member States' embrace of the plan to complete the internal market by the end of 1992 demonstrated both the possibility of dynamic leadership by the Commission, then under the powerful President Jacques Delors, and the need for adjustments to the constitutional framework in order to drive forward ambitious plans. The shift from unanimity as the norm in Council to qualified majority facilitated the adoption of the large package of legislation that the Commission needed to propose in order to convert the patchy state of the market into one apt to realize the full benefits of a single trading space. Member States had therefore been persuaded that the gains accruing from the completion of the internal market made it worthwhile to surrender control of the veto in Council.[7] They would have known too that the rule of unanimity was, anyway, a less powerful brake than might initially be supposed because already by the 1980s the Court of Justice of the European Union ('the Court') had made important contributions which had widened the reach of free movement law and so had diminished, though not eliminated, the need for legislative action.[8]

The new provision – then Article 100a, becoming in 1999 Article 95 and today Article 114 – authorized legislative action in pursuit of the internal market. It did not replace, but rather supplemented, a provision which had always been in the Treaty dedicated to the pursuit of the common market – then Article 100, becoming in 1999 Article 94 and today Article 115. That provision, however, was and remains subject to the lock of unanimity required in Council. Since 1987 what is now Article 114 has in effect taken over the job previously performed by Article 115, mainly because it is so much easier to use because of the more flexible voting rule applicable in Council.

The relationship between the internal market and the common market was left as a deliberately ambiguous compromise. So there were references in the Treaty to both internal market and to common market. With particular reference to legislative harmonization, Article 114 TFEU, which was created by the SEA, referred to the 'internal market', while Article 115 TFEU, the older provision dating back to the Treaty of Rome, retained the 'common market' at its core. This discrepancy persisted until 2009, as the following section explains.

One could take the view that the internal market was a narrower concept than the common market in that it was overtly focused on removing barriers to inter-state trade to the relative neglect of common policy-making. Or one could argue that the internal market was a more ambitious project because it made a firmer commitment to ridding the EU of physical obstacles to mobility at national frontiers than did the common market. The narratives are not mutually exclusive. But the key point is that the Treaty offered no resolution. It simply embraced both a common market and an internal market without making clear any distinction. Although the change generated some dismay at the time,[9] in practice nothing significant appears to have turned on the distinction. The best guess as to why such a clumsy solution was reached in the SEA is that most Member States were adamantly hostile to diluting the existing commitment to a common market, whereas the UK was eager to emphasize deregulation while seeking to avoid stronger policy-making in common, and so the internal

---

[7] Moravcsik, 'Negotiating the Single European Act: National Interests and Conventional Statecraft in the European Community', 45 *International Organisation* (1991) 19 was an influential exploration of why and how the deal was done, though some have criticized it for its over-emphasis on intergovernmental bargaining. For a good account of the process, including appraisal of the copious (mainly political science) literature, see S. Bulmer and K. Armstrong, *The Governance of the Single European Market* (1998), Ch. 1.

[8] See especially Chapter 12 on the intimate connection between the Court's ruling in Case 120/78, *Cassis de Dijon* and the Commission's 1985 White Paper.

[9] Pescatore criticized 'the one-sided notion of an "internal market" based on an arbitrary selection of the Treaty objectives', in 'Some Critical Remarks on the Single European Act', 24 *Common Market Law Review* (1987) 8, at 11.

market, as a shorthand compromise that would satisfy both camps, was grafted on to the existing system. The point was political: to free up QMV in Council as the voting rule for harmonization in the internal market while leaving untouched other aspects of the system on which there was no agreement. The concept of the internal market was introduced into the Treaties as a convenient camouflage. It was not a legal or economic term of art; it was, instead, shorthand for the area of shared purpose, i.e., deepened economic integration – the full implications of which were calculatedly left to one side for future debate. Here lies ambiguity.

The Treaty was left in an odd shape, with provisions driven by the internal market scattered apparently haphazardly throughout the Treaty alongside provisions driven by the common market. It was not really haphazard – the choice of label revealed whether the provision was a 1987 addition or part of the original settlement of the 1950s. There is no call to provide an exhaustive list here because none of this matters any longer: as the next section explains, the Lisbon Treaty changed all references to the 'common market' to references to the 'internal market', with effect from 2009. But this background history is important as it reveals that the 'internal market' was, and is, a concept that suited political compromise. It lacked, and lacks, legal or economic precision.

C. The Treaty of Lisbon and the Political Bargain

The definitional conundrum was swept away by the Lisbon Treaty, which entered into force in 2009. This eliminated the 'common market' from the text of the Treaty, converting all references to it to references to the 'internal market'. There is today no worth in trying to attach any significance to provisions that were once connected to the 'common market' as distinct from those connected to the 'internal market', although admittedly knowing the background helps to explain some thoroughly perplexing apparent overlaps and idiosyncrasies. So, for example, the difference in purpose between Article 114 TFEU – harmonization pursuant to the ordinary legis-lative procedure in order to achieve the internal market objectives set out in Article 26 – and Article 115 TFEU – harmonization by unanimous vote in Council in order to promote the internal market – is utterly baffling unless the reader knows the back-ground, in order to appreciate both the SEA's trick which added (what is now) Article 114 alongside the pre-existing Article 115 and the Lisbon Treaty's alignment under the concept of the 'internal market' of provisions that had previously referred to either the internal market or the common market. Today, it is the internal market that is the defining legal concept. But this is not because any sort of ideological battle on behalf of a particular vision of the EU market has been won, or even fought. In fact the 'internal market' as a legal concept is an exercise in *avoiding* that battle at the constitu-tional level and leaving its elaboration instead to the judicial and legislative institutions of the EU. The internal market is, and remains, an ambiguous legal concept.

Economic integration was the route chosen by the founders of the system to promote interdependence among participating states: it was the concrete project on which agreement could be readily reached in order to grant initial momentum to the process. But the deeper purpose was to use that process as a vehicle for increasing interdependence – 'an ever closer Union', as the Preamble stated and still states. Over time, the material at the beginning of the Treaties has been padded and, especially as a result of the Lisbon Treaty, reorganized. The simplicity of Article 2 EEC has been lost. The prominence of economic integration has been reduced as the early parts of the Treaty on European Union (TEU) give expression to far grander visions and values. Article 3(3) TEU today directs that the Union shall establish an internal market, but this is located *beneath* Article 3(1) TEU which identifies the Union's aim as to promote peace, its values (as listed in Article 2 TEU) and the well-being of its peoples. However, Article 3(3) TEU, though tucked away, declares that '[t]he Union shall establish an internal market', which is to assert it as an end, rather than simply the means to an end that it originally was. But it remains clear that economic integration, and the project of creating an internal market for the EU, is only one element in the EU's endeavours.

The Lisbon Treaty did, however, add its own new ambiguities. As mentioned, Article 3 TEU provides inter alia that '[t]the Union shall establish an internal market'. Pre-Lisbon, so before December 2009, Article 3(l)(g) EC provided that the activities of the EC shall include 'a system ensuring that competition in the internal market is not distorted'. The Lisbon Treaty removed the reference to undistorted competition from the Treaty proper and placed it instead in a protocol attached to both the TEU and the TFEU, which states that the internal market 'includes a system ensuring that competition is not distorted'. A protocol is legally binding, so in this sense one could treat this as a re-arrangement without legal significance. However, one might argue that what is, in effect, a relegation of the reference to undistorted competition from its previous prominence at the beginning of the Treaty adjusts the constitutional balance in favour of socially motivated public regulation at the expense of market competition, and that this should be taken into account in the interpretation of the key Treaty articles. Article 3(3) TEU's embrace of the 'social market economy' and the binding effect attributed to the Charter of Fundamental Rights might be similarly employed to argue that the constitutional character of the internal market has been altered by the Lisbon Treaty. How to choose? The change appears to have been made largely at the behest of President Sarkozy so that he could present the Lisbon Treaty to the people of France as qualitatively different from the Treaty establishing a Constitution, with the result that, in the matter of its ratification, he could avoid any need to conduct a referendum of the type that had sunk the Treaty establishing a Constitution in 2005.[10] So it is another political trick. There is no clear-cut understanding here, and the point is probably that the impact of the package of 'soft' reforms wrought by the Lisbon Treaty becomes part of the political debate and the pattern of judicial interpretation, rather than serving as a decisive re-orientation of the rules of the internal

---

[10] See, e.g., B. Van Rompuy, *Economic Efficiency: The Sole Concern of Modern Antitrust Policy?* (2012), at 125–128; Drexl, 'Competition Law as Part of the European Constitution', in A. Von Bogdandy and J. Bast, *Principles of European Constitutional Law* (2nd ed., 2010), at 659–669.

market.[11] The ambiguity is remarkable and once again reveals the dynamic potential of the internal market as a legal concept. This volume will identify the circumstances in which this tension emerges or may emerge.

D. The Economics of the Internal Market

The internal market serves as one of the EU's best claims to have transformed the relationship between the states of Europe. That the transformation has been *for the better* is a key element in the claim too, and even if no realistic account of the EU can possibly evade the misery that has accompanied the recent travails of the Eurozone, it remains the case that there is little appetite in most affected Member States for quitting the EU and going it alone, even if there is anger and frustration directed at policies conducted in its name.

Economic integration has always been central to the EU's motivation, even if, as mentioned above, its constitutional status is more elusive, and melding a more competitive EU market out of the pattern of previously fragmented national markets has always been central to the EU's claim to legitimacy. Economic prosperity is what it claims to deliver more effectively and sustainably than can its Member States acting without the support of the EU's rules. In practice, much of the EU's activity has been dedicated to the achievement of economic integration among the Member States. And, as sketched above and elaborated below, the TFEU is choked with provisions that are sharply focused on the pursuit of economic integration through legal rules.

As a project it is driven by assumptions about the virtues of eliminating the economic significance of political boundaries. Securing the free movement of goods, persons, services and capital between Member States should, as a matter of economic theory, generate an intensification of competition, the release of economies of scale and patterns of industrial restructuring stimulated by specialization and achievement of comparative advantage, thereby causing improvements in the quality of goods and services and a reduction in price. Trade should no longer be distorted by the chance fact of crossing a political border. Ultimately, the consumer should win.[12]

In this sense the insistence in the discussion above that, at least until 2009, economic integration in the EU was a means to an end and not an end in itself may be treated as constitutionally proper but unhelpfully, even misleadingly, formalist. So when in 2011 the Court in *FA Premier League et al.* v. *QC Leisure et al.*, *Karen*

---

[11] Cf., e.g., Nic Shuibhne, 'Margins of Appreciation: National Values, Fundamental Rights and EC Free Movement Law', 34 *European Law Review* (2009) 230; Semmelmann, 'The European Union's Economic Constitution under the Lisbon Treaty: Soul-searching Shifts the Focus to Procedure', 35 *European Law Review* (2010) 516; Schiek, 'The EU Constitution of Social Governance in an Economic Crisis: In Defence of a Transnational Dimension to Social Europe', 20 *Maastricht Journal of European and Comparative Law* (2013) 185; Lianos, 'Competition Law in the European Union after the Treaty of Lisbon', in D. Ashiagbor, N. Countouris and I. Lianos (eds), *The European Union after the Treaty of Lisbon* (2013).

[12] For a good summary for lawyers see C. Barnard, *The Substantive Law of the EU: The Four Freedoms* (4th ed., 2013), Ch. 1; and, beyond the particular case of the EU, M. Trebilcock, *Understanding Trade Law* (2011), Ch. 1. The economics are introduced in relatively gentle fashion by El-Agraa, *supra* note 5, Chs 1 and 5.

Murphy v. *Media Protection Services Ltd* stated that completion of the internal market is 'the fundamental aim of the Treaty'[13] it was *in form* every bit as *wrong* as it was fully 40 years earlier in *Deutsche Grammophon* when it declared the 'essential purpose of the Treaty' to be 'to unite national markets into a single market'.[14] But this, though constitutionally exaggerated, was to tell us something important about the market-driven centrality of the EU's activities *in practice*.

Most of the time, however, the Court does not engage in such flights of fancy and rhetoric. Lawyers are, in any event, not trained to provide deep critical appraisal of the economic assumptions of the project, and must take some of these virtuous claims on trust, while certainly remaining open to more critical concerns about, for example, the potential disregard for sustainable growth that may flow from this economic energy. As a minimum, however, lawyers should be able to reflect on whether the legal rules are being designed and interpreted in order to meet the economic expectations underpinning the internal project.

On occasion the economic context emerges in a judgment of the Court. In *Walter Rau* v. *de Smedt* it was asked to consider whether Belgian rules which required that margarine be packed in the shape of a cube acted as an impediment to inter-state trade.[15] The background was the exclusion from the Belgian market of margarine produced in Germany and packed in a cone. The ruling is unusual, but helpful, for the Court's explicit reference to the economic assumptions that underpin the law of free movement. It noted that the Belgian rule was not an absolute barrier to the importation of margarine into Belgium, but that it rendered 'the marketing of those products more difficult or more expensive either by barring them from certain channels of distribution or owing to the additional costs brought about by the necessity to package the products in question in special packs which comply with the requirements in force on the market of their destination'.[16] The Belgian market was separated from the wider EU internal market by the rule. And the Court added that 'the protective effect of the Belgian rules is moreover demonstrated by the fact . . . that despite prices appreciably higher than those in some other Member States there is practically no margarine of foreign origin to be found on the Belgian market'.[17] Rarely does the Court make such explicit empirical observations, but here it lays bare core economic assumptions about the EU's purpose in reviewing national measures that obstruct the creation of its internal market, in which, in such a case, Belgian margarine producers would be subject to cross-border competition and Belgian consumers could expect more choice and cheaper products.

In *Commission* v. *France*, the so-called '*Tourist Guides*' case, the Court offered a glimpse beyond legal formalism in a case concerning the services sector.[18] The case concerned French rules governing the qualification of tourist guides. Just as imported margarine could be sold in Belgium but only on condition that it was packed accord-

---

[13] Joined Cases C-403/08 and C-429/08, *FA Premier League et al.* v. *QC Leisure et al., Karen Murphy* v. *Media Protection Services Ltd*, [2011] ECR I-9083 (ECLI:EU:C:2011:631), at para. 115.

[14] Case 78/70, *Deutsche Grammophon* v. *Metro*, [1971] ECR 487 (ECLI:EU:C:1971:59), at para. 12.

[15] Case 261/81, *Walter Rau* v. *de Smedt*, [1982] ECR 3961 (ECLI:EU:C:1982:382).

[16] *Ibid.*, at para. 13.   [17] *Ibid.*, at para. 14.

[18] Case C-154/89, *Commission* v. *France*, [1991] ECR I-659 (ECLI:EU:C:1991:76).

ing to Belgian law, so too guides from outside France could work in France but only on condition that they acquired a French qualification. The Court drew explicit attention to the effect on choice in the market for services of the French rules: '... that legislation prevents both tour companies from providing that service with their own staff and self-employed tourist guides from offering their services to those companies for organized tours. It also prevents tourists taking part in such organized tours from availing themselves at will of the services in question.'[19] So, it added, as a result tourists may 'not have a guide who is familiar with their language, their interests and their specific expectations'.[20] The Court was not impressed by the argument advanced in defence of the rules that they maintained quality of service. This, the Court believed, would be adequately ensured by the unregulated market. It noted that 'the profitable operation of such group tours depends on the commercial reputation of the operator, who faces competitive pressure from other tour companies; the need to maintain that reputation and the competitive pressure themselves compel companies to be selective in employing tourist guides and exercise some control over the quality of their services'.[21]

This emphasis on the virtues of consumer choice has occasionally reached the surface of the reasoning of the Court elsewhere in its free movement case law. *Commission* v. *Germany* involved the German *Reinheitsgebot*: an ancient law which confined use of the name 'Bier' to products brewed using *only* malted barley, hops, yeast and water.[22] The Commission challenged the rule on the – entirely convincing – basis that such strict rules governing the permissible ingredients of *Bier* unlawfully restricted the commercial opportunities in Germany of producers brewing beer elsewhere according to different recipes and traditions. The Court explicitly remarked that 'consumers' conceptions which vary from one Member State to the other are... likely to evolve in the course of time within a Member State'.[23] The *Reinheitsgebot* served to block such evolution. The Court noted that 'the establishment of the common market is... one of the factors that may play a major contributory role in that development', and, referring explicitly to an earlier judgment in a case of tax discrimination,[24] it stated that the legislation of a Member State must not 'crystallize given consumer habits so as to consolidate an advantage acquired by national industries concerned to comply with them'.[25] The Court's point is not that German consumers should be denied the possibility to exercise a preference for 'pure' beer, but rather that they should be permitted the opportunity to express a different preference. That end will be realized by requiring that German law may not be applied to exclude differently produced beers originating in other Member States. Choice in a competitive market prevails over governmental regulation of that market.

In competition law too, the Court on occasion spells out the economic context to the application of legal rules. Agreement to reduce capacity in the beef-processing sector in Ireland would doubtless increase profitability by limiting output, but this preference for co-operation between undertakings over the risks of competition

---

[19] *Ibid.*, at para. 13.   [20] *Ibid.*, at para. 19.   [21] *Ibid.*, at para. 20.
[22] Case 178/84, *Commission* v. *Germany*, [1987] ECR 1227 (ECLI:EU:C:1987:126).
[23] *Ibid.*, at para. 32.
[24] Case 170/78, *Commission* v. *United Kingdom*, [1980] ECR 417 (ECLI:EU:C:1980:53).
[25] Case 178/84, *supra* note 22, at para. 32.

would, the Court pointed out, lead to price increases and the exclusion of potential new entrants into the market.[26]

Commonly, however, the Court does not interrogate these types of underlying issues. Certainly it feels no need to make any consistent tie between legal analysis and case-specific economic effects. This is understandable from the point of view of expertise: lawyers are rightly cautious when invited to think like economists. And legal rules require a degree of predictability of application which is served by the adoption of standard formulas and presumptions. But even more so, the Court's caution is influenced by the constitutional unreliability of the internal market as an anchor. It is an ambiguous legal concept.

E. The Internal Market beyond Economics Alone

The Court's occasional engagement with underlying economic questions and its depiction of completion of the internal market as 'the fundamental aim of the Treaty'[27] should not be taken as a claim that the internal market, or the EU generally, is *solely* about economic concerns. In fact, its point is best understood in terms that treat the internal market as a legal concept that is – in an ambiguous way – *more* than narrowly economic in character and purpose. The Court's case law is spotted with remarks directed at the special significance of the process of economic integration within the EU. It is not always clear exactly what the Court intends to convey by such remarks, but they are typically to be found in circumstances where it is concerned to contrast the relatively ambitious aims of the EU with less profound expectations underlying other arrangements. In its Opinion on the draft agreement relating to the creation of the European Economic Area (EEA) it found that the system of judicial supervision which the agreement proposed to establish was incompatible with EU law, and so renegotiation of the EEA's legal foundation was required.[28] In reaching its negative verdict, the Court took the view that even though the provisions of the draft agreement and corresponding provisions in (what was then) EC law were identically worded this did not entail that they should be interpreted identically. The objectives, in the light of which a Treaty falls to be interpreted according to the Vienna Convention of 1969, were quite different. The planned EEA agreement was concerned with the application of rules on free trade and competition in economic and commercial relations between the contracting states. The EU is bolder: its rules on free movement and competition are not an end in themselves, but rather they are means for attaining wider objectives, ultimately, as the Court noted, to contribute together to making concrete progress towards European unity.[29] Much more recently in *Demirkan*, Ms Demirkan, a Turkish national, had been refused a

---

[26] Case C-209/07, *Competition Authority* v. *Beef Industry Development Society Ltd*, [2008] ECR I-8637 (ECLI:EU:C:2008:643).

[27] Joined Cases C-403/08 and C-429/08, *supra* note 13.

[28] Opinion 1/91, [1991] ECR I-6079 (ECLI:EU:C:1991:490). For an introduction to the law of the EEA, see P. Oliver (ed.), *Oliver on Free Movement of Goods in the European Union* (5th ed., 2010), Ch. 14.

[29] Opinion 1/91, *supra* note 28, at para. 17, citing Art. 1 of the Single European Act.

visa to visit her stepfather, who lived in Germany.[30] The question arose whether she could claim a right to visit Germany as a recipient of services under the relevant agreements between the EU and Turkey. Such a right would plainly exist were a national of an EU Member State making the same claim against Germany, for the Court treats a right to receive services as a necessary supplement to the right to provide services which is explicitly found in Article 56 TFEU.[31] The EU's agreement with Turkey explicitly recognized the freedom to provide services, but, in the absence of any explicit direction to that effect, the Court refused to use the interpretation it has embraced as appropriate in EU internal market law by analogy to the interpretation of the EU–Turkey agreement. Even if the same wording is found, this does not necessarily dictate that the same interpretation be placed on those words, and the Court insisted on the need for a 'comparison between the objectives and context of the agreement and those of the Treaty'.[32] The agreement, the Court concluded, pursued a solely economic purpose; it establishes no general principle of freedom of movement of persons between Turkey and the EU. By contrast, EU law protects passive freedom to provide services, which 'is based on the objective of establishing an internal market, conceived as an area without internal borders, by removing all obstacles to the establishment of such a market'; and it is 'precisely that objective which distinguishes the Treaty from the Association Agreement, which pursues an essentially economic purpose'.[33] This is a little obscure in detail, but it conveys the notion that the internal market project *within* the EU possesses a certain, if ambiguously expressed, depth of ambition.

In 1976 the Court in *Defrenne* v. *SABENA* described (what was then) the Community as 'not merely an economic union, but is at the same time intended, by common action, to ensure social progress and seek the constant improvement of the living and working conditions of their peoples'.[34] So the EU here pursues 'a double aim, which is at once economic and social'.[35] Over 30 years later, in *Viking Line* the Court declared that the EU has 'not only an economic but also a social purpose', which means that 'the rights under the provisions of the Treaty on the free movement of goods, persons, services and capital must be balanced against the objectives pursued by social policy'.[36] There is a risk that this is rhetorical flourish, and in *Viking Line* this apparent embrace of a social market was immediately confronted by the substance of the judgment which caused serious harm to orthodox assumptions about the importance of the potential for collective labour action as a defence of social concerns (see Chapter 9.B). As a minimum, however, there are visible fragments to be found in the Court's case law that project the internal market as an endeavour that is bolder than merely an exercise in market-making.

[30] Case C-221/11, *Demirkan*, judgment of 24 September 2013, not yet reported (ECLI:EU:C:2013:583).
[31] E.g., Joined Cases 286/82 and 26/83, *Luisi and Carbone*, [1984] ECR 377 (ECLI:EU:C:1984:35). See further Chapter 5.A.
[32] Case C-221/11, *supra* note 30, at para 47.
[33] *Ibid.*, at para 56. See also Case C-102/09, *Camar Srl*, [2010] ECR I-4045 (ECLI:EU:C:2010:236).
[34] Case C-43/75, *Defrenne* v. *SABENA*, [1976] ECR 455 (ECLI:EU:C:1976:56), at para. 10. See more fully at Chapter 14.B.1.
[35] *Ibid.*, at para. 12.
[36] Case C-438/05, *Viking Line*, [2007] ECR I-10779 (ECLI:EU:C:2007:772), at para. 79.

4

Principal Themes and Structure

Quite how much gain should be truly associated with the project of economic integration in the EU is contested in the economic literature.[1] Moreover, the construction of the EU's internal market is no one-off, but rather an iterative process. The Single European Act added a new provision directing that measures with the aim of progressively establishing the internal market, defined as an area without internal frontiers in which the free movement of goods, persons, services and capital is ensured, should be adopted over a period expiring on 31 December 1992. This was the birthplace of what is now Article 26 TFEU, but in tribute to lengthened horizons the reference to 1992 was deleted with effect from 2009 by the Treaty of Lisbon. 'Deadline 1992' was an important focus of attention, and it helped to generate political momentum, but legally, politically and economically it was no finishing point. In fact it pushed new challenges on to the agenda: stubborn gaps (especially in the services sector, taxation and in public contracting), new priorities (including technological change), uneven implementation deficits in the Member States, and imperfect judicial and administrative expertise. A great deal of the practical management of the internal market depends on administrative co-operation between agencies charged with the regulation of the market across the territory of the 28 Member States, and the required dense networks of co-operation cannot be invented or wished into existence from above, but rather will take a great deal time to evolve, within the frameworks set by EU law. More generally there are certainly blockages that are more deep-rooted in some areas than others, such as language and culture. Writing in 1998, Mortelmans accurately identified that the 'creation of the internal market is a dynamic process'.[2] In 2002 the European Commission ('the Commission') declared that the internal market will never be 'completed' and that '[t]he effort to maximise its performance is a process, not an event'.[3] In 2007 it added that '[t]he single market is evolving, it will never be finalised', and reminded that it is 'a means; it is not an end'.[4] In 2012, in *The Single Market Act II, Together for New Growth*, the Commission declared that '[t]he development of the single market is a continuous exercise'.[5]

---

[1] See Chapter 3.B.

[2] Mortelmans, 'The Common Market, the Internal Market and the Single Market, What's in a Market?', 35 *Common Market Law Review* (1998) 101, at 102.

[3] Commission's Internal Market Scoreboard No. 11, 11 November 2002.

[4] *A Single Market for Citizens – Interim Report to the Spring 2007 European Council*, COM (2007) 60, February 2007, at 3, 10.

[5] COM (2012) 573, at 4.

The Internal Market as a Legal Concept. First Edition. Stephen Weatherill.
© Stephen Weatherill 2017. Published 2017 by Oxford University Press.

The internal market is not 'complete' in any absolute sense. However, it is not just the economics that are incomplete, dynamic and ambiguous. The internal market as a legal concept is incomplete, dynamic and ambiguous too. The compromises and incremental pattern of Treaty revision, examined earlier, provide one set of reasons why the internal market is imbued with ambiguity. The approach taken by the Court of Justice of the European Union ('the Court') adds a further dimension too. The Court's treatment of the internal market in a dynamic, sometimes even unpredictable, manner, is in many respects understandable and excusable, because the Treaty itself leaves the concept of the internal market open. Most of all, an abiding theme in this volume, this is true of both vertical questions about the distribution of competences between the EU and the Member States and horizontal questions about the distribution of powers between EU's judicial and its political institutions.

In *Deutsche Grammophon* the Court interpreted the Treaty provisions on free movement of goods and competition law so as to avoid an approach 'which would legitimize the isolation of national markets', and instead focused on the aim 'to unite national markets into a single market'.[6] In *Gaston Schul* it described the concept of a common market as involving 'the elimination of all obstacles to intra-Community trade in order to merge the national markets into a single market bringing about conditions as close as possible to those of a genuine internal market'.[7] These might plausibly be treated as the roots of the 'internal market' as a concept, but such definitional rhetoric is in fact just as evasive as the internal market found in Article 26 TFEU. Most of all, it evades the choices that need to made about the shape of this market. The law of the internal market is built on two distinct but complementary sets of Treaty provisions – those that stop public and private actors from impeding cross-border trade and those which grant competence to the EU to adopt its own common rules which will govern the terms of that cross-border trade. As introduced earlier, these may be understood as negative and positive law, the sense that they forbid particular (national) practices and adopt particular (EU) standards respectively. Negative law comprises most prominently the Treaty provisions on free movement (of goods, persons, services and capital) and competition law. The impact on the internal market is obviously deregulatory. Positive law is most prominently shaped by way of legislative harmonization, but also includes other more sector-specific legislative competences in areas such as social policy, labour market regulation, environmental protection and consumer policy. It is deregulatory too, in so far as it distils diverse national rules to a single common EU rule, but at the same time it adds a regulatory layer to the internal market where EU rules replace national rules (in whole or in part). Negative and positive law work together – what survives the discipline of free movement law and yet causes fragmentation of the market may be cured by the adoption of EU harmonized rules through the legislative process. However, the relevant Treaty provisions on both negative and positive law are typically written with remarkable economy. They leave open many key questions about, in particular, how aggressively the negative law provisions will be promoted. The

---

[6] Case 78/70, *Deutsche Grammophon v. Metro*, [1971] ECR 487 (ECLI:EU:C:1971:59), at para. 12.
[7] Case 15/81, *Gaston Schul*, [1982] ECR 1409 (ECLI:EU:C:1982:135).

more work is undertaken through this route, the deeper the deregulatory impact on national regulatory autonomy (the vertical issue) and the stronger the emphasis on judicially applied provisions at the expense of the role of the EU legislative institutions (the horizontal issue); vice versa, the more cautious the control exercised under negative law, the greater the room allowed to national regulatory autonomy (the vertical issue) and the more pressing the need for the judicially applied provisions to be supplemented by political action pursued through the legislative process (the horizontal issue), which will in turn bring to the fore contested questions about the proper intensity of, for example, social policy-making.

So Norbert Reich, writing in 1991 under the title 'Binnenmarkt als Rechtsbegriff' – 'internal market as legal concept' – from which the inspiration for this book's title is drawn, convincingly explained that the label 'internal market' tends to conceal a whole range of highly complex problems of legal interpretation and application.[8] The story has become ever more intricate since the publication of this insight, and, moreover, the target is not static: the internal market is in many respects a dynamic work in progress. Damian Chalmers, another author who appreciated at an early stage the significance of the shaping of legal rules for the process of economic integration, noted in 1995 that '[f]or a lawyer the principal dilemma posed by the single market is that it is a concept whose outer limits require constant redefinition'.[9] This remains true!

This connects to a still bigger theme, memorably captured by Koen Lenaerts in his vivid and oft-cited observation that 'there simply is no nucleus of sovereignty that the Member States can invoke, as such, against the' EU.[10] The internal market, as a dynamic and ambiguous legal concept, is a major reason for the breadth of the EU's reach and the constraints placed on those who would wish to find reliable means to hold its influence over national choices at bay. It is anxiety that this is a major structural deficiency in EU law that led to attention being paid to this issue at the Convention on the Future of Europe, in particular to the possibility of reform. Adjustments made with effect from 2009 by the Treaty of Lisbon to the pattern whereby the EU is granted competence are, however, slight and, if more than cosmetic, then certainly not structural. This is examined in Chapter 13.H.3. And the basic framework of the legal rules governing the internal market has not been changed at all.

The basic idea is clear. Some practices harm the creation of an internal market. Some will be incompatible with it and may not be applied: leaving a regulatory vacuum or gap. Some will be justified. At that point, legislative harmonization may intervene.

This now leads to the structure of the detailed legal analysis that follows: how to understand the internal market as a concept which animates the legal rules. The concept of the 'internal market' *empowers* the EU and it *limits* the EU. Article 26

---

[8] Reich, 'Binnenmarkt als Rechtsbegriff', 7 *Europäische Zeitschrift für Wirtschaftsrecht* (1991) 203.

[9] Chalmers, 'The Single Market: From Prima Donna to Journeyman', in J. Shaw and G. More (eds), *New Legal Dynamics of European Union* (1995) 55.

[10] Lenaerts, 'Constitutionalism and the Many Faces of Federalism', 38 *American Journal of Comparative Law* (1990) 205.

TFEU defines the internal market, but in an ambiguous way. It leaves open the precise relationship between EU and Member State competences (the vertical issue) and between judicial and legislative powers (the horizontal issue).

These are the two principal ambiguities. *First*, the vertical issue: what type of national measures threaten the achievement of the internal market, and therefore what will be the scope of intervention, or, put another way, where does EU internal market law end and State autonomy begin? There are two main sub-sets of this investigation – the internal *market* (when is there an economic context?) and the *internal* market (when is there a cross-border dimension?) – and inquiry is also needed into the personal scope of the provisions. Then, it must be asked what scope is allowed for justification of national measures that are treated as barriers to trade in the internal market. These are matters for courts, both the Court of Justice of the European Union ('the Court') and (given that the provisions are directly effective) the national courts in the Member States. The Commission too has important powers in the field of competition law (including state aid). *Secondly*, the horizontal issue: the ambiguity here asks how, in circumstances where Member State autonomy is subjected to review in the name of EU internal market law, it is decided whether the Court resolves the matter or instead the matter falls for legislative intervention? This is a horizontal issue – it goes to the relationship between the EU's judicial and political institutions. The more eagerly the Court applies free movement and competition law, the less is left for the legislative process and vice versa. This is a question of institutional power, but it is also serves to determine the shape of the internal market and, in particular, the balance between deregulation and reregulation. Also at stake is the definition of the permitted scope of the legislative competence to harmonize (and of other conferred legislative competences too) and an understanding of how the content and quality of those common rules adopted at EU level are determined.

Both ambiguities have at their core a definitional conundrum – what is this 'internal market' which drives the legal rules? In each instance the issue is that there are limits, as follows unavoidably from the principle of conferral, but they are broadly drawn, sometimes ambiguous and sometimes frankly hard to treat as wholly rational. There is a law of the internal market, but it is not smooth-edged nor homogenous.

The choices made are constitutionally significant as well as economically and politically significant. All internal markets across the globe wrestle with these challenges. But not all make the same choices. There is a broad band of possible internal markets, ranging from one which is radically decentralized as a result of a choice in favour of unrestricted inter-jurisdictional competition, which means that units may adopt different rules but may never apply them to impede imports, to, at the other extreme, one which is radically centralized in the sense that lawmaking competence has been completely stripped away from the constituent units in favour of the central authority. Within that spectrum there is a huge range of options, varying according to institutional choice and regulatory intensity. Moreover the different freedoms within the internal market may themselves not be understood in the same way. This offers a further choice.

The point, then, is not that the EU's internal market is, as a matter of empirical observation, fragmented, in that some sectors are a good deal more aggressively integrated on an EU scale than others – though this is certainly true – the point is that in its constitutional meaning and loading the 'internal market' is not fixed or homogenous as a concept.

And this is exactly the focus of this volume's inquiry. The provisions on free movement, on competition law and on legislative harmonization are all driven by the project of creating an internal market – but that very project is itself contested. So the concept that is supposed to inform an understanding of the reach of the provisions on free movement, on competition law and on legislative harmonization, does not offer a precise benchmark, but rather a range of choices. And then the choices made about the reach of the provisions on free movement, on competition law and on legislative harmonization come to determine the shape of the internal market – which is a reversal of the initial assumption that the internal market itself is the shaping concept. This is a functional challenge to the vitality of the principle of conferral.

So, given the plurality of models of an internal market which may be imagined, the question arises which is the one chosen by the EU – and why. The concern is with the internal market as a legal concept under EU law.

The location of the most vigorous activity in the shaping of the law of the internal market is the Court. Over an extended period it has actively developed the law of the internal market in such a way that it is impossible to get a true sense of the impact of EU law on national regulatory autonomy without a secure grasp of the case law. Its approach is necessarily built around the basic structure envisaged by the Treaty – particular practices are prohibited, subject to the possibility that they may be shown to be justified and that there is a supplementary role for legislative intervention in the name of harmonization or under the sector-specific regulatory competences. But the case law is a great deal more elaborate than the Treaty. And the case law is not static – the Court has on occasion changed its mind, though it has not always confessed to doing so (and perhaps it has not always even noticed it is doing so). This has implications both vertically – in fixing the extent to which EU law curtails national (public or private) autonomy – and horizontally – in determining the relationship between the Court and the EU's legislative institutions. In part, the ambiguity of the internal market defined in Article 26 TFEU is to blame, and too many of the key provisions such as Article 34 TFEU are skeletal and terse, which means that much autonomy is delegated to the Court by the Treaty design. It is, however, vital to grasp that the Court has been, and remains, highly influential in shaping the law of the internal market. This does not mean that the Court's case law is 'law' in the way that an orthodox common lawyer would understand it, but it does mean that the Court's case law has more vitality and significance than an orthodox civil lawyer might expect. It is, in fact, a hybrid – the Court famously hailed and thereby created the EU legal order as a 'new legal order',[11] by which it meant to distance it from traditional international law – but here too, in the weight of authority of its own case law, there is something distinctive about EU law as crafted in Luxembourg.

---

[11] Case 26/62, *Van Gend en Loos*, [1963] ECR 1 (ECLI:EU:C:1963:1); Case 6/64, *Costa v. ENEL*, [1964] ECR 585 (ECLI:EU:C:1964:66).

5

The Internal *Market*

The pursuit of an internal market assumes there is a 'market' element to the national provision or practice under challenge. Absent any such necessary economic dimension the matter escapes the scope of application of EU internal market law.

Clearly the 'market' is functionally broad: all sectors are in principle covered. The only explicit adaptation found in the Treaty on the Functioning of the European Union (TFEU) is Article 38 TFEU which adds that the internal market 'shall extend to agriculture, fisheries and trade in agricultural products'; that '[s]ave as otherwise provided in Articles 39 to 44, the rules laid down for the establishment and functioning of the internal market shall apply to agricultural products'; and that 'the operation and development of the internal market for agricultural products must be accompanied by the establishment of a common agricultural policy'. But this merely reflects the particular importance of the agricultural sector in the EU's history. Its explicit treatment in this fashion is not of any great *general* legal significance. All sectors of the economy are in principle covered by the TFEU. It is plain that products, workers and services normally easily and uncontroversially fall within the scope of internal market law and so national measures adopted by public authorities or private practices that address them in such a way as to impede cross-border trade require justification by the regulator.

The interesting question, then, is when does EU law *not* apply? This is where the true test of the internal market as a legal concept that serves to put Article 5 TEU's principle of conferral into practice emerges most vividly.

A. The Breadth of the Market as a Legal Concept

The road was initially smooth, perhaps deceptively so. In its pioneering early case law the Court of Justice of the European Union ('the Court') tended to find no reason at all to hesitate at this stage of the analysis. The Court's very first ruling which concerned the free movement of goods was delivered in December 1961. It was an application by the Commission under what is today the Article 258 TFEU infringement procedure, and it concerned Italian measures which caused a suspension in the importation of pigs and pig products.[1] It was perfectly plain there was the required economic dimension to the matter. The Italian intervention was unarguably of

---

[1] Case 7/61, *Commission* v. *Italy*, [1961] ECR 317 (ECLI:EU:C:1961:31).

a type that exerted an effect prejudicial on the market for pigs and pig products and in fact one of the – entirely fruitless – arguments raised by Italy in its attempt before the Court to resist the Commission's application was that it was concerned to address the problem of artificially low prices in the sector. This was economic protectionism in its most naked and unjustified form.

In February 1963 the Court delivered its first preliminary ruling concerning the free movement of goods. This was one of the most celebrated of all its judgments: it was *Van Gend en Loos*, one of the key cases in which the Court developed a constitutional discourse about EU law which was designed to distance it – and did distance it – from orthodox public international law.[2] It is for the deduction and elaboration of the principle of direct effect that the decision is remembered, but in its substantive context it concerned the internal market. In that respect it was, in fact, a thoroughly trivial case about the imposition of customs duties on urea-formaldehyde imported into the Netherlands. Obviously and unarguably the matter was about a 'market'. Today the relevant Treaty provision would be Article 28 TFEU.

There rarely is a problem finding a 'market'. Bees are 'goods'.[3] The Court has found the notion of 'goods' to cover waste, and this is true whether or not the waste is recyclable and so reusable.[4] After all, disposing of waste has a price and so any restriction on its cross-border movement interferes with commercial activity and accordingly requires justification. The Court has developed a consistent formula which insists that the concept of 'worker' within the meaning of Article 45 TFEU has an autonomous meaning specific to EU law and, moreover, that given its role in defining the scope of a fundamental freedom it should be interpreted broadly to cover pursuit of effective and genuine economic activity.[5] So, for example, part-time or low-waged work will do[6] and payment in kind counts too, so a migrant living in a community who received food and accommodation in return for work within the community is covered.[7] An activity must not be provided for nothing, but a person need not be seeking to make a profit.[8] Pursuant to this calculatedly broad interpretative approach the Court ruled that an employed woman who gave up work less than three months before the birth of her child and then returned to work three months after the birth did not lose her status of 'worker' within the meaning of Article 45 TFEU.[9]

In similar expansive vein, although Article 56 TFEU refers only to the freedom to *provide* services in another Member State, the Court has found no difficulty in treating it also as covering the freedom to *receive* services in another Member State, breezily and sweepingly observing that this interpretation was necessary to fulfil 'the

---

[2] Case 26/62, *Van Gend en Loos*, [1963] ECR 1 (ECLI:EU:C:1963:1).
[3] Case C-67/97, *Ditlev Bluhme*, [1998] ECR I-8033 (ECLI:EU:C:1998:584).
[4] E.g., Case C-2/90, *Commission v. Belgium*, [1992] ECR I-4431 (ECLI:EU:C:1992:310).
[5] E.g., Case 66/85, *Lawrie-Blum*, [1986] ECR 2121 (ECLI:EU:C:1986:284); Case C-413/01, *Ninni-Orasche*, [2003] ECR I-13187 (ECLI:EU:C:2003:600).
[6] E.g., Case C-53/81, *Levin*, [1982] ECR 1035 (ECLI:EU:C:1982:105); Case C-139/85, *Kempf*, [1986] ECR 1741 (ECLI:EU:C:1986:223).
[7] Case 196/87, *Steymann*, [1988] ECR 6159 (ECLI:EU:C:1988:475).
[8] Case C-281/06, *Jundt*, [2007] ECR I-12231 (ECLI:EU:C:2007:816) (which concerns Art. 56 TFEU). See also Case C-301/14, *Pfotenhilfe-Ungarn e.V.*, judgment of 3 December 2015, not yet reported (ECLI:EU:C:2015:793) (which concerns Reg. 1/2005, based on what is now Art. 43 TFEU).
[9] Case C-507/12, *Saint Prix*, judgment of 19 June 2014, not yet reported (ECLI:EU:C:2014:2007).

objective of liberalizing all gainful activity not covered by the free movement of goods, persons and capital'.[10] So Article 56 TFEU includes 'passive' freedom to provide services, meaning the freedom for recipients of services to go to another Member State in order to receive a service there. This means that tourists, persons receiving medical treatment and persons travelling for the purpose of education or business are to be regarded as recipients of services who are protected by EU law.[11]

Article 57 TFEU directs that services within the meaning of EU law are 'normally provided for remuneration' but pursuant to a similarly thematically broad interpretation this covers not only services for which the user pays directly but also services for which no direct payment is made, as long as remuneration is in some way provided. Medical treatment provided by a hospital counts as a 'service' in this sense where it is funded by sickness insurance schemes including fixed fee rates, even though the patient may not pay directly for treatment received.[12] This is the route to promoting patient mobility through reliance on free movement law, considered in Section C, and which prompted the subsequent adoption of Directive 2011/24,[13] which is, in fact, largely a rather pedestrian codification of the Court's position on prior authorization of treatment and reimbursement of costs incurred. The Court has been a little less aggressive in addressing provision of secondary and higher education. This constitutes the fulfilment of a state's social duties towards its population and where it is funded essentially out of the public purse, it will not count as a service for these purposes.[14] This shows that there *are* limits. However, private education will plainly attract a different interpretation and even the limit asserted in the matter of public education is vulnerable to subsequent breach by reliance on the Court's more expansive logic employed in the cases on medical treatment.[15]

In *Schindler* the Court rejected the arguments of several governments that lotteries are not an 'economic activity' within the meaning of the Treaty.[16] The Court focused on the relevance of remuneration in the form of the price paid for the lottery ticket. There were, the Court observed, services provided by the operator of the lottery to enable purchasers of tickets to participate in a game of chance with the hope of winning. The Court agreed that lotteries are subject to particularly strict regulation in many Member States and it went so far as to note that 'the morality of lotteries is at least questionable',[17] but it refused to 'substitute its assessment for that of the legislatures of the Member States where that activity is practised legally'.[18] In consequence, the viability of national regulation of lotteries and gambling services more

---

[10] Joined Cases 282/82 and 26/83, *Luisi and Carbone* v. *Ministero del Tesoro*, [1984] ECR 377 (ECLI:EU:C:1984:35), at para. 10.
[11] E.g., Case 186/87, *Cowan* v. *Le Tresor Public*, [1989] ECR 195 (ECLI:EU:C:1989:47); Case C-274/96, *Bickel and Franz*, [1998] ECR I-7637 (ECLI:EU:C:1998:563); Case C-348/96, *Calfa*, [1999] ECR I-11 (ECLI:EU:C:1999:6).
[12] E.g., Case C-157/99, *Smits and Peerbooms*, [2001] ECR 5473 (ECLI:EU:C:2001:404).
[13] OJ 2011 L 88/45.
[14] Case 263/86, *Humbel*, [1988] ECR 5365 (ECLI:EU:C:1988:451); Case C-109/92, *Wirth*, [1993] ECR I-6447 (ECLI:EU:C:1993:916).
[15] See, e.g., Opinion of A.G. Stix-Hackl in Case C-76/05, *Herbert Schwarz*, [2007] ECR I-6849 (ECLI:EU:C:2007:492).
[16] Case C-275/92, *Schindler*, [1994] ECR I-1039 (ECLI:EU:C:1994:119).
[17] *Ibid.*, at para. 32.   [18] *Ibid.*, at para. 32.

generally under EU law rested on showing a justification for such intervention. Justification is examined more fully in Chapter 8.

The main theme visible in the Court's case law is its <u>unwillingness at the stage of determining whether there is a restriction on cross-border economic activity to offer any sector-specific treatment</u>. So, by way of typical example, in *Webb* it was asked to deal with Dutch rules that required governmental authorization for the use of what the judgment calls (rather anachronistically) 'manpower'.[19] It found this constituted an obstacle to the free movement of services from other Member States. It was faced by submissions by the French government to the effect that such services were 'special' because their treatment engaged both social policy and the free movement of persons, but the Court briskly noted that 'the special nature of certain services does not remove them from the ambit of the rules on the freedom to supply services'.[20] This is readily understood as the Court's application of the system envisaged by the Treaty. The internal market as a legal concept militates against a sensitivity to the particular context in the matter of finding a restriction on economic activity. That sensitivity is, instead, located and visible at the stage of justification.

In competition law the 'undertaking' which is the subject of express reference in Articles 101 and 102 TFEU is interpreted by the Court to cover any entity that is engaged in an economic activity, regardless of the legal status of that entity and the way in which it is financed. So any activity consisting in offering goods and services on a given market is an economic activity.[21] This is a wide, if not quite all-embracing, definition. <u>Activities which fall within the exercise of public powers are not of an economic nature justifying the application of the Treaty rules of competition.</u> The Court found Eurocontrol's function to establish and collect charges levied on users of air navigation services in accordance with an international agreement was connected with the exercise of powers relating to the control and supervision of air space which are typically those of a public authority, and so they were not of an economic nature such as to fall within the competition rules.[22] So, too, the Court has been willing to treat the management of the public social security system as an activity which does not belong to the sphere of economic activity.[23] This, however, is a limit to the reach of internal market law which is far more readily breached than respected. Where there is a market or even a *potential* market to the activity, the threshold is crossed.

Ambulanz Glöckner is an example that is as powerful as it is typical.[24] The applicant was refused authorization to provide patient ambulance transport services in a

---

[19] Case 279/80, *Webb*, [1981] ECR 3305 (ECLI:EU:C:1981:314).

[20] *Ibid.*, at para. 10, citing Case 33/74, *Van Binsbergen*, [1974] ECR 1299 (ECLI:EU:C:1974:131).

[21] E.g., Case C-41/90, *Höfner and Elser*, [1991] ECR I-1979 (ECLI:EU:C:1991:161); Joined Cases C-264/01, C-306/01, C-354/01 and C-355/01, *AOK-Bundesverband and Others*, [2004] ECR I-2493 (ECLI:EU:C:2004:150); Case C-205/03P, *FENIN* v. *Commission*, [2006] ECR I-6295 (ECLI:EU:C:2006:453).

[22] Case C-364/92, *SAT* v. *Eurocontrol*, [1994] ECR I-43 (ECLI:EU:C:1994:7); Case C-113/07P, *SELEX Sistemi*, [2009] ECR I-2207 (ECLI:EU:C:2009:191).

[23] E.g., Joined Cases C-159/91, C-160/91, *Poucet and Pistre*, [1993] ECR I-637 (ECLI:EU:C:1993:63).

[24] Case C-475/99, *Firma Ambulanz Glöckner* v. *Landkreis Sudwestpfalz*, [2001] ECR I-8089 (ECLI:EU:C:2001:577).

German region because two medical aid organizations entrusted with the public ambulance service in the area operated at only 26 per cent of their capacity and so did not wish to suffer competition. The Court found that the provision of such services constituted an economic activity provided by undertakings for the purposes of the application of the Treaty competition rules. The Court accepted that public service obligations may render the services provided by a given medical aid organization less competitive than comparable services rendered by other operators not bound by such obligations, but that fact cannot prevent the activities in question from being regarded as economic activities nor the providers from being treated as undertakings. The most striking dimension to the ruling is the Court's focus on the fact that the transport services 'have not always been, and are not necessarily, carried on by such organisations or by public authorities'.[25] So where there is *potentially* a market, EU competition law applies.

This obviously entails that a body which is not profit-making may be an 'undertaking'. So, for example, a scheme set up through collective negotiation between both sides of industry in a particular sector for the purpose of reimbursing healthcare costs incurred by employees was not for profit and, as the Court fully accepted, in pursuit of a social objective, but this was not enough to exclude its designation as an 'undertaking'.[26] It would escape subjection to EU competition law only provided that, in addition, it acted on the basis of the principle of solidarity and was subject to state supervision and control. Absent such features, its capability to act in competition with other providers of such services means that EU competition law bites.

Injecting competition into markets previously dominated by monopoly suppliers, commonly state-owned, is a policy which brings with it an increased profile for the disciplining force of competition law, but on the Court's logic even in the absence of any injection of competition the sector and, in particular, the monopoly supplier may be subject to review conducted pursuant to competition law. This means that in many circumstances bodies which provide public services such as health care are 'undertakings' and so are subject to the discipline of EU competition law.[27] A formal status as a body that is public or private is not in point: this is a manifestation of EU law's insouciance to classifications cherished under national law. Universities may be 'undertakings' where they attract funding for research activities.[28] Broadcasting provides another example. The Court long ago rejected the contention that public broadcasters 'fulfil a task which concerns the public and is of a cultural and informative nature' and so are not 'undertakings'.[29] They *are* undertakings, although in so

---

[25] *Ibid.*, at para. 20.

[26] Case C-437/09, *AG2R Prévoyance*, [2011] ECR I-973 (ECLI:EU:C:2011:112).

[27] See, e.g., Van de Gronden and Sauter, 'Taking the Temperature: EU Competition Law and Health Care', 38 *Legal Issues of Economic Integration* (2011) 213; Sauter, 'The Impact of EU Competition Law on National Healthcare Systems', 38 *European Law Review* (2013) 457; Odudu, 'Are State Owned Healthcare Providers That Are Funded by General Taxation Undertakings Subject to Competition Law?', *European Competition Law Review* (2011) 231.

[28] See Gideon, 'Blurring Boundaries between the Public and the Private in National Research Policies and Possible Consequences from EU Primary Law', 11 *Journal of Contemporary European Research* (2015) 50.

[29] Case 155/73, *Sacchi*, [1974] ECR 409 (ECLI:EU:C:1974:40), at para. 13.

far as they are entrusted with a service of general economic interest they may enjoy the shelter provided by what is now Article 106(2) TFEU, to the effect that the rules on competition apply to them only insofar as that does not obstruct the performance of the particular tasks assigned to them. They may enjoy exclusive rights conferred by law, but their exercise must comply with EU internal market law.

The mainstream of practice readily brings commercial operators within the scope of the Treaty competition rules as 'undertakings' even where they exercise a form of regulatory power. It is apt to catch bodies which perform regulatory functions where there is a sufficient commercial context. So, for example, in *Ministero dello Sviluppo economic* v. *SOA* a commercial undertaking entrusted with supplying certification services, as provided for by Italian legislation, did not escape.[30] Certificates were provided in return for remuneration and exclusively on the basis of demand. The undertaking assumed the financial risks involved in the exercise of that activity. This was, in short, a market. EU competition law accordingly applied. In similar vein, the Court in *Wouters* treated rules of the Dutch bar prohibiting multi-disciplinary partnerships as within the scope of the competition rules on the basis that members of the Bar provide services for a fee while bearing the financial risks attaching to the performance of those activities, and the Bar itself was acting as the regulatory body of a profession, the practice of which constitutes an economic activity.[31] The Court refused to find that the Dutch bar was fulfilling a social function based on the principle of solidarity or exercising powers which are typically those of a public authority. The Court's ruling in *Wouters* underlines its thematic reluctance to adopt a sector-specific approach to the jurisdictional question of whether internal market law is engaged. Its finding was not affected by the 'complexity and technical nature of the services they provide and the fact that the practice of their profession is regulated',[32] a view the Court had already adopted in relation to medical practitioners.[33]

Meca-Medina and Majcen v. *Commission*, which concerned anti-doping rules in swimming, was decided on the basis that the IOC was an 'undertaking' and, within the Olympic Movement, as an association of international and national associations of undertakings.[34] And in *Motosykletistiki Omospondia Ellados NPID (MOTOE)* v. *Elliniko Dimosio* the Court, dealing with a sports governing body's exclusive right to decide whether or not to sanction the staging of new events, considered that even if it was non-profit-making as a matter of legal form, it was subject to Article 102 TFEU where it went beyond the status of impartial regulator by organizing and commercially exploiting its own events.[35] It competed with bodies which were seeking to make a profit. It was an 'undertaking'.

---

[30] Case C-327/12, *Ministero dello Sviluppo economico* v. *SOA Nazionale Costruttori*, judgment of 12 December 2013, not yet reported (ECLI:EU:C:2013:827).

[31] Case C-309/99, *Wouters*, [2002] ECR I-1577 (ECLI:EU:C:2002:98).

[32] *Ibid.*, at para. 49.

[33] E.g., Joined Cases C-180/98 to C-184/98, *Pavlov and Others*, [2000] ECR I-6451 (ECLI:EU:C:2000:428).

[34] Case C-519/04 P, *Meca-Medina and Majcen* v. *Commission*, [2006] ECR I-6991 (ECLI:EU:C:2006:492).

[35] Case C-49/07, *Motosykletistiki Omospondia Ellados NPID (MOTOE)* v. *Dimosio*, [2008] ECR I-4863 (ECLI:EU:C:2008:376).

In all these circumstances the point is not that the practices are unlawful. The point is jurisdictional: these activities fall within the scope of EU law because of their effects in the market and there is only a relatively narrow zone of 'non-economic activity' which escapes. This loads a heavy weight on to the subsequent stage of the analysis, which asks whether such practices which fall within the scope of internal market law are *justified* or not. This engages Treaty provisions such as Articles 36 and 52 TFEU and, of especial significance to public services, Article 106(2) TFEU as well as the Court's more generous elaboration of justification in the public interest, where *Wouters* is a particular landmark. This is examined in Chapter 8. It is only at the stage of justification, not at the stage of identifying a 'market' in the first place, that the particular purpose or sector-specific context of the activities breaks the surface of internal market law.

B. The Limits of the 'Market'

Just occasionally the limits to the muscular reach of internal market become visible in the mountain of case law. But these occasions are so rare and sometimes so eccentric that they tend to highlight rather than contradict the claim that EU internal market law is extraordinarily broad and ambiguous. They show, with an eye to Article 5 TEU's principle of conferral, that it is more marked as an empowering than as a limiting concept.

SPUC v. *Grogan* is one of the best-known examples: the decision is as illuminating as it is atypical.[36] Action was taken pursuant to highly restrictive Irish laws to prevent students' unions in Dublin from providing information about abortion services available in London. In the first place the Court resisted the argument advanced by SPUC that the matter fell outwith the scope of the Treaty on the basis that the provision of abortion 'cannot be regarded as being a service, on the grounds that it is grossly immoral and involves the destruction of the life of a human being, namely the unborn child'.[37] The Court did not agree. Services fall within the meaning of the Treaty where they are normally provided for remuneration, and the termination of pregnancy, lawful in several though not all Member States, counts as a medical activity which is normally provided for remuneration. The Court had nothing in detail to say about the moral issues save only to hold that it was not for it to substitute its assessment for that of the legislature in those Member States where abortion is practised legally. Exactly this approach would subsequently be adapted in *Schindler* to cover lotteries.[38] EU law applies: this was an economic activity.

But the Court was able to avoid the looming and extremely awkward question whether the restriction on free movement was justified. In *Grogan* the Court refused to allow the Irish intervention to be tested against the Treaty rules governing the free movement of services on the basis that the students' union involved had no commercial

---

[36] Case C-159/90, *Society for the Protection of Unborn Children Ireland* v. *Grogan*, [1991] ECR I-4685 (ECLI:EU:C:1991:378).

[37] *Ibid.*, at para. 19.

[38] Case C-275/92, *supra* note 16. Para. 32 cites *Grogan, supra* note 36.

motivation in providing the information. So abortion services are an economic activity, but *the union* was not engaged in an economic activity. The fragility of this protection afforded to the Irish regime is plain when one appreciates that had the students' union accepted even a token payment by a clinic in London in return for providing the information, then the Court would have been denied its convenient escape route.[39] So *Grogan* reveals a glimpse of the limits of the 'market' as a concept which empowers EU law, but it confirms how tenuous and ad hoc those limits truly and typically are.

Marc Michel Josemans v. *Burgemeester van Maastricht* bears a similar stamp.[40] The case addressed the licensing of 'coffee shops' in Maastricht (where buying and smoking marijuana is tolerated in those shops). Under amended rules introduced locally in 2005, only 14 such shops are allowed and their use is restricted to local residents. The rule's aim was to restrict 'drug tourism' and to improve the quality of life of the citizens of Maastricht, but in doing so it impeded inter-state trade (in drugs and in drug tourists). The Court declared that 'the harmfulness of narcotic drugs, including those derived from hemp, such as cannabis, is generally recognised' and that accordingly 'there is a prohibition in all the Member States on marketing them, with the exception of strictly controlled trade for use for medical and scientific purposes', citing several of its own previous decisions in support.[41] Outside the cited strictly controlled channels, narcotic drugs were, in the Court's view, 'prohibited from being released into the economic and commercial channels of the European Union',[42] and so it was not open to a coffee-shop proprietor to rely on the freedoms of movement or the principle of non-discrimination to challenge local rules affecting the sale of cannabis. This was beyond the reach of the EU law. The problem with the Court's analysis is that there clearly *was* trade in such products. It may not have been completely lawful and certainly it was not unregulated, but it was evidently tolerated: that was undeniably clear from the facts of the case itself. The rule in question had been enacted to protect the citizens of Maastricht only because there was a lot of such (tolerated) trade in soft drugs. Moreover, the previous case law cited by the Court in *Josemans* did not in fact offer useful support for the finding that internal market law did not apply. *Horvath*, for example, concerned heroin, which, unlike cannabis, is plainly tolerated nowhere in Europe,[43] while *Einberger* v. *Hauptzollamt Freiburg* was a case about the liability to tax of morphine smuggled illegally into Germany.[44] *Josemans* was not of this type at all. It did not concern a product or service that was clearly and systematically banned.

Both *Grogan* and *Josemans* suggest a Court eager to find a convenient way to evade adjudicating a thoroughly awkward collision between commercial freedom and

---

[39] So momentum for change was not stalled by this litigious failure; on subsequent reform of Irish law, treating it as a story of value pluralism within the EU, see Nic Shuibhne, 'Margins of Appreciation: National Values, Fundamental Rights and EC Free Movement Law', 34 *European Law Review* (2009) 230.

[40] Case C-137/09, *Marc Michel Josemans* v. *Burgemeester van Maastricht*, [2010] ECR I-3019 (ECLI:EU:C:2010:774).

[41] *Ibid.*, at para. 36.

[42] *Ibid.*, at para. 42.

[43] Case 50/80, *Horvath*, [1981] ECR 385 (ECLI:EU:C:1981:34).

[44] Case 294/82, *Einberger* v. *Hauptzollamt Freiburg*, [1984] ECR 1177 (ECLI:EU:C:1984:81).

local social and moral choices: neither ruling asserts or reveals any principled excavation of space for national regulatory autonomy unaffected by internal market law. The 'market' gets *almost* everywhere.

Elisabeta Dano concerned a Romanian national resident in Germany who had been refused social benefits for her and her son by the public authorities in Leipzig.[45] The Court noted that she had not worked in Germany or Romania and that although her ability to work was not in dispute, there was no evidence that she had looked for a job.[46] The Court explained that the principle of non-discrimination laid down Article 18 TFEU has been given more specific expression in Article 24 of Directive 2004/38 on the right of citizens of the Union and their family members to move and reside freely within the territory of the Member States, and it proceeded to examine the matter from the perspective of that measure. That Directive makes separate provision for three types of migrant: those resident in another Member State for up to three months; those resident for more than three months but less than five years; and, finally, those resident for more than five years in the host Member State. Dano was in the second category, but, as the Court stressed, she was 'economically inactive',[47] and under the Directive this meant she was required to possess sufficient resources of her own in order to enjoy a right of residence in the host State. The Court concluded that it was permitted under EU law for the German authorities to refuse 'to grant social benefits to economically inactive Union citizens who exercise their right to freedom of movement solely in order to obtain another Member State's social assistance although they do not have sufficient resources to claim a right of residence'.[48] The Court's ruling was high profile. It is loosely correct to treat it as having closed the door to the protection of 'benefit tourism' under EU law, although there is in fact little evidence that the phenomenon of 'benefit tourism' occurs on any significant scale[49] and so the facts of *Dano* are probably abnormal. The ruling is thematically abnormal too. It is rare to find refusal to allow a migrant to rely on EU law: Advocate General Wathelet described *Dano* as having caused an 'unusual stir . . . in the European media' in his Opinion in *Alimanovic*, the first case that tasked the Court with exploring the implications of *Dano* beyond the case's particular facts.[50] However, as with *Grogan* and *Josemans*, the most striking aspect of *Dano* is how unusual it is to discover a niche where EU law does not help. It would have been different had she been *looking* for work: the Court long ago insisted on the need to adopt a broad interpretation of the scope of the law on the free movement of workers and accordingly treated (what is now) Article 45 TFEU as apt to cover the person seeking a job in another Member State.[51] It is rare to find someone wholly economically inactive – applicants in future will doubtless be able to learn from *Dano* and do what they can

---

[45] Case C-333/13, *Elisabeta Dano*, judgment of 11 November 2014, not yet reported (ECLI:EU: C:2014:2358).
[46] *Ibid.*, at para. 39.   [47] *Ibid.*, at para. 73. See also paras 39, 40 and 66.
[48] *Ibid.*, at para. 78.
[49] For Commission studies, see http://ec.europa.eu/social/main.jsp?langId=en&catId=89&newsId =1980&furtherNews=yes.
[50] Case C-67/14, *Jobcenter Berlin Neukölln* v. *Alimanovic*, Opinion of 26 March 2015 (ECLI:EU: C:2015:210).
[51] Case C-292/89, *Antonissen*, [1991] ECR 745 (ECLI:EU:C:1991:80).

to avoid falling into that category, where EU law does not come to the rescue. And in any event the limits of the logic and reach of *Dano* itself should be appreciated: the Court decided she could be refused access to particular social benefits, but it did not rule more generally that she was wholly outwith the scope of protection envisaged by EU law. If, for example, Germany wished to remove Ms Dano from its territory she would surely be entitled to the procedural protections envisaged by the Directive.[52]

Similarly, in competition law it is rare to find the Court willing to place activity with economic effects outwith the reach of internal market law and when it does so it tends to create surprise for its atypicality. *Albany International* counts as an – illustrative but isolated – example of the occasional but rare readiness of the Court to restrain the force of the internal *market* as a (self-) empowering legal concept.[53] The Dutch public authorities made affiliation to a sectoral pension fund compulsory at the request of organizations representing employers and workers. Albany wished to attack the request by management and labour as an anti-competitive agreement contrary to what is now Article 101(1) – and also, though of less present relevance, to attack the state intervention too. The core of Albany's case was that the compulsory nature of the scheme shut down opportunities for other providers to compete in the pension insurance market. The Court found a way to defeat the claim. It placed the competition rules in the Treaty alongside the Treaty's expressed concern for a high level of employment and of social protection. It could not, and did not, deny that 'certain restrictions of competition are inherent in collective agreements between organisations representing employers and workers' but added that 'the social policy objectives pursued by such agreements would be seriously undermined if management and labour were subject to Article 85(1) [now 101(1)] of the Treaty when seeking jointly to adopt measures to improve conditions of work and employment'.[54] With this one bound it was free: expressing a concern for an effective and consistent interpretation of the Treaty *as a whole,* it stated that collective negotiations between management and labour did not fall within the scope of what is today Article 101(1).[55] The Court thereby creatively found a way to protect social dialogue from competition law. This contextual approach is dictated by a concern to prevent the Treaty competition rules damaging other objectives set by the Treaties: the Court on occasion does treat particular circumstances as 'special'. It can do it if it tries.[56]

This 'Albany exception' is, however, limited in scope. It demands the presence of both collective action and the improvement of conditions of work and the Court does not seem minded to expand it as an escape route applicable beyond the specific

---

[52] For discussion of this and other points see Thym, 'When Union Citizens Turn into Illegal Migrants: The *Dano* Case', 40 *European Law Review* (2015) 249.

[53] Case C-67/96, *Albany International*, [1999] ECR I-5751 (ECLI:EU:C:1999:430).

[54] *Ibid.*, at para. 59.   [55] *Ibid.*, at para. 60.

[56] For comment at the time, see, e.g., Van den Bergh and Camesasca, 'Irreconcilable Principles? The Court of Justice Exempts Collective Labour Agreements from the Wrath of Antitrust', 25 *European Law Review* (2000) 492. See also B. Van Rompuy, *Economic Efficiency: the Sole Concern of Modern Antitrust Policy? Non-Efficiency Considerations under Article 101 TFEU* (2012), Ch. 4, especially at 221–223; R. Whish and D. Bailey, *Competition Law* (7th ed., 2012), Ch. 3 sec. 4; and (seen from the other direction) C. Barnard, *EU Employment Law* (4th ed., 2012), at 193–197.

problem it faced in *Albany*. For example, in *FNV Kunsten Informatie en Media* it refused to apply the logic of *Albany* to a collective labour agreement setting minimum fees for musicians acting as substitutes in an orchestra.[57] The reason was that the musicians were self-employed, not workers, and therefore, in contrast to *Albany*, the Court was not willing to treat this as a case where the unions were acting as social partners in the sense of *Albany*. It would only be different if the self-employed individuals were not truly independent undertakings, but were, in truth, workers.

Overall, there is a strong 'marketizing' pull in EU internal market law, as a result of the breadth of economic effects. Very few activities truly escape the scope of application of EU economic law. It is normally a low threshold to insist that EU economic law applies only where there is an internal *market* element. So the regulatory autonomy of the Member States is respected in principle, but not reliably and certainly not generously in practice. What this means, in particular to those seeking to defend practices that collide with the impetus to create an internal market for the EU, is that they must seek to show justification for their regulatory choices. To persuade the Court that they do not fall within the scope of EU law *in the first place* is a tough task.

C. The Internal Market as a Concept Which Takes the Scope of Negative Law beyond That of Positive Law

The matter is taken further by the point that the free movement and competition provisions are in no sense confined in their scope of application to areas in which the EU enjoys a legislative competence conferred by the Treaties. There is no protection for national regulatory autonomy where its exercise contradicts the demands of the internal market even if the EU is disabled (in part or completely) from intervening through a *legislative* act. Negative law – free movement law, competition law – goes further than positive law, because it is driven by the functionally broad concern to make an internal market. This is a further reason why the promises made by the principle of conferral found in Article 5 TEU are far less helpful to the preservation of national autonomy than they may first appear.

The factual background to the Court's ruling in *ex parte Watts* concerns a British national's receipt of medical treatment in another Member State. In its ruling the Court adopted an approach which is of general application in circumstances where the scope of EU internal market law exceeds the limits of EU legislative competence:

> . . . although . . . [Union] law does not detract from the power of the Member States to organise their social security systems and decide the level of resources to be allocated to their operation, the achievement of the fundamental freedoms guaranteed by the Treaty nevertheless inevitably requires Member States to make adjustments to those systems. It does not follow that this undermines their sovereign powers in the field.[58]

---

[57] Case C-413/13, *FNV Kunsten Informatie en Media* v. *Staat der Nederlanden*, judgment of 4 December 2014, not yet reported (ECLI:EU:C:2014:2411).

[58] Case C-372/04, *Watts*, [2006] ECR I-4325 (ECLI:EU:C:2006:325), at para. 121.

The Court has adopted this as a standard formula in cases where the achievement of economic integration comes into conflict with national practices in fields where the Union is not competent (at all or only under limited conditions) to act as a substitute legislator. Health care, the matter at stake in *ex parte Watts*, is a good example: there is no question of the EU assuming any general responsibility for the organization, management and still less the funding of health care, but nevertheless where such arrangements shaped at national level have an effect on the internal market, EU law is engaged and the national practices require justification. This approach is found with structural similarity in areas such as social security[59] and taxation.[60] A powerful example is found in the maintenance of public order. Plainly this is the responsibility of state authorities, not the EU, but where failure to take proper action to suppress disorder leads to impediments to free movement across borders, the EU asserts a role in reviewing the national (in)action.[61] Free movement law stops states (and to some extent private parties: see Chapter 9) acting in the absence of justification for chosen practices that impede cross-border trade, even where the fields in question are beyond the bounds of EU legislative competence.

It is readily arguable that the Court's formula is at best disingenuous, and at worst downright deceptive. The declaration that the achievement of the Treaty's fundamental freedoms requires an adjustment by the Member States which does not undermine 'their sovereign powers in the field' begs the question of what sovereign powers truly entail in this context. Used in this way, EU internal market law circumscribes the scope of sovereign state choices and makes pivotal the allowed scope of justification which is available and recognized under EU law. So, for example, the impetus towards cross-border patient mobility which was the result of the ruling in *ex parte Watts* ruling confronted health care authorities with genuinely awkward questions associated with budget management: waiting lists are a feature of the allocation of scarce resources which are upset by the intervention of a claim based on EU law.[62] However, the Court's choice is based on a perception of the logic of the Treaty itself. The Treaty does not place particular sectors of economic activity beyond the reach of its basic rules. Quite the reverse: the Treaty asserts a very broad functional reach. The Court therefore interprets EU trade law in an expansive manner. When one is engaged in some form of economic activity it is very difficult to construct an argument which is effective in securing insulation from the application of EU law. In internal market law the principal arguments tend to surround the question whether a particular practice is justified or not. Typically, and thematically clearly, there is negligible scope for arguing that EU law does not apply *at all*.

Sport offers a particularly vivid example, not least because of the long-standing and loud protests of governing bodies that they should *not* be subjected to the demands

[59] E.g., Case C-512/03, *J E J Blankaert*, [2005] ECR I-7685 (ECLI:EU:C:2005:516); Case C-255/09, *Commission* v. *Portugal*, [2011] ECR I-10547 (ECLI:EU:C:2011:695).
[60] E.g., Case C-446/03, *Marks and Spencer* v. *Halsey*, [2005] ECR I-10837 (ECLI:EU:C:2005:763).
[61] E.g., Case C-265/95, *Commission* v. *France*, [1997] ECR I-6959 (ECLI:EU:C:1997:595); Case C-112/00, *Schmidberger* v. *Austria*, [2003] ECR I-5659 (ECLI:EU:C:2003:333).
[62] E.g., Newdick, 'Citizenship, Free Movement and Health Care: Cementing Individual Rights by Corroding Social Solidarity' 43 *Common Market Law Review* (2006) 1645.

of EU law. Sport itself is the subject of reference in the TFEU. Article 165 TFEU is the relevant provision, which declares inter alia that account shall be taken of 'the specific nature of sport' and which equips the EU with a carefully limited legislative competence (which explicitly excludes harmonization). However, this provision is an innovation of the Treaty of Lisbon. Up until 2009 sport was not mentioned *at all* in the Treaties. Sport is, however, part of the economy. In fact, it has famously become very big business indeed in recent years, as technological advances coupled to deregulation have dramatically altered the broadcasting sector to which high-level professional sport is so tightly connected. In this vein, the Court has consistently refused to accept the submissions of the relevant governing bodies that their game should lie beyond the reach of EU law. *Bosman* is the most famous example.[63] The Court was asked in that case to consider the compatibility of the transfer system for footballers with EU law. As a preliminary point, the Belgian football association had argued that that only the major European football clubs may be regarded as undertakings, whereas by contrast the economic activity pursued by smaller clubs is 'negligible'[64] while the German government pressed, in similar vein, that in most cases football is not an economic activity.[65] The Court did not disagree. It stated that sport is subject to EU law only in so far as it constitutes an economic activity within the meaning of the Treaty. But it found that this readily applied to the activities of professional or semi-professional footballers.[66] The application of EU law could not be excluded in principle. On the matter that was the subject of Bosman's principal complaint, the transfer system, it plainly is not for the EU to impose a shape on football's transfer system. That lies beyond its legislative competence, then as now. However, it *is* for the EU – specifically its Court – to rule on how football shall *not* shape its transfer system. That means that it must not violate EU internal market law. In *Bosman* the Court concluded that the system challenged in the case contravened free movement law. It was unnecessarily restrictive and inadequately focused on its identified and (in the Court's view) legitimate purpose to *maintain a balance between clubs by preserving a certain degree of equality and uncertainty as to results and to encourage the recruitment and training of young players.*[67] The instructive dimension of the ruling is that the Court was forced to engage with the purpose of a transfer system in football and to express a view on its legitimate reach, even though the Treaty was utterly barren of any reference to sport at all. It is the broad reach of EU law into matters that form part of the 'market' that causes this.

The same pattern is visible in the application of the Treaty competition rules to sport. *Meca-Medina and Majcen* v. *Commission* concerned the suspension of swimmers from competition as a result of a ban imposed for doping offences.[68] The Court

---

[63] Case C-415/93, *Bosman*, [1995] ECR I-4921 (ECLI:EU:C:1995:463). The first step, however, was Case 36/74, *Walrave and Koch* v. *Union Cycliste Internationale*, [1974] ECR 1405 (ECLI:EU: C:1974:140); its wide understanding of the material scope of EU law was stressed at the time by Ubertazzi, 'Le domaine du droit communautaire. A propos de l'arrêt Walrave, Union cycliste internationale', 12 *Revue trimestrielle de droit européen* (1976) 635.
[64] Case C-415/93, *supra* note 63, at para. 70.   [65] *Ibid.*, at para. 72.
[66] *Ibid.*, at paras 73–74.   [67] *Ibid.*, at para. 106.
[68] Case C-519/04 P, *supra* note 34.

was on familiar ground: it began by asserting that sport is subject to EU law 'in so far as it constitutes an economic activity'.[69] It admitted that the Treaty prohibitions against restrictions on free movement 'do not affect rules concerning questions which are of purely sporting interest and, as such, have nothing to do with economic activity'[70] and applied a parallel approach to the competition rules, but the *effect* of a practice is what drives EU internal market law and rules that are 'purely sporting' in effect are, in truth, extremely rare. At stake was 'the difficulty of severing the economic aspects from the sporting aspects of a sport':[71] in most circumstances *both* aspects inform the practices of governing bodies. A ban imposed on an athlete had a clear economic effect – on that athlete's livelihood. Not only that, but the purpose of doping rules is not only to ensure that sport is clean but also to make it attractive to sponsors and broadcasters, as the Court itself noted in its ruling.[72] The constitutional constraint of the principle of conferral is thus seen in its true context: in practice, the EU Treaty is structured to bring a very wide range of activities actually or potentially within its scope.

The consequence of the wider reach of negative over positive law is the need to create a policy where the Treaty (by definition) does not offer one in order to decide whether challenged national rules shall be permitted under EU internal market law. This is why and where questions of justification for trade-restrictive measures become acutely important. There is a pressing need for the Court to be sensitive to the disturbance potentially wrought by EU law *especially* when free movement and competition law collides with areas where the EU's legislative competence is thin or non-existent. This is explored further in Chapter 8.

Even the few tentative attempts in the Treaty to seal off particular sectors or interests from the influence of EU law have been treated by the Court as largely ineffective, precisely because of its driving concern to protect the project of creating an internal market. Article 345 TFEU provides that the Treaties 'shall in no way prejudice the rules in Member States governing the system of property ownership'. This is simply the current version of a proviso which has been part of the system ever since the original Treaty of Rome entered into force in 1958. But it plays a negligible role. This first became visible in the 1970s in cases in which national rules governing intellectual property – patents, copyright and trademarks – were challenged as restrictions to inter-state trade in goods. The Court, forced to reckon with the effect of (what is now) Article 345 TFEU, acknowledged that 'the Treaty does not affect the existence of [property] rights recognized by the legislation of a Member State', but then found that 'the exercise of those rights may . . . be restricted by the prohibitions in the Treaty'.[73] This approach has much in common structurally with that subsequently adopted in *ex parte Watts*, the case on patient mobility discussed earlier.[74] There is something disingenuous about the Court's claim to be leave intact the *existence* of property rights when at the same time the effect of its approach is to curtail the *use*

---

[69] *Ibid.*, at para. 22.   [70] *Ibid.*, at para. 25: it draws on Case 36/74, *supra* note 63.
[71] *Ibid.*, at para. 26.   [72] *Ibid.*, at paras 40, 46.
[73] E.g., Case 119/75, *Terrapin* v. *Terranova*, [1976] ECR 1039 (ECLI:EU:C:1976:94), at para. 5.
[74] Case C-372/04, *supra* note 58.

to which they may be put. But the heart of its concern is to ensure that review of the impact of intellectual property rights on the functioning of the internal market is not placed beyond the reach of EU law. This is, once again, to glimpse the thematic empowering effect of the internal market as a legal concept.

More recently, the Court adopted a comparable approach in *Essent* when asked to address Dutch rules prohibiting privatization in the gas sector.[75] The Court accepted that Article 345 TFEU guaranteed the neutrality of EU law as far as property ownership within the Member States was concerned, but it did not extend this interpretation of Article 345 TFEU to involve a conferral of immunity from the basic control exercised by the rules of free movement and non-discrimination. And accordingly, and in familiar vein, this placed a heavy emphasis on the Court's treatment of justifications for the chosen national measures which it had readily found to fall within the scope of EU internal market law. In *Essent* this drew it into inquiry into the reasons for public ownership, such as its capacity to combat cross-subsidization, to promote transparency and to encourage investment. To criticize this as judicial inflation of the reach and content of EU law must reckon with the functional logic embedded in the Treaties which are bare of unambiguous 'Halt!' signs. The internal market is *meant* to be a broad empowering concept. In very similar vein, Article 153(5) TFEU's direction that 'the provisions of this Article shall not apply to pay, the right of association, the right to strike or the right to impose lock-outs' was treated by the Court in *Viking Line* and *Laval* as no barrier to the review under free movement law of industrial action.[76] This once again made vivid the wider reach of negative over positive law: Article 153(5)'s carefully drawn limit applied to the latter but not the former. This is not inconsistent with the principle of conferral found in Article 5 TEU, but rather it exposes its practical frailties as a means to reserve a zone of autonomy to Member States.

Subsidiarity as a legal principle is similarly inapt to achieve insulation from the dauntingly broad reach of internal market law. *Bosman* offers a simple illustration of the Court's attitude. The German government, seeking to restrain scrutiny of sporting practices in the name of EU internal market law, cited the principle of subsidiarity to frame an argument that intervention by public authorities, including those of the EU, must be confined to what is strictly necessary.[77] The Court did not disagree with this as a matter of principle, but it ruled that the principle of subsidiarity cannot lead to a situation in which the freedom of private associations to adopt sporting rules restricts the exercise of rights conferred on individuals by the Treaty.[78] This is fully in line with the Court's orthodox interpretation of the structure of internal market law. Restrictive practices with economic effects do not escape scrutiny under EU law. The real test is typically whether or not they are justified.

Respect for the regulatory autonomy of the Member States is limited and unreliable. That seems to be the very nature of the Treaty system. In particular, the principle

---

[75] Joined Cases C-105/12 to C-107/12, *Essent*, judgment of 22 October 2013, not yet reported (ECLI:EU:C:2013:677).

[76] Case C-438/05, *Viking Line*, [2007] ECR I-10779 (ECLI:EU:C:2007:772); Case C-341/05, *Laval*, [2007] ECR I-11767 (ECLI:EU:C:2007:809).

[77] *Ibid.*, at para. 73.   [78] *Ibid.*, at para. 81.

of conferral's practical elaboration in Articles 2–6 TFEU, entitled 'Categories and areas of Union competence', possesses two main deficiencies: first, it ignores the impact of free movement and competition law operating beyond the scope of *legislative* competence; and, secondly, while it sets out three forms of competence – the EU's exclusive, shared and supporting competences – it makes no mention at all of the fourth category that must logically (pursuant to Articles 4(1) and 5(2) TEU) also exist, which is exclusive Member State competences. But the fact that the EU system does not offer any hard protection of such exclusive Member State competences is the reason that they are so difficult to identify and to protect. This expansionist trend is strongly driven by the internal market as an empowering legal concept.

Perhaps there is virtue in placing certain things and activities beyond the market.[79] EU internal market law is a really unpromising place to search for examples of any moral preference of this type. This *market* element in the development of EU internal market law is a major reason why Koen Lenaerts was right to conclude that 'there simply is no nucleus of sovereignty that the Member States can invoke, as such, against the' Union.[80] Looking at the matter from the other direction (with equally shrewd insight), Loïc Azoulai has observed that this approach serves as a 'vehicle for the totalization of the process of integration'.[81] Markets, on some accounts, may debase dignity and moral worth, but in the EU legal order they have enormous competence-empowering force and the constitutional consequences – in both the vertical and the horizontal dimension – are profound.

[79] For recent inquiry into a very old set of questions see M. Sandel, *What Money Can't Buy: The Moral Limits of Markets* (2012); D. Satz, *Why Some Things Should Not Be for Sale: The Moral Limits of Markets* (2010).

[80] In 'Constitutionalism and the Many Faces of Federalism', 38 *American Journal of Comparative Law* (1990) 205.

[81] Azoulai, 'The 'Retained Powers' Formula in the Case Law of the European Court of Justice: EU Law as Total Law?', 4 *European Journal of Legal Studies* (2011) 192.

6

The *Internal* Market

The examination of the internal market conducted in the previous chapter showed
that the *market* serves in principle to place a limit on the scope of application of EU
law, in line with the dictates of the principle of conferral found in Article 5(1) TEU,
but in practice that limit is drawn extraordinarily broadly. The *market* is more conspicuously an empowering rather than a limiting concept. The concern in this chapter is with the *internal* market. A starting-point in understanding the reach of EU
law of free movement and competition is that because the rules are in the service of
the internal market project, their application ends where the demands of the internal market end. A situation that is 'purely internal' to a single Member State falls
outwith the scope of the rules of the internal market. It is a matter of local concern.
But here too this limit is in practice not as firm and reliable as it may seem in
principle.

A. Limits, What Limits?

EU law does not prevent restrictions being placed on the sale of domestic goods or
services. So Article 34's purpose 'is to eliminate obstacles to the importation of goods
and not to ensure that goods of national origin always enjoy the same treatment as
imported or reimported goods'.[1] For workers too, the Treaty rules governing freedom of movement cannot be applied to cases in which all elements are purely internal
to a single Member State. So in *Land Nordrhein Westfalen* v. *Uecker, Jacquet* German
nationals who resided and worked in Germany and who had never exercised the
right to freedom of movement within the EU could not rely on EU law to protect
the position of their family members faced with discriminatory treatment.[2] Any
discrimination fell to be tackled under German law. Similarly, in *Saunders* EU law
was no help to a British national who, in consequence of conviction for theft, had
been required to proceed to Northern Ireland and not to return to England or Wales
within three years.[3] The Court of Justice of the European Union ('the Court')
declared that this was a situation 'wholly internal to a Member State . . . where there

---

[1] Case 355/85, *Michel Cognet*, [1986] ECR 3231 (ECLI:EU:C:1986:410), at para. 10.
[2] Case C-64/96 and C-65/96, *Land Nordrhein Westfalen* v. *Uecker, Jacquet*, [1997] ECR I-3171
(ECLI:EU:C:1997:285).
[3] Case 175/78, *Saunders*, [1979] ECR 1129 (ECLI:EU:C:1979:88).

is no factor connecting them to any of the situations envisaged' by EU law.[4] *Hans Moser* v. *Land Baden-Württemberg* involved a challenge by Moser to the refusal of the authorities of the Land Baden-Württemberg to allow him to undertake the post-graduate training necessary to secure entry to the teaching profession.[5] The reason was his membership of the German Communist Party. This, it was argued, might deprive Moser of the possibility of applying for teaching posts in other Member States. Citing *Saunders*, the Court noted that Article 48 EEC (now Article 45 TFEU) 'cannot be applied to situations which are wholly internal to a Member State, in other words where there is no factor connecting them to any of the situations envisaged by Community law'.[6] Moser's was such a case. His claim, the Court found, was based on a 'purely hypothetical prospect of employment in another Member State' which did not 'establish a sufficient connection with Community law'.[7] The message in this and many other of the cases on this jurisdictional boundary is that EU law offers no solution to a dispute that falls for resolution under national law, if necessary conditioned and supplemented by the law of the European Convention on Human Rights.

Competition law does not touch a practice that has no effect on inter-state trade patterns. This is made plain on the face of the relevant provisions in the Treaty. Article 101 TFEU requires that practices 'affect trade between Member States'. Article 102 TFEU controls conduct 'in so far as it may affect trade between Member States'. This is a jurisdictional requirement which serves in particular to demarcate EU competition law from national competition law. A practice that exerts a solely domestic impact lies beyond the reach of the Treaty.

These are the limits of EU internal market law, which grant concrete shape to the dictates of Article 5(1) EU's principle of conferral. Exactly what is at stake in locating and policing this jurisdictional boundary was little tested in the early years, as initially the case law tended to raise few difficulties of this type.

1. Early Years, Easy Years

The early years seldom generated any need for awkward inquiry into the existence of a cross-border dimension. Finding an inter-state element was usually very easy, indeed scarcely worth addressing. As mentioned earlier, the first ruling concerning the free movement of goods arrived in December 1961 and since it concerned Italian measures suspending the importation of pigs and pig products on to Italian territory, the inter-state trigger was obviously pulled.[8] So too in *Van Gend en Loos*, the first preliminary ruling concerning the free movement of goods, the fact that customs duties on imported products were at stake made it obvious that a cross-border element was present and correct in the case.[9] This was the nature of the types of dispute seen ini-

---

[4] *Ibid.*, at para. 11.
[5] Case 180/83, *Hans Moser* v. *Land Baden-Württemberg*, [1984] ECR 2539 (ECLI:EU:C:1984:233).
[6] *Ibid.*, at para. 15. [7] *Ibid.*, at para. 18.
[8] Case 7/61, *Commission* v. *Italy*, [1961] ECR 317 (ECLI:EU:C:1961:31).
[9] Case 26/62, *Van Gend en Loos*, [1963] ECR 1 (ECLI:EU:C:1963:1).

tially. Litigation was largely targeted at border controls, administrative formalities and customs duties which amounted to obvious physical obstacles to inter-state trade.[10] Discriminatory practices were also addressed. So – of course – offering subsidies to encourage the purchase of agricultural machinery on terms that favoured locally produced machines damaged the very basis of an internal market in which quality not origin should determine purchasing decisions, and so fell readily within the scope of free movement law.[11] Mapping and categorizing the types of measures that are caught is an immense job,[12] but most of the issues of principle surrounding physical barriers to trade and discriminatory practices are now relatively well settled and case law exposing such blatant violations of EU internal market law are infrequent today.

2. *Dassonville*

A key theme in the law of the internal market is that the areas immune from its influence are few and shrinking. In part this is because it is perfectly logical that the process of eliminating the economic significance of national frontiers should reduce the number of matters that are of truly local significance alone. It is also because the Court is on occasion remarkably quick to find an inter-state element, in some cases because it has allowed itself to be bamboozled by the ingenious and well-funded private litigants who are predatorily ubiquitous in EU law. The *internal* market criterion for the triggering of EU law tends to deceive as a reliable limiting feature, just as does the internal *market* criterion examined in the previous chapter.

Litigation concerning the free movement of goods provided the Court with ammunition. The relevant provision, today Article 34 TFEU, states that '[q]uantitative restrictions on imports and all measures having equivalent effect shall be prohibited between Member States'. This is absolutely typical of the spare style in which the relevant Treaty provisions are written. This pattern delegates a generous margin of interpretative autonomy to the Court, and there is minimal legislative amplification. Commission Directive 70/50 provided some limited direction, but the Court has rarely relied on it.[13] The 'quantitative restriction' – or quota – is tolerably straightforward. It refers to a numerical limit placed on imports. A complete ban, where the number would be zero, would simply amount to the most extreme version of the quota and certainly falls within the scope of Article 34.[14] The 'MEQR' (i.e., the measure having equivalent effect to a quantitative restriction) is not as straightforward a concept, but it is apt to catch the very wide range of devices that tend to restrict imports, stretching far beyond the conventional quota. The Court stepped in, and, allowed a choice between, at one extreme, a focus only on the prohibition of

---

[10] E.g., Cases 51-54/71, *International Fruit Company*, [1971] ECR 1107 (ECLI:EU:C:1971:128).

[11] Case 192/84, *Commission v. Greece*, [1985] ECR 3967 (ECLI:EU:C:1985:497).

[12] So, e.g., P. Oliver (ed.), *Oliver on Free Movement of Goods in the European Union* (5th ed., 2010) covers 31 different types of measure of equivalent effect in Ch. 7.II; L. Gormley, *EU Law of Free Movement of Goods and Customs Union* (2009) has 28 in Ch. 11.B.2.

[13] OJ Sp. Ed. L 13/29. Its effects were in any event formally exhausted at the end of the transitional period in 1970.

[14] E.g., Case 34/79, *Henn and Darby*, [1979] ECR 3795 (ECLI:EU:C:1979:295), at para. 12.

discrimination and, at the other, a wide claim to review any national measure that impedes the exercise of commercial freedom, it chose an approach towards, but not at, the wider end of the spectrum. But this story of judicially driven development of internal market law is uneven.

In *Geddo* v. *Ente* the Court described the scope of (what is now) Article 34 TFEU as covering 'measures which amount to a total or partial restraint of…imports, exports or goods in transit…measures having equivalent effect not only take the form of restraint described: whatever the description or technique employed, they can also consist of encumbrances having the same effect'.[15] Then in its 1974 ruling in *Dassonville* the Court brought 'all trading rules enacted by Member States which are capable of hindering, directly or indirectly, actually or potentially, intra-Community trade' within the scope of Article 34 TFEU.[16] Of enduring thematic significance is the fact that the Court in this, the so-called *Dassonville* formula, chose to emphasize as the key jurisdictional trigger the *effect* of the national measure on the internal market, not its form.

The significance of this ruling is appreciated only by comparing it closely with the text of Article 34 TFEU. Its wording is infused with assumptions familiar in international trade law. The General Agreement on Tariffs and Trade (GATT) entered into force in 1948, precursor of the World Trade Organization established in 1995, and its Article XI was entitled *General Elimination of Quantitative Restrictions*. On its own terms, a focus on quantitative restrictions or quotas could be interpreted as a mere anti-discrimination norm. Article 34's extra textual limb, measures *having equivalent effect*, offers a lure to move beyond discrimination, but it is an imprecise phrase, and it was in *Dassonville* that the Court chose to make that decisive and bold extra step. It does not exaggerate to identify *Dassonville* as a ruling which nurtured a specifically *EU* understanding of free movement in a way that resembles the construction of a distinctively *EU* constitutional law, distanced from and deeper than the demands made by orthodox international law, as seen in *Van Gend en Loos* and *Costa* v. *ENEL*.[17] *Dassonville* by no means solved or explained everything, but it was, and remains, a landmark choice with immense implications for the shape of the internal market.

This was certainly appreciated at the time. In an article published in the *Common Market Law Review* in 1976, Meij and Winter surveyed the existing case law and academic writing in order to expose choices open to the Court in addressing the questions referred to it for answer in *Dassonville*.[18] They highlighted how the Court had elected to move beyond a focus on discrimination, with the consequence that its ruling served to curtail the scope of the powers of the Member States 'to regulate commerce or even to conduct economic policies of their own'.[19] True, the Court has

---

[15] Case 2/73, *Geddo* v. *Ente*, [1973] ECR 865 (ECLI:EU:C:1973:89).

[16] Case 8/74, *Dassonville*, [1974] ECR 837 (ECLI:EU:C:1974:82).

[17] Case 26/62, *supra* note 9; Case 6/64, *Costa* v. *ENEL* [1964] ECR 585 (ECLI:EU:C:1964:66).

[18] Meij and Winter, 'Measures Having an Effect Equivalent to Quantitative Restrictions', 13 *Common Market Law Review* (1976) 76. See Oliver *supra* note 12, at paras 6.44–6.47 for summary of the competing academic views at the time; also unusually insightful on the choices available to the Court is Weiler, 'The Constitution of the Common Market Place: Text and Context in the Evolution of the Free Movement of Goods', in P. Craig and G. De Búrca, *The Evolution of EU Law* (1999) Ch. 10.

[19] Meij and Winter, *supra* note 18, at 81; also in the same vein at 103 and 104 on depletion of state 'reserved powers'.

subsequently deviated in detail from this thread from time to time (as is explored later), but it has never retreated from the core narrative pioneered in *Dassonville* that locates free movement law as a control over national practice that is more intrusive than merely to require equal treatment between imported goods and services and their domestically produced counterparts.

On its facts, *Dassonville* was a case about a discriminatory practice, though the Court's formula was not focused on discrimination as a necessary element in EU free movement law. The next big step taken by the Court was the application of the law governing the free movement of goods to national technical standards even in the absence of any explicit reference on the face of such measures to the origin of goods. *Disparities between national laws* may themselves generate measures having equivalent effect within the meaning of Article 34 TFEU. They have the potential for *protectionist* effect.

This was when the Court's choice and its sense of interpretative ambition became still more evident; when the surge beyond anti-discrimination as a basis for the scope of application of free movement law became most plain. This was *Cassis de Dijon*.

3. *Cassis de Dijon*

The ruling in the famous *Cassis de Dijon* case – more properly, *Rewe-Zentrale AG* v. *Bundesmonopolverwaltung für Branntwein* – demonstrates how Article 34 TFEU controls local regulatory autonomy in setting technical standards in so far as it may impede the building of Europe's internal market.[20] *Cassis de Dijon*, like *Dassonville*, is an unavoidable point of reference in understanding the shape of the EU's internal market. It is crucial to the vertical issue – it determines the extent to which national regulatory autonomy falls to be disciplined by EU internal market law – and also to the horizontal issue – it determines how heavy a load is undertaken by judicial institutions in tackling obstructions to inter-state trade and how much instead is reserved for the supplementary attention of the political institutions, acting most prominently through the role of legislative harmonization.

The litigation involved Cassis de Dijon, a blackcurrant fruit liqueur which was made in France with an alcohol content of between 15 and 20 per cent. It could not be sold in Germany because it did not comply with German law, which by contrast required that such products should have a minimum alcohol content of 25 per cent. Germany did not target its rules against imports *at all*. A German-made product with the same relatively low level of alcohol as the French-made product would equally have been excluded from the German market. The German rule did not concern itself with the origin of products, only with their composition. The problem was simply that German product standards were *different* from French standards and so, in consequence, typical French products were different (weaker in alcoholic strength) than typical German products of similar type. And the consequence of that regulatory diversity was an obstacle to the free movement of goods and the

---

[20] Case 120/78, *Rewe-Zentrale AG* v. *Bundesmonopolverwaltung für Branntwein*, [1979] ECR 649 (ECLI:EU:C:1979:42).

fragmentation of the internal market along national lines. The effects-based emphasis of the '*Dassonville* formula' is plain: diversity between national technical rules had the *effect* of impeding inter-state trade, and consequently the German rule could be applied only if shown to be justified.

The heart of the Court's ruling is paragraph 8, which is so intricate and beautifully structured as to deserve full citation:

> In the absence of common rules relating to the production and marketing of alcohol – a proposal for a regulation submitted to the Council by the Commission on 7 December 1976 (Official Journal C 309, p. 2) not yet having received the Council's approval – it is for the Member States to regulate all matters relating to the production and marketing of alcohol and alcoholic beverages on their own territory. Obstacles to movement within the Community resulting from disparities between the national laws relating to the marketing of the products in question must be accepted in so far as those provisions may be recognized as being necessary in order to satisfy mandatory requirements relating in particular to the effectiveness of fiscal supervision, the protection of public health, the fairness of commercial transactions and the defence of the consumer.

The structure of this paragraph is based on a clever inversion of the allocation of regulatory competence between the 'home state' (here, France) and the 'host state' (here, Germany). Paragraph 8 begins by stating that it is for the Member States to regulate matters on their own territory. This is a concession to 'host state' competence to set rules governing the composition of products. The Court continues in the same vein: obstacles to movement resulting from disparities between national laws 'must be accepted'. But all of a sudden the judgment bites. Acceptance of host state regulatory autonomy is conditional. The host state's obstructive rules are put to the test, and they may be applied only where necessary in order to satisfy mandatory requirements – in short, only where they are *justified*. In the absence of such justification the host state is denied the competence to apply its rules to impede imports, and in consequence the trader is allowed to penetrate the market of the host state merely by virtue of having complied with the rules of the home state. Yielding to unconditional 'host state' regulatory autonomy would have allowed persisting fragmentation of the national market, pending EU legislative intervention, while accepting unconditional 'home state' regulatory autonomy would have swept aside even legitimate claims to regulate the host state market according to local preference, but the Court goes to neither extreme. Neither home state nor host state control is absolute. The model is more nuanced and sophisticated. It is frequently described as 'the principle of mutual recognition' – even sometimes by the Court itself[21] – but

---

[21] The offence is committed in Case C-110/05, *Commission* v. *Italy*, [2009] ECR I-519 (ECLI:EU:C:2009:66), at para. 34; Case C-108/09, *Ker-Optika*, [2010] ECR I-12213 (ECLI:EU:C:2010:725), at para. 48; Case C-484/10, *Ascafor*, judgment of 1 March 2012, not yet reported (ECLI:EU:C:2012:113), at paras 53, 70; Case C-456/10, *ANETT*, judgment of 26 April 2012, not yet reported (ECLI:EU:C:2012:241), at para. 33; Case C-385/10, *Elenca Srl*, judgment of 18 October 2012, not yet reported (ECLI:EU:C:2012:634), at para. 23. Most textbooks sin, and C. Janssens, *The Principle of Mutual Recognition in EU Law* (2013) has much to commend it but not its title. For a grumpy critique, see Weatherill, 'Why There is No "Principle of Mutual Recognition" in EU Law (and Why that Matters to Consumer Lawyers)', in K. Purnhagen and P. Rott (eds), *Varieties of European Economic Law and Regulation: Liber Amicorum for Hans Micklitz* (2014) 401.

this is profoundly *wrong*. Its interpretation casts Article 34 TFEU as a provision laying down a *conditional* or *non-absolute* rule of 'mutual recognition' of the adequacy of technical standards set by the Member States. The free movement provisions of the Treaty serve as instruments for the allocation of regulatory competence. They create a non-absolute principle of home country control.

Accordingly, in *Cassis de Dijon* the trade barrier was put to the test. This did not detain the Court for long, which may be one reason why the importance of the point that any principle of mutual recognition is not absolute is sometimes overlooked or at least left to one side. The reason is that in the case itself Germany's arguments in support of its rules were remarkably weak. The rules were, in the view of the Court, not justified, principally because the Court could simply not accept that consumers needed protection from an admittedly unfamiliar product through the imposition of a prohibition on liqueurs that were made according to a slightly different recipe. This intervention in the market went too far. Much closer attention will be paid later to the way in which EU law approaches the question of when the rules of the 'host state' are justified (see Chapter 8), but the main point in *Cassis de Dijon* is its shaping of Article 34 TFEU as a basis for review of diversity in technical standards between Member States which obstructs inter-state trade, and without resting the analysis on notions of discrimination.

Cassis was, in a sense, no novelty. It is simply a logical application of the *Dassonville* ruling, delivered five years earlier, to examine the *effects* of a national measure as a basis for the invocation of Article 34 TFEU. Nevertheless, *Cassis de Dijon* was the first case to deal directly with inter-state divergence in non-discriminatory technical standards as a barrier to trade in goods. Moreover, it was the first case to set out with clarity the test which is still commonly used in the judgments of the Court today more 35 years since *Cassis de Dijon*. *Cassis de Dijon* was a case initiated strategically by Gert Maier, the astute advocate acting on behalf of the supermarket Rewe-Zentrale, but why the case was selected by the Court as a springboard for this innovative and transformative leap is not clear.[22] Whatever the origins, viewed then and even more viewed now, *Cassis de Dijon* fully merits its iconic status in EU internal market law.

The approach taken in *Cassis* is readily applicable beyond the area of the free movement of goods. In fact the Court had already deployed language close to that now used in *Cassis* in an earlier case arising in the services sector, *Van Binsbergen*.[23] The '*Tourist Guides*' case mentioned earlier, *Commission* v. *France*, fits perfectly easily into the *Cassis* model: provision of services in the host state (France) was restricted not because France targeted its licensing rules at out-of-state providers in a discriminatory fashion but simply because the French rules were different from those applied in other Member States.[24] As in *Cassis*, the restrictive effect on inter-state trade of diversity between technical rules cast an obligation on France to justify its rules; like Germany in *Cassis*, it could not do so.

---

[22] See Barnard, 'The Mysterious Origins of the Principle of Mutual Recognition', forthcoming.

[23] Case 33/74, *Van Binsbergen*, [1974] ECR 1299 (ECLI:EU:C:1974:131).

[24] Case C-154/89, *Commission* v. *France*, [1991] ECR I-659 (ECLI:EU:C:1991:76). See similarly Case C-76/90, *Manfred Säger* v. *Dennemeyer & Co. Ltd*, [1991] ECR I-4221 (ECLI:EU:C:1991:331).

The Court's approach is perfectly consistent with the Treaty. Articles 34 and 56 TFEU prohibit barriers to inter-state trade. This favours home state control. Then Articles 36 and Articles 62 and 52 TFEU soften the prohibition by allowing the host state to show justification for its regulatory intervention. The pattern of the Treaty is therefore one of conditional mutual recognition or non-absolute home state control – which is the same as that developed by the Court in *Cassis.* The Treaty cements the law of free movement into a model that envisages the possibility of shared regulatory responsibility between home and host states, though a close inspection of the particular circumstances is required to determine whether the host state has an adequate justification for maintaining restrictive rules. *Cassis* elaborated and elucidated the legal treatment of host State measures under EU law: it did not represent anything wholly novel. Dual regulation by both home and host state is excluded in the absence of justification – as is well illustrated by *Cassis* itself.

However, although the Court's ruling is readily understood as compatible with the structure mapped out by the Treaty, it is important to appreciate that it was not inevitable. A different approach, but one also not incompatible with the structure of the Treaty, would have refused to bring technical standards within the scope of free movement law on the basis that the free movement rules touch only physical barriers to trade and overtly discriminatory practices. That would, of course, have left in place the German rules as obstacles to the marketing in Germany of the French-made Cassis, but the Treaty envisaged and envisages a means to address that problem, which is legislative harmonization.[25] What the Court in fact did in *Cassis de Dijon* was to choose an approach that enhanced the significance of free movement law as means to cleanse the internal market of the trade-restrictive rules of the type encountered in the case, at the expense of the need to introduce common harmonized EU standards. This, in turn, has the consequence that the judicial role is increased at the expense of the legislative process.

Having made that choice, the real significance of the Court's *Cassis de Dijon* case law is that it offers an attempt to move beyond the spare text of the Treaty. It aspires to a much more elaborate approach to shaping the internal market and, in particular, to balancing the competing interests of local regulatory autonomy, which is served by holding host State rules untouched by or compatible with the Treaty, and market integration, which is served by holding host state rules incompatible with the Treaty. The Court has converted the Treaty rules into a subtle, flexible and intrusive set of instruments for advancing market integration which also take account of legitimate national interests in regulatory protection. And cases of the *Cassis de Dijon* type, where technical standards partition the internal market along national lines, have been abundant in the Court's reports ever since 1979, revealing just how deeply rooted are such obstacles to trade – often the product of centuries of accumulated regulatory diversity in a colourfully fragmented Europe. *Walter Rau* (Belgian rules on the packaging of margarine) and *Commission* v. *Germany* (beer purity) were

---

[25] This was exactly the argument advanced by the Bundesmonopolverwaltung in *Cassis*: see the Opinion of A.G. Capotorti in the case.

mentioned earlier.[26] They are fully in line with the *Cassis* analytical model and good examples of its application to the review of national technical standards. The glory of *Cassis* is that, assuming (as in that case and in many others, including *Walter Rau, Commission* v. *Germany* and '*Tourist Guides*') such measures are not shown to be justified, Europe's diversity is not diminished. Regulatory diversity is sustained: but it may not be applied in a way that excludes products made or services provided according to different standards in other Member States. German blackcurrant liqueur competes with the French version on the German market, so too German beer, and so on: consumer choice is increased. There is no call or need for legislative action at EU level: no harmonization, no centralization, no product homogenization. *Cassis de Dijon* is about the vertical tension – the extent to which EU law circumscribes state autonomy in the internal market – but it stands in this sense also as a major judgment on the horizontal distribution of powers within the EU, for it asserts a powerful place for judicially applied prohibitions without a need for supplementary legislative action. And, crucially, the turn the Court chose in 1979 was not forced on it by the Treaty. The Court, faced with an ambiguity about the reach of free movement law and its relationship with legislative harmonization, made a choice that privileged the former over the latter, which in turn promoted a model of regulatory plurality and consumer choice in the market over a vision of legislatively defined harmonized 'Europroducts'.

quite a paean.

4. Competition Law

The Court has never attempted to make a systematic connection between competition law and free movement law in its treatment of the required inter-state element. Wisely so. Both are key elements in the legal framework of the internal market, but there are differences of detail between them that demand to be taken seriously. Competition law rests heavily on finding concerted practices, on Article 101(3) TFEU's criteria of exemption and on market analysis, and there are clear differences in the personal scope of the free movement and the competition provisions. So it would be quite wrong for the Court to re-write the Treaty in order to force alignment between competition law and free movement law. Exploration of the relationship between free movement and competition law is the job of academic analysis, and this has been undertaken with gusto and skill.[27]

However, the inquiry into the *internal* market as an organizing concept applies here too. Analogies are visible. Article 101 TFEU is concerned only with practices that 'affect trade between Member States', whereas Article 102 TFEU prohibits abusive conduct only where it 'may affect trade between Member States'. Article 107(1)

---

[26] Case 261/81, *Walter Rau* v. *de Smedt*, [1982] ECR 3961 (ECLI:EU:C:1982:382); Case 178/84, *Commission* v. *Germany*, [1987] ECR 1227 (ECLI:EU:C:1987:126).

[27] E.g., J. Baquero Cruz, *Between Competition and Free Movement: The Economic Constitutional Law of the European Community* (2002); Mortelmans, 'Towards Convergence in the Application of the Rules on Free Movement and Competition?', 38 *Common Market Law Review* (2001) 613; Hatzopoulos, 'The Economic Constitution of the EU Treaty and the Limits between Economic and Non-Economic Activities', *European Business Law Review* (2012) 973.

TFEU applies to aid granted by a Member State or through state resources only 'in so far as it affects trade between Member States'. EU competition law goes no further: there is room for national competition law to make its own choices about how to address practices that exert a solely domestic impact.

One of the Court's earliest judgments in the field, *Consten and Grundig* v. *Commission*, delivered in 1966, addressed the jurisdictional divide between national and EU competition law.[28] The Court, dealing with the reach of what is now Article 101 TFEU, focused on 'whether the agreement is capable of constituting a threat, either direct or indirect, actual or potential, to freedom of trade between Member States in a manner which might harm the attainment of the objectives of a single market between States'. *Dassonville* lay eight years in the future![29] The Court's approach meant that even where sales across borders increased as a result of the deal, the application of EU law was triggered. This set EU competition law on a relatively interventionist road and, in particular, it shaped it as apt to intervene in deals involving territorial separation within the EU. In general, the Court has long emphasized the importance of a careful and realistic legal and economic assessment of the effect of particular practices on the patterns of (inter-state) trade. So account should be taken of a combination of factors which, taken separately, are not necessarily decisive: most prominently the nature of the agreement or practice at issue, the nature of the goods or services concerned and the position and the importance of the parties on the market.[30]

Practices isolated to a national market alone are rare – all the more so as the project of market integration in the EU deepens. Most of the time it is rather easy to find the cross-border aspect which is required to bring EU law into play. Even where the matter is on its face confined to the territory of a single Member State, it is still possible to treat this as a deception. This has deep roots in EU competition law. *Cooperative Stremsel- en Kleurselfabriek* v. *Commission*, decided in 1981, involved a co-operative of producers in the dairy sector which required all its members to buy exclusively from each other.[31] All the members were Dutch, and together they accounted for more than 90 per cent of Dutch cheese output. But this was not exclusively a Dutch matter. The European Commission ('the Commission') held that an effect on inter-state trade had been established, and the Court agreed. The inquiry into the agreement's liability to affect trade between Member States required

---

[28] Joined Cases 56 and 58/64, *Consten and Grundig* v. *Commission*, [1966] ECR 429 (ECLI: EU:C:1966:41). See also (and equally foundational) Case 56/65, *STM* v. *Maschinenbau Ulm*, [1966] ECR 235 (ECLI:EU:C:1966:38).

[29] This analogy between free movement and competition law is pressed by A.G. Van Gerven in Case 145/88, *Torfaen BC*, considered in Section C.1, but the Court, perhaps unwisely (for reasons explained in that section), ignored the inquiry.

[30] E.g., Case C-3/14, *Prezes Urzędu Komunikacji Elektronicznej, Telefonia Dialog sp. z o.o.* v. *T-Mobile Polska SA*, judgment of 16 April 2015, not yet reported (ECLI:EU:C:2015:232), at para. 53; Joined Cases C-295/04–C-298/04, *Vincenzo Manfredi and Others*, [2006] ECR I-6619 (ECLI:EU:C:2006:461); Case C-49/07, *Motosykletistiki Omospondia Ellados NPID (MOTOE)* v. *Dimosio*, [2008] ECR I-4863 (ECLI:EU:C:2008:376). See R. Whish and D. Bailey, *Competition Law* (7th ed., 2012), Chs 3.179–3.196.

[31] Case 61/80, *Cooperative Stremsel- en Kleurselfabriek* v. *Commission*, [1981] ECR 851 (ECLI:EU:C:1981:75).

a determination on whether it was 'possible to foresee with a sufficient degree of probability that it may have an influence, direct or indirect, actual or potential, on the pattern of trade between Member States'.[32] The echo of *Consten and Grundig* mediated through the '*Dassonville* formula' is certainly no accident. This serves both to assert the project of internal market-making which is shared by free movement law and competition law, and also to confirm how relaxed in practice is the threshold that must be crossed before jurisdiction is claimed by the EU. The point, when this test was applied in the case, was that practices which tied up the Dutch market in this way tended to confine opportunities for other parties to trade into the Netherlands. The rules of the co-operative were 'precisely of such a nature as to reinforce the partitioning of markets on a national basis, thereby holding up the economic interpenetration which the Treaty is designed to bring about'.[33] The thematic concern which drives the analysis of whether the EU is able to claim jurisdiction is isolation of national markets – not formalism. So here competition law has obvious similarities with free movement law.

An illuminating and influential insight into law and practice may be obtained from the Commission's 'Guidelines on the effect on trade concept contained in Articles 81 and 82 of the Treaty'.[34] These make explicit that what is at stake 'is a jurisdictional criterion, which defines the scope of application of Community competition law'.[35] So EU competition law 'is not applicable to agreements and practices that are not capable of appreciably affecting trade between Member States'.[36] The required threshold of an *appreciable* affect has been shaped by the Court's case law and it is granted fuller expression in the Commission's 'Notice on agreements of minor importance which do not appreciably restrict competition', the so-called 'De Minimis Notice'.[37] This, then, is a limit to the intrusion of EU law into national autonomy. But, revealingly, the Guidelines then turn to show how readily this jurisdictional criterion is met, not how it is *not* met. So, for example, '[i]f the agreement as a whole is capable of affecting trade between Member States, there is Community law jurisdiction in respect of the entire agreement, including any parts of the agreement that individually do not affect trade between Member States';[38] '[i]t is not necessary, for the purposes of establishing Community law jurisdiction, to establish a link between the alleged restriction of competition and the capacity of the agreement to affect trade between Member States';[39] and '[w]here a dominant undertaking adopts various practices in pursuit of the same aim, for instance practices that aim at eliminating or foreclosing competitors, in order for Article 82 [now 102] to be applicable to all the practices forming part of this overall strategy, it is sufficient that at least one of these practices is capable of affecting trade between Member

---

[32] *Ibid.*, at para. 14.   [33] *Ibid.*, at para. 15.
[34] OJ 2004 C 101/81.
[35] *Ibid.*, at para. 12, citing as fn. 'See e.g. Joined Cases 56/64 and 58/64, Consten and Grundig, [1966] ECR p. 429, and Joined Cases 6/73 and 7/73, Commercial Solvents, [1974] ECR p. 223'.
[36] *Ibid.*, at para. 12.
[37] OJ 2014 C 291/1. See Whish and Bailey, *supra* note 30, Chs 3.164–3.178.
[38] OJ 2014 C 291/1, at para. 14.   [39] *Ibid.*, at para. 16.

States'.[40] In similar vein, later parts of the Guidelines carefully trace the application of these principles to cases that seem to relate to the territory of a single Member State but follow this thematic reluctance to treat EU law as inapplicable. So, for example, horizontal cartels covering the whole of a Member State are normally capable of affecting trade between Member States; horizontal co-operation agreements which are confined to a single Member State and which do not directly relate to imports and exports require careful individual examination, and may, in particular, be capable of affecting trade between Member States where they have foreclosure effects.[41]

The Guidelines note that the influence of agreements and practices on patterns of trade between Member States can be 'direct or indirect, actual or potential',[42] which once again echoes both *Consten and Grundig* and *Dassonville*.

The overall conclusion is that there are limits to the reach of internal market law rooted in the need to demonstrate that the challenged practices exert an adequate (appreciable) impact on cross-border trade patterns. But these limits are crossed with remarkable ease. For competition law as for free movement law, cross-border economic activity is broadly understood. The internal market is an empowering legal concept.

B. Where Do the Limits Lie?

The problem with this trend is to determine where it stops. If the internal market is used in this empowering manner, where does the reserved area of national autonomy promised by Article 5 TEU's principle of conferral begin? At one level the answer is simple: it begins where the needs of the internal market end, and most obviously it begins where the matter is of purely internal concern within a particular Member State. So Moser's exclusion from the teaching profession in Germany was a matter between him and the German authorities, and the opportunistic claim that he *might* be prevented from teaching in another Member State did not avail.[43]

But cases like *Moser* are rare. Compare a case such as *Mary Carpenter*.[44] Mrs Carpenter, a national of the Philippines, was threatened with deportation from the UK. She was married to Peter Carpenter, a British national. She, as a third country national, had no EU law rights. He did, if he was engaged in cross-border economic activity. He was a national of the UK and he was living in the UK, but the Court fastened on to the point that in his business activity (selling advertising space in journals and providing publishing services) he sold to persons established in other Member States and occasionally travelled outside the UK on business. This was enough to bring the matter within the scope of EU free movement law, and so the restriction he faced – the intended deportation of Mrs Carpenter – had to be justified (and was not). It is striking in the judgment how little effort the Court makes to

---

[40] *Ibid.*, at para. 17.   [41] *Ibid.*, at paras 78–84.
[42] *Ibid.*, at para. 36.   [43] Case 180/83, *supra* note 5.
[44] Case C-60/00, *Mary Carpenter*, [2002] ECR I-6279 (ECLI:EU:C:2002:434).

establish a connection between the threatened deportation and the perceived impediment to trade. EU free movement law applies with astonishing ease, and this is also true for goods. In part, the trigger is easily pulled thanks to the reliance on not only *actual* but also *potential* effects in the '*Dassonville* formula'. In *Commission* v. *France*, it did not matter that hardly any *foie gras* was imported into France: the *potential* effect of restrictive French rules governing product composition was enough to bring Article 34 into play.[45] This pushes aside any need for conscientious assembly of empirical evidence about a measure's effect on cross-border trade patterns. So, for example, *Berlington Hungary and Others* concerned Hungarian operators of slot machines affected by restrictive rules introduced by the Hungarian authorities, but the Court found the necessary inter-state element by noting that some of the customers of the operators were EU citizens holidaying in Hungary and adding that it was 'far from inconceivable' that operators established in Member States other than Hungary might be interested in opening amusement arcades in Hungary.[46] It offered no empirical evidence for this at all, but in this way the jurisdictionally necessary connection with inter-state trade was established. The striking element in the case, which is not at all atypical,[47] is the *ease* with which it is established. This has much in common with the reading of competition law that insists on a dynamic approach to the building and maintenance of the internal market. The limits of the internal market as a legal concept are close to vanishing.

The problem of defining the limits of the *internal* market closely resembles that associated with defining the limits of the internal *market*. They are there, but they are hard to find and, most of all, it is hard to pin them down in an operationally useful matter. Just as pursuit of economic activity is immensely broad as a trigger to EU internal market law, so too the expectation of a restriction to inter-state trade throws a wide-mouthed net over national practices.

The examination conducted above could be summarized as the search for the meaning of a 'restriction' for the purposes of determining the type of national measure that falls to be examined by EU internal market law. Physical frontiers and discriminatory practices are covered and so are technical regulations of the *Cassis* type. In this sense, the *Cassis* story is just one chapter in a longer interrogation of the proper scope of review. *Bosman* occupies a different chapter.[48] In that case, the basic problem faced by the footballer was a restriction to his movement across a border, since he wished to move from a Belgian club to a French club, but could not do so

---

[45] Case C-184/96, *Commission* v. *France*, [1998] ECR I-6197 (ECLI:EU:C:1998:495).

[46] Case C-98/14, *Berlington Hungary and Others*, judgment of 11 June 2015, not yet reported (ECLI:EU:C:2015:386), at para. 27.

[47] The same insouciance ('far from inconceivable') may be seen in, e.g., Case C-470/11, *Garkalns*, judgment of 19 July 2012, not yet reported (ECLI:EU:C:2012:505), at para. 21 (gambling in Latvia); Case C-367/12, *Susanne Sokoll-Seebacher*, judgment of 13 February 2014, not yet reported (ECLI:EU:C:2014:68), at para. 10 (pharmacies in Austria); Case C-327/12, *Ministero dello Sviluppo economic* v. *SOA*, judgment of 12 December 2013, not yet reported (ECLI:EU:C:2013:827), at para. 48 (certification services in Italy). See also Joined Cases C-197/11 and C-203/11, *Eric Libert*, judgment of 8 May 2013, not yet reported (ECLI:EU:C:2013:288), at para. 34; Case C-168/14, *Grupo Itelevelesa*, judgment of 15 October 2015, not yet reported (ECLI:EU:C:2015:685), at para. 36.

[48] Case C-415/93, *Bosman*, [1995] ECR I-4921 (ECLI:EU:C:1995:463); Case C-384/93, *Alpine Investments*, [1995] ECR I-1141 (ECLI:EU:C:1995:126) also belongs in the *Bosman* chapter.

even though his contract of employment had come to an end because of the restrictive effect of the transfer system in the sport. However, he would have been faced by exactly the same problem had he been trying to join another *Belgian* club. The problem was not a 'dual burden' in the sense of *Cassis*; nor was the problem that practices differed between Member States – they did not differ. His problem was the very existence of the system which prevented him gaining access to the employment market in France (or anywhere else), but this was enough for the Court to treat the matter as falling within the scope of EU law as a restriction within the meaning of Article 45 TFEU. A similar approach would apply to authorization requirements imposed by the public authorities of a state as a pre-condition to establishing a business in that state or providing services on its territory: *all* traders would be subject to the rule, but its very existence as a restriction is enough to bring free movement law into play.[49] A complete ban on goods imposed in a Member State counts as a restriction within the meaning of Article 34 TFEU;[50] a ban on working or setting up a business or providing services in a Member State counts as a restriction within the meaning of Article 45 TFEU. What rules happen to apply in *other* Member States do not matter for these purposes. There is some sort of threshold, lower than that prevailing in cases of the *Cassis* type, which brings measures that affect access to the regulated market within the scope of free movement law. But what is that threshold, exactly?

There are, in fact, two distinct though connected lines of inquiry. First, how far should the control exercised by free movement law reach? And, secondly, is the jurisdictionally crucial notion of 'restriction' treated in the same way across the entirety of free movement law?

In *Kraus* the Court ruled that what were then Articles 48 and 52 EEC (now Articles 45 and 49 TFEU) precluded any national measure governing the conditions under which an academic title obtained in another Member State may be used where that measure, even though applicable without discrimination on grounds of nationality, is liable to hamper or to render less attractive the exercise by EU nationals, including those of the Member State which enacted the measure, of fundamental freedoms guaranteed by the Treaty.[51] This was a broad approach, comfortably applicable in principle to a restriction of any of the Treaty freedoms, and, as that very paragraph of *Kraus* made clear, it placed the emphasis on the obligation of the regulating state to show a justification recognized by EU law in order to maintain its practices. The Court has made relatively frequent use of the formula that 'measures which prohibit, impede or render less attractive' the exercise of free movement rights are caught as restrictions.[52] It has, however, chosen to reserve its use for cases involv-

---

[49] E.g., Joined Cases C-570/07 and C-571/07, *Blanco Pérez and Chao Gómez*, [2010] ECR I-4629 (ECLI:EU:C:2010:300); Case C-217/09, *Polisseni*, [2010] ECR I-175 (ECLI:EU:C:2010:796).

[50] Case 34/79, *supra* note 14.

[51] Case C-19/92, *Kraus*, [1993] ECR I-1663 (ECLI:EU:C:1993:125), at para. 32. See also Case C-55/94, *Gebhard*, [1995] ECR I-4165 (ECLI:EU:C:1995:411), especially para. 37.

[52] E.g. Case C-686/13, *X*, judgment of 10 June 2015, not yet reported (ECLI:EU:C:2015:375), with references at paras 27, 28. A search against this phrase conducted on 1 March 2016 at http://curia.europa.eu/juris/recherche.jsf?language=en yields 39 judgments of the Court of Justice.

ing free movement or services and capital and the right of establishment. There is no obvious reason not to use the same formula in cases involving goods, and it seems that the Court does not wish to adopt a single all-embracing convergent approach. In similar vein in a case involving services, *DKV Belgium*, the Court framed the restriction to arise because '... undertakings entering the market of a Member State which has introduced [measures] ... are obliged, if they want to be able to access that market under conditions which comply with the legislation of that Member State, to re-think their business policy and strategy...'.[53] This describes the problem in *Cassis de Dijon* perfectly well! But here, too, the Court seems resistant to adopting a formula of general application.

It is well over 20 years since 'convergence' of the freedoms has been debated in the academic literature.[54] In some instances convergence is admittedly more-or-less uncontested. Justification of barriers to trade in goods and in services runs along identical lines and on occasion, where both freedoms are involved, the Court simply fuses its exploration of whether restrictions are justified.[55] In other areas convergence is excluded by the Court: this is true of the personal scope of the free movement provisions (see Chapter 9). The preoccupation of this chapter – the search for a reliable definition of 'restriction' on trade of a type that falls within the scope of EU internal market law – lies in the middle: convergence is neither embraced nor rejected, but rather may be traced and pieced together from the incremental drift of the Court's case law over time. At stake are demanding questions about *both* the reach of EU law into national autonomy (the definitional/competence question) *and* the proper scope for common interpretation of the relevant Treaty provisions (the convergence question).

It was mentioned earlier that Meij and Winter, writing in 1976 about the impact of *Dassonville*, drew attention to the reduction in Member State regulatory autonomy as a result of the Court's determined advance beyond a test based purely on forbidding discrimination.[56] This anxiety becomes a great deal more acute as one surveys the expanding, though ambiguous, understanding of when a restriction to inter-state trade exists. The tremors certainly did not go unappreciated in Luxembourg. In 1993 Advocate General Tesauro began his Opinion in *Ruth Hünermund and Others* v. *Landesapothekerkammer Baden-Württemberg* in attention-grabbing fashion: is (what is now) Article 34 'a provision intended to liberalize intra-Community trade or is it intended more generally to encourage the unhindered pursuit of commerce in individual Member States'?[57] 'The former!' was the essence

---

[53] Case C-577/11, *DKV Belgium*, judgment of 7 March 2013, not yet reported (ECLI:EU:C:2013:146), at para. 36.

[54] The starting-point is probably Behrens, 'Die Konvergenz der wirtschaftlichen Freiheiten im europäischen Gemeinschaftsrecht' *Europarecht* (1992) 145 and important feeding stations along the way include Oliver and Roth, 'The Internal Market and the Four Freedoms', 41 *Common Market Law Review* (2004) 407 and E. Dubout and A. Maitrot de la Motte, *L'unité des libertés de circulation: In Varietate Concordia* (2012). There probably is no finishing point.

[55] E.g., Case C-390/99, *Canal Satélite Digital*, [2002] ECR I-607 (ECLI:EU:C:2002:34).

[56] Meij and Winter, *supra* note 18, at 76, 103.

[57] Case C-292/92, *Ruth Hünermund and Others* v. *Landesapothekerkammer Baden-Württemberg*, [1993] ECR I-6787 (ECLI:EU:C:1993:932).

of his answer. He would not interpret 'the *Dassonville* test' to catch a measure causing 'potential reduction in imports caused solely and exclusively by a more general (and hypothetical) contraction of sales', and his interpretative guide was what he thought needed to achieve a 'single integrated market'.[58] Advocate General Jacobs in *Leclerc-Siplec* rooted his analysis in 'the Treaty's concern to establish a single market' and went so far as to exclude a discrimination (only) test as 'inconsistent as a matter of principle with the aims of the Treaty', because it would permit fragmentation along national lines where national rules differed.[59] He was well aware of the thematic tension that this might lead to 'excessive interference in the regulatory powers of the Member States' but proposed to address this by requiring that the national measure act as a 'substantial restriction on access to the EU market'.[60] The word *substantial* carries a heavy load: it is a form of *de minimis* test. Advocate General Tizzano's Opinion several years later in *CaixaBank France* counts as another insightful uncovering of the tensions at stake.[61] The case concerned the freedom of establishment, but he did not confine his comments to that particular freedom. Reflecting on (inter alia) *Kraus* and *Gebhard* he admitted the case law is 'difficult to reduce to a consistent whole'.[62] He expressed anxiety to avoid a test that would catch measures for the sole reason that they reduce the economic attractiveness of pursuing that activity. Crossing the threshold has to require more than just profit margins narrowed by the impugned national measure. If it did *not*, even simply levying tax would immediately be allowed only if justified. He placed reliance explicitly on the internal market as a *limiting* legal concept. The widened reading which he wished to reject would 'would be tantamount to bending the Treaty to a purpose for which it was not intended: that is to say, not in order to create an internal market in which conditions are similar to those of a single market and where operators can move freely, but in order to establish ... a market in which rules are prohibited as a matter of principle, except for those necessary and proportionate to meeting imperative requirements in the public interest'.[63] He preferred a narrower approach which would catch only measures that were discriminatory or which directly affected access to the regulated market. This limit, designed to preclude measures from being classified as restrictions where their effects 'are merely hypothetical or entirely uncertain and indirect',[64] would, he thought, 'reconcile the objective of merging the different national markets into a single common market with the continuation of Member States' general powers to regulate economic activities'.[65]

The Court has never attempted to articulate a systematic or convergent formula for determining when there is a 'restriction' within the meaning of free movement law. It has, however, responded in an *ad hoc* manner to these concerns and these prescriptions. It is necessary to engage with the case law in order to acquire a secure

---

[58] *Ibid.*, at paras 25, 28 of his Opinion.
[59] Case C-412/93, *Leclerc-Siplec*, [1995] ECR I-179 (ECLI:EU:C:1995:26), para. 40.
[60] *Ibid.*, at para. 42.
[61] C-442/02, *CaixaBank France*, [2004] ECR I-8961 (ECLI:EU:C:2004:586); Opinion (ECLI: EU:C:2004:187).
[62] *Ibid.*, at para. 57.   [63] *Ibid.*, at para. 63.   [64] *Ibid.*, at para. 75.
[65] *Ibid.*, at para. 68.

feel for just how the Court has tried to draw the line – that Article 5 TEU says it must draw – between practices that require review for their effect on the internal market and those which are simply an expression of national regulatory autonomy that lie beyond the reach of the EU. Put another way, the point is that it is not enough that national laws differ for free movement law to bite.[66] There must be something more. But how much more?

Two case studies beg for attention: the first concerns the free movement of goods, where the Court has staggered awkwardly across a swamp largely of its own making in an attempt to define a shore of preserved national autonomy; the second concerns the free movement of persons, where the Court has broken open the limiting factor of the purely internal situation where EU law does not apply but without abandoning it completely. These are vivid stories which risk drowning the matters of principle in the eccentricity of the case law. The attempt here is to navigate a course between the two, but it will be seen that the internal market as a legal concept has drawn the Court, and therefore the legal scholar, inescapably into this fact-driven teasingly shaky terrain.

C. Mis-steps and Re-sets

By the mid-1980s the law of free movement clearly embraced physical barriers to trade such as frontier controls, practices that discriminated on the basis of origin, and technical standards of the *Cassis* type. These, it was well settled, constituted trade barriers within the meaning of the law of the internal market. The Court, having shaped its effects-based *Dassonville* formula in 1974 which could be coupled to the direct effect and primacy of the relevant provisions before national courts, had in effect recruited an army of vigilant police – those parties, mainly cross-border traders, whose commercial interests were the subject of interference by protectionist national measures of local market regulation. Their self-interested litigious activity before national courts in turn empowered the Court in Luxembourg.[67]

There is no reason at all for litigants to halt their charge when they reach the outer limits of discrimination, protectionism and associated practices which harm the internal market. To the contrary, there is every reason for them to seek to exploit these Court-created toys to try and force market deregulation within the Member States ever deeper. And the Court was left wrong-footed – in fact, it wrong-footed itself.

This is in its detail old news. But no apology is needed for telling the story because it reveals much about the ambiguous relationship between national autonomy and

---

[66] It is surprising (and perhaps revealing) how rarely the Court makes this point in explicit terms; for an example see Case C-565/08, *Commission v. Italy*, [2011] ECR I-2101 (ECLI:EU:C:2011:188), at para. 49.

[67] For an influential telling of this story (which reaches beyond the law of the internal market) from the political science perspective see Burley and Mattli, 'Europe before the Court: A Political Theory of Legal Integration', 47 *International Organization* (1993) 41; also A. Stone Sweet, *The Judicial Construction of Europe* (2004).

the law of the internal market and about the momentum that drives it, which is decisive in the EU's endemic tendency to curtail national regulatory autonomy.

1. *Sunday Trading*

The most high-profile illustrative cases were the pair of so-called '*Sunday Trading*' cases. In England and Wales (but not Scotland) there were an assortment of peculiar statutory restrictions on the times shops could open on Sundays and on the types of product that could be sold. The maze of rules was the product of centuries of incremental drift and defied rational explanation, but, given in particular the religious lobby's desire to keep Sunday 'special' combined with trade union objections to increased commercial activity on Sunday, the system was resistant to change through Parliament. Traders, especially big supermarkets, were convinced there was a 'Sunday pound' – in other words, that liberalization of selling on Sunday would lead to more sales, not simply a spread of the same volume of sales across the whole week. They turned to EU law as part of strategy designed to provoke change. In particular, they argued that the restrictions on Sunday trading depressed the volume of sales, including sales of goods imported from other Member States.

The matter was the subject of a preliminary reference by a court in South Wales to the Court. This was *Torfaen BC* v. *B&Q plc*, where Torfaen was a public authority charged with upholding the law, and B&Q was a supermarket relying on EU law to defeat the allegation it had broken it.[68] The Court blundered.

selling — It noted that 'national rules prohibiting retailers from opening their premises on Sunday apply to imported and domestic products alike' and that in principle 'the marketing of products imported from other Member States is not therefore made more difficult than the marketing of domestic products'.[69] The Court has here put its finger *precisely* on why this is a qualitatively different type of obstacle to commerce from that addressed in *Cassis de Dijon* and its progeny. In *Cassis* the problem was that selling imports was more difficult than selling home-produced goods, because imports, having complied with the specifications laid down in their 'home state', were faced with the further demand to comply with the (different) rules of the host state – rules with which the home-produced goods naturally already complied. Put another way, in *Cassis* imports faced a dual regulatory burden, whereas home-produced goods faced only a single burden. That is why there was an obstacle to the construction of the internal market. In *Sunday Trading* all products were subject to the same burden – the single burden of not being able to compete for the 'Sunday pound'. It was not the same. But the Court failed to grasp or develop the distinction. It simply concluded that EU law does not prohibit 'national rules prohibiting retailers from opening their premises on Sunday where the restrictive effects on Community trade which may result therefrom do not exceed the effects intrinsic to rules of that kind'.[70]

---

[68] Case 145/88, *Torfaen BC* v. *B&Q plc*, [1989] ECR 765 (ECLI:EU:C:1989:593).
[69] *Ibid.*, at para. 11.   [70] *Ibid.*, at para. 17.

This wilfully obscure formula led to understandable bemusement at national level. Some English and Welsh courts decided the Sunday trading rules were compatible with EU law, others took the opposite view.[71] Opportunistic litigants exploited the confusion: in *R* v. *Birmingham City Council ex p Wesson*, for example, siting roadworks in front of a shop was attacked as an obstacle to trade in goods contrary to EU law.[72] On the particular issue of Sunday trading, a second reference was made to the Court in *Stoke on Trent and Norwich City Councils* v. *B&Q plc* and on this occasion the Court cleared up *some* of the confusion,[73] giving a ruling which was far more concrete and helpful. It ruled that the restrictions, as a reflection of national choices relating to particular socio-cultural characteristics, pursued a legitimate aim under EU law and ultimately that national legislation prohibiting retailers from opening their premises on Sundays was not prohibited by EU law.

This solved the *small* problem. Courts could now confidently dismiss the 'Eurodefence' advanced by Sunday traders, although the confusion wrought by the litigation was a factor which led to Parliament being induced to reform the system in order to make the Sunday trading laws more coherent (and more liberal). The use of EU law was, in this sense, part of a wider political strategy.[74] But the ruling did not solve the *big* problem. The big problem was that the Court had extended the reach of free movement law beyond a true understanding of the intent of the '*Dassonville* formula', which insisted on an effect on *intra-Community* trade, and beyond the 'dual burden' at stake in a case such as *Cassis de Dijon*. The Court now seemed prepared to treat free movement law as apt to encompass any restriction on commercial freedom.

'Obviously', it had been written in 1976 in the aftermath in *Dassonville*, that (what is now) Article 34 TFEU 'should not be construed in such a way that it could gobble up, like some sort of a octopus, the reserved powers of the member States'.[75] Obvious that may be – but in the *Sunday Trading* cases the Court had converted Article 34 into that octopus. The Court had lost sight of the internal market as a legal concept that *limits* the scope of EU law. This is why the saga, though now ancient history, retains instructive value. The Sunday trading rules restricted commercial freedom, but they did not have any particular impact on cross-border trade. All goods were equally affected. In similar vein, the roadworks in Birmingham restricted the amount of goods sold in the shop, but did not exert any particular effect on *imported* goods. The Court had lurched beyond the free movement rules as a means to construct an integrated European economic space and was teetering on the brink of treating them as a general charter of economic constitutional review applicable to any national measure, even if unassociated with the particular phenomenon of

[71] See Arnull, 'What Shall We Do on Sunday?', 16 *European Law Review* (1991) 112.
[72] *R* v. *Birmingham City Council ex p Wesson* [1992] 3 CMLR 377.
[73] Case C-169/91, *Stoke on Trent and Norwich City Councils* v. *B&Q plc*, [1992] ECR I-6635 (ECLI:EU:C:1992:519).
[74] Cf. H.-W. Micklitz, *The Politics of Judicial Co-operation in the EU – the Case of Sunday Trading, Equal Treatment and Good Faith* (2005).
[75] Meij and Winter, *supra* note 18, at 103–104.

cross-border trade. At this point the existence of national regulatory autonomy promised by Article 4(1) and 5(2) TEU risks complete obliteration.

2. The Readjustments

The Court needed to rise to the challenge or else see the legitimacy of internal market law gravely imperilled by its insertion into disputes which had no evident connection to the project of creating a market without internal frontiers, as mapped by Article 26 TFEU.

Already the Court had dabbled with methods for curtailing the reach of (what is now) Article 34 TFEU. Asked to apply it to national legislation prohibiting the sale of lawful sex articles from unlicensed sex establishments – again, litigation pursued to propel unblocking of odd and old laws that Parliament would not readily touch – the Court found that the sale of imported products was made no more difficult than the sale of domestic products and that the rules were not of such a nature as to impede trade between Member States.[76] Accordingly, questions of justification of national rules simply did not arise, in contrast to the *Sunday Trading* cases. There were other, older, cases where it had similarly found rules that restricted commercial freedom – governing working hours in bakeries and the hours of delivery, and restraint on the sale of strong spirits for consumption – did not have the necessary connection with the importation of the products.[77] And both long ago and more recently the Court has adopted a functionally similar willingness to treat national rules as too remote or uncertain in their effects on inter-state trade to demand justification in the light of Article 34 TFEU.[78] There were, in short, ad hoc examples of the Court's disinclination to treat the internal market as that suffocating octopus. It was October 1993 when Advocate General Tesauro's Opinion in *Ruth Hünermund and others*, mentioned earlier, revealed a degree of contrition about mechanical application of *Dassonville* to catch measures even where restrictive effects on trade were hypothetical and unsubstantiated.[79] And four weeks later the Court began to dance to a different tune. In the matter of rules affecting the marketing of particular products the Court had the chance to provide a bolder formula in *Keck and Mithouard*.[80] And – in part – it took it.

The case concerned national (French) legislation imposing a general prohibition on resale of particular products at a loss. This legislation resembled the Sunday trading rules: at stake was apparently an 'equal burden' shared by all products and all

---

[76] Case C-23/89, *Quietlynn Ltd* v. *Southend on Sea BC*, [1990] ECR I-3059 (ECLI:EU:C:1990:300); Case C-350/89, *Sheptonhurst* v. *Newham BC*, [1991] ECR I-2387 (ECLI:EU:C:1991:194).

[77] Case 155/80, *Oebel*, [1981] ECR 1993 (ECLI:EU:C:1981:177); Case 75/81, *Blesgen* v. *Belgium*, [1982] ECR 1211 (ECLI:EU:C:1982:117) respectively.

[78] E.g., Case C-339/89, *Alsthom Atlantique*, [1991] ECR I-107 (ECLI:EU:C:1991:28); Case C-93/92, *CMC Motorradcenter*, [1993] ECR I-5009 (ECLI:EU:C:1993:838); Case C-291/09, *Guarnieri* [2011] ECR 2685 (ECLI:EU:C:2011:217); Case C-602/10, *SC Volksbank Romania*, judgment of 12 July 2012, not yet reported (ECLI:EU:C:2012:443).

[79] Case C-292/92, *supra* note 57, at para. 14. Also highly influential in provoking a re-think was White, 'In Search of the Limits to Article 30 of the EEC Treaty', 26 *Common Market Law Review* (1989) 235.

[80] Cases C-267/91 and C-268/91, *Keck and Mithouard*, [1993] ECR I-6097 (ECLI:EU:C:1993:905).

traders irrespective of origin. It was *not* like *Cassis de Dijon*: there was no dual burden of a type that placed an extra regulatory burden on imports asked to comply with both home and host state rules while granting protection to local products subject only to their own state's rules. And the Court faced up to this key distinction, as it had failed to face up to it in *Torfaen*. This was a measure which 'deprives traders of a method of sales promotion'.[81] That, however, left open the question 'whether such a possibility is sufficient to characterize the legislation in question as a measure having equivalent effect to a quantitative restriction on imports'.[82] The Court agreed 'it was necessary to re-examine and clarify its case-law'.[83] Its frustration and perhaps its embarrassment spills over at this point in the ruling, as it criticizes the source of the problem as 'the increasing tendency of traders to invoke Article 30 [now 34] of the Treaty as a means of challenging any rules whose effect is to limit their commercial freedom even where such rules are not aimed at products from other Member States'.[84] This is a spiteful remark, because it is the Court's own imprecision, most of all in the *Sunday Trading* cases, that has generated entirely understandable self-motivated litigation by traders seeking to maximize their commercial freedom, relying on the Court's own lovingly nurtured creation, EU law's direct effect. That tantrum out of the way, the Court then homed in on a new and – compared to the *Sunday Trading* cases – narrower test for the invocation of free movement law. Admitting that this was 'contrary to what has previously been decided', it stated that:

16.... the application to products from other Member States of national provisions restricting or prohibiting certain selling arrangements is not such as to hinder directly or indirectly, actually or potentially, trade between Member States within the meaning of the *Dassonville* judgment (Case 8/74 [1974] ECR 837), so long as those provisions apply to all relevant traders operating within the national territory and so long as they affect in the same manner, in law and in fact, the marketing of domestic products and of those from other Member States.

17. Provided that those conditions are fulfilled, the application of such rules to the sale of products from another Member State meeting the requirements laid down by that State is not by nature such as to prevent their access to the market or to impede access any more than it impedes the access of domestic products. Such rules therefore fall outside the scope of Article 30 of the Treaty.

In detail, the judgment is not written with forensic precision and it is almost certainly the product of compromise among the judges. It is 'methodologically rather destitute'.[85] The notion of 'selling arrangements' in paragraph 16 is mystifyingly imprecise; paragraph 17's suggestion that such rules either do not prevent access to the market or impede access no more than they impede the access of domestic products invites the question 'well, which is it?'. However the *general* intent of *Keck* is clear. And, moreover, a warm reception was merited. The Court was anxious lest the scope of internal market law be drawn too broadly, thereby depriving national

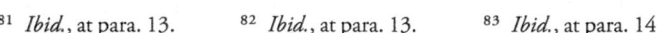

---

[81] *Ibid.*, at para. 13.   [82] *Ibid.*, at para. 13.   [83] *Ibid.*, at para. 14.
[84] *Ibid.*, at para. 14.
[85] Kingreen, 'Fundamental Freedoms', in A. Von Bogdandy and J. Bast, *Principles of European Constitutional Law* (2nd ed., 2010), at 516.

authorities of the competence to select forms of local market regulation which do not interfere with the process of market-building in the EU. *Keck* can convincingly be read as an attempt by the Court to strip out from this area of the law instances where there is no need to pursue a host state/home state analytical framework because in fact the matter can be left for regulation by the host state without any damage being inflicted on cross-border trade patterns. *Keck* rejects EU free movement law as a basis for general review of regulatory choices made at state level even in the absence of evidence of hindrance to the interpenetration of national markets. The jurisdictional point is that where a national measure is excluded from the reach of Article 34 by virtue of the reasoning found in *Keck* then (in contrast to the *Sunday Trading* cases) the national regulator does not even fall under an obligation to justify the measure according to standards recognized by the Court.

Keck shows the Court trying to save itself from itself. The Court was retreating to a purer understanding of the internal market as a legal concept governing the scope of free movement law. Its citation of *Dassonville* in paragraph 16 is a strong indication of its desire to restore the equilibrium it had itself upset in (most of all) the *Sunday Trading* cases. It returns to the gold standard of free movement law.

3. Services

The problem at stake – understanding the reach of the free movement rules and, as corollary, the space allowed for the protection of national regulatory autonomy – is not confined to goods. *Keck*, however, was about goods and the Court has never tried directly to extend the reasoning deployed in that case beyond the sphere of goods. It has, however, developed functionally similar – perhaps functionally identical – vocabulary destined to address the problem when it arises outside the context of goods.

In *Mobistar* and *Belgacom Mobile* the applicants were mobile telephone operators established in Belgium.[86] Their complaints, pursued in two separate sets of proceedings before the Belgian courts, related to taxes imposed on transmission pylons, masts and antennae. They relied on Article 49 EC (now Article 56 TFEU): that is to say, they sought to persuade the Court that the taxes were violations of their right to provide services. The Court adopted its orthodox approach, holding that Member States must exercise their powers in matters of direct taxation consistently with EU law, including free movement law. This is a statement of the wider reach of free movement law compared to the EU's more limited *legislative* competence. The Court then stated a version of its familiarly broad test for the invocation of the Treaty provision on free movement: what is now Article 56 TFEU:

> ... requires not only the elimination of all discrimination on grounds of nationality, against providers of services who are established in another Member State, but also the abolition of any restriction, even if it applies without distinction to national providers of services and to those of other Member States, which is liable to prohibit or further impede the activities of a provider of services established in another Member State where he lawfully provides similar

---

[86] Joined Cases C-544/03 and C-545/03, *Mobistar* and *Belgacom Mobile*, [2005] ECR I-7723 (ECLI:EU:C:2005:518).

services... Furthermore, [it]... precludes the application of any national rules which have the effect of making the provision of services between Member States more difficult than the provision of services purely within one Member State.[87]

But it then immediately addressed the *limits* of Article 56 TFEU. Measures which do no more than create additional costs in respect of the service in question and which affect in the same way the provision of services between Member States and that within one Member State do not fall within its scope.[88]

This is a '*Keck*-like' sense of restraint. But the Court avoided any explicit embrace of a convergent approach between the freedoms. And although resolution of the matter was formally within the gift of the national court, the Court indicated that the tax rules involved seemed to apply without distinction to all owners of mobile telephone installations within the geographical area subject to regulation and did not affect foreign operators either in fact or in law more adversely than national operators; nor did they make cross-border service provision more difficult than national service provision. It seems, then, that the limits of the internal market as a legal concept that place the national regulator under an obligation to justify its practices had been reached.

The Court explicitly adopted the reasoning it had used in *Mobistar* in *Berlington Hungary and Others*.[89] That case concerned the regulation of slot machines in Hungary. One of the questions the Court was asked concerned the introduction of a large increase in the tax payable on slot machines operated in amusement arcades. Was this within the scope of Article 56 TFEU? The judgment reveals the familiar insistence that the fundamental freedoms control choices made about direct taxation by the Member States, coupled to the standard wide definition of Article 56's scope. However, citing *Mobistar*, the Court added that 'measures, the only effect of which is to create additional costs in respect of the service in question and which affect in the same way the provision of services between Member States and that within one Member State, do not fall within the scope of Article 56 TFEU'.[90] Once again, the detailed resolution of the matter belonged with the national court, but the Court noted the absence of any direct discrimination between Hungarian companies and companies established in other Member States operating slot machines in amusement arcades in Hungarian territory.

4. Adjusting the Readjustment

There is, then, a key divide between rules that need to be justified and rules that are expressions of local regulatory autonomy untouched by free movement law. The Court *started* the task of defining and mapping that divide in *Keck*. Since then it has been charged with the task of clarifying the matter further, and it has performed that task in an environment that is often loaded. The cases are typically driven by traders seeking to persuade the Court to nudge the reach of internal market law ever wider,

---

[87] *Ibid.*, at para. 29, 30.   [88] *Ibid.*, at para. 31.   [89] Case C-98/14, *supra* note 46.
[90] *Ibid.*, at para. 36.

so that they may exploit EU law in order to maximize their commercial freedom. The same incentives that motivated the ingenious Sunday traders are still at large. Thus the Court, asked to work with the internal market as a controlling legal concept, is given a hard task.

The Commission in the immediate aftermath of the *Keck and Mithouard* ruling claimed that the Court 'has completed its case law'.[91] Were one feeling charitable one might concede that a broadly familiar pattern has now been established, according to which the Court first considers whether a challenged measure constitutes a trade barrier and then, provided the threshold be crossed and a barrier to inter-state trade shown to exist, the Court proceeds to examine the justifications advanced by the regulator. *Keck* did provide a way to understand and explain the exclusion of equal burden rules from the reach of Article 34 and indeed, soon after *Keck*, the Court decided that rules dictating the opening hours of petrol stations and of shops needed no justification because they did not count as barriers to inter-state trade.[92] This is exactly how the *Sunday Trading* cases *should* have been dealt with. *Keck*, though not perfect, nevertheless is written with sufficient clarity to shield genuine 'equal burden' rules from review in the name of EU law on free movement. Worries about the proper scope of Article 34 can also be set aside in so far as the national rule counts as a measure affecting a commercial practice in trade between business and a consumer within the meaning of Directive 2005/29, because that Directive, a measure of maximum harmonization, provides exhaustive regulation of such matters at EU level, requiring their suppression if unfair and their release if fair.[93]

Keck, however, is only a *partial* revolution. The Court moved quickly to quash any notion that *Cassis de Dijon* was no longer good law, as it sternly rejected attempts to shelter 'dual burden' rules governing the composition of products from review under Article 34 TFEU. The need 'to adapt the products in question to the rules in force in the Member State in which they are marketed' brings the matter within the scope of free movement law.[94] *Keck* did not change that at all. In similar vein, the Court intelligently allowed free movement law to be used to attack restrictions on advertising even where these were applicable to all products where it could be demonstrated that there was an unequal burden in fact – typically, where a ban on advertising could be shown to confer an advantage on a local product with which consumers were familiar at the expense of an unknown imported product that could only effectively compete for market share if allowed to use the lever of advertising.[95] The Court

---

[91] OJ 1993 C 353/6.

[92] Cases C-401 and C-402/92, *Tankstation 't Heukste & JBE Boermans*, [1994] ECR I-2199 (ECLI:EU:C:1994:220) and Joined Cases C-69/93 and C-258/93, *Punto Casa and PPV*, [1994] ECR I-2355 (ECLI:EU:C:1994:226) respectively.

[93] Directive 2005/29 concerning unfair business-to-consumer practices in the internal market, OJ 2005 L 149/22. The material scope of the Directive is broad but to some extent ambiguous: see Chapter 15.C.2.

[94] Case C-390/99, *supra* note 55, at para. 30; Case C-244/06, *Dynamic Medien*, [2008] ECR I-505 (ECLI:EU:C:2008:85), at para. 31. See also, e.g., Case C-470/93, *Verein gegen Unwesen in Handel und Gewerbe Köln* v. *Mars GmbH* [1995] ECR I-1923 (ECLI:EU:C:1995:224); Case C-67/97, *Ditlev Bluhme* [1998] ECR I-8033 (ECLI:EU:C:1998:584).

[95] E.g., Joined Cases C-34/95, C-35/95 and C-36/95, *Konsumentombudsmannen* v. *De Agostini Forlag AB and TV-Shop i Sverige AB*, [1997] ECR I-3843 (ECLI:EU:C:1997:344); Case C-405/98,

is astutely ready to take seriously the contribution of advertising to generating *dynamic* change in the structure of the internal market. So too, gratifyingly resistant to an obstinately formalist reading of *Keck*, the Court instead envisages a detailed inquiry into the factual – equal or unequal – impact of national rules that restrict particular forms of marketing.[96] They *may* affect the internal market. So the Court accepted that Austrian rules banning the selling of jewellery at parties held in the home suppressed a commercially attractive sales technique, but it insisted that this did not suffice to throw the Article 34 net around it.[97] That would occur only if the exclusion of the relevant marketing method affected products from other Member States more than it affected domestic products, which it left for determination by the national court. A realistic examination of its actual impact in the market was required. This is not inconsistent with the judgment in *Keck* itself, but the more recent decisions involving advertising and marketing restrictions have been especially helpful in permitting the Court to provide a more nuanced economic context to the application of EU law in the service of market integration.

Equally, the restraint of application of Article 56 devised in *Mobistar* does not deprive that provision of its role where rules are not in fact equal in application. So in *Berlington Hungary* the Court made clear that Hungarian taxation of slot machines in amusement arcades would *not* escape review where companies operating amusement arcades in the Hungarian market were mainly established in other Member States, for such circumstances would reveal indirect discrimination against service providers established in other Member States;[98] and moreover if it were shown that the effect of taxing the operation of slot machines in amusement arcades was to confine operation of slot machines to casinos, not subject to the tax increase, then this would be a case where the rule was actually liable to prohibit, impede or render less attractive the exercise of the freedom to provide the services of operating slot machines in amusement arcades in Hungary, within the scope of Article 56 TFEU.[99]

In truth, however, case law is never 'completed'.[100] *Keck* left open plenty of enticing questions about exactly when a national measure is immune from challenge. In line with the thematically consistent pattern of EU law, traders quickly moved to exploit the opportunities. And, in line with another consistent theme, the Court was forced to do its best to make sense of the internal market as a legal concept which serves both to empower but also to limit. The toughest test case: national rules that restrict the use of products.

Konsumentombudsmannen v. *Gourmet International Products*, [2001] ECR I-1795 (ECLI:EU:C: 2001:135).

[96] E.g., Case C-239/02, *Douwe Egberts*, [2004] ECR I-7007 (ECLI:EU:C:2004:445); Case C-20/03, *Burmanjer et al.*, [2005] ECR I-4133 (ECLI:EU:C:2005:307)). *Keck* is 'not a magic formula': Rosas, 'Life after Dassonville and Cassis: Evolution but No Revolution', in M. Maduro and L. Azoulai (eds), *The Past and Future of EU Law* (2010), 442.

[97] Case C-441/04, *A-Punkt Schmuckhandels GmbH* v. *Claudia Schmidt*, [2006] ECR I-2093 (ECLI:EU:C:2006:141).

[98] Case C-98/14, *supra* note 46, para. 38.   [99] *Ibid.*, at paras 39–42.

[100] Cf. Commission *supra* note 91.

5. Restrictions on Use

A national rule which *restricts the use* of a product adds an extra dimension to the inquiry. Where a product can be sold, but cannot be used in unlimited fashion, the matter is plainly within the scope of Article 34 TFEU if it is applied in a discriminatory manner, but absent discrimination it seems to restrict commercial freedom to the same degree whether use of domestically produced or imported goods is involved. Where a state bans a product or service completely, there is no legal or factual inequality in application, but there is perfectly obviously a barrier to interstate trade: there is a fragmentation of the internal market along national lines. What is at stake is how much less than a complete ban – a restriction on use – counts as the same problem for the purposes of the scope of application of internal market law.

The conundrum is beautifully captured by the key case in this area, *Åklagaren* v. *Mickelsson, Roos*.[101] Swedish rules restricted the use of (inter alia) jet-skis on particular waterways. There was no discrimination on the basis of the origin of jet-skis or their producers. This was not a problem of the *Cassis de Dijon* type: the Swedish rules were not directed at the composition or shape of jet-skis at all. Nor was there a ban on jet-skis in Sweden, only a restriction on their use. Such a rule doubtless made the purchase of jet-skis in Sweden at least marginally less attractive to consumers than in a State where no such restrictions applied, but there was no evident difference in law or in fact in the rule's application to imported jet-skis as opposed to ones actually or potentially made in Sweden. So could Article 34 TFEU be relevant? The Court observed that:

> Even if the national regulations at issue do not have the aim or effect of treating goods coming from other Member States less favourably, which is for the national court to ascertain, the restriction which they impose on the use of a product in the territory of a Member State may, depending on its scope, have a considerable influence on the behaviour of consumers, which may, in turn, affect the access of that product to the market of that Member State.[102]

So if the national measure has a *considerable* influence on the behaviour of consumers, it falls in principle within the scope of Article 34 TFEU (and, therefore, as a jurisdictional consequence, it requires justification, which in *Åklagaren* v. *Mickelsson, Roos* engaged the protection of the environment). If the influence is not considerable, the measure escapes the scope of application of Article 34 TFEU. So the adjective *considerable* carries heavy constitutional weight: it defines the threshold for the triggering of internal market law. Later in the judgment the Court relied as a test on whether rules prevent users from using jet-skis 'for the specific and inherent purposes for which they were intended or of greatly restricting their use'.[103] So the adverb *greatly* is used as a constitutionally crucial tipping point. There is appeal in using the attitudes of consumers as jurisdictionally significant in defining the reach of the internal market as a legal concept, because ultimately the economic benefits of intensified cross-border competition are intended to be enjoyed by consumers.

---

[101] Case C-142/05, *Åklagaren* v. *Mickelsson, Roos*, [2009] ECR I-4273 (ECLI:EU:C:2009:336). The path was broken by Case C-110/05, *supra* note 21.
[102] *Ibid.*, at para. 26.   [103] *Ibid.*, at para. 28.

But the threshold tests devised by the Court are alarmingly vague. Probably what is required is a restriction on use that is so severe that it approaches the effect of a complete ban on the product, but that is simply another way to ask the question – *what* must be shown, to bring the measure within the scope of Article 34? – rather than to provide an answer.

The Court's use of the adjective 'considerable' and the adverb 'greatly' in defining the reach of Article 34 captures the notion that just because commercial activity is affected by national laws does not of itself mean there is (in short) 'an internal market problem'. The threshold at which a matter of concern for the EU is revealed is higher. Two main objections animate the academic criticism.[104] The *first objection* is that the Court has created a test which simply describes the problem. Internal market law's incursion into national regulatory autonomy has a limit: this necessarily flows ultimately from Article 5 TEU. But rather than providing a *workable* test for determining when those limits are in fact reached, the Court has simply found a way to re-phrase the question. *Roughly* what is at stake is the idea that a restriction which is serious enough to cause the territory of the regulating State to be segmented from the wider internal market requires justification, whereas a restriction that does not prevent access to the regulated market but rather confines commercial freedom within it, does not. This is the limit of the internal market – but it is alarmingly imprecise and ambiguous. One of the consequences of the Court's approach is to require case-by-case analysis, and in practice an elusive task is placed on the shoulders of national judges. The *second objection* is that the Court is coming perilously close to overturning *Keck*. If rules preventing resale of products at a loss (the factual issue in *Keck*) exert a considerable influence on consumer behaviour, is it now correct to conclude that they fall within Article 34 TFEU? This, plainly, will be the way in which litigants will frame a claim, and there seems to be no requirement that a protectionist effect in favour of domestic production must be shown to taint the national rules. *Keck* was a necessary re-balancing of vertical allocation of competence in favour of State autonomy. Indeed, to bring matters unassociated with the project of creating an internal market within the scope of EU law would typically empower commercially powerful actors unable otherwise to induce deregulatory change at national level. Article 26 TFEU provides no authority for that stretch and so neither does Article 5 TEU: the EU's legitimacy in purporting to put such rules to the test is exhausted.[105] What prevents Article 34 having gone full circle and being capable, as in *Sunday Trading*, of application to any restriction on commercial freedom within a Member State is the insistence that there be an influence on consumer demand

---

[104] E.g., Enchelmaier, 'Moped Trailers, Mickelson & Roos, Gysbrechts: The ECJ's Case Law on Goods Keeps on Moving', 29 *Yearbook of European Law* (2010) 190; Lianos, 'In Memoriam Keck: The Reformation of the EU Law on the Free Movement of Goods', 40 *European Law Review* (2015) 225; Horsley, 'Unearthing Buried Treasure: Article 34 TFEU and the Exclusionary Rules', 37 *European Law Review* (2012) 734; Wenneras and Moen, 'Selling Arrangements, Keeping Keck', 35 *European Law Review* (2010) 397; Gormley, 'Inconsistencies and Misconceptions in the Free Movement of Goods', 40 *European Law Review* (2015) 925.

[105] Cf. the (two part) account of Somek, 'The Argument from Transnational Effects', 16 *European Law Journal* (2010) 315 and 375.

caused by the rule that is *considerable* – but that is a very obscure and malleable measurement.

6. Concluding Comments

The project of creating an internal market serves as a basis for the EU's legitimate claim to override national authority. This project and this claim must have limits. They are reached where the national measure in question does not exert an effect on the internal market's creation. The root of the problem of missing definitional precision does not lie principally in the Treaty provisions on free movement. Instead, it lies principally in Article 26 TFEU. The Court is groping for something that the Treaty, and in particular Article 26 TFEU, simply does not give it: a precise and reliable means to determine when there is (in short) an internal market problem. The internal market as a legal concept is not useful in any practical concrete operational sense here. It is broad and ambiguous. The Court's case law conveys that has chosen to treat the free movement rules as *less* than a charter for general review of Member State economic policy but *more* than a mere anti-discrimination rule. This is not in any sense constitutionally right or wrong. The Treaty offers no such benchmark.

D. People and Citizens

Promoting the mobility of people in the EU shares the economic purpose of intensified competition and a better functioning market with promoting the mobility of goods. But people are not simply economic agents. Goods are moved, people move. People have families, goods do not. People have rights, goods do not. In devising an understanding of the reach of free movement law where people are concerned, this could mean that different tests are needed. But this is an inquiry that is delegated to the Court. Nothing in the Treaty spells out how to address this issue. The absence of a reliable anchoring definition of the internal market as a legal concept is the underlying challenge.

1. Remoteness

Hans Moser v. *Land Baden-Württemberg* was encountered earlier, but it deserves revisiting because it is a case which shows – unusually – how a matter is sometimes found with confidence to lie beyond the reach of EU internal market law.[106] Moser had been refused access to post-graduate training required for entry to the teaching profession because of his membership of the German Communist Party. The Court found that the matter was wholly internal to Germany. He had claimed that he might in future wish to work in another Member State, but the Court found this to be a claim based on a 'purely hypo-

---

[106] Case 180/83, *supra* note 5.

thetical prospect of employment in another Member State'.[107] Otherwise put, the matter had no adequate connection with cross-border activity. If it was to be resolved, it should be Germany that should do it.

Finding exercise of the right of freedom of movement to be 'purely hypothetical' is rare in the Court's case law.[108] It is a type of remoteness test, and there are other decisions of the Court which prefer language of this type as the basis for slamming the EU law door shut in the face of over-optimistic litigants. *Volker Graf* v. *Filzmoser Maschinenbau* provides a helpful illustration.[109] The case concerned Austrian rules which denied a worker entitlement to compensation where the worker chose to terminate a contract of employment, whereas compensation was payable where the contract ended without the termination being at the worker's own initiative. Graf had been offered a job in Germany and complained that the Austrian rule deterred his readiness to take up the offer. The obvious retort is that the disadvantage which he certainly faced was one that would have arisen had he sought to take up a new job *anywhere*, even elsewhere in Austria. This was an opportunity for the Court to apply its *Keck* solution also to the free movement of workers. After all, the Austrian rule applied equally in law and in fact to all workers and, in short, it exerted no impact on the creation of an internal market as such, but rather merely restricted their economic freedom. Instead the Court ruled that Austrian rules did not deter a worker from ending a contract of employment in order to take a job with another employer, because the entitlement to compensation on termination of employment was dependent on a future and hypothetical event, namely the subsequent termination of his contract without such termination being at his own initiative. This, the Court ruled, was an event 'too uncertain and indirect a possibility for legislation to be capable of being regarded as liable to hinder freedom of movement for workers'.[110] So the Court embraced the discourse of deterrence, but found the Austrian rule did not have such an effect (on free movement). It also mentioned the jurisdictional importance of showing an obstruction to access to the (labour) market: this was not present. Put another way, this was *not* a case like *Bosman*, considered earlier (see Section B), where such an obstruction was caused by the football transfer system for players. The Court was using a form of remoteness test, and in fact it cited *Krantz* v. *Ontvanger der Directe Belastingen*,[111] a case concerning goods which is in exactly that vein. It avoided *Keck* altogether, even though *Keck* could well be seen as a more sophisticated version of the remoteness test used in *Krantz*, and it is, as a minimum, a functionally similar route to the same outcome – namely, the unavailability of EU free movement law to upset local regulatory autonomy, and a recognition

---

[107] *Ibid.*, at para. 18.
[108] See also Case C-40/11, *Iida*, judgment of 8 November 2012, not yet reported (ECLI:EU:C:2012:691), at para. 77; Case C-299/95, *Kremzow*, [1997] ECR I-2629 (ECLI:EU:C:1997:254), at para. 16.
[109] Case C-190/98, *Volker Graf* v. *Filzmoser Maschinenbau*, [2000] ECR I-493 (ECLI:EU:C:2000:49).
[110] *Ibid.*, at para. 25. See also Case C-542/08, *Friedrich Barth*, [2010] ECR I-3189 (ECLI:EU:C:2010:193); Case C-211/08, *Commission* v. *Spain*, [2010] ECR I-5267 (ECLI:EU:C:2010:340).
[111] Case C-69/88, *Krantz* v. *Ontvanger der Directe Belastingen*, [1990] ECR I-583 (ECLI:EU:C:1990:97).

that simple difference between Member State laws is of itself not an 'internal market problem'.

Advocate General Tizzano's insightful Opinion in *CaixaBank France*, considered in Section B, drew (inter alia) on *Graf* as an example of how, in his view, a limit could and should be placed on the reach of the Treaty provisions on the free movement of workers, and he drew ready analogies with *Keck*.[112] The Court never has done so, at least openly. There may here be a *hidden* convergence of the freedoms, but the Court is intent on cautious avoidance of statements of principle. In exactly this vein, asked in *Pelckmans Turnhout NV* to consider the application of EU law to Belgian rules requiring that shops be closed for at least one day in the week, it found that Article 34 did not apply because the rule affected all traders and all goods in the same way, in law and in fact, and then in the next paragraph relied on a finding that any restrictive effects within the meaning of Article 56 TFEU were too uncertain and indirect for that provision to apply.[113] Same outcome, different language: explicit convergence between the Treaty freedoms evaded!

The really distinctive strain of the case law affecting people, which taxes the location of the limits of the internal market as a legal concept, concerns family (re)unification. This is addressed in Section D.2.

2. People and Families

The *Mary Carpenter* case was discussed earlier, in Section B. It is a startling example of how easy is to trigger EU free movement law with the consequence *not* that an immediate or direct obstacle to cross-border movement may be attacked but rather so that the holder of EU free movement rights may act so as to protect the residence status of a family member who is a third country national (TCN) and so beyond the personal scope of EU law. Mrs Carpenter, a national of the Philippines, was threatened with deportation from the UK, but because her husband, a UK national living in the UK, had *some* association with customers in other Member States in his business activity as a seller of advertising space in journals and of publishing services, *his* free movement rights were treated as prejudiced by *her* plight. His wife's deportation would require him to go to live with her in the Philippines or lead to separation of the family unit if he remained in the UK. In both cases his *business* would be affected. Deportation was therefore challengeable under EU law and, given the significance the Court attached to family life, it was not found to be justified. The Court is perfunctory: it devotes no close attention to establishing a connection between the threatened deportation and the perceived impediment to trade. EU free movement law applies remarkably easily: and when it does protection of fundamental rights immediately becomes part of the assessment. On this logic the individual who shops at an internet site hosted in another Member State becomes a cross-border trader. Moser should have been smarter:[114] litigants in future will be.

---

[112] Case C-442/02, *supra* note 61.
[113] Case C-483/12, *Pelckmans Turnhout NV*, judgment of 8 May 2014, not yet reported (ECLI:EU:C:2014:304).
[114] Case 180/83, *supra* note 5.

The threshold at which national regulatory autonomy becomes subject to review for its prejudicial effect on the EU's internal market is relatively low. The consequence is that EU law is triggered in a case where a Member State is seeking to assert its power to make choices about the residence rights of third country nationals who are part of the family of one of its *own* nationals. This is, admittedly, not wholly new. In *R* v. *IAT and Singh, ex parte Secretary of State* a British national was able to rely on EU law to protect an Indian spouse when returning to the UK after working in Germany.[115] Were it otherwise, workers might be deterred from leaving their country of origin in order to pursue an activity as an employed or self-employed person as envisaged by the Treaty in the territory of another Member State. So – in contrast to cases encountered earlier such as *Uecker, Jacquet*[116] – this was not a situation wholly internal to a one Member State. The Court is anxious to protect the effective enjoyment of free movement rights. *Deterrent* effect on free movement is an important triggering factor.

Cases of this type commonly arise today in the name of the status of 'Citizenship of the Union' (EU citizenship), which by virtue of Article 21 TFEU creates free movement rights which, moreover, are not confined to the economically active. In *O and B* the Court, interpreting Article 21 TFEU, found that the logic of preventing deterrent effect applied generally to citizens with relatives who are third country nationals (TCNs) who have moved from one Member State to another and then returned to the first Member State, but that the residence in another Member State must be sufficiently genuine to create or strengthen family life in the host Member State for EU law to help.[117] In *S and G* the Court took the view that where a national of a Member State who travels to work in another Member State seeks to rely on EU law to protect TCNs against the home Member State, the derived right of the TCN is triggered only if its denial interferes with the exercise of a fundamental freedom.[118] So, for example, where the TCN cares for the workers' children, it would seem likely that action against the TCN would be controlled under EU law because of the damage done to the worker's right. The Court left open other possibilities. In *S and G* the Court expressly relied on *Carpenter*, which concerned what is now Article 56 TFEU, and used it in the context of Article 45 TFEU.

The variety is vivid. Sometimes even a deterrent effect to free movement is not necessary. *Zhu and Chen* provides an example.[119] Catherine Zhu, eight months old, held Irish nationality, although she was born in and had always lived in the UK. But she had in fact been born in Belfast, in Northern Ireland, which entitled her, as a person born on the island of Ireland, to acquire Irish nationality under the relevant rules of the Republic of Ireland. It was in fact clear that Mrs Chen, her mother, had moved to Belfast when pregnant with Catherine precisely to permit the child to acquire Irish nationality and, consequently, to enable the mother to acquire the right

---

[115] Case C-370/90, *R* v. *IAT and Singh, ex parte Secretary of State*, [1992] ECR I-4265 (ECLI:EU:C:1992:296); also Case C-291/05, *Eind*, [2007] ECR I-10719 (ECLI:EU:C:2007:771).
[116] Case C-64/96 and C-65/96, *supra* note 2.
[117] Case C-456/12, *O. and B.*, judgment of 12 March 2014, not yet reported (ECLI:EU:C:2014:135).
[118] Case C-457/12, *S. and G.*, judgment of 12 March 2014, not yet reported (ECLI:EU:C:2014:136).
[119] Case C-200/02, *Zhu and Chen*, [2004] ECR I-9925 (ECLI:EU:C:2004:639).

to reside with her child in the UK.[120] Did EU law protect such a claim? The UK authorities argued it did not, the implication being that the treatment of a Chinese national was its concern alone. The Court refused to accept that the fact that Catherine had never moved from one Member State to another Member State concluded the matter. On the contrary: the situation of a national of a Member State (here, Ireland) who was born in the host Member State (here, the UK) and has not made use of the right to freedom of movement cannot *for that reason alone* be assimilated to a purely internal situation.[121] The Court examined Article 18 EC (now Article 21 TFEU), in conjunction with relevant secondary legislation under an approach which insisted that 'provisions laying down a fundamental principle such as that of the free movement of persons must be interpreted broadly'.[122] In the circumstances, EU law granted Catherine a right to reside for an indefinite period in the UK and her mother, as primary carer, enjoyed the same right. So this was not like *Saunders*.[123] It was not a wholly internal situation. It illustrates how relatively easy it is to trigger the cross-border element which places a burden on the Member State to justify its practices. Acquisition of Irish nationality was enough.

There must be a cross-border dimension before the national rules fall under review, but it is striking how quickly the Court is able to identify an adequate impact. So in this way a state's immigration rules applicable to TCNs become part of the law of the internal market and, in turn, both the Court and courts generally are empowered at the expense of national political processes. This institutional consequence is not at all new in EU law – it is *Cassis de Dijon* in a nutshell! – and it is visible elsewhere in highly sensitive areas such as fundamental rights, where the Court seeks to balance economic rights with social and political rights (see Chapter 11). The risk is that the Court may under-appreciate just how significant the re-allocation of competences and powers between states and the EU and between judges and political processes really is, especially where people rather than goods are involved.

In its Article 21 TFEU case law of more general application, beyond the particular case of the TCN threatened by deportation, the Court has ruled that where a national measure is liable to cause a *serious inconvenience* to an affected person, it falls in principle within the scope of Article 21 TFEU (and requires justification). *Ilonka Sayn-Wittgenstein* v. *Landeshauptmann von Wien* arose out of a difference dating back to 1919 between the rules governing surnames in Austria, which forbids use of noble titles, and Germany, which does away with the associated privileges but allows parts of the noble title to be retained in the surname.[124] The applicant, known in Germany as Ilonka Fürstin von Sayn-Wittgenstein, was advised that in Austria her name had to be stripped down to Ilonka Sayn-Wittgenstein. This constituted serious inconvenience to her commercial activity, which was itself a noble calling: the sale of castles. Austria has accordingly restricted the freedom envisaged by Article 21 TFEU, though as the Court made plain the matter could equally well (also) have been

---

[120] *Ibid.*, at para. 11.   [121] *Ibid.*, at para. 19. See also Case C-148/02, *supra* note 121.
[122] *Ibid.*, at para. 31.   [123] Case 175/78, *supra* note 3.
[124] Case C-208/09, *Ilonka Sayn-Wittgenstein* v. *Landeshauptmann von Wien*, [2010] ECR I-13693 (ECLI:EU:C:2010:806).

treated from the perspective of Article 56 TFEU as a restriction on the free move-ment of services.[125] If the inconvenience is *not* serious, then, as the Court has on occasion made explicit, the measure escapes the scope of application of Article 21 TFEU.[126] So the adjective *serious* carries heavy constitutional weight. This was not an isolated instance of reliance on a test based on the identification of a 'serious inconvenience' as the threshold to reliance on what is now Article 21 TFEU. It was used in the same fashion to require that the refusal of the German authorities to recognize a child's name registered in Denmark to German parents – on the basis that it was double-barrelled, being drawn from both parents' surnames – should be justified.[127] The Court deployed its orthodox formula to note that rules governing a person's surname are matters coming within the competence of the Member States, but this is subject, as ever (Chapter 5.C), to the proviso that they must comply with free movement law. Given that a serious inconvenience on a private and personal level would follow from the discrepancy between surnames, most obviously in mat-ters of proof of identity, Article 21 TFEU put the restrictive German approach to the test, and although resolution of the matter lies formally with the referring national court, the Court's ruling makes it clear that it should *not* be considered justified.

3. Citizenship Too

It was mentioned earlier that in *Land Nordrhein Westfalen* v. *Uecker, Jacquet* the Court held that nationals of a Member State resident and working in that Member State, and who had never exercised a right to free movement within the EU, could not rely on EU law.[128] This was a matter purely internal to one Member State. The Court also took the opportunity in its ruling to reject the submission that the provi-sions on Citizenship of the Union, introduced by the Maastricht Treaty with effect from 1993, made any difference. Citizenship, it declared, is not intended to extend the material scope of the Treaty. It was to the internal legal system of the state in question that the individual must look for legal protection.

This is no longer a fully accurate account of the reach of EU law.

Early in 2011, in *Ruiz Zambrano* the Court dealt with a case of a TCN who was a Colombian national with dependent children who held Belgian nationality and who had never left Belgium.[129] The question was whether the Colombian acquired a right of residence in Belgium via her children, who were EU nationals. This might have seemed to be a situation that was purely internal to Belgium. The children had never crossed a border, so the case seemed much closer to *Moser*, where any impedi-ment to free movement was hypothetical, than to *Carpenter*, where at least there was a small dose of cross-border (economic) activity. Missing too was the special feature

---

[125] *Ibid.*, at para. 40.
[126] E.g., Case C-391/09, *Runevic-Vardyn*, [2011] ECR I-3787 (ECLI:EU:C:2011:291), at paras 76, 78, 81.
[127] Case C-353/06, *Grunkin, Paul*, [2008] ECR I-7639 (ECLI:EU:C:2008:559); also Case C-148/02, *Garcia Avello*, [2003] ECR I-11613 (ECLI:EU:C:2003:539).
[128] Case C-64/96 and C-65/96, *supra* note 2.
[129] Case C-34/09, *Ruiz Zambrano*, [2011] ECR I-1177 (ECLI:EU:C:2011:124).

of a child who was a national of one Member State but resident in other, which had turned the EU law key for *Zhu and Chen*.[130] But the Court created a new test and drew a new line.

It declared that Article 20 TFEU 'precludes national measures which have the effect of depriving citizens of the Union of the genuine enjoyment of the substance of the rights conferred by virtue of their status as citizens of the Union'.[131] This deprivation would occur if the national measure were to force the EU national to leave the territory of the EU. If the deprivation related to the substance of other rights (or for that matter to the rights conferred by virtue of status as EU citizens, but not to the substance of those rights), the measure would escape the scope of application of Article 20 TFEU. A refusal to grant a right of residence to the Colombian would mean the children, who were EU citizens, would have to leave the territory of the EU. As a result they would be unable to exercise the substance of the rights conferred on them by virtue of their status as EU citizens.

EU law applied and, by way of corollary, the autonomy of Belgian immigration law applicable to TCNs was confined. It is the apparent disregard of the *limits* of EU law when confronted by a situation internal to a single Member State which fired much of the critical reaction to *Ruiz Zambrano*. In fact, in the ruling the Court openly acknowledged that it had had pressed on it the absence of any cross-border element to the case and consequently the inapplicability of the free movement provisions,[132] but, startlingly, it completely ignored this principled objection and calmly asserted the matter to fall within the scope of EU law according to its newly minted test focused on deprivation of EU citizens of the genuine enjoyment of the substance of the rights conferred by virtue of their status, which is capable of being met even if the matter appears to raise only issues internal to one Member State.

This is another instance where case law is never 'complete'.[133] *Shirley McCarthy*, decided two months later than *Ruiz Zambrano*, revealed that the Court did not intend a complete abandonment of the very notion of a 'purely internal' situation that escapes the scope of EU law.[134] McCarthy was a dual Irish/ UK national, but she was born and had always lived in the UK. She married a third country national – a Jamaican – who had no leave to remain in the UK. The question was whether she was able to rely on EU law to protect him from deportation. The Court cited *Ruiz Zambrano*, but it found that in this instance the threshold was not crossed: there was no deprivation of genuine enjoyment of the substance of rights conferred by the status of citizenship. 'By contrast' with *Ruiz Zambrano*, and crucially, the UK measure did not oblige her to leave the territory of the EU.[135] So, as Advocate General Kokott's Opinion makes clear, legal protection would have to be sought under English and/or European Convention on Human Rights, not EU law. Plainly, then, the 'purely internal' situation as a category insulated from EU law lives on but in

---

[130] Case C-200/02, *supra* note 119.   [131] *Ibid.*, at para. 42.
[132] *Ibid.*, at para. 37 of the judgment.   [133] Commission, *supra* note 91.
[134] Case C-434/09, *Shirley McCarthy*, [2011] ECR I-3375 (ECLI:EU:C:2011:277).
[135] *Ibid.*, at para. 50.

attenuated form, and, once again, internal market law is revealed as dynamic not static.

Dereci, the Court's third ruling dealing with this issue during calendar year 2011, settled most of the detailed dust.[136] The applicants were all third country nationals who had been refused permission to live with family members who were EU citizens resident in and nationals of Austria. Those EU citizens had never exercised their right to free movement. The Court repeated the test concocted in *Ruiz Zambrano*, then explained that there is a denial of the genuine enjoyment of the substance of the rights conferred by virtue of the status of citizenship where the EU citizen in fact has to leave the territory of the EU as a result of the refusal to grant a right of residence to the family member. By contrast where an individual simply wants to have third country national family members live with him or her for economic reasons or in order to keep a family together in the territory of the EU, this is not enough to support the view that refusal would force the individual to leave the territory of the EU. This, then, is the dividing line. The Court has subsequently added some useful factual clarification about just when the matter will attract the protection of EU law rather than being left to the mercy of national law.[137]

The protection envisaged by the status of EU citizenship projects EU law into a situation which is apparently internal to one Member State – but only where otherwise the EU citizen will be forced to leave the EU entirely. That is where the line is drawn. This is doubtless how an individual seeking the protection of EU law should seek to frame such an argument in future.

The jurisdictional matter seems somehow loosely connected with the importance of EU citizenship. The Court's relatively generous approach, eroding the 'purely internal' situation, could plausibly be driven by the widened aims of the EU and deepened commitments to fundamental rights accepted under the Lisbon Treaty.[138] Perhaps people are more important than goods and so the free movement rules are triggered more quickly where they are concerned. Perhaps people are actually or potentially more independently mobile than goods, so the free movement provisions are triggered more quickly where they are concerned. There is a long-standing flavour in the case law that EU citizenship in some ambiguous way eases free movement law towards inflation by reducing the jurisdictional centrality of migration,[139] but in its case law the Court evades any statements of clarifying or organizing principle. In an especially vigorous critique Hailbronner and Thym noted the opaque nature of the test newly introduced by *Ruiz Zambrano*, and observed that neither has the

---

[136] Case C-256/11, *Dereci*, [2011] ECR I-11315 (ECLI:EU:C:2011:734).

[137] E.g., Case C-40/11, *supra* note 108; Case C-87/12, *Ymeraga*, judgment of 8 May 2013, not yet reported (ECLI:EU:C:2013:291); Case C-86/12, *Alokpa*, judgment of 10 October 2013, not yet reported (ECLI:EU:C:2013:645).

[138] See in particular the Opinion of A.G. Sharpston in *Ruiz Zambrano*.

[139] Cf., e.g., Nic Shuibhne, 'The Outer Limits of EU Citizenship: Displacing Economic Free Movement Rights?', in C. Barnard and O. Odudu (eds), *The Outer Limits of European Union Law* (2009) Ch. 8; E. Spaventa, 'Seeing the Wood Despite the Trees? On the Scope of Union Citizenship and its Constitutional Effects', 45 *Common Market Law Review* (2008) 13; Caro de Sousa, 'Quest for the Holy Grail – Is a Unified Approach to the Market Freedoms and European Citizenship Justified?', 20 *European Law Journal* (2014) 499.

Court shown it to fit with existing case law nor has its future scope of application been made clear, and concluded that '[a] Supreme Court should behave more responsibly'.[140] Simply to note that EU law has often been developed in this dynamic way is, though true, no adequate response to this rebuke, given the significant institutional and constitutional consequences, both horizontal and vertical in nature, which flow from this assertion of an EU judicial power to rule on sensitive matters of state immigration policy. This is yet another area of internal market law that is unsettled both descriptively and normatively. Even if what is at stake here is more aggressive control of 'internal' national practices in the name of citizenship, rather than the more restrained control in the name of the internal market covered elsewhere in this volume, the thematic core of the structural inquiry remains the same as that pursued elsewhere in this volume: there is a hard-to-fix dividing line between national practices that require justification under EU law and those that do not and, by way of corollary, there is an unreliably protected zone of national autonomy to decide on the fate of TCNs wishing to enjoy residence rights.

E. State Aid

EU law governing state aid offers further rich illustrative fare. The intent here is not to offer any exhaustive survey of the field; rather, it is to pick out two particular instances where the internal market as a legal concept is not drawn with sufficient precision to provide clear answers to questions about the scope of EU law and, its corollary, the protection of national autonomy. The thematic link to the previous discussion is also that the Court is as a result granted remarkable interpretative room for manoeuvre.

Article 107(1) TFEU applies to 'any aid granted by a Member State or through State resources in any form whatsoever which distorts or threatens to distort competition by favouring certain undertakings or the production of certain goods... in so far as it affects trade between member States'. Such aid is to be treated as 'incompatible with the internal market' unless either found to fall within the list of types of aid that are to be treated as compatible with the internal market (Article 107(2) TFEU) or may be so treated after inspection by the Commission (Article 107(3) TFEU).

It is fully in line with the orthodoxy of internal market law, and therefore not at all surprising, that the Court has long emphasized that the effect, not the form, of the national measure is the focus. Its definition of aid is more general than that of a subsidy, because it includes not only positive benefits, such as subsidies themselves, but also state measures across a wide spectrum which mitigate the charges which are normally included in the budget of an undertaking. Such practices may not be subsidies in the strict sense of the word, but the Court recognizes them as similar in

---

[140] Hailbronner and Thym, 'Annotation', 48 *Common Market Law Review* (2011) 1253, 1259. See also N. Nic Shuibhne, *The Coherence of EU Free Movement Law: Constitutional Responsibility and the Court of Justice* (2013), Ch. 4.

character and having the same effect, and so apt to be treated as 'aid'.[141] There is a whiff of *Dassonville* here.[142]

Embedded within these rules is a restraint of pure inter-jurisdictional competition in the granting of state subsidies, under the rather vague notion of preventing the 'distortion' of competition mentioned but not elucidated in Article 107.[143] It is seen elsewhere in internal market law too, perhaps most strikingly in Article 114 (see Chapter 13.G.4). It has some analogy with social dumping and the rationale for labour market regulation (see Chapter 14.B.2); and the General Court has explicitly observed that the harmonization of national fiscal legislation shares with the state aid rules the objective of combating distortions of competition as part of the project to promote the proper functioning of the internal market.[144] The point is that attaching the label 'distortion' is not simply a pejorative slur which reflects dismay at inter-jurisdictional competition in the grant of aid: it is, in EU law terms, a competence-enhancing claim. Finding 'distortion' entails that diversity between national laws and practice is in short an 'internal market problem'. Quite when difference becomes distortion is, however, not defined. That 'distortion' needs to be addressed – whatever it actually is – is a reflection of the EU's concept of an internal market not being based on radical decentralization as a result of a choice in favour of unrestricted inter-jurisdictional competition, but rather that it embraces a concern to review and curtail certain policies adopted at national level which are treated as harmful. The question is – *exactly when?*

So, given that the state aid rules do *not* apply to advantages which result from the simple fact of difference between Member State practices, key definitional questions surround the question of just what it is that states are permitted to do without being obliged to fit within the gateways to compatibility mapped by the Treaty and supervised by the Commission. That is, there is here too a borderline between on the one hand measures of national regulatory policy that do not count as state aid for the purposes of EU law and therefore belong within the sphere of national regulatory autonomy, and on the other, measures that count as state aid and which therefore need approval in line with the supervisory scheme planned by the Treaty if they are to proceed. There are two particularly awkward twists. The purpose is not to provide

---

[141] E.g., Case 78/76, *Steinike and Weinlig* v. *Germany*, [1977] ECR 595 (ECLI:EU:C:1977:52); Case 39/94, *SFEI* v. *La Poste*, [1996] ECR I-3547 (ECLI:EU:C:1996:285); Case C-143/99, *Adria-Wien Pipeline GmbH*, [2001] ECR I-8365 (ECLI:EU:C:2001:598); Cases C-106/09 P and C-107/09 P, *Commission and Spain* v. *Government of Gibraltar and United Kingdom*, [2011] ECR I-11113 (ECLI:EU:C:2011:732); Case C-5/14, *Kernkraftwerke Lippe-Ems GmbH*, judgment of 4 June 2015, not yet reported (ECLI:EU:C:2015:354).

[142] Case 8/74, *supra* note 16.

[143] See, e.g., C. Quigley, *EU State Aid Law and Policy* (2nd ed., 2009), Ch. 2; L. Hancher, T. Ottervanger and P.-J. Slot, *EU State Aids* (4th ed., 2012), Ch. 3; L. Rubini, *The Definition of Subsidy and State Aid: WTO and EC Law in Comparative Perspective* (2009), Ch. 14.

[144] Case T-50/06, *Ireland* v. *Commission*, judgment of 21 March 2012, not yet reported (ECLI:EU:C:2007:325): the Court set aside the judgment in Case C-272/12 P, *Commission* v. *Ireland*, judgment of 10 December 2013, not yet reported (ECLI:EU:C:2013:812) on the basis that it disregarded the distinct roles of the Council and Commission in the two areas, but did not disagree with this point.

an exhaustive examination: other sources provide that admirably.[145] The concern here is to show that state aid law is another area where the internal market as a legal concept does not offer an unambiguous basis for determining just how far EU law should reach in curtailing national regulatory autonomy and that accordingly important but difficult tasks are delegated to the Court.

1. Aid Must Be Granted 'Granted Directly or Indirectly Through State Resources'

Aid must be granted 'granted directly or indirectly through state resources' to fall within Article 107 TFEU. *Kirsammer-Hack* v. *Hurhan Sidal* explores the *limits* of this notion.[146] The German system of protection of workers against unfair dismissal excluded small businesses, defined as those with no more than five employers. The aim was plainly to alleviate regulatory costs shouldered by such businesses, at the expense of worker protection and to the disadvantage of slightly larger businesses in competition with the benevolently treated small business. Was this any of the EU's concern or was it simply a matter of German policy? The Court focused on the Treaty requirement that advantages must be granted directly or indirectly through state resources. So not all advantages granted by a state, whether financed through state resources or not, constitute aid: there is a line to draw. The Court disposed of the matter briefly. It ruled that:

the exclusion of a category of businesses from the protection system in question does not entail any direct or indirect transfer of State resources to those businesses but derives solely from the legislature's intention to provide a specific legislative framework for working relationships between employers and employees in small businesses and to avoid imposing on those businesses financial constraints which might hinder their development.[147]

It was not, the Court concluded without any further elaboration, a measure which constituted a means of granting directly or indirectly an advantage through state resources.

This is more assertion than legal analysis. The claim made by the Court in the extracted quote above is to state the problem, not to solve it. Had the state paid compensation owed by small businesses instead of granting them an immunity from it, then presumably that would count as 'aid'. In those circumstances the state would have paid out money and the workers would have received it – but the effect on small businesses and their competitors would have been no different.[148] So the criticism is

[145] E.g., Quigley, *supra* note 143, Chs 1–3; Hancher, Ottervanger and Slot, *supra* note 143, Chs 1–3; Rubini, *supra* note 143, Ch. 5.

[146] Case C-189/91, *Kirsammer-Hack* v. *Hurhan Sidal*, [1993] ECR I-6185 (ECLI:EU:C:1993:907). See similarly Joined Cases C-72/91 and C-73/91, *Sloman Neptun*, [1993] ECR I-887 (ECLI:EU:C:1993:97). It is certainly no coincidence that these jurisdictionally restrained rulings are so close in time to *Keck*, *supra* note 80; see Davies, 'Market Integration and Social Policy in the Court of Justice', 24 *Industrial Law Journal* (2005) 49; Ross, 'State Aids: Maturing into a Constitutional Problem', 15 *Yearbook of European Law* (1995) 82.

[147] *Ibid.*, at para. 17.

[148] For close analysis at the time of the rulings in *Kirsammer-Sack* and *Sloman Neptun* see Bacon, 'State Aids and General Measures', 17 *Yearbook of European Law* (1997) 269, rightly hailed as a 'classic' by Biondi, 'State Aid is Falling Down, Falling Down: An Analysis of the Case Law on the

that the Court has adopted a formalist means to limit the reach of state aid law which pays inadequate regard to the operation of the market. The German scheme was not a direct subsidy to small business, but by releasing them from regulatory burdens it clearly provided an advantage. The ruling is open to criticism for misunderstanding that the state has a range of techniques for intervening in the market which are more subtle than taxation and financial support. And yet such criticism might itself be vulnerable to the counterpunching accusation that it ignores the restraining influence of Article 5 TEU's principle of conferral and the consequent constitutional obligation to find *some* limit to the reach of the state aid rules. Two different worlds – the economics of regulation and constitutional law – come into collision here.

The Court took a similar approach in *PreussenElektra AG* v. *Schleswag AG*.[149] German rules required suppliers of electricity to purchase electricity produced from renewable energy sources at minimum prices. This conferred an advantage on producers of that type of electricity, since, as the Court put it, 'it guarantees them, with no risk, higher profits than they would make in its absence'.[150] The Court focused on (what is now) Article 107's definitional need for advantages to be granted directly or indirectly through state resources. So some advantages granted by a state are not aid. Here, in the Court's assessment, was such a case. There was no direct or indirect transfer of state resources to undertakings which produced electricity from renewable sources. The state had intervened to place a financial burden on private suppliers to the advantage of private producers (of renewable energy). But that is not aid. Advocate General Jacobs, after considering but rejecting the case for adopting a wide interpretation of an 'aid' that *would* catch such measures, concluded that 'it seems preferable that legislation regulating the relationship between private actors is as a matter of principle excluded from the scope of the State aid rules'.[151] It would have been aid had the state subsidized suppliers of renewable energy directly in the amount achieved by the minimum price guarantee.[152] But what was really a scheme shaped by the state but financed by private undertakings was not aid. Yet, either way, the effect on the market position of suppliers of renewable energy and their competitors would have been identical. The scheme was also checked for compliance with the free movement rules: its environmental credentials allowed it to survive that inspection (see Chapter 8.E).

These cases demonstrate that the Court can find ways to call a halt to internal market law's incursion into state regulatory autonomy. Lines are drawn: the boundary beyond which national regulatory autonomy is respected does exist. At the same time, they show that in order to do so the Court must resort to some rather formalist reasoning, of a type which it shuns in the mainstream of internal market law. In this

---

Notion of Aid', 50 *Common Market Law Review* (2013) 1719, 1724 (itself an article deserving such accolade).

[149] Case C-379/98, *PreussenElektra AG v. Schleswag AG*, [2001] ECR I-2099 (ECLI:EU:C:2001:160).

[150] *Ibid.*, at para. 54.

[151] *Ibid.*, at para. 157.

[152] See Case C-262/12, *Association Vent de Colère!*, judgment of 19 December 2013, not yet reported (ECLI:EU:C:2013:851), where the Court was able to 'distinguish' the case from *Preussen Elektra* (para. 34).

sense they confirm rather than deny the ambiguously malleable character of the internal market as a legal concept.

2. Selectivity

Aid must favour certain undertakings or the production of certain goods when compared with others which, in the light of the objective pursued by the regime, are in a comparable factual and legal situation. Take away that focused favouritism and one is left with a measure of general tax or economic policy applicable to all economic operators which will not count as a state aid (though it may feasibly come within the scope of the free movement rules and may be the subject of harmonization). This criterion is in short a requirement of *selectivity* as the trigger to the application of EU law.[153] Plainly the more general the scheme, the more likely it is to escape classification as an aid within the meaning of Article 107 TFEU: only where such a scheme confers an advantage to the exclusive benefit of certain undertakings or certain sectors of activity does the net close. By contrast where aid is granted on an individual basis, the identification of economic advantage is, in principle, sufficient to support the presumption that it is selective.[154] Then the focus turns to whether the aid is justified. Lines of a jurisdictionally critical nature are therefore drawn by the criterion of selectivity.

There are myriad examples but one will suffice. In *Eventech* the Court was faced by the claim that the UK was granting state aid to London's black cabs by permitting them to use bus lanes from which minicabs were banned.[155] This was doubtless litigation designed to promote a political campaign targeted at liberalization of the sector, and the Court neatly dodged the invitation to become involved. It found no selective advantage enjoyed by black cabs, because they were in a different factual and legal situation when compared to minicabs. The Court innocently declared it would offer the referring court 'guidance' – and then made very concrete its view that there was no comparability, given that only black cabs may ply for hire, must be wheelchair-friendly, must be metered and must have drivers possessing 'the Knowledge' (of London's streets).[156] So black cabs were not being selected ahead of minicabs – they were different. That, of course, was the minicabs owners' principal gripe. But the Court's approach denied them the lever of EU state aid law, and (by implication) directed them to local political and legal processes to achieve reform instead. This was one of those rare instances where EU internal market law did not offer any direct help. Put another way, the Court was carefully aware of the limits of its own institutional role.

---

[153] E.g., Case C-143/99, *supra* note 141; Cases C-106/09 P and C-107/09 P, *supra* note 141; Joined Cases C-393/04 and C-41/05, *Air Liquide Industries Belgium SA*, [2006] ECR I-5293 (ECLI: EU:C:2006:403).

[154] E.g., Case C-15/14 P, *Commission* v. *MOL Magyar*, judgment of 4 June 2015, not yet reported (ECLI:EU:C:2015:362).

[155] Case C-518/13, *Eventech*, judgment of 14 January 2015, not yet reported (ECLI:EU:C:2015:9).

[156] *Ibid.*, at paras 3–11, 60.

3. Making Connections and Re-Shaping Lines

These tensions are not unconnected. One possible way to resolve the awkwardness is to prioritize use of the selectivity test and to set aside the focus on when a transfer of resources by the state has occurred.

In *Sloman Neptun*, Advocate General Darmon's very thoughtful Opinion, informed by comparative discussion of inter alia US and GATT law, proposed use of the criterion of selectivity to distinguish aid from general measures. Aid, he thought, would be found where the measure constituted a derogation from the scheme of the general system in which it was set.[157] This approach is definitionally slippery and hard to apply and it did not tempt the Court, although, as mentioned earlier, the Court's own 'test' in cases of this type, focused on finding a transfer of state resources, is no less vulnerable to such criticism. The Opinion of Advocate General Maduro a decade later in *Enirisorse SpA* shows that Mr Darmon's call had not gone unnoticed and provides a vision of what the Court could, but prefers not to, do.[158] He wanted to focus state aid law on the grant of preferential treatment to an undertaking or a class of undertakings which involves a departure from the state's general legislative policy and, of particular relevance to the examination presented above, he feared that to favour a test founded on the direct transfer of public funds over a test focused on selectivity would be to tempt states 'to use their regulatory powers to encourage or compel private sector enterprises to alleviate the costs of certain undertakings', which would risk 'a significant portion of State measures having all the *effects* of State aid' escaping scrutiny.[159] His proposed test was based on identification of special treatment meted out to certain situations, resulting in an economic advantage being conferred on economic agents in those situations, where that special treatment cannot be justified on the basis of a general system or where it does not result from a consistent application of the system to which it belongs. It is another definitionally slippery threshold.

Academic writing, too, has sought a better way. De Cecco, for example, has advocated a test whereby there is no aid where the link between the advantages conferred and the commitment of public resources is 'too uncertain and indirect'.[160] This would allow an easy connection to similar limiting terminology used in free movement law,[161] and even if it is yet another test that is likely to be hard to apply in practice, it has the merit of forcing appreciation that there must *be* limits to the reach of state aid supervision.

This debate plainly carries significance in the intriguing world of state aid law, but moreover the inclination and motivation of these jurists fits beautifully into the thesis of this more broadly focused volume: there must be *limits* to the internal market as a legal concept, but locating them is no easy task. In *Enirisorse* Advocate General Maduro

---

[157] Joined Cases C-72/91 and C-73/91, *supra* note 146, at para. 50.
[158] Case C-237/04, *Enirisorse SpA*, [2006] ECR I-2843 (ECLI:EU:C:2006:197), Opinion (ECLI:EU:C:2006:21).
[159] *Ibid.*, at para. 50 of his Opinion, emphasis is in the original.
[160] F. De Cecco, *State Aid and the European Economic Constitution* (2013), 110–115.
[161] See Sections B, D.1 and F.

was *not at all* intending to criticize the Court's attempts to find limits to the reach of EU state aid law – he considered them 'entirely legitimate'[162] – he was concerned only to adjust the detailed choice and application. He was concerned to endorse the need for the scope of the aid rules 'to be carefully circumscribed' for otherwise the rules would be 'broadened to cover distortions of competition that are simply the result of differences in legislative policy between Member States' which would 'encroach on powers reserved to the Member States'.[163] Principle was joined to practice. In an echo of the Court's disapproving reference in *Keck* to the 'increasing tendency' of traders to invoke Article 34 (see Section C.2), he added that 'over extension of the State aid rules... would also result in a substantial increase in the workload of the... supervisory authorities, the Commission and the Court'.[164]

Defining the 'aid' is another quest to draw lines which serve to protect national regulatory autonomy from internal market law, as mandated by Article 5 TEU. State aid law has a different tone from most other areas examined in this volume: grey areas tend to be resolved more readily in favour of national regulatory autonomy rather than the grip of EU law. Thematically, however, the connecting factor is that the internal market as a legal concept helps little in fixing the precise location of the relevant lines. The most vivid point is to confirm that there are profound – vertical and horizontal, institutional and constitutional – choices involved in whatever interpretation is preferred.

F. Conclusion: The Limits of the *Internal* Market

As stated earlier (Section B): this inquiry addresses *both* the reach of EU law into national autonomy (the definitional/competence question) *and* the proper scope for common interpretation of the relevant Treaty provisions (the convergence question).

The Court has clearly and consciously taken free movement law beyond tests rooted in discrimination. Equally, it has decided not to permit any restriction on commercial freedom within a Member State to be subject to review in the name of EU law. This is – roughly summarized – how this aspect of internal market law pushes hard to accelerate inter-state economic integration while remaining faithful to the limiting dictates of Article 5 TEU's principle of conferral. The awkward step is to move from rough summary to forensic precision. Advocate General Tizzano, in his Opinion in *CaixaBank France*,[165] wanted to find a test that would avoid too *vague* a formulation of the concept of restriction, for fear that, without such a control, measures would be caught even where their effects on free movement were merely hypothetical or entirely uncertain and indirect. His express concern was with preservation of a legitimate zone of national regulatory autonomy, which we would today treat as the corollary of the principle of conferral. The Court thinks along these lines too: but it has not provided clarity.

---

[162] Case C-237/04, *supra* note 158, para. 47 of his Opinion.
[163] *Ibid.*, at paras 43 and 45 of his Opinion.   [164] *Ibid.*, at para. 45 of his Opinion.
[165] Case C-442/02, *supra* note 61; see Section B.

There is an extraordinary variety of terminology in use, sometimes reflecting context-ual distinction but sometimes apparently haphazard and sometimes muddled further by divergences among the Chambers of the Court[166] and also translation oddities between different language versions.[167] For example, the word 'entrave' does not appear in the French version of the Treaty provisions dealing directly with free movement[168] but it is in regular use by the Court in its case law, where, as with English words such as 'barrier' and 'restriction', it lacks precision.[169] A forest of words and phrases describe the circum-stances where EU internal market law does apply and where it does not. So, to collect together from the account above, a restriction on use must exert a *considerable* influence, not simply an influence, on consumer behaviour; an inconvenience must be *serious*; a measure's effect on inter-state trade must not be *indirect* or *remote or uncertain*; an obs-tacle must not be purely *hypothetical*. Article 101 TFEU depends on an *appreciable* effect on inter-state trade. Aid must *distort* competition and it must be *selective*. The *purely internal* situation is within the grip of State autonomy, but even that safe harbour has been invaded in part, most of all in the name of protecting the genuine enjoyment of the substance of the rights conferred by virtue of the status of EU citizenship. All these *limits* on the reach of EU law are ambiguous and malleable.

And sometimes the Court really should take more care. So, for example, in *Bonnarde*, which was not a case concerning a restriction on use but rather a classic *Cassis* 'dual burden' type of case, the Court unhelpfully relied explicitly on its case law dealing with restrictions on use but cited the wrong test: Article 34 TFEU catches rules that 'may influence the behaviour of consumers and, consequently, affect the access of those [products] ... to the market' of the regulating State, which drops the qualification that the influence on consumer behaviour must be *consider-able* and so hurls the doors of Article 34 TFEU wide open.[170] This is simply a mis-take and has not been repeated, but such blips are not conducive to legal certainty in an area that is already fraught with analytical difficulty.[171]

The abiding problem remains that it is easy to state imprecisely what is at stake, but it is hard to provide concrete and operationally useful tests for separating practices that trigger review in the name of the internal market from those that do not. It is about more than discrimination; it is about hindering access to the market to a sufficient degree as opposed to simply structuring the operation of the market in a way that is factually and legally even in application. But what *exactly* does that mean? 'Without an analytical framework to go with it, market access is a useless addition to the law of free movement of goods'.[172] If there

---

[166] Woods, 'Consistency in the Chambers of the ECJ: A Case Study on the Free Movement of Goods', 31 *Civil Justice Quarterly* (2012) 339; Nic Shuibhne, *The Coherence, supra* note 140, 54–62.

[167] E.g., Jansson and Kalimo, 'De Minimis meets Market Access: Transformations in the Substance – and the Syntax – of EU Free Movement Law?', 51 *Common Market Law Review* (2014) 523.

[168] It does appear in Arts 114(6) and 326 TFEU.

[169] See L. Azoulai (ed.), *L'entrave dans le droit du marché intérieur* (2011).

[170] Case C-443/10, *Bonnarde*, [2011] ECR I-9327 (ECLI:EU:C:2011:641).

[171] Case C-108/09, *supra* note 21 is another ruling that is poorly written: see Caro de Sousa, 'Through Contact Lenses, Darkly' 37 *European Law Review* (2012) 79. See also *supra* note 21 for cases citing the (non-existent) principle of mutual recognition.

[172] Sibony, 'Can Market Access Be Taken Seriously?', *European Journal of Consumer Law* (2012) 323, 341. See also Davies, 'Understanding Market Access: Exploring the Economic Rationality of Different Conceptions of Free Movement Law', 11 *German Law Journal* (2010) 671; Snell, 'The Notion of

is such a framework, it seems more intuitive than analytical: rules that close off the regulated market are caught, rules that limit exercise of commercial freedom within it are not. This is a rough fit for most of the case law[173] but the margin between 'closing off' access to the market and restricting exercise of commercial freedom within it is not precise, and it is exactly here in defining the borderline that the Court reaches for its scattergun: *considerable* influence, *serious* inconvenience, an effect that is not *indirect* or *remote* or *uncertain*, an obstacle that is not *hypothetical*, and so on. The evasion of convergence is troubling too, given that the basic issue to be addressed certainly applies in common irrespective of which economic freedom is at stake: it asks what is the threshold at which national regulatory autonomy becomes subject to review for its prejudicial effect on the EU's internal market, which in turn has constitutional and institutional consequences that are both vertical and horizontal. The Court's multiple tests stand accused of tending to conceal rather than reveal. Its Advocates General have periodically tried without success to push the Court onto firmer ground.[174] The Court has never attempted to provide a systematic or convergent approach to defining a 'restriction'. Its case law is, frankly, very hard work.[175]

It is well said that 'an obligation to sustain case law coherence stems from the constitutional responsibilities of the Court of Justice'.[176] Admittedly, not all of this hard work is equally important. *Keck* and its ill-shapen progeny are intellectually fascinating as an attempt by the Court to re-boot its own understanding of the limits of Article 34, but it is easy to exaggerate the impact of *Keck*. It is far from the forefront in most cases on which the Court is asked to rule in the area of free movement of goods, still less in internal market law generally. And what's the worst that can happen? The EU will survive a malfunctioning market for jet-skis in Sweden. The cases concerning people and, most of all, those associated with family (re-)unification are quite different. They concern vulnerable people and deeply sensitive issues. Indeed, rulings such as *Carpenter, Zhu and Chen* and the stream initiated in *Ruiz Zambrano* suggest the Court is eager to find an adequate connection to EU law precisely so it can offer protection in supplement to that which might be available under national law or the European Convention on Human Rights, but which, as evidenced by the very fact that the matter has reached Luxembourg, has presumably fallen short of the applicant's aspirations. The cases suggest the Court is nudging towards treating the right to move as having a 'converse . . . right

Market Access: a Concept or a Slogan?', 47 *Common Market Law Review* (2010) 437; Connor, 'Market Access or Bust? Positioning the Principle within the Jurisprudence on Goods, Persons, Services and Capital', 13 *German Law Journal* (2012) 679.

[173] E.g., caught – goods, Case 34/79, *supra* note 14, workers, Case C-415/93, *supra* note 48; not caught – goods, Joined Cases C-267/91 and 268/91, *supra* note 80, workers, Case C-190/98, *supra* note 109.

[174] Several are mentioned in Section B; also notable is A.G. Maduro in Cases C-158/04 and C-159/04, *Alfa Vita*, [2006] ECR I-8135 (ECLI:EU:C:2006:562).

[175] See, e.g., working hard on where the limits of the *internal* market lie, Barnard, *supra* note 22, especially Chs 4, 5, 8; Oliver, *supra* note 12, at paras 6.56–6.94; Tryfonidou, 'The Notions of "Restriction" and "Discrimination" in the Context of the Free Movement of Persons Provisions: From a Relationship of Interdependence to One of (Almost Complete) Independence', 33 *Yearbook of European Law* (2014) 385; Enchelmaier, 'Always at Your Service (Within Limits): The ECJ's Case Law on Article 56 TFEU (2006–2011)', 36 *European Law Review* (2011) 615; Lianos, 'Shifting Narratives in the European Internal Market: Efficient Restrictions of Trade and the Nature of "Economic" Integration', *European Business Law Review* (2010) 705.

[176] Nic Shuibhne, *The Coherence, supra* note 140, 31.

not to move without being unduly penalized'.[177] Another way to frame such incursion into the apparently 'internal situation' would be to argue that where EU law creates legal rights for the migrant, EU law should not be blind to the discrimination against non-migrants which it has thereby caused within the national order.[178] But: should *EU law* really expect so much of itself, should it really have so little trust in other sources of protection within the Member States? The tension is between sensitivity to individual rights and sensitivity to the limits of EU competence; between the empowering force of the concept of the internal market combined with that of EU citizenship and preservation of national autonomy. The Court's stance seems heavily influenced by the context: so for example in state aid law it is cautious about empowering the EU (most of all the Commission and the Court) to rule on general economic policy, in the law concerning persons it is a great deal more intrusive.

There is no single descriptive narrative that fits all the Court's case law. On a normative plane, much depends on one's preferred understanding of the proper reach of free movement and competition law into national regulatory autonomy and the proper reach of the judicial role in relation to the legislative role. The constitutional and institutional – vertical and horizontal – implications of the choices made are certainly profound,[179] but the current ambiguous Treaty background and most of all the ambiguous nature of the internal market as a legal concept precludes identification of any *single* correct model. A test is needed which leaves space for recognition of the dynamic process of market integration (the empowering dimension of the internal market) while also showing respect for Article 5 TEU's principle of conferral and the value of national autonomy which it enshrines (the limiting dimension). In this vein the 'negative law' of the internal market should be built on control of discriminatory and physical barriers, technical standards which cause market fragmentation along national lines simply because they are different and other rules which act as a direct or substantial hindrance to access to the regulated market.[180] This does not solve the problem of deciding precisely what 'direct' and 'substantial' means for these purposes – it is admittedly simply to place a heavy constitutional load on (yet) more adjectives – but it ensures the right questions are being asked about how to navigate a course between the internal market as an empowering and a limiting concept.

---

[177] *Wyatt and Dashwood's European Union Law* (6th ed., 2011), at 491.

[178] Cf. Maduro, 'The Scope of European Remedies: The Case of the Purely Internal Situations and Reverse Discrimination', in C. Kilpatrick, T. Novitz and P. Skidmore, *The Future of Remedies in Europe* (2000) Ch. 5.

[179] E.g., Caro de Sousa, 'Negative and Positive Integration in EU Economic Law: Between Strategic Denial and Cognitive Dissonance', 13 *German Law Journal* (2012) 979; Saydé, 'One Law, Two Competitions: An Inquiry into the Contradictions of Free Movement Law', 13 (2010–11) 365; Snell, 'Varieties of Capitalism and the Limits of European Economic Integration', 13 *Cambridge Yearbook of European Legal Studies* (2010–11) 415.

[180] I stick with the test proposed in Weatherill, 'After *Keck*: Some Thoughts on How to Clarify the Clarification', 33 *Common Market Law Review* (1996) 885.

7

The Personal Scope

The competition rules in the Treaty on the Functioning of the European Union (TFEU) apply directly to private parties and, in so far as they constitute 'undertakings', they may apply to public bodies too. Other competition rules in the TFEU make particular provision for state practices, most notably the state aid rules. The personal scope of the free movement provisions is a good deal more awkward. All the provisions of the TFEU which deal with free movement apply to the acts of public authorities in the Member States. By contrast, the provisions on free movement of workers and services apply directly to private parties, albeit that the precise scope appears not to have remained static, but the provisions on free movement of goods do not. This is not stipulated by the TFEU – it is the consequence of the choices made by the Court of Justice of the European Union ('the Court') in its case law. But the Court has never explained just why there is no convergence in the personal scope of application of the free movement rules.

This absence of convergence between the several Treaty freedoms is now so ingrained and so lacking in judicial explanation that it does not deserve exhaustive examination. This area of EU internal market law seems locked into its odd shape. It is, however, an enduring illustration of how the internal market as a legal concept leaves key issues confusingly open.

Walrave and Koch v. *UCI*, a decision of the Court in 1974, provides a good starting-point.[1] The Court was asked to consider the governing rules of an international sports (cycling) federation. Such bodies are typically powerful and, in order to ensure sport is played everywhere according to common rules, they tend to be monopoly regulators, but they do not hold the status of a public authority. The Court however brought their practices within the scope of EU law. It concluded that the prohibition of discrimination based on nationality pursuant to (what were then) Articles 7, 48 and 59 EEC (now after amendment Articles 18, 39 and 56 TFEU) 'does not only apply to the action of public authorities but extends likewise to rules of any other nature aimed at regulating in a collective manner gainful employment and the provision of services'.[2] The Court provided two principal reasons for this finding. The first: the Treaty objective of tackling obstacles to inter-state trade would be 'compromised if the abolition of barriers of national origin could be neutralized by obstacles resulting from the exercise of their legal autonomy by associations or

---

[1] Case 36/74, *Walrave and Koch*, [1974] ECR 1405 (ECLI:EU:C:1974:140).
[2] *Ibid.*, at para. 17.

The Internal Market as a Legal Concept. First Edition. Stephen Weatherill.
© Stephen Weatherill 2017. Published 2017 by Oxford University Press.

organizations which do not come under public law'.[3] The second: given the diversity between Member States on the scope of and relationship between public regulation and private agreements, limiting the Treaty provisions 'to acts of a public authority would risk creating inequality in their application'.[4]

This is logical and it is forceful. Both arguments – which one may usefully label an 'effectiveness' rationale and an 'equality' rationale respectively – carry weight.

The Court has made this its orthodox approach to the personal scope of the Treaty provisions dealing with the free movement of persons and services. So, following this approach, it subjected trade unions to obligations imposed by the Treaty rules on free movement. In *Viking Line* it stated that Article 43 EC (now Article 49 TFEU), 'is to be interpreted as meaning that, in principle, collective action initiated by a trade union or a group of trade unions against an undertaking in order to induce that undertaking to enter into a collective agreement, the terms of which are liable to deter it from exercising freedom of establishment, is not excluded from the scope of that article'.[5] So collective labour action of this type falls to be tested against EU free movement law in so far as its exercise obstructs cross-border corporate mobility and it is lawful only where it is shown to comply with standards of justification recognized by EU law. The Court has been criticized for this ruling as much as for any it has ever delivered: the criteria governing justification seem peculiarly insensitive to the legitimate demands of trade unions. This is considered more fully in Chapter 9.B. But for present purposes the ruling in *Viking Line* sits in the orthodox line of case law which targets (what are now) Articles 45, 49 and 56 TFEU not only at the actions of public authorities but also 'rules of any other nature aimed at regulating in a collective manner gainful employment, self-employment and the provision of services'.[6] And, in line with comments made frequently in this volume about the wide reach of the free movement and competition rules, the thematic point is that the heavy load is therefore carried by justification. The restriction falls easily within the scope of internal market law in the first place.

The Court has gone further on occasion. In *Angonese* it ruled that 'the prohibition of discrimination on grounds of nationality laid down in Article 48 of the Treaty [now Article 39 TFEU] must be regarded as applying to private persons as well'.[7] It did not confine this to a case where *collective* action was taken by private parties. This appears to mean that unilateral action by a private employer or service provider may be controlled under the Treaty provisions on free movement.[8] However, the Court has not routinely adopted this formula and it would be a mistake to assume that EU law definitely goes that far.

By stark and complete contrast Article 34 TFEU has never been interpreted as imposing obligations on private parties. *Schmidberger v. Austria* involved private

---

[3] *Ibid.*, at para. 18.   [4] *Ibid.*, at para. 19.

[5] Case C-438/05, *Viking Line*, [2007] ECR I-10779 (ECLI:EU:C:2007:772), at para. 55; Case C-341/05, *Laval*, [2007] ECR I-11767 (ECLI:EU:C:2007:809), at para. 98.

[6] *Ibid.*, at para. 33.

[7] Case C-281/98, *Angonese*, [2000] ECR I-4139 (ECLI:EU:C:2000:296), at para. 36.

[8] See also Case C-94/07, *Andrea Raccanelli*, [2008] ECR I-5939 (ECLI:EU:C:2008:425); Case C-379/09, *Maurits Casteels* v. *British Airways*, judgment of 10 March 2011, not yet reported (ECLI:EU:C:2011:131).

parties obstructing the passage of goods through the Brenner Pass in protest at the environmental damage done by such traffic.[9] The Court found that Article 34 TFEU was in principle apt to form the basis for review of the Austrian authorities' failure to intervene to suppress the protests, but Article 34 TFEU would not apply directly to the private parties themselves. The Grand Chamber took the same approach more recently in *Ålands Vinkraft AB* in which it cited *Schmidberger* in treating inaction by public authorities rather than private actions as the true target of Article 34.[10] In *Sapod Audic* the Court could not have made it plainer.[11] An obligation arising out of a private contract cannot be regarded as a barrier to trade for the purposes of (what is now) Article 34 TFEU 'since it was not imposed by a Member State but agreed between individuals'.[12] In support of this implacable statement of the limits of the personal scope of Article 34 the Court reached back as far as one of the great classics of the free movement pantheon, *Dassonville*, in which it had confined the reach of the law governing the free movement of goods to trading rules 'enacted by Member States'.[13] Admittedly, a smattering of cases tease at the borderline: in *Fra.bo SpA* a private law entity was held to be subject to obligations arising under Article 34 TFEU, but closer inspection reveals that it was a private law entity in form only, since its functions included a quasi-regulatory power conferred by the (German) state to certify products wishing to gain admittance to the German market of the products in question (which are copper fittings for joining pipes together).[14] It is old news that Article 34 applies to the activities of a private company where it is backed by public funding and its mission is dictated by the state.[15] Nothing in *Fra.bo* wishes to apply Article 34 to 'true' private parties.

In sum, private practices that interfere with cross-border trade in goods have always been treated as the preserve of the Treaty rules on competition law, in contrast to private practices affecting people, which are assessed from the perspective of both competition law and free movement law.

This is very hard to understand and nothing in the Court's case law tries to dispel the sense of confusion. A convergent approach is perfectly feasible in principle. In particular the 'effectiveness' and the 'equality' rationales set out earlier as the key contributions of *Walrave and Koch* seem in principle capable of application with just as much force to the free movement of goods as they do to the free movement of persons. All the freedoms could enjoy the same personal scope, whether that be a complete embrace of the obligations of private parties in all circumstances, application to private parties only where they act collectively, or a complete immunity for

---

[9] Case C-112/00, *Schmidberger* v. *Austria*, [2003] ECR I-5659 (ECLI:EU:C:2003:333).

[10] Case C-573/12, *Ålands Vinkraft AB*, judgment of 1 July 2014, not yet reported (ECLI:EU:C:2014:2037).

[11] Case C-159/00, *Sapod Audic*, [2002] ECR I-5031 (ECLI:EU:C:2002:343).

[12] *Ibid.*, at para. 74.

[13] Case 8/74, *Dassonville*, [1974] ECR 837 (ECLI:EU:C:1974:82), at para. 5.

[14] Case C-171/11, *Fra.bo SpA*, judgment of 12 July 2012, not yet reported (ECLI:EU:C:2012:453). On how the ruling may apply to standards-setters, see Schepel, 'The New Approach to the New Approach: The Juridification of Harmonised Standards in EU Law', 20 *Maastricht Journal* (2013) 521.

[15] E.g., Case 249/81, *Commission* v. *Ireland*, [1982] ECR 4005 (ECLI:EU:C:1982:402). See also Oliver, 'L'Article 34 TFUE peut-il avoir un effet direct horizontal?', 50 *Cahiers de droit européen* (2014) 77.

private parties. Choosing which model would involve some sort of assessment of the strength of the Court's predilection for the 'effectiveness' and 'equality' rationales, on the one hand, and EU law's respect for private autonomy on the other. Perhaps, by contrast, there is a case for distinguishing between the freedoms and for, with the Court, interpreting the personal scope of the Treaty provisions on the free movement of persons more broadly than those governing the free movement of goods. *People*, as beneficiaries of EU law, should perhaps enjoy more generous treatment than goods. On the other hand, this immediately runs up against counter-arguments rooted in the autonomy of the people against whom such rights would be asserted.[16]

There are truly intriguing questions about whether, and if so to what extent, constitutional or public law values should govern private autonomy and contractual freedom.[17] But the current system applicable to the personal scope of EU free movement law, whereby some freedoms have a broader personal scope than others and yet in circumstances where no attempt is made to explain why, is very hard to defend. The driving question here should involve inquiry into the internal market as a legal concept and also the strength of claims to private autonomy. These are admittedly ambiguous materials, but the Court has done an inconsistent job in using them in this area.

---

[16] Cf., e.g., (with different views) Prechal and De Vries, 'Seamless Web of Judicial Protection in the Internal Market', 34 *European Law Review* (2009) 5; Müller-Graff, 'Die horizontale Direktwirkung der Grundfreiheiten', 49 *Europarecht* (2014) 3; Schepel, 'Constitutionalising the Market, Marketising the Constitution, and to Tell the Difference: On the Horizontal Application of the Free Movement Provisions in EU Law', 18 *European Law Journal* (2012) 177; Davies, 'Freedom of Movement, Horizontal Effect and Freedom of Contract', 20 *European Review of Private Law* (2012) 805; Caro de Sousa, 'Horizontal Expressions of Vertical Desires: Horizontal Effect and the Scope of the EU Fundamental Freedoms', 2 *Cambridge Journal of International and Comparative Law* (2013) 479; Krenn, 'A Missing Piece in the Horizontal Effect Jigsaw: Horizontal Direct Effect and the Free Movement of Goods', 49 *Common Market Law Review* (2012) 177; Van Leeuwen, 'Private Regulation and Public Responsibility in the Internal Market', 33 *Yearbook of European Law* (2014) 277.

[17] This is particularly well developed in Schepel, 'Freedom of Contract in Free Movement Law: Balancing Rights and Principles in European Public and Private Law', 21 *European Review of Private Law* (2013) 1211.

8

Justification

Where a measure does not constitute a barrier to inter-state trade, national regulatory autonomy is preserved. There is no need to justify the measure. Where a measure is treated as a barrier to inter-state trade, it is by no means inevitable that the state will be disentitled from applying it, but it must show that it is justified. And because the matter has been found to fall within the scope of EU internal market law, the terms according to which justification is assessed are set by EU law itself. Competition law displays a structural similarity. The importance of understanding the methodology of justification is accentuated by the explanation above of the relative rarity with which national practices are treated as entirely unaffected by internal market law.

A. Structure

Where a trade barrier exists in the sense examined above, national regulatory autonomy is *conditional* – conditional on showing an adequate justification for placing the local regulatory choice ahead of the momentum of cross-border trade. Just how generous EU law is in assessing justification has consequences for the vertical allocation of competences between the EU and the Member States. A typically sceptical attitude to claimed justification would tend to release cross-border trade at the expense of choices made at national level, whereas a permissive view tends to assume the virtue of local regulatory initiatives to the detriment of the internal market, left fragmented along national lines. The more cramped the room allowed for justification, the more deregulated the EU's internal market. Also at stake is the horizontal allocation of powers between the judicial and the legislative process in the EU. The more that national measures are condemned as unjustified trade restrictions, the less need there is for the EU to adopt legislative solutions to replace varied national rules: conversely, the retention of national measures on the basis that they are treated as justified despite their trade-restrictive effects thrusts the emphasis on the need for legislative action at EU level, in order to introduce common rules apt to serve as the foundation of the internal market. So, the deeper the Court of Justice of the European Union ('the Court') cuts, the more deregulated the EU's internal market. The internal market, as a site of shared competence, is built on both national and EU rules, but just as rulings like *Cassis de Dijon*[1] and

---

[1] Case 120/78, *Rewe-Zentrale AG* v. *Bundesmonopolverwaltung für Branntwein*, [1979] ECR 649 (ECLI:EU:C:1979:42).

The Internal Market as a Legal Concept. First Edition. Stephen Weatherill.
© Stephen Weatherill 2017. Published 2017 by Oxford University Press.

Keck[2] reveal how choices about the reach of the basic prohibitions intimately affect the shape of the internal market being created, so too choices about the generosity of justification applied to trade barriers in turn dictate how regulated or deregulated the texture of the EU's internal market will be.

The broad approach taken by the Court to the material, geographical and personal scope of internal market law, examined in previous chapters, means that assessment of whether rules are justified becomes pivotally important in determining just how far in practice national autonomy may survive the deregulatory bite of free movement and competition law. Because not much national regulatory practice escapes the law of the internal market, its fate – and whether it is subjected to deregulatory prohibition or to the potential for re-regulatory legislative intervention at EU level – hangs on the availability of justification.

This is the EU as 'market state'. This is where EU internal market law – based on individual rights – is open to critical scrutiny as apt to subvert often hard-won interventions in the market designed to address its malfunctioning and its inequities. Protection of public health and the consumer, environmental protection, social policy and labour market regulation are all achieved at national level as a result of political contestation and have been extracted over time, but such promotion of collective interests is subject to review where it collides with cross-border economic activity. Structurally, a lot is therefore asked of the modifying influence of justification in internal market law to make real the commitments in Article 3(3) TEU to a social market economy in which, according to Article 4(2) TEU, the national identities of the Member States are respected and in which, more broadly, the values, rights and principles set out in the Charter of Fundamental Rights are recognized and observed. This is the inquiry embedded within assessment of the justification of trade barriers. Full appreciation of where this leads must involve assessment of the *quality* of the space left to justify such practices that collide with market opening. This is examined in the chapters that follow, before Chapter 12 offers a qualitative assessment.

B. Principles

The Treaty on the Functioning of the European Union (TFEU) does not dictate that a trade barrier is unlawful. Rather, it requires that it be shown to be justified, and the burden of demonstrating such justification is placed on the regulator.[3]

Article 36 TFEU allows room to justify national measures 'on grounds of public morality, public policy or public security; the protection of health and life of humans, animals or plants; the protection of national treasures possessing artistic, historic or archaeological value; or the protection of industrial and commercial property'. It adds in its second paragraph that such national action shall not 'constitute a means

---

[2] Cases C-267 and C-268/91, *Keck and Mithouard*, [1993] ECR I-6097 (ECLI:EU:C:1993:905).

[3] E.g., Case 227/82, *Van Bennekom*, [1983] ECR 3883 (ECLI:EU:C:1983:354); Case C-14/02, *ATRAL SA*, [2003] ECR I-4431 (ECLI:EU:C:2003:265).

of arbitrary discrimination or a disguised restriction on trade between Member States'. For persons, Article 45(3) TFEU envisages that rights may be limited where that is justified 'on grounds of public policy, public security or public health' and Article 45(4) TFEU excludes the matter of 'employment in the public service'. Grounds of 'public policy, public security or public health' are also cited in Article 52(1) TFEU as reasons to treat foreign nationals in a special way in relation to the right of establishment and this caveat is extended into the sphere of the free movement of services by Article 62 TFEU.

The Court does not regard these exceptions as being subject to the interpretation placed on them that a regulating Member State deems most suitable for its particular purposes in the exercise of a reserved jurisdiction. This would be to concede too much. Instead, they permit national measures only up to the point that they are justified as necessary to meet the objectives contained therein.[4] Article 36's second sentence cautions against 'arbitrary discrimination' and the Court has fastened on to this as a basis for a generally applicable approach which refuses to accept that a Member State may justify repressive measures against imports where it takes no serious measures to restrict supply of local products or services of the same type.[5] So too a Member State which has a choice between various measures to attain the same objective is required to choose the measure which least restricts free movement. Otherwise the choice is disproportionately restrictive.[6]

FA Premier League et al. v. *QC Leisure et al.*, *Karen Murphy* v. *Media Protection Services Ltd* offers a simple example of how this principle is used to weed out and reject justifications that might make convenient good sense from the perspective of the regulating body, but which cannot be allowed to stand in the face of the impetus to free movement, given that they are not necessary to achieve the end in view.[7] The case concerned restrictions placed on the cross-border provision of satellite broadcasting services, and in particular attempts to prevent English football matches that were broadcast in other Member States being available to view also in England. This entailed market fragmentation within the EU, but it was attempted, largely without success, to justify the restrictions. One such claim was based on encouraging the public to attend football matches 'live'. There is to this end a 'closed period' rule which prohibits the broadcasting in the UK of football matches on Saturday afternoons. If cross-border provision of services were released, then television viewers in the UK would be able freely to watch the Premier League matches which broadcasters transmitted from other Member States and, it is claimed, they would no longer go to watch Crewe or Colchester or Kidlington play on a Saturday afternoon. This is doubtless true to some extent, but the Court simply observed that if the football authorities wished to achieve this objective they could do so by incorporating

---

[4] E.g., Case 72/83, *Campus Oil*, [1984] ECR 2727 (ECLI:EU:C:1984:256).

[5] E.g., Case 121/85, *Conegate*, [1986] ECR 1007 (ECLI:EU:C:1986:114), at para. 15; Cases 115/81 and 116/81, *Adoui and Cornuaille*, [1982] ECR 1665 (ECLI:EU:C:1982:183), at para. 8.

[6] E.g., Case 261/81, *Walter Rau*, [1982] ECR 3961 (ECLI:EU:C:1982:382), at para. 12; Case C-189/95, *Harry Franzén*, [1997] ECR I-2471 (ECLI:EU:C:1997:504); Case 72/83, *supra* note 4.

[7] Joined Cases C-403/08 and C-429/08, *FA Premier League et al.* v. *QC Leisure et al.*, *Karen Murphy* v. *Media Protection Services Ltd*, judgment of 4 October 2011, not yet reported (ECLI:EU:C:2011:631).

a contractual limitation in the licence agreements between the right holders and the broadcasters, under which the latter would be required not to broadcast those Premier League matches at all during closed periods. No doubt this would depress the price of the broadcasting rights, which is why the football authorities wanted to avoid doing this and preferred instead to try to impede the cross-border provision of services. But an economic motivation for preferring a more restrictive regime over a less restrictive one that would achieve the desired end (keeping television screens in the UK bare of football on Saturday afternoons) could not be accepted.

Exactly the same control is exercised over measures of *public* authorities. *Klas Rosengren* concerned the Swedish retail monopoly over alcohol, in particular a block on importation of goods bought by a consumer in Spain.[8] The justification advanced was public health. But the system does not reduce consumption – it simply increases costs. The Court did not rule out that a system targeted on the particular need to protect the health of young people might be justified, but nothing in the system was so targeted. In the absence of any such targeting the control was treated as dispropor-tionately restrictive of cross-border trade.

It is plain that the more aggressive the Court is in requiring that national measures be based on a consistent and coherent plan to achieve particular goals, the more it curtails local regulatory autonomy where its expression impedes cross-border trade. In similar vein, the more exacting the standard of proof to which the regulator is held, the less likely that it will be able to fend off the deregulatory bite of free movement law.[9] On the other hand, although EU internal market law puts national measures that impede inter-state trade to the test, it is not a charter for remorseless deregula-tion. Justification is closely scrutinized, but it is of central structural significance that it is in principle available. The Court asserts that 'the fact that one Member State imposes less strict rules than another Member State does not mean that the latter's rules are disproportionate and hence incompatible' with EU law, a statement of principle which the Court has endorsed with equal application to both the free move-ment of services and the free movement of goods.[10] Given that states differ in mat-ters of moral or cultural choice and given diversity in prevailing social circumstances, the Court avoids an aggressively intolerant attitude to justification which would lead to regulatory standards being forced down to the level of the lowest common denominator found among the Member States. States have a 'margin of discretion'.[11] Justification is exactly the device that prevents free movement law from operating as an exclusively deregulatory exercise.

Traders have no absolute right to access the entire EU market simply because they meet the standards demanded by their 'home' state; a regulating state in which they wish to become active (i.e., a 'host state'), may set tougher standards than its

---

[8] Case C-170/04, *Klas Rosengren*, [2007] ECR I-4071 (ECLI:EU:C:2007:313).

[9] Cf. Nic Shuibhne and Maci, 'Proving Public Interest: The Growing Impact of Evidence in Free Movement Case Law', 50 *Common Market Law Review* (2013) 965.

[10] E.g., Case C-3/95, *Reisebüro Broede* v. *Gerd Sanker*, [1996] ECR I-6511 (ECLI:EU:C:1996:487); Case C-294/00, *Deutsche Paracelsus Schulen*, [2002] ECR I-6515 (ECLI:EU:C:2002:442).

[11] E.g., Case C-244/06, *Dynamic Medien*, [2008] ECR I-505 (ECLI:EU:C:2008:85); Case C-434/04, *Ahokainen and Leppik*, [2006] ECR I-9171 (ECLI:EU:C:2006:609); Case C-390/12, *Pfleger*, judgment of 30 April 2014, not yet reported (ECLI:EU:C:2014:281).

competitors – if it can justify them. It has to show, as the Court has put it in a neat turn of phrase, that there is a legitimate public interest objective which merits being pursued by national 'legislation, rather than the law of the market'.[12] The wider the scope allowed to the possibility to justify barriers to trade, the more room for manoeuvre is handed back to national regulatory autonomy – and the more weight is placed on the process of legislative harmonization at EU level as the way to advance integration – and vice versa. But what this means in practice can be revealed only by close inspection of the case law.

C. Breadth

The scope of justification is not confined to the matters recognized explicitly by the Treaty provisions mentioned earlier, namely Articles 36, 45, 52 and 62 TFEU.

1. Breadth – Free Movement Law

In *Cassis de Dijon*[13] the Court not only embraced variation between technical standards as a reason to engage Article 34 TFEU, thereby casting its net beyond a discrimination-only understanding of the reach of free movement law, it also accepted that a wide range of justifications in the public interest may be advanced by a regulating authority, stretching beyond the specific and limited list found in the TFEU.

In paragraph 8 of the judgment in *Cassis de Dijon* the Court, referring to the room allowed to the host state to justify its trade-restrictive rules, endorsed 'mandatory requirements relating in particular to the effectiveness of fiscal supervision, the protection of public health, the fairness of commercial transactions and the defence of the consumer'.

This is a peculiarly unfortunate turn of phrase. The notion of 'mandatory requirements' as a means to capture this wider pattern of justification has endured in the literature, but to no good effect, because it is little more than a poor translation into English of the German *Zwingenden Erfordnisse* and the French *exigences imperatives*. A superior rendition into English would be something like 'compelling interests' and, in fact, later in the judgment itself the Court offers a more satisfying formulation: the true question is whether the purposes pursued by the national measure that restricts inter-state trade 'serve a purpose which is in the general interest and such as to take precedence over the requirements of the free movement of goods'.[14] This, then, signals the adoption of a general public interest test, and it has meant that in principle when examining whether a national measure is justified the Court has long been prepared to admit a wide range of interests and values that are left unmentioned in Articles 36, 45, 52 and 62 TFEU. So trade integration may collide with national initiatives to protect the economic interests of consumers,[15] to secure protection of

---

[12] Case C-456/10, *ANETT*, judgment of 26 April 2012, not yet reported (ECLI:EU:C:2012:241), at para. 52.
[13] Case 120/78, *supra* note 1.   [14] Para. 14 of *Cassis*.
[15] In *Cassis* itself and, as discussed in Section F, frequently since.

the environment,[16] to conserve biodiversity,[17] to defend and promote culture and artistic property,[18] to preserve and promote press diversity,[19] to secure respect for human dignity,[20] to protect the child,[21] to promote concern for animal welfare,[22] to take care of the particular features of sport,[23] to ensure the survival of small and medium-sized businesses,[24] and to protect workers and the right to take collective action[25] and yet, even though the provisions on free movement themselves do not accommodate explicit direction to take account of such concerns, the Court has ensured that it is open in principle to national (public and private) regulators to draw on the full breadth of their purposes in interfering with the integration of product and service markets in the EU as they seek to demonstrate that they should be treated as justified.

In 1976 Meij and Winter, examining *Dassonville*, had highlighted the 'inherent difficulty' in the Court's approach in that case, which they diagnosed as the severe curtailment of the states' regulatory autonomy.[26] Their analysis – and their anxiety – assumes throughout that the sole location of potential justification for restrictive rules affecting trade in goods within the meaning of *Dassonville* was (what is now) Article 36 TFEU. And in 1976 no other conclusion could possibly have been reached. The point of *Cassis* is to release that tension by widening the scope of available justifications in tandem with adopting a widened view of the concept of the trade barrier subject to review.

The scope of justification is not completely open-ended. The Court refuses to accept that economic justifications are available to defend trade-restrictive practices. This goes back to its very earliest judgments. In 1961 Italy made no headway at all in seeking to justify a suspension in the importation of pigs and pig products on the basis that inter-state trade was causing competition and low prices in the sector.[27] So it should! But even this limit on the scope of available justifications is misleading. Where a Member State refuses to agree to fund a national's medical treatment in another Member State in order to contain the costs of providing health care and to balance the budget of the social security system, it may appear that impermissible

---

[16] E.g., Case 302/86, *Commission* v. *Denmark*, [1988] ECR 4607 (ECLI:EU:C:1988:421): Case C-379/98, *PreussenElektra AG* v. *Schleswag AG*, [2001] ECR I-2099 (ECLI:EU:C:2001:160).
[17] Case C-67/97, *Ditlev Bluhme*, [1998] ECR I-8033 (ECLI:EU:C:1998:584).
[18] E.g., Case C-250/06, *United Pan-Europe Communications Belgium SA*, [2007] ECR I-11135 (ECLI:EU:C:2007:783); Case C-531/07, *Fachverband/ LIBRO*, [2009] ECR I-3717 (ECLI:EU:C:2009:276); Case C-200/96, *Metronome Musik GmbH*, [1998] ECR I-1953 (ECLI:EU:C:1998:172).
[19] Case C-368/95, *Vereinigte Familiapress Zeitungsverlags- und vertriebs GmbH* v. *Heinrich Bauer Verlag*, [1997] ECR I-3689 (ECLI:EU:C:1997:325).
[20] Case C-36/02, *Omega Spielhallen*, [2004] ECR I-9609 (ECLI:EU:C:2004:614).
[21] Case C-244/06, *supra* note 11.
[22] Case C-219/07, *Nationale Raad van Dierenkwekers en Liefhebbers*, [2008] ECR I-4475 (ECLI:EU:C:2008:353).
[23] Case C-415/93, *Bosman*, [1995] ECR I-4921 (ECLI:EU:C:1995:463).
[24] Case C-464/05, *Maria Geurts*, [2007] ECR I-9325 (ECLI:EU:C:2007:631).
[25] Case C-438/05, *Viking Line*, [2007] ECR I-10779 (ECLI:EU:C:2007:772); Case C-341/05, *Laval*, [2007] ECR I-11767 (ECLI:EU:C:2007:809).
[26] Meij and Winter, 'Measures Having an Effect Equivalent to Quantitative Restrictions', 13 *Common Market Law Review* (1976) 76, at 103.
[27] Case 7/61, *Commission* v. *Italy*, [1961] ECR 317 (ECLI:EU:C:1961:31).

economic aims are at stake. However, the Court admits that the risk of seriously undermining the financial balance of the social security system may constitute an overriding reason in the general interest, and that maintaining a balanced medical and hospital service open to all, albeit an objective linked to the method of financing the social security system, may fall within the derogations on grounds of public health.[28] In similar vein, the regulation of gambling through the grant of licences and taxation is typically a helpful source of revenue for public authorities in the Member States, and the Court has held that this objective alone cannot permit an intervention which serves as a restriction of the freedom to provide services in the gambling sector.[29] However, the same rulings reveal that the Court does not take the view that this economic motivation for intervention which may harm free movement deprives the regulator of the possibility to justify its choices where there are objectives relating to overriding reasons in the public interest, typically engaging the protection of consumers against gambling addiction and the prevention of crime and fraud linked to gambling. In this sense the Court *translates* economic justifications, which it will not recognize in principle, into justifications of a different type which fall within the acknowledged sweep of available justifications.[30] And so that net is once again revealed to be vast.

As with the notion of a barrier to trade, so too here with the notion of justification: the Court, while remaining faithful to the basic structural ideas contained in the TFEU, has elaborated a much more complex and sophisticated set of principles according to which to adjudicate between the competing interests at stake when the lust for inter-state trading freedom clashes with national regulatory choices. In this way the Court has made free movement law *porous*. It is not only about free movement, and it is not only about market solutions. It also recognizes the limits of market solutions. This is certainly strongly supported today by the grant of binding force to the Charter. Since, as the Court puts it, the 'applicability of EU law entails applicability of the fundamental rights guaranteed by the Charter'[31] the application and interpretation of the free movement and competition rules must be informed by Charter rights and principles, including, for example, Articles 22 (culture), 35 (health), 37 (environment) and 38 (consumer). But these are readily aligned with orthodox justifications embraced in the Court's case law. *Cassis de Dijon* itself, after all, involved assessment of the worth of (rather unconvincing) measures of consumer protection, and, as mentioned earlier, there is nothing groundbreaking about treating matters of environmental protection, health and cultural policy pursued at national level as

[28] Case 158/96, *Kohll*, [1998] ECR I-1931 (ECLI:EU:C:1998:171). See also on access to education Case C-73/08, *Nicolas Bressol*, [2010] ECR I-2735 (ECLI:EU:C:2010:181).

[29] E.g., Case C-243/01, *Gambelli and Others*, [2003] ECR I-13031 (ECLI:EU:C:2003:597); Joined Cases C-338/04, C-359/04 and C-360/04, *Massimiliano Placanica*, [2007] ECR I-1891 (ECLI:EU:C:2007:133); Case C-390/12, *supra* note 11; Case C-98/14, *Berlington Hungary and Others*, judgment of 11 June 2015, not yet reported (ECLI:EU:C:2015:386).

[30] See also Oliver, 'When, if Ever, Can Restrictions on Free Movement Be Justified on Economic Grounds?', 41 *European Law Review* (2016) 147; Arrowsmith, 'Rethinking the Approach to Economic Justifications under the EU's Free Movement Rules', 68 *Current Legal Problems* (2015) 307.

[31] Case C-617/10, *Fransson*, judgment of 26 February 2013, not yet reported (ECLI:EU:C:2013:280), at para. 21.

potential justifications for trade barriers. In truth 2009, the date on which the Charter acquired binding status, is a deceptive landmark. In *Dynamic Medien* the Court accepted that German controls over image storage media could be justified as measures to protect children from harmful content and, in so placing child protection within the sphere of legitimate justification, it relied on the EU Charter of Fundamental Rights ('the Charter') *even though it was not yet binding.*[32]

So the Charter is *presentationally* innovative in free movement law. The Court has taken to treating challenged national measures as restrictive not only from the point of view of free movement law but also limitations from the perspective of Articles 15–17 of the Charter dealing with the freedom to choose an occupation, the freedom to conduct a business and the right to property. But it has then typically declared that no need arises for separate examination of the Charter-based claims, for analysis runs in perfect alignment with the Court's pre-Charter practice: the Charter is not *substantively* transformative.[33] Precisely the same pattern applies to justification: the Court's citation of the Charter as a source of values that might serve an interest of higher significance than trade integration should not be taken to represent any change of *substance.*[34]

The Charter's main importance is as a *confirmation* of the Court's choices and, in particular, its resistance to treat the internal market as an aggressively deregulatory project. The integration objectives set out in the Charter and in the TFEU preclude any argument that the Court's case law is ephemeral and could be altered. The Court led, the process of Treaty revision followed, and the regulatory constitutional foundations are thereby entrenched.

This is not at all to suggest the Court has an easy job. The host state enjoys *conditional* regulatory autonomy – the precise determination of whether or not it has met the necessary *conditions* belongs with the Court. Frequently the TFEU offers little, if any, help in defining just what EU law should make of, for example, the value of press diversity or animal welfare. In particular, in connection with the cases that have set economic rights embedded in the TFEU against social and political rights and freedoms guaranteed under national law (and recognized within EU law) concerns are properly raised about the Court's strained legitimacy in assuming an adjudicative task.[35] This tension is endemic in EU internal market law given the absence of 'hard' limits to its reach dictated by the TFEU. The Court's choices dictate the shape of the internal market and they raise questions about it as a legal concept.

2. Breadth – Competition Law

The Court has performed a structurally and functionally similar adjustment to the competition rules in the TFEU. Competition law too shows an openness – a porosity – that transcends the Treaty's explicit terms and shape.

---

[32] Case C-244/06, *supra* note 11.

[33] E.g., Case C-390/12, *supra* note 11; Case C-98/14, *supra* note 29.

[34] E.g., Case C-28/09, *Commission v. Austria*, judgment of 21 December 2011, not yet reported (ECLI:EU:C:2011:854): see Section E.

[35] See further Chapters 9 and 11.

Article 101 TFEU forbids restrictive practices as defined by its first paragraph, but allows for carefully confined exemption pursuant to the four criteria (two positive two negative), inscribed in its third paragraph. Article 102 TFEU has no explicit exemption provision, but the determination of whether or not an 'abuse' of a dominant position has been committed allows room to assess the context. For undertakings entrusted with the operation of services of general economic interest, Article 106(2) TFEU envisages a partial protection from the keen blast of the competition rules which arises where those rules obstruct the performances of the tasks assigned to them.[36] This creates Treaty-recognized, albeit imprecisely defined, space to preserve the value of public services or, put another way, to call a halt of sorts to the tide of market competition.[37]

As a general observation, the breadth of the notion of 'undertaking' combined with the ease with which an effect on inter-state trade may be identified, considered earlier,[38] means that the scope allowed for justification under these provisions is of critical importance.

However, the Court has, in effect, extended still further the room allowed to justify practices. It has, in particular, written into Article 101(1) TFEU an opportunity to justify practices that are undeniably restrictive of competition where they serve an interest of sufficient importance. *Wouters* is the most prominent landmark.[39] The Court found that a Dutch rule forbidding the creation of multi-disciplinary partnerships involving barristers and accountants restricted competition, because it suppressed the possibility to offer a wider range of services, which would be apt to generate economies of scale, and was liable to limit production and technical development in the field. But the Court then added that the content and the objectives of the restriction matter in determining the application of Article 101(1). The Court asked 'whether the consequential effects restrictive of competition are inherent in the pursuit of those objectives'.[40] And that then led it to accept that the motivation for prohibiting partnerships between barristers and accountants, which was to guarantee the independence and loyalty to the clients of members of the Bar as part of a broader concern to secure the sound administration of justice, was sufficient to prevail over the finding that the prohibition exerted effects restrictive of competition. Moreover, the rule did not go beyond what was necessary in order to ensure the proper functioning of the legal profession in the Netherlands. There was, in short, no breach of EU competition law.

In similar vein, the Court in *Meca-Medina and Majcen* found that a doping ban imposed on swimmers by a sports governing body did not necessarily constitute

---

[36] See, e.g., Case C-475/99, *Firma Ambulanz Glöckner v. Landkreis Sudwestpfalz*, [2001] ECR I-8089 (ECLI:EU:C:2001:577).

[37] This cannot be explored exhaustively here but is in itself a vast and intriguing field of inquiry. See, e.g., R. Whish and D. Bailey, *Competition Law* (7th ed., 2012), Chs 6.048–6.066; M. Cremona (ed.), *Market Integration and Public Services in the European Union* (2011); Sauter, 'Public Services and the Internal Market: Building Blocks or Persistent Irritant?', 21 *European Law Journal* (2015) 738.

[38] See Chapter 5.A and Chapter 6.A.4 respectively.

[39] Case C-309/99, *J.C.J. Wouters, J.W. Savelbergh, Price Waterhouse Belastingadviseurs BV v. Algemene Raad van de Nederlandse Orde van Advocaten*, [2002] ECR I-1577 (ECLI:EU:C:2002:98).

[40] *Ibid.*, at para. 97.

a forbidden restriction of competition within the meaning of (what is now) Article 101 TFEU, since it was 'justified by a legitimate objective', which was that of (in short) clean sport.[41] Moreover, penalties were necessary to ensure enforcement of the doping ban, so the effect of a suspension from competition on athletes' freedom of action was considered inherent in the anti-doping rules, although a requirement that it be proportionate applied.[42]

In *Consiglio nazionale dei geologi* the Court relied on *Wouters* as it insisted on the need for a contextual assessment of the regulation of prices charged for services carried out by a professional association (of Italian geologists).[43] This clearly had a pernicious whiff of horizontal price-fixing, but the Court instructed the national court to assess whether the practice might be saved in the light of its claimed objective to maintain the 'dignity' of the profession – though even if such a (frankly implausible) objective were accepted, the rule would need to be no more restrictive than needed to attain it. This is in essence the Court's backstop protection and it is thematically fully in line with the case law dealing with free movement.[44]

The Court's approach has caused disquiet for fear it may dilute the purity of economic analysis on which some competition lawyers would pride themselves,[45] but it represents a readiness to place the economic objectives of EU internal market in their wider social and economic contexts for the purposes of the interpretation of the basic prohibition. The structure of the analysis, whereby the Court performs a full contextual examination of the challenged measure and is willing to locate it outwith the reach of Article 101(1) TFEU without the need to consider it in the light of Article 101(3), is aligned to the *Cassis*-inspired approach taken under Articles 34 and 56 TFEU, whereby national rules which serve a sufficiently important interest may be treated as justified trade barriers without explicit recourse to the derogations foreseen by the Treaty in Articles 36, 52 and 62 TFEU. That is, just as *Cassis* is a supple interpretation of Article 34 rather than an inflated application of Article 36, so too *Wouters* is a supple interpretation of Article 101(1) rather than an inflated interpretation of Article 101(3). The outcome is an internal market law that is structurally porous to wider non-economic concerns.

Albany, considered earlier,[46] is different from *Wouters* in that the Court in *Albany* placed collective negotiations between management and labour outwith the reach of competition law entirely, rather than, as in *Wouters*, admitting a restrictive effect but finding it objectively justified in the context in which it was applied. But functionally *Wouters* and *Albany* share an ambition to prevent a rigid application of competition

---

[41] Case C-519/04 P, *Meca-Medina and Majcen v. Commission*, [2006] ECR I-6991 (ECLI:EU:C:2006:492), at para. 45.

[42] *Ibid.*, at para. 44.

[43] Case C-136/12, *Consiglio nazionale dei geologi*, judgment of 18 July 2013, not yet reported (ECLI:EU:C:2013:489).

[44] See Section B.

[45] A full survey escapes the scope of this volume: see, with no allegation of either purity or impurity, e.g., Whish and Bailey, *supra* note 37, Chs 3.128–3.143; C. Townley, *Article 81 EC and Public Policy* (2009); B. Van Rompuy, *Economic Efficiency: The Sole Concern of Modern Antitrust Policy?* (2012), Ch. 4; Witt, 'Public Policy Goals under EU Competition Law: Now is the Time to Set the House in Order', 8 *European Competition Journal* (2012) 443.

[46] Case C-67/96, *Albany International*, [1999] ECR I-5751 (ECLI:EU:C:1999:430). See Chapter 5.B.

law serving to disable pursuit of other distinct and worthwhile objectives. The internal market is malleable as a legal concept.

D. Public Health

Many of the early cases reaching the Court focused on the justification recognized by Article 36 whereby states may act to protect the health and life of humans, animals or plants. The Court has described the health and life of humans as 'foremost among the interests' protected by the TFEU.[47] There is a hint here of rhetorical flourish: whatever type of justification is advanced, the structure of the analysis is identical, and the Court does not mean to permit national measures to escape review when they impede inter-state trade simply because public health is claimed to be at stake. However, as a minimum it suggests that the Court will demonstrate a particular sensitivity to justifications rooted in health protection. But what matters is the quality of the arguments advanced in particular cases. And the Court has been faced with some pretty shoddy attempts to defend protectionist rules dressed up in the implausible garb of public health.

Commission v. *United Kingdom* captures this gist of this periodic absurdity.[48] British restrictions on the importation of turkeys from France were defended as necessary to prevent the spread of contagious poultry disease. The Court was not impressed. It noted that the UK government 'had been subject to pressure from British poultry producers to block these imports' and that the policy had been introduced hurriedly 'with the result that French Christmas turkeys were excluded from the British market for the 1981 season'.[49] This was not 'part of a seriously considered health policy'.[50] It was commercially motivated – it was an attempt to protect British farmers from competition at the expense of cross-border traders and British turkey buyers.

Commission v. *Portugal* involved a measure which prohibited the affixing of any type of tinted film designed to filter light to the windscreen and the windows alongside the passenger seats in motor vehicles.[51] In classic *Cassis de Dijon* fashion, this constituted a technical standard that tended to exclude imported products from the Portuguese market. Portugal had argued that its rule enabled seat belt use by a passenger to be checked by means of a simple observation conducted from outside the vehicle, but the good sense of this initiative was wholly subverted by Portugal's admission that it in any event it allowed the marketing of motor vehicles fitted *from the outset* with tinted windows. So the Court concluded that the 'ban must be regarded as being excessive and, therefore, disproportionate with respect to the objectives pursued'.[52] The laughable attempt made by Germany in *Cassis de Dijon* to persuade the Court that a ban on weak alcoholic drink was a justified measure of public health

---

[47] E.g., Case C-170/04, *supra* note 8, at para. 39; Case C-367/12, *Sokoll-Seebacher*, judgment of 13 February 2014, not yet reported (ECLI:EU:C:2014:68), at para. 26.

[48] Case 40/82, *Commission* v. *United Kingdom*, [1982] ECR 2793 (ECLI:EU:C:1982:285).

[49] *Ibid.*, at para. 37.   [50] *Ibid.*, at para. 38.

[51] Case C-265/06, *Commission* v. *Portugal*, [2008] ECR I-2245 (ECLI:EU:C:2008:210).

[52] *Ibid.*, at para. 47.

protection when it cheerfully allowed much stronger alcoholic drinks on to the market is typically treated as the very height of absurdity observable in the Court's case law, but the sad truth is that over the years plenty of regulating authorities in the EU have run it close by wasting the Court's time, and that of cross-border traders and consumers, by trying to defend trade restrictions that serve only the vested interests of local suppliers and producers.

Use of the proportionality principle in such cases allows the Court to avoid impugning the good intentions that may lie behind a national measure – even where, as in the two cases explained earlier, there are none. But sometimes there are good reasons, and the Court is able to accept the virtue of public health policies while requiring that they be tailored to meet the demands of the internal market. *Klas Rosengren*, concerning the Swedish retail monopoly over alcohol, was mentioned earlier: the Court accepted the worth in principle of a policy designed to protect young people, but condemned the applicable and very broad system because it was *not* so designed.[53] In *Scotch Whisky Association* the Court suggested that the fixing of minimum prices as a means to curtail consumption of alcohol could not be justified because of the availability of a method to achieve the end in view which would be less restrictive of competition, namely increased taxation, though it properly left the ultimate decision to the referring (Scottish) court.[54] In similar vein, the Court did not agree that Austrian rules prohibiting the marketing of blood for which payment had been made were justified: the Court took particular account of the fact that a number of other Member States reimburse blood donors' costs and could see no public health reason for Austria's refusal to accept such a possibility.[55] So the Austrian rules went beyond what was necessary to achieve the end in view.

EU law exercises a tight grip: the principle that the least restrictive means must be used by a regulator has a real controlling bite. But the Court is not dismissive of justification, provided that the regulating authority approaches its responsibilities to make choices in the light of the demands of the internal market with a degree of coherence and care.

In *Eyssen* the Dutch authorities were sufficiently anxious about the danger to human health presented by the use of a particular type of preservative in cheese that they introduced a ban.[56] Other less cautious Member States were prepared to allow such additives. The Dutch ban impeded trade in cheeses manufactured in more permissive states, but the Court accepted that regulatory attitudes could legitimately vary in such circumstances of scientific uncertainty and did not find the Netherlands to have acted unlawfully, even though it had intervened in the market more vigorously than the norm elsewhere. So a product acceptable to State X may be justifiably excluded by State Y. The 'precautionary principle', explicitly recognized in Article 191(2) TFEU as a basis for EU policy, tends to be used to capture this approach

[53] Case C-170/04, *supra* note 8. See also, e.g., Case C-434/04, *supra* note 11.
[54] Case C-333/14, *Scotch Whisky Association*, judgment of 23 December 2015, not yet reported (ECLI:EU:C:2015:845).
[55] Case C-421/09, *Humanplasma GmbH* v. *Austria*, judgment of 9 December 2010, not yet reported (ECLI:EU:C:2010:760).
[56] Case 53/80, *Eyssen*, [1981] ECR 409 (ECLI:EU:C:1981:35).

today[57] and a great deal of the necessary assessment of risk in the shadow of pre-caution has been transplanted from national level to EU level by the increasingly complex and dense network of secondary legislation in the field of medicines, phar-maceuticals, foodstuffs and cosmetics. Here too the precautionary principle per-forms a key if controversial role in shaping regulatory responses in cases of scientific uncertainty.[58]

Commission v. *France* provides a particularly vivid demonstration of the Court's willingness to be persuaded by hard evidence that there is a genuine divergence in regulatory tradition among the Member States which justifies refusal to impose a common solution in the name of integrating markets.[59] France refused to accept on to its markets woodworking machines that were freely available and used in Germany because it claimed they were unsafe. This plainly restricted inter-state trade. France did not seek to claim it had higher standards of protection than did Germany. Rather, and more subtly, it claimed that techniques of protection differed between the two states. The French rules were based on the aim of protecting users from their own mistakes and therefore curtailed scope for intervention in the machine's func-tioning by the user. Germany preferred to train users so they were able to deal with any malfunctioning. France demanded machines be foolproof on an understanding that users were likely to be fools, whereas Germany trained operators to acquire the necessary skills. In such circumstances of demonstrated factual heterogeneity the Court refused to find that the German system would lead to the same level of safety as that prevailing in France, and so France's restriction on trade in machines was treated as justified.

The insistence on articulated and coherent justification is equally visible in con-nection with restrictions on the free movement of services, where no material differ-ence in approach exists. In two cases the Court was asked to consider the French *Loi Evin*, pursuant to which France required that television broadcasts in France by French broadcasters of sports events occurring in other Member States should not feature advertisements for alcohol.[60] This plainly restricted the free movement of services, by requiring interference with broadcasts in the case of games taking place in jurisdictions outside France where shirt or poster advertising of alcoholic drinks was permitted. The Court found the rules to be a justified contribution to the pro-tection of public health. The European Commission and the UK had pressed on the Court that because the rules concerned only television advertising, and did not extend to advertising for alcoholic drinks visible in the background on film sets, and moreover did not extend to advertising for tobacco, they should be regarded as

---

[57] E.g., Case C-192/01, *Commission* v. *Denmark*, [2003] ECR I-9693 (ECLI:EU:C:2003:492); Case C-95/01, *John Greenham*, [2004] ECR I-1333 (ECLI:EU:C:2004:71); Case C-333/08, *Commission* v. *France*, [2010] ECR I-757 (ECLI:EU:C:2010:44).

[58] See, e.g., E. Fisher, J. Jones and R. Von Schomberg (eds), *Implementing the Precautionary Principle: Perspectives and Prospects* (2006); Berends and Carreño, 'Safeguards in Food Law – Ensuring Food Scares Are Scarce', 30 *European Law Review* (2005) 386; Von Schomberg, 'The Precautionary Principle: Its Use within Hard and Soft Law', 3 *European Journal of Risk Regulation* (2012) 147.

[59] Case 188/84, *Commission* v. *France*, [1986] ECR I-419 (ECLI:EU:C:1986:43).

[60] Case C-429/02, *Bacardi* v. *TF1*, [2004] ECR I-6613 (ECLI:EU:C:2004:432); Case C-262/02, *Commission* v. *France*, [2004] ECR I-6569 (ECLI:EU:C:2004:431).

inconsistent and therefore unworthy of being treated as a justified expression of public health policy. The Court was not so strict. Such choices fell within the discretion of the regulating Member State. Market deregulation has its limits: justification sets those limits.

E. Environmental Protection

The Court's readiness to entertain justifications for barriers to inter-state trade rooted in concern to secure protection of the environment dates back to the 1980s. In fact environmental protection became one of the most immediately prominent types of justification that were treated as in principle available to a regulating state by the Court under the widened notion of justification pioneered in *Cassis de Dijon*. Environmental protection was not – is not – listed in Article 36 TFEU. But in 1988, in *Commission* v. *Denmark*, the Court declared that 'the protection of the environment is a mandatory requirement which may limit the application of Article 30 [now 34] of the Treaty'.[61] Today, this connection between environmental concerns and, inter alia, the EU's project of building an internal market is confirmed by Article 11 TFEU and Article 37 of the Charter, and moreover a great many issues are addressed through a relatively dense network of secondary legislation giving shape to EU environmental law, but the Court was the pioneer. This is particularly strongly emphasized by the realization that although in *Commission* v. *Denmark*, decided in 1988, the Court was able to draw on the Single European Act's introduction of environmental protection into the list of EU competences with effect from 1987.[62] In fact the Court had in 1985 already declared that the protection of the environment belonged among the EU's 'essential objectives', even though the Treaty at that time made no mention at all of the environment.[63]

The concern here is not to provide an exhaustive examination.[64] Instead, the concern is to show how the internal market as a legal concept has become a more intricate matter than trade liberalization alone as a result of the interpretative choices boldly made by the Court. In the 'Walloon Waste' case the Court instructively meshed concerns about promoting trade integration with the particular anxieties associated with environmental protection.[65] The public authorities in the French-speaking region of Belgium prohibited importation of waste on to its territory. This was, in short, designed to forestall 'waste tourism', but it clearly impeded cross-border economic activity (in waste disposal). However, it is good environmental practice that pollution be rectified as a priority at source, a principle that was recognized in the Treaty at the time, albeit not in the part that deals with free movement, as well as under international law instruments. It is today recognized by Article 191(2) TFEU on environmental protection. This, the Court concluded, was enough to justify the

---

[61] Case 302/86, *supra* note 16.   [62] *Ibid.*, at para. 8 of the judgment.
[63] Case 240/83, *Procureur de la République* v. *Association de défense des brûleurs d'huiles usages*, [1985] ECR 531 (ECLI:EU:C:1985:59).
[64] See, e.g., N. De Sadeleer, *EU Environmental Law and the Internal Market* (2014), Ch. 5.
[65] Case C-2/90, *Commission* v. *Belgium*, [1992] ECR I-4431 (ECLI:EU:C:1992:310).

measures as contributions to the protection of the environment. It was explained earlier that the Court is typically chilly when asked to insulate a particular sector from the scrutiny of internal market law. It is much warmer when such an invitation is made in the context of justification. Where waste and pollution are involved, environmental protection and free trade are in tension in a way that 'normal' trade would not be, and the Court absorbs and reflects that in assessing the justification for trade barriers.

In *PreussenElektra AG* v. *Schleswag AG* German rules required suppliers of electricity to purchase electricity produced from renewable energy sources at minimum prices.[66] Citing the '*Dassonville* formula', the Court found this was a national measure capable of hindering, directly or indirectly, actually or potentially, intra-Community trade. Where an obligation is placed on traders in a Member State to obtain a certain percentage of their supplies of a given product from a national supplier, the result is to limit the possibilities for importers to satisfy that demand. The Court, however, found that the scheme was justified. The use of renewable energy sources for producing electricity protects the environment by contributing to the reduction in emissions of greenhouse gases which are amongst the main causes of climate change, and the Court cited a number of relevant EU and international legal instruments in order to situate its assessment of justification in free movement law in a context wider than simply trade liberalization.[67] It also drew on the requirement to integrate environmental protection requirements into the definition and implementation of other policies, which is today commanded by both Article 11 TFEU and Article 37 of the Charter. In *Preussen Elektra* the Court also added that the nature of electricity as a product justified a territorial limitation of the type employed by Germany in its scheme. The problem is that, once electricity has been allowed into the transmission or distribution system, it is difficult to identify the source of energy from which it was produced. It is not possible to attach a label to electricity produced virtuously from renewable sources. So the German system, which linked the obligation to buy to the location of the producer, was lawful.

The receptivity to territorial limitation, justified in the light of the particular context of the generation of electricity and the difficulty otherwise in tracing the origin of electricity once it is released into the distribution system, has become orthodox in the Court's case law.[68] So electricity is a special case – but this is recognized not at the stage of deciding whether the matter falls within the scope of internal market law, but instead at the stage of justification.

The Charter confirms the constitutional significance in EU law of a high level of environmental protection in its Article 37, but, given the Court's long track record in its free movement case law, the Charter is not transformative. In *Commission* v. *Austria* Austria had banned lorries over 7.5 tonnes from carrying certain goods – those with

---

[66] Case C-379/98, *supra* note 16. [67] Especially *ibid.*, at para. 74.
[68] E.g., Case C-573/12, *Ålands Vindkraft*, judgment of 1 July 2014, not yet reported (ECLI:EU:C:2014:2037); Joined Cases C-204/12 to C-208/12, *Essent Belgium*, judgment of 11 September 2014, not yet reported (ECLI:EU:C:2014:2192).

an 'affinity to rail' – from using a section of motorway in the Inn valley.[69] This was found to have a substantial effect on the free movement of goods between Northern Europe and Northern Italy. In assessing whether the intervention was justified, the Court referred to (what were then) Articles 2, 3, 6 and 152(1) EC and Articles 35 and 37 of the Charter as sources of respect for health and environmental protection. But it then found the 'radical' traffic ban to go too far.[70] Austria had not sufficiently considered alternative less restrictive methods of achieving its ends, including applying a lower permanent speed limit in preference to the prevailing variable speed limit. The ruling demonstrates how the Charter fits easily into the familiar structure of free movement law as an amplification of the relevant material relied on to assess whether a restriction is justified. The Charter is confirmation, not transformation, of judicial practice.

An irritating twist in the case law is that for fully 35 years the Court has insisted that the wider *Cassis*-created justifications for trade barriers may be deployed only where the national measures in question are not discriminatory.[71] Where they are discriminatory, then only exceptions listed in Article 36 TFEU may be relied on. But what the Court *says* does not seem to accord with what it *does*. In cases where environmental protection is at stake, the Court allows the wider *Cassis* justifications to be deployed even where national measures are discriminatory on the basis of origin. Initially, the Court found a contorted way to claim the measures were not in fact discriminatory after all. This was 'Walloon Waste', where it claimed that waste created locally and transported waste were simply not the same thing.[72] Latterly, it seems perfectly content to accept the presence of discrimination but to find the measures justified in the service of environmental protection if they are part of a rationally structured system. This is plain in the cases mentioned earlier on territorial limitations written into rules that favour production of energy from renewable sources. This peculiar niche is a stain on the Court's record: here the ambiguity of the internal market is no excuse for the mess. It would be a service were the Court to abandon its claim that discrimination matters for these purposes, as it has set aside an emphasis on discrimination in free movement law generally ever since *Dassonville* (see Chapter 6.A.2). It should instead simply accept that any trade barrier may be justified by a public interest claim, with discrimination relegated to one element in the assessment (and militating against finding a measure justified, especially outwith the particular context of environmental protection).[73]

---

[69] Case C-28/09, *supra* note 34.   [70] *Ibid.*, para. 140.

[71] E.g., Case C-113/80, *Commission v. Italy*, [1981] ECR 1625 (ECLI:EU:C:1981:139); Joined Cases C-1 and 176/90, *Aragonesa de Publicidad Exterior*, [1991] ECR I-4151 (ECLI:EU:C:1991:327); Joined Cases C-344/13, C-367/13, *Blanco, Fabretti*, judgment of 22 October 2014, not yet reported (ECLI:EU:C:2014:2311); Case C-375/14, *Rosanna Laezza*, judgment of 28 January 2016, not yet reported (ECLI:EU:C:2016:60).

[72] Case C-2/90, *supra* note 65.

[73] For an exasperated but ignored plea to the Court openly to embrace this change see A.G. Bot in Joined Cases C-204/12 to C-208/12, *supra* note 68. He is no lone voice, see also, e.g., A.G. Jacobs in Case C-136/00, *Danner*, [2002] ECR I-8147 (ECLI:EU:C:2002:558).

F. Protection of the Economic Interests of Consumers

Case law involving inspection of national measures that purport to offer protection to the economic interests of consumers provides another helpful testing ground within which to understand how far the Court will go in insisting on deregulation in the name of market-making and, by way of corollary, what scope is allowed to national measures resistant to free movement. Once again, the crucial element is the quality and sincerity of the justifications advanced by the Member State for the inspection of the Court.

The economic protection of consumers is not listed as a derogation recognized by Article 36 TFEU, but the structure of the analysis resembles those cases raising justifications associated with public health, which is listed, and both are areas which attract a heap of plainly absurd claims by regulating authorities. In *Cassis de Dijon* justification rooted in the claimed public health threats of weak alcohol was dismissed with contempt by the Court, but claims that the introduction of Cassis onto the German market would cause harm to the economic interests of consumers fared little better. The Court did not deny that consumers might be confused by the appearance on the (German) market of a new and unfamiliar product, which might in principle justify an intervention in the market designed to protect consumers from spending money unwisely or without full awareness that (in casu) that they are buying a sickly sweet and weak alcoholic drink that the robust German palate will promptly spit out in revulsion. But transparency in the market could be achieved by requiring the disclosure of information about alcohol content and composition more generally on the product packaging. It went too far to fix a minimum level of alcohol content which, if not met, led to the complete exclusion of the product from the (German) market.

This is an application of the Court's orthodox demand that the means used to achieve a particular end shall be the least restrictive of trade that are necessary to achieve it – a version of the principle of proportionality.[74] Each case demands assessment in its own particular context, but the trend in the case law is to assume the regulatory virtue of mandatory information disclosure over product composition rules. So there is a deregulatory impulse, and it is visible within a pile of case law. So, for example, in the 'Beer Purity' case, considered earlier,[75] German law confined use of the name 'Bier' to products brewed using only malted barley, hops, yeast and water. This unlawfully restricted the commercial opportunities in Germany of producers brewing elsewhere according to different recipes and traditions. The Court did not exclude intervention in the market designed to protect consumers expecting their 'Bier' to have a particular taste and quality, but it did exclude a rule so rigid as to have the effect of keeping differently constituted beers off the market altogether. Labelling would do the job: it is the least restrictive means to achieve the end in view, that of consumer protection.

---

[74] See Section B.
[75] Case 178/84, *Commission* v. *Germany*, [1987] ECR 1227 (ECLI:EU:C:1987:126). See Chapter 3.D.

'*Tourist Guides*', another case met earlier,[76] illustrates the same preference for market solutions, not public regulation, in the services sector. France required tourist guides to hold a local qualification as a pre-condition of offering their services on French territory. The Court observed that competition between tour operators would ensure the hiring of competent guides and that accordingly a state licensing regime governing access to the profession could not be justified. Choice was the leitmotif: the Court noted that the French rule '... prevents tourists taking part in such organized tours from availing themselves at will of the services in question'.[77] The market would take care of consumers: 'the profitable operation of such group tours depends on the commercial reputation of the operator, who faces competitive pressure from other tour companies' and 'the need to maintain that reputation and the competitive pressure themselves compel companies to be selective in employing tourist guides and exercise some control over the quality of their services'.[78] It is not that consumers *have* to buy or use unfamiliar imports but rather that they can *choose* to do so. These decisions use free movement to transfer the decision over whether a particular product or service shall be accessible away from the regulator to the consumer. Competition law applied in particular to market sharing does something similar, by ensuring a shift from the interest of producers to cross-border competition favouring consumer choice. There is potential too in the application of a comparable analysis to the Treaty rules on state aids and state monopolies which have also been relied on to shake up often long-standing and cosily anti-competitive domestic public sector arrangements.[79]

There is a strong sense of regulatory absurdity, as EU law is used to sweep away the deadwood and detritus of centuries. The judges in Luxembourg must have been perplexed and frustrated as their time was taken up with attempts to argue that consumers need to protected by rules which required margarine to be packed only in a cube,[80] that Edam cheese be regulated according to strict minimum fat rules,[81] that bleach must cross a defined threshold of strength,[82] that 'shallots' must be reproduced directly from bulbs and cannot be applied to seedling vegetables,[83] and that advertising medical and surgical treatments be banned on national television networks but permitted on local television networks.[84] The Court can be forgiven for coming close to losing its temper with bone-headed regulatory inertia: what a sorry tale of wasted resources emerges from a case like *Eric Libert*, in which Flemish rules restricting the acquisition of property by those without a 'sufficient connection' to

---

[76] Case C-154/89, *Commission* v. *France*, [1991] ECR I-659 (ECLI:EU:C:1991:76).

[77] *Ibid.*, at para. 13.   [78] *Ibid.*, at para. 20.

[79] E.g., Case C-41/90, *Höfner and Elser*, [1991] ECR I-1979 (ECLI:EU:C:1991:161); see also, e.g., Smith, 'In Pursuit of Selective Liberalization: Single Market Competition and Its Limits', 8 *Journal of European Public Policy* (2001) 519; Clifton, Díaz-Fuentes and Revuelta, 'The Political Economy of Telecoms and Electricity Internationalisation in the Single Market', 17 *Journal of European Public Policy* (2010) 988.

[80] Case 261/81, *supra* note 6.

[81] Case 286/86, *Deserbais*, [1988] ECR 4907 (ECLI:EU:C:1988:434).

[82] Case C-358/01, *Commission* v. *Spain*, [2003] ECR I-13145 (ECLI:EU:C:2003:599).

[83] Case C-147/04, *de Groot*, [2006] ECR I-245 (ECLI:EU:C:2006:7).

[84] Case C-500/06, *Corporación Dermoestética SA*, [2008] ECR I-5785 (ECLI:EU:C:2008:421).

the local commune were defended as a means to hold down costs to prevent the exclusion of socially and/or economically disadvantaged locals.[85] The Court accepted this protective aim as legitimate in principle, as it has been prepared to do in other free movement cases,[86] but in fact, on closer inspection, the rules in question attached no significance whatsoever to affluence, so even well-off locals would meet the requirement. This is not the Court undermining locally determined social welfare choices – this is the Court exposing regulatory mendacity.

The list of such cases is not endless, but it is long. The Court frequently uses the 'reasonably circumspect' consumer as a benchmark in these cases,[87] in the sense that national measures which it regards as unnecessary for such a consumer are normally not justified. The consumer is used instrumentally in such circumstances: as a lever to prise open national regulatory choices in order to free up trade and expand a distinct vision of the consumer interest, that of choice in the internal market. On the face of it there is something unsettling about decisions of a transnational court that require the setting aside of national regulatory decisions. However, once one realizes just how weak are the arguments in support of such rules, one can appreciate how EU internal market law draws legitimating force from its cleansing of Member State rulebooks, and the fact that Member States troubled to make the trek to Luxembourg to defend protectionist absurdities and anachronisms of the type summarized earlier is solid proof that leaving the matter to be resolved through national political processes would have been fruitless. In truth, such rules, defended as measures of consumer protection, were simply measures of protection to the benefit of local producers. One might wonder why on earth a national regulator would bother to defend such a fatuous rule: the answer probably lies not in an expectation or even a desire to win the case but rather in the need to be seen to be taking the side of politically influential local producers.[88] EU law, as a correcting force, rescues not only consumers and out-of-state traders, but also local political actors trapped by vested interests. Further reflection on the role of internal market law in addressing the mis-match between political processes tied to the state and affected interests beyond the state is reserved for Chapter 12.

The approach taken in *Cassis de Dijon* is immensely helpful to those seeking to challenge the thickets of regulatory intervention that have accumulated over the centuries in Europe. This deregulatory tendency also has an important institutional consequence. Free movement law exerts a prodigious effect on trade-restrictive technical standards, far beyond a discrimination-only focus. Legislative harmonization could be confined to national laws having an impact on the functioning of the internal market where the barriers to trade which need to be removed arise from national

---

[85] Joined Cases C-197/11 and C-203/11, *Eric Libert*, judgment of 8 May 2013, not yet reported (ECLI:EU:C:2013:288).

[86] E.g., Case C-370/05, *Festersen*, [2007] ECR I-1129 (ECLI:EU:C:2007:59), Case C-452/01, *Margarethe Ospelt and Schlössle Weissenberg Familienstiftung*, [2003] ECR I-9743 (ECLI:EU:C:2003:493) (rules on property ownership designed to protect agricultural communities in Denmark and Austria respectively).

[87] E.g., Case C-470/93, *Verein gegen Unwesen in Handel und Gewerbe Köln v. Mars GmbH*, [1995] ECR I-1923 (ECLI:EU:C:1995:224).

[88] There is little empirical work in this vein: it would be intriguing.

provisions which are shown to be justified. So the judicial process takes the strain and there is a diminished need for legislative action. But this is not cost free. This is a reminder that the costs saved by reducing the weight of the harmonization programme are to be weighed against those incurred by the absence of harmonized standards and consequent reliance on ad hoc litigation to keep Member States honest in their fidelity to the Court's vision of non-absolute mutual recognition. Here, too, further comment is reserved for Chapter 12.

Only if information disclosure will not suffice to protect the consumer will more intrusive intervention be permitted. The Court's model makes some powerful assumptions about the capacity of the consumer to acquire, digest and act up on disclosed information. It is that image of the consumer which allows it to treat so much national practice as unlawful over-regulation of national markets. Much properly depends on appreciation of just how serious will be the harm done if consumers (or at least some consumers) are not alert: if they are forced, by learning from mistakes, to surrender the 'crystallization' of their habits which the Court has identified as the blockage against which free movement is targeted.[89] A disappointingly tasteless bottle of beer or a bland cheese is not the same as a medicine that, if not taken in a particular dosage, is dangerous. In the vividly illustrative ruling in *Drei Glocken* v. *USL Centro-Sud* the Court found no adequate justification for Italian rules requiring use of durum wheat in pasta, and must be taken to have been profoundly unimpressed by the views pressed on it by its Advocate General, Mr Mancini, to the effect that the release on to the Italian market of differently made German pasta would have left the Italian consumer utterly bemused, given the depth of cultural expectation in Italy about pasta, its many forms of presentation and the exclusive use in Italy of durum wheat.[90] The Court presumably thought the Italian consumer could cope with the uncertainty.[91] What's the worst that could happen? But a case like *Eyssen* shows how a public health concern increases the Court's readiness to treat local choices as justified even where they suppress trade and so consumer choice.[92]

The key thematic point for the purposes of this volume is that the internal market as a legal concept draws the Court into developing a vision of how markets operate and how consumers behave, and this has both descriptive and normative dimensions. But some national rules survive the Court's inspection. The internal market is a more nuanced project than a process of automatic deregulation – it is based on shared competence. *Buet* concerned a French rule which went beyond giving consumers the right of cancellation required by the so-called 'Doorstep Selling' Directive (85/577), which mandated only minimum rules.[93] France prohibited canvassing at

---

[89] Case 178/84, *supra* note 75, at para. 32.

[90] Case 407/85, *Drei Glocken* v. *USL Centro-Sud*, [1988] ECR 4233 (ECLI:EU:C:1988:401).

[91] The Court's ruling is not based exclusively on assumptions. It rejected the claim that permitting the release of German-made pasta on to the market would harm the very viability of future production of pasta made from durum wheat by pointing to statistics supplied to it which showed that in other Member States pasta made from durum wheat typically acquired an enlarged market share when faced by competition from differently made pasta (at para. 27).

[92] Case 53/80, *supra* note 56.

[93] Case 382/87, *Buet*, [1989] ECR 1235 (ECLI:EU:C:1989:198). The Directive has now been replaced by Directive 2011/83 which does *not* allow stricter rules.

private dwellings for the sale of educational material. The Court treated this as an obstacle to inter-state trade by a firm that sold English-language teaching material which earned 90 per cent of its turnover by such canvassing at private dwellings.[94] Was the French rule justified? It protected consumers against hasty purchases to a degree that surpassed the level that the EU legislature had thought necessary and, moreover, it was more restrictive than the choices made in most of the other Member States. The Court, however, was persuaded that the rules were justified, because they revealed a planned and targeted form of consumer protection. The Court drew attention to the greater risk of an ill-considered purchase 'when the canvassing is for enrolment for a course of instruction or the sale of educational material ... [because] the potential purchaser often belongs to a category of people who, for one reason or another, are behind with their education and are seeking to catch up'.[95] That, the Court observed, 'makes them particularly vulnerable'.[96] It noted too that the French ban had been enacted 'as a result of numerous complaints caused by such abuses, such as the sale of out-of-date courses'.[97] It added that 'since teaching is not a consumer product in daily use, an ill-considered purchase could cause the purchaser harm other than mere financial loss that could be longer lasting'.[98]

Piecing together these analytical fragments, the Court resisted the opportunity to deploy free movement law in such a way as to deregulate the (French) market. Instead, it was interpreted to grant respect to the local regulatory choice designed to protect particularly vulnerable consumers.

A-Punkt Schmuckhandels GmbH v. *Claudia Schmidt* has a similar flavour.[99] Parties in the home where jewellery was offered for sale were banned in Austria. If this were found to be a barrier to inter-state trade, a matter for the national court to determine,[100] then the Court of Justice was open to the possibility of finding it to be justified despite its restrictive effect on commercial freedom. The Court noted that the rule was apt to:

take account of the specific features associated with the sale of silver jewellery in private homes, in particular the potentially higher risk of the consumer being cheated due to a lack of information, the impossibility of comparing prices or the provision of insufficient safeguards as regards the authenticity of that jewellery and the greater psychological pressure to buy where the sale is organised in a private setting.[101]

The leeway afforded to heavier regulators may encompass respect for divergent assessment of the same risk or it may cover a case where local conditions dictate that the threat is peculiarly sensitive. For example, in *Estee Lauder Cosmetics*[102] the Court accepted that in deciding whether a commercial practice forbidden under national

---

[94] *Ibid.*, para. 2. The ruling pre-dates the Court's re-examination of such questions in Cases C-267 and 268/91, *supra* note 2 above.

[95] *Ibid.*, at para. 13.   [96] *Ibid.*, at para. 13.   [97] *Ibid.*, at para. 13.

[98] *Ibid.*, at para. 14.

[99] Case C-441/04, *A-Punkt Schmuckhandels GmbH* v. *Claudia Schmidt*, [2006] ECR I-2093 (ECLI:EU:C:2006:141).

[100] Another question that invites 'post-*Keck*' re-appraisal: cf. Chapter 6.C.4, although in fact the matter would now seem to fall within the material scope of Directive 2005/29 concerning unfair business-to-consumer practices in the internal market, OJ 2005 L 149/22.

[101] *Ibid.*, at para. 29.

[102] Case C-220/98, *Estee Lauder Cosmetics*, [2000] ECR I-117 (ECLI:EU:C:2000:8).

rules is 'misleading' – and its suppression therefore potentially justified despite the damage inflicted on cross-border trade – it is necessary to take into account the presumed expectations of an average consumer who is reasonably well informed and reasonably observant and circumspect. This is the Court's orthodox benchmark, but the Court did not stop there. It added that 'social, cultural or linguistic factors' may justify special local anxiety about particular practices tolerated elsewhere. A degree of local regulatory diversity is envisaged in the application of the Treaty provisions on free movement.

Buet involved a class of consumers vulnerable for want of education, *A-Punkt* concerned consumers who may be vulnerable in a particular setting (at home). These rules were, in stark contrast to those tackled in *Cassis* and the many other maddening cases considered earlier, targeted at particular sensitivities and particular products. Where the national regulator has identified a particular need for protection and crafted a law that is appropriately nuanced and specific, the Court responds by judging with due respect for that nuance. The same theme is found in recent cases in the services sector.

DKV Belgium concerned Belgian rules restraining an increase in premium rates for 'individual room' coverage in hospitalization insurance.[103] The Court found this was a restriction on the right of establishment and the freedom to provide services, but it showed receptivity to the justification of the rules. It referred to the permissible objective of protecting consumers against sharp, unexpected increases in insurance premiums, though it left it the national court to ascertain whether or not the chosen system of national regulation went beyond what is necessary in order to achieve that objective.

Citroën Belux concerned a commercial practice consisting of a free offer of comprehensive insurance for six months on the purchase of a Citroën vehicle.[104] This was treated under Belgian law as a prohibited 'combined offer'. The matter fell within the material scope of Directive 2005/29 on unfair commercial practices, which applies a regime of maximum harmonization, and so would normally provide a complete answer to the question of whether the practice is fair or not, to the exclusion of Belgian preference. However, Article 3(9) of the Directive excludes financial services from the maximum harmonization regime and states instead that Member States are allowed room to choose to apply more restrictive rules, because, as its Preamble makes explicit, financial services engage 'complexity and inherent serious risks'. This already suggests a receptivity to the virtue of supplementary protection in this sector, should a Member State choose to provide it. The Court took the legislative hint and found stricter Belgian rules to be justified. It accepted that 'financial services are, by nature, complex and entail specific risks with regard to which the consumer is not always sufficiently well informed'.[105] It added that a combined offer of which one component is a financial service tends to lack transparency as regards the conditions,

---

[103] Case C-577/11, *DKV Belgium*, judgment of 7 March 2013, not yet reported (ECLI:EU:C:2013:146).

[104] Case C-265/12, *Citroën Belux*, judgment of 18 July 2013, not yet reported (ECLI:EU:C:2013:498).

[105] *Ibid.*, at para. 39.

the price and the exact content of that service. So the Court agreed that 'such an offer may well mislead consumers as to the true content and actual characteristics of the combination offered and, at the same time, deprive them of the opportunity of comparing the price and quality of that offer with other corresponding services from other economic operators'.[106]

Such rulings contradict depiction of the Court as an institution that is uniformly ruthless in interpreting free movement law in order to force deregulation on national markets. The internal market as a legal concept embraces nuance.

Exhaustive examination is here unfeasible, but it is not only in these richly vivid cases about consumer protection that the Court displays its tolerance of national measures that are sceptical of the virtue of unregulated markets. *Essent NV* concerns Dutch rules prohibiting privatization in the gas sector.[107] The Court embraced justifications rooted in consumer protection and energy security, and it lards the judgment with vigorous endorsement of the virtues of public ownership as a means to address matters such as cross-subsidization, promoting transparency and ensuring investment.[108] EU law does not require such intervention but it permits it, should a Member State so choose, even where harm to trade integration ensues.

The overall message holds, first, that sector-specific claims to need special treatment under internal market are fed in at the stage of justification, not in the determination of whether there is in the first place a jurisdictional trigger; and, secondly, that, once one looks beyond the blizzard of absurd defences of protectionist and anachronistic national measures that litter the *European Court Reports*, what emerges is a model of justification which is porous to sincere and targeted national initiatives which respond to the inadequacy or inequity of market solutions.

---

[106] *Ibid.*, at para. 39.
[107] Joined Cases C-105/12 to C-107/12, *Essent*, judgment of 22 October 2013, not yet reported (ECLI:EU:C:2013:677).
[108] Especially *ibid.*, at paras 56, 58, 59, 65.

9

Creativity in the Gap between Negative and Positive Law

The Principle of Conferral Unleashed

The wider the scope of the justification interrogated, the more intricate becomes the challenge faced by the Court of Justice of the European Union ('the Court') in finding a basis for adjudicating between the competing interests. What is striking in the cases examined in Chapter 8 is the Court's need to develop its own conception of legitimate public health, environmental protection and consumer protection – and to do so with relatively little assistance from the Treaty on the Functioning of the European Union (TFEU). Because the free movement provisions are written with reference to the functional end of market-making, they control national measures across a wide range of areas, some of which lie beyond EU legislative competence. So EU competence reaches beyond positive law. This was examined earlier: the disingenuous formula adopted by the Court in *ex parte Watts* is central to the inquiry.[1] Then, in the need to assess whether those national measures attain the standard of justification required under EU law, it is incumbent on the Court to proceed to shape its own understanding of the worth and role of matters to which the TFEU, by definition, gives little or no policy direction. This elucidates the full extent of the challenge that the law of the internal market presents in practice for the vitality of the principle of conferral. Sometimes the extraordinary breadth of the Court's mandate tends to be concealed by its readiness to decide cases with reference to the proportionality principle, where it offers no quarrel with the national regulatory choice in principle but, instead, objects only to the detailed way in which it is pursued in the particular circumstances. So the Court does not exclude that Member States have room to protect their consumers or to tackle pollution even where they take actions which will impede cross-border trade, but the least restrictive measure that will achieve the end in view must be chosen. But sometimes the Court must dig deeper into the essence of the regulatory choices.

---

[1] Case C-372/04, *Watts*, [2006] ECR I-4325 (ECLI:EU:C:2006:325). See Chapter 5.C generally.

The Internal Market as a Legal Concept. First Edition. Stephen Weatherill.
© Stephen Weatherill 2017. Published 2017 by Oxford University Press.

A. Sport as a Case Study

Sport provides a fine case study.[2] The famous ruling concerning the transfer system for football players in *Bosman* is spectacularly instructive.[3] At the time of the dispute, over 20 years ago, the EU had no explicit legislative competence in the field of sport (and even today its competence, introduced in 2009 by the Treaty of Lisbon, is thin: Article 165 TFEU). However, as explained earlier, the Court ruled that sport is subject to EU law in so far as it constitutes an economic activity. Moreover, it found that practices applicable at the time in football associated with the transfer system and the selection of non-national players violated EU law on free movement and non-discrimination. But the judgment is richer than that. It sought to shape an understanding of what may be 'special' about sport, even in the admitted absence of any Treaty guidance. The Court ruled that 'the aims of maintaining a balance between clubs by preserving a certain degree of equality and uncertainty as to results and of encouraging the recruitment and training of young players must be accepted as legitimate'.[4] This, then, is the extent to which EU law admits that sport is 'special' – this is, in the vocabulary found in the Treaty since 2009, the 'specific nature of sport' which is mentioned in Article 165 TFEU – but its source is not the TFEU nor indeed any other legal document. It is the Court's own invention, which it had to develop because sport's collision with EU internal market law forced the Court to engage with the question of what a sport transfer system is for. There is an incremental drift of this type driven by litigation. The transfer system was duly amended in a less restrictive direction – not by EU legislative act, which would have been a constitutional step too far, but by processes internal to the sport, operating in the shadow of the Court's ruling and EU internal market law more generally.[5] In *Bosman* the question also arose whether nationality based discrimination in club football was incompatible with the Treaty. The football authorities argued for the need to maintain a link between club and country, in order to give supporters a means of identification with their favourite team. One might ask: how could the Court possibly disagree? No material in the Treaty or in any other relevant EU law text offered it a base on which to make a judgement about the soundness of this argument. Advocate General Lenz led the way. In his Opinion he states that supporters are more interested in the success of their team than its composition, and refers to four 'foreign' players who were/are especially popular, not less popular, with their club's fans.[6] The Court too rejected the arguments of the football authorities, albeit in less vivid terms than its Advocate General. And so nationality rules affecting club football had to be immediately abandoned as far as players who were EU nationals were concerned.

---

[2] See, e.g., S. Weatherill, *European Sports Law: Collected Papers* (2nd ed., 2014).
[3] Case C-415/93, *Bosman*, [1995] ECR I-4921 (ECLI:EU:C:1995:463).
[4] *Ibid.*, at para. 106.
[5] The current 'master version' is FIFA's *Regulations on the Status and Transfer of Players*, available via http://www.fifa.com/governance/transfers/index.html.
[6] Case C-415/93, *supra* note 3, Opinion, at para. 143: Radenkovic (TSV1860), Keegan (HSV), Cantona (Manchester United), Klinsmann (Spurs).

Something similar has happened in relation to anti-doping, albeit that competition law provides the legal context. Penalties imposed pursuant to anti-doping rules may interfere with commercial freedom. EU law, given its orthodox claim to functional breadth, is potentially engaged. *Meca-Medina and Majcen* v. *Commission*, a decision of July 2006,[7] sustains *Bosman*'s thematic receptivity to sport's special concerns in the application of EU law. A sporting practice falls to be tested against the demands of EU competition law where it exerts economic *effects*. But the Court took the view that the general objective of the rules was to combat doping in order for competitive sport to be conducted on a fair basis; and the adverse effect of penalties on athletes' freedom of action must be considered to be inherent in the anti-doping rules. This was, in short, the '*Wouters* route' to shaping internal market law in a style sensitive to the particular context (see Chapter 8.C.2) but, more generally, it underlines the scale of the Court's ambition. It aspires to an internal market law that, in the room left for justification of restrictive measures, is informed by the peculiarities and sensitivities of the very many areas which it touches.

B. Collective Labour Action as a Case Study

This is not to assert that the Court's approach is unfailingly respectful of the sensitive balances that are demanded. Any argument that the Court is not locked into a congenital tendency to prioritize economic rights over social and political rights must reckon with the abominable December 2007 rulings of the Grand Chamber of the Court of Justice in *Viking Line* and *Laval*.[8]

The two cases had their factual and contextual twists, but, stripped down to the core, they involved the question whether EU free movement law protected a shipping firm wishing to 'reflag' ships from their homes in Finland and in Sweden ('old' Member States) to Estonia and Latvia ('new' Member States). The alleged trade barrier was collective action taken or threatened by labour unions aimed at deterring this corporate migration. The potential losers were Finnish and Swedish workers. The potential winners were corporate interests seeking lower costs; and Estonian and Latvian workers, at least in the short term. In the longer term, the balancing of these winners and losers plainly invited assessment of the type of internal market that is being built under the propulsion of EU free movement law. Is it freedom to trade? Or freedom to act collectively to compete effectively against corporate power? Loss of the latter would immediately hit Finns and Swedes, but Estonians and Latvians hoping to seize those jobs might need to be careful what they wish for: they might be the next potential victims of ruthless corporate cost-cutting once this freedom has been unleashed.

---

[7] Case C-519/04 P, *Meca-Medina and Majcen* v. *Commission*, [2006] ECR I-6991 (ECLI:EU:C:2006:492).

[8] Case C-438/05, *International Transport Workers' Federation* v. *Viking Line ABP*, [2007] ECR I-10779 (ECLI:EU:C:2007:772); Case C-341/05, *Laval un Partneri*, [2007] ECR I-11767 (ECLI:EU:C:2007:809).

The Court followed its own internal market orthodoxy which should be highly familiar from the examination pursued earlier in this volume. It quickly and easily found that the matter engaged the jurisdiction of the EU with the result that the tension fell to be resolved by exploration of possible justification for trade union practices. So, in line with its long-established case law considered earlier (see Chapter 7), the union action fell within the scope of Article 43 EC (now Article 49 TFEU), even though private parties, unions, were responsible. The right to strike, though explicitly excluded from the scope of EU *legislative* competence in the social policy field (by what is now Article 153(5) TFEU), was not sealed off from free movement law by this proviso.

It therefore followed that collective action which restricts inter-state trade may be taken only on condition that it meets standards recognized by EU law. But in shaping those standards of justification the Court had no mandate set out in the Treaty. Worse, the Treaty actively distanced EU legislative action from any association with this awkward matter of policy through the – *in casu* ineffective – exclusion of the right to strike, found now in Article 153(5) TFEU. So the Court was on new and uncharted territory.

The Court accepted in principle that the right to take collective action to protect workers is a legitimate interest which justifies a restriction of economic freedoms guaranteed by the Treaty. It added that the Community, now Union, has 'not only an economic but also a social purpose'.[9] For those fearful of EU free movement law's deregulatory bite, this is the cheerful part of the judgment. Here the Court seems careful to avoid any rhetorical claim that economic rights and freedoms enjoy any priority over other rights and interests – it is an apparent embrace of the porous nature of free movement law. But then the Court adopted a highly controversial approach. It excluded from the permissible scope of justified practices, collective action taken where jobs or conditions of employment were not jeopardized or under serious threat.[10] So collective action which lacks an intimate connection with the nuts and bolts of a particular labour dispute and which instead has a more long-term strategic and political objective would appear to be unjustifiable in so far as it impedes cross-border commercial activity.

That the EU becomes so heavily involved in such affairs in the name of advancing the internal market is a concern, but it is not structurally out of line with the Court's usual expansive reading of the scope of the free movement provisions. It is the Court's cramped understanding of the possible scope of justification that is out of line with its own practice. Its test which significantly favours corporate interests over worker protection is not the porous law of the internal market so carefully nurtured elsewhere by the Court. And, disturbingly, the Court did not follow the model regularly preferred in the case law considered earlier: it leaves wholly out of account any margin of appreciation apt to permit recognition of local circumstances. The test of justification chosen by the Court in *Viking Line*, which limits the scope of labour unions' autonomy, shows scant regard for the exercise of established routes to

---

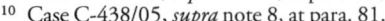

[9]   Case C-438/05, *supra* note 8, at para. 79; Case C-341/05, *supra* note 8, at para. 105.
[10] Case C-438/05, *supra* note 8, at para. 81.

achieve social protection built up over time at national level and often only after struggle and sacrifice by marginalized groups in society. Social constitutional law clashes with economic considerations and emerges bloodied, as locally determined political choices are undermined.[11] And this occurs in circumstances where there is no serious possibility for the balances at stake to be readdressed through the political process at EU level. The astringency of this anxiety has been accentuated in the wake of the judgments. Hopeful, even wistful, nagging by the European Commission ('the Commission') to the effect that 'Political forces have to engage in a search for a solution, in line with the Treaty objective of a social market economy'[12] led to 'Monti II', the Commission Proposal for a Regulation on the exercise of the right to take collective action within the context of the freedom of establishment and the freedom to provide services,[13] which was designed to achieve a modest clarification of the law in this area. It could not be advanced under Article 153 in the TFEU's Title on *Social Policy*, because of Article 153(5)'s exclusion of application to the right to strike, a barrier over which the Court had been able to skip in interpreting free movement law but which stopped *legislative* action dead. So Article 352 TFEU was used instead, which, dauntingly, requires unanimity in Council. The proposal, although in no sense radical in its substance, generated sufficiently fierce political resistance among some Member States, national Parliaments and the European Parliament for the Commission to feel the need to withdraw it.[14] The Commission has absolutely no appetite to try again.

The Court is revealed as immensely powerful. Its orthodox model insists on a very broad reach to free movement law which is then conditioned by a relatively sensitive and context-specific approach to justification. But what if one believes the Court, in assessing justification, has got it *wrong*? Legislative paralysis throws the matter on the mercy of free movement law. And decisions of the Court which interpret primary law – such as *Viking Line* and *Laval* – are not easily shifted because unanimity at the time of Treaty revision needs to be assembled. This is difficult and highly unusual, and should sharpen awareness of the constitutional and institutional choices at stake whenever the Court makes a judgement about how far to push the deregulatory

---

[11] Cf., e.g., Azoulai, 'The Court of Justice and the Social Market Economy: The Emergence of an Ideal and the Conditions for Its Realisation', 45 *Common Market Law Review* (2008) 1335; Davies, 'One Step Forward, Two Steps back? The *Viking* and *Laval* Cases in the ECJ', 37 *Industrial Law Journal* (2008) 126; Joerges and Rödl, 'Informal Politics, Formalised Law and the "Social Deficit" of European Integration: Reflections after the Judgments of the ECJ in *Viking* and *Laval*', 15 *European Law Journal* (2009) 1; Ashiagbor, 'Unravelling the Liberal Bargain: Labour and Social Welfare Law in the Context of EU Market Integration', 19 *European Law Journal* (2013) 303; Nicol, 'Europe's Lochner Moment', *Public Law* (2011) 308; McCann, 'The CJEU on Trial: Economic Mobility and Social Justice', 22 *European Review of Private Law* (2014) 729.
[12] *A New Strategy for the Single Market: At the Service of Europe's Economy and Society*, the 'Monti Report' of May 2010, at 68–69, http://ec.europa.eu/internal_market/strategy/index_en.htm.
[13] COM (2012 130) 21 March 2012.
[14] For the Commission's explanation, see Annual Report 2012 on Subsidiarity and Proportionality, COM (2013) 566, at 6–8; see also 'The Adoptive Parents, 'The Life of a Death Foretold: The Proposal for a Monti II Regulation', in M. Freedland and J. Prassl (eds), *EU Law in the Member States: Viking, Laval and Beyond* (2014) Ch. 5; Fabbrini and Granat, 'Yellow Card But No Foul: The Role of the National Parliaments Under the Subsidiarity Protocol and the Commission Proposal for an EU Regulation on the Right to Strike', 50 *Common Market Law Review* (2013) 115.

consequences of internal market law. And it may also generate exactly the resistance from *national* constitutional courts which in other areas, most notably fundamental rights but also to some extent competence control, has provoked the Court to exercise cautiously responsive sensitivity in its shaping of EU law.

In such circumstances it may be only the Court that can save the Court from itself. Most of all, the mis-step made in *Viking Line* and *Laval* could be corrected by reliance on the reforms made subsequently by the Treaty of Lisbon. The commitment to undistorted competition in the Treaty was there shifted out of the Treaty 'proper' and into a Protocol. This may readily be reckoned to adjust the constitutional balance in favour of socially motivated public regulation at the expense of market competition. So, too, Article 28 of the Charter of Fundamental Rights provides inter alia that workers have the right to take collective action to defend their interests, including strike action – and this is now binding. Moreover, Article 3(3) TEU now commits the EU to inter alia a 'social market'. These do not amount to *definitive* changes to the heartland of internal market law, but were one seeking to defend the (trade-restrictive) expression of social and political freedom in circumstances such as those which arose in *Viking Line* and *Laval*, one would now argue that post-Lisbon the emphasis has shifted. Two Advocates General – Cruz Villalón in *Santos Palhota and others* and Trstenjak in *Commission* v. *Germany*[15] – have already tried to push the Court in these directions, albeit so far without success. What is at stake is to re-balance priorities. There are two distinct routes. The first, the conventional internal market lawyer's approach, would insist on exactly this more refined re-balancing of priorities with consequences sympathetic to social protection.[16] An approach driven by more vigorous scepticism about the credentials of internal market law to show adequate respect for labour rights would draw on the Court's ruling in *Albany*, considered earlier,[17] and press instead for recognition of an immunity from EU law in such circumstances.[18] But the differences between the two routes should not be over-stated. Re-balancing is performed by the Court, but '*Albany* immunity' is also immunity on the terms granted by the Court. Both routes depend on how the internal market as a legal concept is framed. And so both routes run through Luxembourg.

C. Justification and Sensitivity

Viking Line is a serious threat to the legitimacy of the Court's case law. The criticism that the deregulatory cutting edge, which demonstrably cannot be fully compensated for by re-regulation because of a constitutional asymmetry between negative

---

[15] A.G. Cruz Villalón in Case C-515/08, *Santos Palhota and Others*, Opinion (ECLI:EU:C:2010:245); A.G. Trstenjak in Case C-271/08, *Commission* v. *Germany*, Opinion (ECLI:EU:C:2010:183).

[16] See Weatherill '*Viking* and *Laval*: The EU Internal Market Perspective', in Freedland and Prassl, *supra* note 14, Ch. 2. See also Chapter 3.C, especially references in note 11.

[17] Case C-67/96, *Albany International*, [1999] ECR I-5751 (ECLI:EU:C:1999:430). See Chapter 5.B.

[18] See Bogg, '*Viking* and *Laval*: The International Labour Law Perspective', in Freedland and Prassl, *supra* note 14, Ch. 3.

and positive law and because of political blockages to the exercise of such competences as do exist, is met by an orthodox EU internal market lawyer by protesting that EU law guards against *excessive* deregulation by, first, asserting that the reach of EU law has its limits and, secondly, (and frankly much more operationally significant) that there is always space to justify obstructive rules and, where justification is polycontextual, a soft standard of review (engaging a margin of appreciation) is applied. *Viking Line* just cannot be explained in this way: it does not fit. And this is the point on which to conclude. One would certainly understand that if the Court does choose to repent, it will use the reforms made by the Lisbon Treaty as its excuse. That, indeed, is exactly how both Advocates General mentioned earlier structured their Opinions. But the point about *Viking Line* is that even when delivered it was not typical of internal market orthodoxy: it was a perversion of it. The intersection between labour law and EU internal market law should have followed, and should follow, the general pattern whereby sensitive national practices and concerns are treated with care in the light of their impact on the internal market. The Charter of Fundamental Rights (in particular) allows the Court an excuse to backtrack, but the flaws in *Viking Line* and *Laval* are not endemic to internal market law, but rather arise from the Court's own misguided, one-sided approach in those rulings, which even at the time of the rulings was sorely out of line with the orthodoxy of free movement law. The Court's normal approach to justification of obstacles to inter-state trade is context-specific and sensitive.

10

Abuse

It has already been explained how easy it is to create a cross-border dimension to a case, as a means to bring EU law into play, and thereby put the rule-maker on the defensive by requiring it to demonstrate a justification for its practices. Singh was able to challenge his own state's practices because he was returning from another state where he had worked.[1] Carpenter was able to do the same, even though he was still resident in his own state but simply providing services (occasionally) to other Member States.[2] *Ruiz Zambrano*[3] and *Dereci*[4] do not do away with the 'purely internal' situation, but, as explained in Chapter 6.D.3, confine still further the space it occupies.

Is there a risk that it is so easy to invent a cross-border element that in fact the wholly internal situation, whereby a Member State may assert autonomy, is in practice emptied of content?

Is there an overarching 'abuse' control which precludes the obligation cast on a regulator to show justification? The answer is that there is, but it is an ambiguous concept on top of another ambiguous concept, that is, the internal market itself.

'Fictitious' free movement does not count. *Leclerc* v. *Au Blé Vert* concerned French rules requiring books to be sold at the retail price fixed by the publisher.[5] This discouraged the marketing of books published in France but sold elsewhere and then re-imported into France, since it prevented the importer from passing on any advantage resulting from a lower price in the exporting State. It was consequently treated as a barrier to inter-state trade in goods. However, this did not apply to books exported from France 'for the sole purpose of re-importation in order to circumvent legislation of the type at issue'.[6] What seems to be at stake here is the crossing of a frontier as a means to seek to evade the rules of what was the home state and which the migration has converted into the host state – but with no subjection to the rules of the 'new' home state. This is a sham: it is not a cross-border situation at all. EU law does not help. But this situation will be rare, and *Leclerc v Au Blé Vert* is of no general significance to the structure of the law of the internal market.

---

[1] Case C-370/90, *R* v. *IAT and Singh, ex parte Secretary of State*, [1992] ECR I-4265 (ECLI:EU:C:1992:296).

[2] Case C-60/00, *Mary Carpenter*, [2002] ECR I-6279 (ECLI:EU:C:2002:434).

[3] Case C-34/09, *Ruiz Zambrano*, [2011] ECR I-1177 (ECLI:EU:C:2011:124).

[4] Case C-256/11, *Dereci*, [2011] ECR I-11315 (ECLI:EU:C:2011:734).

[5] Case 229/83, *Association des Centres distributeurs Édouard Leclerc et al.* v. *SARL 'Au Blé Vert' et al.*, [1985] ECR 1 (ECLI:EU:C:1985:1).

[6] *Ibid.*, at para. 27.

The Internal Market as a Legal Concept. First Edition. Stephen Weatherill.
© Stephen Weatherill 2017. Published 2017 by Oxford University Press.

Much more interest emerges from cases where the Court has *refused* to allow protests of 'abuse' to shelter the regulatory authority from the obligation to show justification for practices that restrict inter-state trade. This is where the *empowering* force of internal market law shines – and where the trouble in locating its *limits* is plain.

Centros is a gem of an illustration.[7] Centros Ltd was a private limited company registered in England, but since its formation it had never traded in the UK. Its existence was entirely the result of its two shareholders, who were Danish nationals resident in Denmark, realizing they could take advantage of the favourable provisions of company law applicable in the UK compared to that of Denmark, most of all the absence of any requirement relating to a minimum paid-up share capital for such a company. The Danish authorities objected to this strategy, which was plainly designed to exploit for commercial advantage the different burdens imposed by the company laws of the two relevant Member States. They refused to register a *branch* of Centros Ltd in Denmark, insisting that the reality of the matter was attempted evasion of the Danish rules concerning, in particular, the paying-up of minimum capital for a company *established* in Denmark. But the refusal was found to violate EU free movement law. The Court cited – inter alia – *Leclerc v Au Blé Vert*, and stated that:

although, in such circumstances, the national courts may, case by case, take account – on the basis of objective evidence – of abuse or fraudulent conduct on the part of the persons concerned in order, where appropriate, to deny them the benefit of the provisions of Community law on which they seek to rely, they must nevertheless assess such conduct in the light of the objectives pursued by those provisions.[8]

This, in *Centros* itself, was not abuse! In fact, choosing to register a company according to the régime of company law in the EU which was reckoned to be most favourable (i.e., that of the UK), and then to set up a branch in another Member State (i.e., Denmark), was not an abuse, but to the contrary it was the exercise of a choice 'inherent in the exercise, in a single market, of the freedom of establishment guaranteed by the Treaty'.[9] And the Court, interpreting the Treaty in this way to protect free movement by corporate entities, simply treated it as 'of little consequence' that company law was not harmonized across the EU.

The ruling has something in common with the cases on consumer protection considered in Chapter 8.F: the Court accepts that, in principle, a targeted control on fraud or related pernicious practices could be lawfully applied by Denmark even where a restriction to free movement follows, but the blanket refusal to admit branches onto Danish territory simply because of non-compliance with host state rules went too far. This was no abuse: this was the internal market in vigorous action. *Centros* does not assert complete transfer of regulatory responsibility away from the host state to the home state. The free movement rules never, in principle, go so far. Firmly in line with the *Cassis* model of conditional mutual recognition, this promotes inter-jurisdictional competition and choice (here, in matters of company law) by upholding access to the wider EU market in reliance on home state rules, excepting only

---

[7] Case C-212/97, *Centros*, [1999] ECR I-1459 (ECLI:EU:C:1999:126).
[8] *Ibid.*, at para. 25.   [9] *Ibid.*, at para. 27.

circumstances where a host state is able to show a coherent and sincere justification for insisting on the application of its own local rules.[10]

Abundant case law has clarified just when restrictions on corporate mobility in these type of circumstances are treated as justified: exhaustive treatment goes beyond the scope of this volume.[11] The general picture, however, suggests that 'abuse' is not a helpful *new* notion in internal market law. In fact, it is another way to frame the basic structural point that a State wishing to place a restriction on free movement must demonstrate an adequate justification for its practices. An allegation of 'abuse' of free movement invites an assessment of whether the host state rules are apt for application to the alleged abuser. The mere fact that a trader has chosen to operate in another jurisdiction and then to target its original jurisdiction is not of itself abusive: it does not automatically disentitle the trader from putting the obstructive rules of the original jurisdiction to the test set by the law of the internal market.

The Court needs to be alert to the risk that invocation of 'abuse' amounts to the last refuge of the scoundrel regulator. In *Torresi and Torresi* an Italian Bar Council refused to register lawyers who held an Italian law degree, and had then obtained a Spanish law degree and secured registration in Spain.[12] This, the Bar Council argued with reference to the Court's case law, was an abuse. But it was not. It was, the Court correctly concluded, simply the exercise of a fundamental freedom. 'Abuse' remains part of the Court's case law and it deploys it in particular in tax law, where in *SICES* it brought together a stream of its own case law to rule that EU law does not protect 'abusive practices by economic operators, that is to say transactions carried out not in the context of normal commercial operations, but solely for the purpose of wrongfully obtaining advantages under EU law', adding that a finding of abusive practices requires a combination of objective and subjective elements.[13] The case law, however, resists simple explanation.[14] In general, internal market law is not obviously improved by adoption of a discrete line of inquiry rooted in 'abuse'. It is best treated as another basis on which to initiate an inquiry into whether a host state's rules which restrict inter-state trade are justified.

[10] Cf. Schammo, 'Arbitrage and Abuse of Rights in the EC Legal System', 14 *European Law Journal* (2008) 351; Saydé, 'One Law, Two Competitions: An Inquiry into the Contradictions of Free Movement Law', 13 (2010–11) 365; B. Gabor, *Regulatory Competition in the Internal Market: Comparing Models for Corporate Law, Securities Law and Competition Law* (2013).

[11] See, e.g., *Wyatt and Dashwood's European Union Law* (6th ed., 2011), at 649–658.

[12] Cases C-58/13 and C-59/13, *Torresi and Torresi*, judgment of 17 July 2014, not yet reported (ECLI:EU:C:2014:2088).

[13] Case C-155/13, *SICES and Others*, judgment of 13 March 2014 (ECLI:EU:C:2014:145), at paras 30–33. See also especially Case C-255/02, *Halifax plc, Leeds Permanent Development Services Ltd, County Wide Property Investments Ltd* v. *Commissioners of Customs & Excise*, [2006] ECR I-1609 (ECLI:EU:C:2006:121); Case C-196/04, *Cadbury Schweppes plc, Cadbury Schweppes Overseas Ltd* v. *Commissioners of Inland Revenue* [2006] ECR I-7995 (ECLI:EU:C:2006:544).

[14] For thorough treatment, see A. Saydé, *Abuse of EU Law and Regulation of the Internal Market* (2014).

11

Fundamental Rights and National Identity in the Internal Market

In *Fransson* the Court of Justice of the European Union ('the Court') declared that '[t]he applicability of EU law entails applicability of the fundamental rights guaranteed by the Charter'.[1] And this must cover also internal market law, in both its positive and its negative aspects: it must be compliant with fundamental rights. So free movement law is not only about free movement; competition law is not only about competition. But this is not new. It has, in fact, been one of the thematic underpinnings of the narrative presented in this volume. Economic rights recognized by the Charter of Fundamental Rights ('the Charter') run in parallel to the free movement rights contained in the Treaty on the Functioning of the European Union (TFEU).[2] And they are equally capable of being shown to be justifiably restricted by national measures. Here, as shown already in Chapter 8 in connection with matters such as health, environmental and consumer protection, the story is of how the Charter confirms and consolidates the Court's commitment to respect for regulatory values expressed through national choices and viewed through the prism of justification, but the Charter is not transformative of internal market law. But this, in common with the examination conducted earlier, does *not* mean that the detailed task of adjudication pressed on and accepted by the Court is simple. This is explored here in circumstances where the national measures that restrict inter-state trade engage matters associated with the protection of nationally recognized fundamental rights and with national identity. Free movement was itself described in *Cassis de Dijon* as 'one of the fundamental rules' of the EU,[3] so here it now collides with quite differently motivated social and political but also fundamental values. The truth is that the Court has been rather promiscuous and indiscriminate in attaching the label 'fundamental' to the provisions on free movement and competition. There is a normative case to be made that it should separate out those rights which protect the individual

---

[1] Case C-617/10, *Fransson*, judgment of 26 February 2013, not yet reported (ECLI:EU:C:2013:280), at para. 21.
[2] Especially Arts 15, 16 and 17 of the Charter. See Case C-390/12, *Pfleger*, judgment of 30 April 2014, not yet reported (ECLI:EU:C:2014:281) (Art. 56 TFEU); Case C-98/14, *Berlington Hungary and Others*, judgment of 11 June 2015, not yet reported (ECLI:EU:C:2015:386) (Art. 56 TFEU); Case C-367/12, *Susanne Sokoll-Seebacher*, judgment of 13 February 2014, not yet reported (ECLI:EU: C:2014:68) (Art. 49 TFEU).
[3] Case 120/78, *Rewe-Zentrale AG* v. *Bundesmonopolverwaltung für Branntwein*, [1979] ECR 649 (ECLI:EU:C:1979:42), at para. 14.

The Internal Market as a Legal Concept. First Edition. Stephen Weatherill.
© Stephen Weatherill 2017. Published 2017 by Oxford University Press.

person from those of less weight associated with goods and capital, and which are instrumentally confined to the construction of the internal market.[4] Not the least of the advantages would be to allow a sharper focus on choice of priorities. But, in practice, the Court's inquiry into justification gives it the opportunity to convert the rather imprecisely generous recitation of the language of fundamental rights into something more concrete and context-specific, as it has to decide when interests expressed through national rules are strong enough to withstand the deregulatory impacts of free movement law. Blackcurrant liqueur may have been the source, but the taste is richer now.

A. Early Years, Early Cases

The emergence and development of fundamental rights principles within the EU legal order is a familiar tale, but its nurturing mainly occurred in the context of review of EU *legislative* measures. The issue here is to establish how 'porous' are the free movement rules to fundamental rights.

The first ruling was as late as 1991. In *ERT* v. *Dimotiki* the Court insisted on an interpretation of the scope of the freedom to provide services 'in the light of the general principle of freedom of expression embodied in Article 10 of the European Convention on Human Rights'.[5] This means that the space allowed under internal market to national authorities seeking to justify measures that restrict inter-state trade (here, in television broadcasting) is conditional on compliance with the fundamental rights guaranteed under EU law (here, freedom of expression).

This set the tone. Free movement law was not divorced from fundamental rights; rather, the two were intimately connected in that the former was infused by the obligation to respect the latter. Case law opened up room for the Court to elaborate what was at stake. *Vereinigte Familiapress Zeitungsverlags- und vertriebs GmbH* v. *Heinrich Bauer Verlag* involved Austrian rules preventing the inclusion of inter alia prize crosswords in newspapers for fear that such strategies, if unleashed, would allow a small number of large and powerful (presumably German) publishers to acquire control of the Austrian market.[6] The Court accepted that maintenance of press diversity, which is a means to promote the vibrancy of democratic contestation, may constitute a justification for a restriction on free movement of goods because such diversity helps to safeguard freedom of expression, which itself counts as one of the fundamental rights guaranteed by EU law. But this, it agreed, might interfere with the rights of free movement enjoyed by publishers accustomed to offering prize crosswords – and they too had a plausible claim to exercise freedom of expression.

---

[4] Cf. De Cecco, 'Fundamental Freedoms, Fundamental Rights and the Scope of Free Movement Law', 15 *German Law Journal* (2014) 383; J. Baquero Cruz, *Between Competition and Free Movement: The Economic Constitutional Law of the European Community* (2002); Kingreen, 'Fundamental Freedoms', in A. Von Bogdandy and J. Bast, *Principles of European Constitutional Law* (2nd ed., 2010).

[5] Case C-260/89, *ERT* v. *Dimotiki*, [1991] ECR I-2925 (ECLI:EU:C:1991:254), at paras 43, 45.

[6] Case C-368/95, *Vereinigte Familiapress Zeitungsverlags- und vertriebs GmbH* v. *Heinrich Bauer Verlag*, [1997] ECR I-3689 (ECLI:EU:C:1997:325).

Fundamental rights armed *both* the regulator *and* the cross-border trader: the Court left to the referring national court the awkward choice as to which side should prevail. The lesson of the case, however, is that the rich diet of cases fed to the Court causes internal market law to require an interpretation that is sensitive to the demands of fundamental rights. The Court in *Herbert Karner GmbH* v. *Troostwijk GmbH* began to embroider the account by ranking *commercial* freedom of expression below its *political* counterpart, meaning that review of interference by national authorities with the former would be less intrusive than the latter.[7] This sense of priority was, the Court made plain, intended to align internal market law with the case law of European Court of Human Rights.[8]

B. *Schmidberger* and *Omega*

Schmidberger v. *Austria* offered the Court a beautifully simple opportunity to address some fiendishly awkward questions of principle.[9] The Austrian authorities decided to permit a protest which attempted to draw attention to environmental damage by blocking the movement of transport carrying goods through the Brenner Pass, a key north-south transalpine route. This led to an obstacle to trade in goods for almost 30 hours while the protest continued, and fell within the scope of Article 34 as a measure (not) taken by a public authority.[10] But was it justified? It was, after all, motivated by a concern to protect the freedom of assembly and freedom of expression of those wishing to object to such trade. This inevitably drew the Court into areas of adjudication that are sensitive and difficult for any court, let alone a transnational court.

The Court declared that:

since both the Community and its Member States are required to respect fundamental rights, the protection of those rights is a legitimate interest which, in principle, justifies a restriction of the obligations imposed by Community law, even under a fundamental freedom guaranteed by the Treaty such as the free movement of goods …[11]

So free movement law encompasses fundamental rights which conflict – the economic versus the political. They are fundamental rights, but they are not absolute rights, for both free movement and freedom of expression may justifiably be limited. But, to resolve the case, one or the other must prevail. The Court ruled that 'the interests involved must be weighed having regard to all the circumstances of the case in order to determine whether a fair balance was struck between those interests' and it added that '[t]he competent authorities enjoy a wide margin of discretion in that regard'.[12]

---

[7] Case C-71/02, *Herbert Karner GmbH* v. *Troostwijk GmbH*, [2004] ECR I-3025 (ECLI:EU: C:2004:181).

[8] *Ibid.*, para. 51.

[9] Case C-112/00, *Schmidberger* v. *Austria*, [2003] ECR I-5659 (ECLI:EU:C:2003:333).

[10] The protesters – private parties – were *not* caught: see Chapter 7.

[11] Case C-112/00, *supra* note 9, at para. 74.

[12] *Ibid.*, at paras 81–82.

The Court then proceeded actively to assess the 'balance' to which it referred. It noted that the obstruction was to a single route, on a single occasion and for a limited period (of 30 hours), and that advance notice had been given to allow traders to make alternative plans. The Court was impressed in particular that there was no 'general climate of insecurity such as to have a dissuasive effect' on intra-EU trade.[13] In this, in particular, it was able to make more vivid its point by contrasting the situation in Austria with the unjustified failure of the French authorities to suppress regular violent protests against and destruction of imported fruit and vegetables by farmers in an earlier case.[14] The Court made plain that the Austrian (lack of) action against those conducting the protests did not constitute a violation of EU law. The restrictive effect on cross-border trade in goods, though fully acknowledged, was treated as justified. The national authorities, enjoying a wide margin of discretion, were entitled to conclude that a ban on the protest would have been an unacceptable interference with the fundamental rights of the demonstrators.

The Court's readiness to permit justification is structurally consistent with its approach throughout the law governing free movement, but the discourse of 'balancing' adds something new and reflects the sensitivities at stake. It is common for the Court to rely on the proportionality principle to find a polite way to reject justifications which are plain stupid. So, for example, in *Walter Rau* v. *de Smedt* the Court accepted that in principle legislation designed to prevent butter and margarine from being confused in the mind of the consumer would be justified, but achieving that objective through mandatory rules on use of a specific kind of (cube-shaped) packaging 'considerably' exceeded the requirements of the object in view.[15] The Court could have been more rude about a rule that was simply inappropriate in an integrating market. But ultimately there are much more genuine conflicts of values that fall to be addressed by internal market law and *Schmidberger* provides an example. A discourse of 'balancing' allied to a margin of appreciation granted to the regulator, which carries a flavour of general human rights law rather than the more intense, even sceptical, review conventionally associated with the Court's case law in the often protectionist economic heartland of free movement law, is the Court's way to embed sensitivity to the complexity of the calculations at stake in the interplay of economic integration with social and political freedoms.

Further insight into the Court's technique is provided by *Omega Spielhallen*.[16] The Bonn police authority imposed a ban on a game involving simulated killing, called 'Laserdrome', on the basis that such practices offended against standards of respect for human dignity that were constitutionally protected in Germany. The Court treated the matter as a restriction on the free movement of services from the UK. The Court had 'no doubt that the objective of protecting human dignity' was compatible with EU law and added that it was 'immaterial in that respect that, in Germany, the principle of respect for human dignity has a particular status as an independent

---

[13] *Ibid.*, at para. 88
[14] Case C-265/95, *Commission* v. *France*, [1997] ECR I-6959 (ECLI:EU:C:1997:595).
[15] Case 261/81, *Walter Rau* v. *de Smedt*, [1982] ECR 3961 (ECLI:EU:C:1982:382), at para. 17.
[16] Case C-36/02, *Omega Spielhallen*, [2004] ECR I-9609 (ECLI:EU:C:2004:614).

fundamental right'.[17] In this way the Court nimbly avoided constructing the matter as EU free movement law *versus* protection of human dignity under German law, but instead viewed it as EU free movement law *versus* protection of human dignity under EU law. Today it could confirm this approach by citing Article 1 of the Charter, which expressly embraces human dignity as inviolable, but in *Omega*, fully five years in advance of the grant of binding effect on the Charter, the Court was able to shape an EU recognition of a standard of protection in the context of examining the justification advanced according to the particular sensitivities emerging in one Member State. Other Member States are less fastidious than Germany about such games, but the Court, in its treatment of justification, ensured that German anxieties about the damaging effect of trade integration were accommodated as EU anxieties. Human dignity matters more than cheese, but *structurally* this is just the same as *Eyssen*![18] The internal market as a legal concept is porous to non-economic values, and the Court added explicitly that 'the competent national authorities must therefore be allowed a margin of discretion within the limits imposed by the Treaty'.[19]

C. National Identity

The Lisbon Treaty, which came into force in 2009, re-shaped and expanded a provision which is a candidate for framing the whole debate about competing values and the role of national autonomy within the internal market. According to Article 4(2) TEU:

The Union shall respect the equality of Member States before the Treaties as well as their national identities, inherent in their fundamental structures, political and constitutional, inclusive of regional and local self-government. It shall respect their essential State functions, including ensuring the territorial integrity of the State, maintaining law and order and safeguarding national security. In particular, national security remains the sole responsibility of each Member State.

This is the successor to Article 6(3) TEU which, pre-Lisbon, provided that '[t]he Union shall respect the national identities of its Member States'. Article 4(2) TEU counts as a significantly elaborated version and offers itself as a basis for showing a higher level of respect for national diversity than previously, inter alia in connection with free movement law's application to national restrictions. On the other hand, rulings such as *Omega Spielhallen* and *Schmidberger* challenge any claim that prior to 2009 justification of trade barriers has *not* been receptive to the possibility of showing just why national constitutional sensitivities should be tolerated even where they impede cross-border trade. So, once again, the impact of the Lisbon Treaty on internal market law is probably best seen as confirmatory rather than transformative.

Ilonka Sayn-Wittgenstein v. *Landeshauptmann von Wien*, already addressed in Chapter 6, offers a testing ground.[20] The dispute was caused by a difference dating

---

[17] *Ibid.*, at para. 34. [18] Case 53/80, *Eyssen*, [1981] ECR 409 (ECLI:EU:C:1981:35).
[19] *Ibid.*, at para. 31.
[20] Case C-208/09, *Ilonka Sayn-Wittgenstein* v. *Landeshauptmann von Wien*, [2010] ECR I-13693 (ECLI:EU:C:2010:806), see Chapter 6.D.2.

back to 1919 between Austria, which prohibits use of noble titles, and Germany, which has abolished the associated privileges without completely banning use of parts of a noble title in a person's surname. So in Austria, the applicant could not use the name she was known by in Germany. This was a restriction of the freedom envisaged by Article 21 TFEU, the heart of the ruling, although Article 56 TFEU on the free movement of services was readily engaged too. It was the scope for justification of the Austrian rule that really mattered.

The Court was receptive to the Austrian concern, expressed at a constitutional level, to abolish titles in the service of equality of citizens before the law. It referred in this vein to Article 20 of the – by this time binding – Charter of Fundamental Rights, which concerns equality, and it then observed that in accordance with Article 4(2) TEU the EU is to respect the national identities of its Member States and that it did not appear disproportionate for a Member State to seek to attain the objective of protecting equal treatment by prohibiting use of titles of nobility.[21]

The Court's approach has much in common with that which it took in *Omega Spielhallen*. As in that case, it converted an appeal to *national* constitutional values into assessment of justification recognized by *EU* law: equality under the Charter plus Article 4(2)'s direction to respect concern for national identity. Moreover, it cited *Omega Spielhallen* in treating this as a sensitive issue, where national authorities are permitted a 'margin of discretion'.[22]

Article 4(2) acts as the gateway through which national constitutional concerns enter EU law in general and internal market law in particular *as specifically EU concerns*. It is not that EU law defers to national law as a superior norm, but rather it is that EU law has within it an EU conception of deference to national constitutional values. Internal market law is porous. This cannot mean *automatic* subjection to a state's appeal to its constitutional values. A test of justification softened to such a degree would destroy the aim of market integration completely. Too broad a view of national identity (whether at EU or at national level) disables the very core of the EU's mission and method of functioning, while too narrow an approach reduces national identity to impotent symbol (and may, if perpetrated by the Court in Luxembourg, risk provoking national courts to aggressive protection of their conceptions of national identity). Sinisa Rodin has in this vein intelligently argued for a separation between national identity writ large and national identity writ small – and he also argues for a check on resort to national identity informed by Article 2 TEU, meaning that a state could not claim to protect national identity in circumstances where that would contradict the EU's *values*.[23] Defence of constitutional identity must not be permitted to become the last desperate catch-all attempt by a regulator to defend the status quo against the cleansing effect of EU

---

[21] *Ibid.*, at paras 92–93. See also Case C-391/09, *Runevic-Vardyn*, [2011] ECR I-3787 (ECLI:EU:C:2011:291); Case C-202/11, *Anton Las*, judgment of 16 April 2013, not yet reported (ECLI:EU:C:2013:239).

[22] Case C-208/09, *supra* note 20, at para. 87.

[23] Rodin, 'National Identity and Market Freedoms after the Treaty of Lisbon', 7 *Crotian Yearbook of European Law and Policy* (2011) 11.

trade law.[24] So the Court needs to be rigorous in forestalling the transformation of feeble economic and social justifications into claimed protection of national identity, while also, as in *Omega* and *Sayn-Wittgenstein* and other cases too,[25] taking seriously its more valid pretensions. Article 4(2) frames this debate, nudging respect for national identity but not acting as a 'hard' protection of exaggerated national reliance upon it.

Article 4(2) EU must not be used in opportunistic fashion. But used with sincerity – both in Luxembourg *and* by national courts – it is able to serve as the pivot: it is a means to open up EU law to national constitutional concerns while still laying formal claim to the supremacy of EU law over national law.[26] It has a functional similarity to the margin of appreciation which, as explained earlier, has infiltrated EU law but which has been more fully elaborated in European human rights law: the purpose is to mediate the struggle between pluralism and uniformity.[27] True, there is risk here of complacent anticipation that all is for the best in the best of all possible worlds, but the interpretation *so far* placed on Article 4(2) is vivid proof of the Court's ambition to ensure the porous nature of the EU's internal market as a legal concept even – perhaps especially – where national constitutional values are invoked.

---

[24] Cf. also on the need to avoid absolute reservations on the reach of EU law applied at national level, e.g., AG Maduro in Case C-213/07, *Michaniki*, [2008] ECR I-9999 (ECLI:EU:C:2008:731), at para. 33; A.G. Cruz Villalón in Case C-62/14, *Gauweiler*, judgment of 16 June 2015, not yet reported (ECLI:EU:C:2015:7), at para. 59.

[25] See also, e.g., Case C-156/13, *Digibet*, judgment of 12 June 2014, not yet reported (ECLI:EU:C:2014:1756): the federal division of competence in Germany may not be called into question by free movement law.

[26] Cf. Von Bogdandy and Schill, 'Overcoming Absolute Primacy: Respect for National Identity under the Lisbon Treaty', 48 *Common Market Law Review* (2011) 1417; Guastaferro, 'Beyond the Exceptionalism of Constitutional Conflicts. The Ordinary Functions of the Identity Clause', 31 *Yearbook of European Law* (2012) 263; Dobbs, 'Sovereignty, Article 4(2) TEU and the Respect of National Identities: Swinging the Balance of Power in Favour of the Member States?', 33 *Yearbook of European Law* (2014) 298; Konstadinides, 'Dealing with Parallel Universes: Antimonies of Sovereignty and the Protection of National Identity in European Judicial Discourse', 34 *Yearbook of European Law* (2015) 127; Van der Schyff, 'The Constitutional Relationship between the European Union and its Member States: The Role of National Identity in Article 4(2) TEU', 37 *European Law Review* (2012) 37.

[27] Cf. Spielmann, 'Whither the Margin of Appreciation?', 67 *Current Legal Problems* (2014) 49.

12

The Internal Market as a Site of Diversity

The cases which engage fundamental rights and national identity as justifications for trade barriers are a long stretch from the problems posed by blackcurrant liqueur, tourist guides and packs of margarine. The Court of Justice of the European Union ('the Court'), building in a margin of discretion for the regulator and embracing 'balancing', does not alter the structure of its older, more sceptical, approach – it looks for a trade barrier and assesses whether it is justified – but, in reflection of the nature of the far more sincere arguments advanced, it ensures that free movement law has become a more texturally rich landscape in response to the richer diet provided by its caseload. Assessing justification demands a creative Court: 'balancing' is a delightfully dignified notion, but a stern test of practical adjudication. The internal market as a legal concept, built on a shared competence to open up markets and to regulate them, forces the Court to develop its own notion of what is proper and tolerable when pursued at national level. This too is not new as such: it is a rhythm that tends to be concealed in the many cases argued before the Court involving frankly stupid – or, more politely, disproportionate – national measures, but it is visible in the cases on public health, environmental law, consumer protection and, extending to competition law, sport and professional regulation, in which seriously considered national policies have been entrusted to the Court's review in the framework of justification. The law of the internal market is not *exclusively* concerned with levering open national restrictions on cross-border trading freedom and, indeed, if one is prepared to accept the good faith of the Court in these cases which engage a margin of discretion and balancing, it is not even *mainly* about cross-border trading freedom. It is a site of diversity.

The internal market as a site of diversity is shaped by the super-structure provided by the Treaty on the Functioning of the European Union (TFEU), but it is also heavily dependent on the particular interpretative approaches chosen by the Court. There is *the diversity of products and services* that prevails in the market where the Court rules that an obstructive national measure may not be applied to restrain importation because it is not justified. And there is *the diversity of national rules* that prevails when the Court rules that a national measure is beyond the reach of free movement law or where it rules that an obstructive national measure is justified and so may be applied within the internal market despite its prejudicial impact on trade integration.

The Internal Market as a Legal Concept. First Edition. Stephen Weatherill.
© Stephen Weatherill 2017. Published 2017 by Oxford University Press.

The Court's interpretation of the scope of free movement law is generally broad. The approach pioneered in and sustained since *Dassonville*[1] and *Cassis de Dijon*[2] reduces the scope of national regulatory autonomy (the vertical issue) while also eliminating the need for political intervention at EU level to introduce harmonization legislation (the horizontal issue). It has profound implications for the shape of the internal market. The European Commission ('the Commission') grasped this immediately. It published a Notice in 1980 which was vividly perceptive on the vertical and horizontal implications of the ruling in *Cassis*: 'Member States, when drawing up commercial or technical rules liable to affect the free movement of goods, may not take an exclusively national viewpoint and take account only of requirements confined to domestic products' and 'The Commission's work of harmonization will henceforth have to be directed mainly at national laws having an impact on the functioning of the common market where barriers to trade to be removed arise from national provisions which are admissible under the criteria set by the Court'.[3] So pleased was the Commission with *Cassis* that it made exactly this thematic readiness to reduce the intensity of the programme of legislative harmonization and instead to place heavier reliance on judge-driven free movement law, central to the agenda set by the White Paper on completion of the internal market, published in June 1985.[4] In its 'Internal Market Strategy' of 2003 it described conditional mutual recognition as 'a corner stone of the Internal Market'.[5]

Had the Court in *Cassis* declined to employ Article 34 TFEU in the case of diverse but non-discriminatory technical standards, then a vast amount of harmonization would have been required to tackle such market-fragmenting regulatory diversity. This, as the Commission put it in 1985, would have been 'over-regulatory...inflexible and could stifle innovation'.[6] The Court protects the EU's internal market from this outcome by its willingness to let directly effective free movement law bite even where legislative intervention has not: it did it in *Cassis de Dijon*[7], it did it in *Centros*[8] and it did it in *Reyners*, one of its earliest judgments on recognition of professional qualifications driven by the Treaty freedoms without a need for their legislative amplification.[9] This is a vivid insight into how the Court's interpretation of free movement law is capable of affecting the allocation of constitutional and institutional power within the EU.[10]

---

[1] Case 8/74, *Dassonville*, [1974] ECR 837 (ECLI:EU:C:1974:82).

[2] Case 120/78, *Rewe-Zentrale AG* v. *Bundesmonopolverwaltung für Branntwein*, [1979] ECR 649 (ECLI:EU:C:1979:42).

[3] OJ 1980 C 256/2. See Mattera, 'Protectionism Inside the European Community: Decisions of the European Court', 18 *Journal of World Trade Law* (1984) 283.

[4] COM (85) 310, especially paras 57 et seq. *Cassis* is the 'founding myth' of the single market programme: Nicolaïdis, 'Kir Forever?', in M. Maduro and L. Azoulai (eds), *The Past and Future of EU Law* (2010) 449.

[5] COM (2003) 238.   [6] White Paper *supra* note 4, para. 64.

[7] Case 120/78, *supra* note 2.

[8] Case C-212/97, *Centros*, [1999] ECR I-1459 (ECLI:EU:C:1999:126).

[9] Case 2/74, *Reyners*, [1974] ECR 631 (ECLI:EU:C:1974:68).

[10] Cf. e.g., Snell, 'Who's Got the Power? Free Movement and Allocation of Competences in EC Law', 22 *Yearbook of European Law* (2003) 323; Weatherill, 'Pre-Emption, Harmonisation and the Distribution of Competence to Regulate the Internal Market', in J. Scott and C. Barnard (eds), *The Law of the Single European Market* (2002) Ch. 2; Bernard, 'La libre circulation des marchandises, des person-

This is not simply an abstract remark. The point that internal markets take different shapes the world over is made with force by comparing the EU experience with that of Canada. There is no equivalent to *Cassis de Dijon* in Canada. The reach of federal inter-state trade law is limited to judicial control of discriminatory measures. In 1995 the AIT (the Agreement of Internal Trade) was struck to extend control beyond discrimination between the provinces. So Canada does by political process what the EU does through courts – and Canada, though doubtless possessing an internal market and clearly a state in its own right, possesses a space that is less economically integrated than the EU.[11] Other jurisdictions would tell stories that are structurally familiar but different in detail.[12] WTO law, too, faces structurally analogous questions about the reach of its review power over national regulatory autonomy and, as a general observation founded on its relatively less ambitious political aims and much thinner rule-making capacity, it tends to show a more restrained attitude than the EU.[13] Such questions of design are also among the many provoking controversy in the negotiation of a 'Transatlantic Trade and Investment Partnership' (TTIP) between the EU and the United States: how much regulatory autonomy should be broken open and subjected to review, by whom and according to what standards?[14]

This extends beyond an exercise in empowering the judiciary and private litigants at the expense of the EU legislature. The Court's choice also had significant implications for the map of the internal market. More harmonization would have meant more uniformity: more 'Europroducts' produced according to uniform standards. The Court's preference for more a generous application of Article 34 TFEU means more variety and choice in the internal market – different kinds of liqueur, beers, tourist guides and cheese. This institutional implication was made very clear in the

---

nes et des services dans le Traité CE sous l'angle de la compétence' 34 *Cahiers de droit européen* (1998) 11; Saydé, 'One Law, Two Competitions: An Inquiry into the Contradictions of Free Movement Law', 13 *Cambridge Yearbook of European Legal Studies* (2010–11) 365.

[11] Hinarejos, 'Free Movement, Federalism and Institutional Choice: A Canada-EU Comparison', 71 *Cambridge Law Journal* (2012) 537.

[12] E.g., Staker, 'Free Movement of Goods in the EEC and Australia: A Comparative Study', 10 *Yearbook of European Law* (1990) 209; Knook, 'Guns and Tobacco: The Effect of Interstate Trade Case Law on the Vertical Division of Powers', 11 *Maastricht Journal* (2004) 347. The store of 'comparative integration studies' is relatively meagre – it is especially surprising that more has not been done to follow up the trail blazed by M. Cappelletti, M. Seccombe and J. Weiler (eds), *Integration through Law: Europe and the American Federal Experience* (1986), though the earth is not entirely scorched, see, e.g., K. Nicolaidis and R. Howse, *The Federal Vision: Legitimacy and Levels of Governance in the United States and the European Union* (2001); D. Augenstein (ed.), *Integration through Law Revisited: The Making of the European Polity* (2012); E. Fahey and D. Curtin (eds), *A Transatlantic Community of Law: Legal Perspectives on the Relationship between the EU and US Legal Orders* (2014).

[13] See, e.g., Diebold, 'Standards of Non-Discrimination in International Economic Law', 60 *International and Comparative Law Quarterly* (2011) 831; Ming Du, 'The Rise of National Regulatory Autonomy in the GATT/ WTO Regime', 14 *Journal of International Economic Law* (2011) 639; S. Gaines, B. Olsen and K. Sorensen (eds), *Liberalising Trade in the EU and the WTO* (2012).

[14] See, e.g., Lester and Barbee, 'The Challenge of Cooperation: Regulatory Trade Barriers in the Transatlantic Trade and Investment Partnership', 16 *Journal of International Economic Law* (2013) 847; and more generally still Correia de Brito, Kauffmann and Pelkmans, 'The Contribution of Mutual Recognition to International Regulatory Co-Operation', OECD Regulatory Working Papers No. 2 (2016).

Italian pasta case, *Drei Glocken*, discussed earlier.[15] Advocate General Mancini, who would have found the rigid Italian product composition rules to be justified as means of consumer protection, advocated, instead, that the matter of how to make pasta should await legislative treatment at EU level. The Court's judgment, holding the Italian rules to be an unjustified barrier to importation of differently made pasta, buried the banal spectre of 'Europasta'.

An appealing consequence of this model is that the competence to regulate is not left exclusively in the hands of either the home or the host state, nor is it transferred to the EU's legislature. Instead, the model of conditional or non-absolute host state control involves a distribution of regulatory competences consequent on scrutiny of the merits of the competing claims. The host state regulates the matter – as long as it shows it has a sufficient reason to do so. It may not simply point to its rulebook and tell an importer 'this is how we do things here': it must *justify* its rulebook. So internal market law gives private parties what they do not possess politically: an ability to put trade restrictions adopted in their target state *to the test*.[16] In the absence of adequate justification, home state control is treated as adequate and costly dual regulation within the internal market is thereby averted. Improved economic performance is pushed by directly effective *legal* rights vindicated by parties with no *political* voice in the regulating jurisdiction. And regulatory diversity, promoting choice and variety in the product and service markets of the EU, persists free of the imposition of common rules 'from above', by the EU as (harmonized) lawmaker.

The Court's model reduces the costs of harmonization, measured both in the energy that must be expended by the lawmakers, and the suppression of diverse preference and innovative potential. But cost *free* it is not. Costs are delayed, and they arise when traders find they can break down rules which are stubbornly defended by national regulators only by resort to litigation. Under a harmonized regime traders would have a higher degree of confidence they can penetrate markets in other Member States than prevails under the model of non-absolute mutual recognition. The anxiety, then, is that the elegance *on paper* of *Cassis de Dijon* in particular, and free movement law generally, is not matched by its practical worth. These costs are hard to quantify, not least because they need to be measured in failure even to bother incurring the costs of litigation with an uncertain outcome in order to try to penetrate new markets, and not simply in thwarted attempts and in delayed success. Some respite has been provided by legislative requirements imposed on Member States to notify planned technical standards and other product-specific interventions to the Commission with a view to promoting a screening process apt to prevent

---

[15] Case 407/85, *Drei Glocken v. USL Centro-Sud*, [1988] ECR 4233 (ECLI:EU:C:1988:401). See Chapter 8.F.

[16] No more than a nod to a rich literature is possible here: see, e.g., M. Maduro, *We, The Court: The European Court of Justice and the European Economic Constitution* (1998); Joerges, 'A New Type of Conflicts Law as the Legal Paradigm of the Postnational Constellation', in C. Joerges and J. Falke (eds), *Karl Polanyi, Globalisation and the Potential of Law in Transnational Markets* (2011); Chalmers, 'Administrative Globalisation and Curbing the Excesses of the State', in C. Joerges and U. Petersmann (eds), *Constitutionalism, Multilevel Trade Governance and International Economic Law* (2nd ed., 2011); Somek, 'The Argument from Transnational Effects', 16 *European Law Journal* (2010) 315 and 375.

trade barriers coming into being in the first place,[17] and that regime has been strengthened further by the Court's astute finding that un-notified measures are unenforceable before national courts.[18] Moreover the Court has also strengthened the Commission's supervisory powers by agreeing that a technical standard governing product composition shall include (what it called) a 'mutual recognition clause' permitting products lawfully marketed in another Member State to be marketed in the regulated territory.[19] But the regime of obligatory notification is neither comprehensive nor unerringly adhered to by Member State authorities and the same is true of the obligation to include a (so-called) mutual recognition clause. The road to effective management of and administrative co-operation in the internal market is well-intentioned but rocky.[20] Therefore a heavy weight still rests on reactive litigation to root out many unmeritorious obstacles to the functioning of the internal market.

But the biggest questions associated with any *qualitative* assessment of the Court's chosen model for the internal market surround its treatment of justification. This is where priorities are revealed and entrenched. The inquiry is already intriguing in cases such as *Cassis de Dijon* and its progeny, where the Court has decided to bite without awaiting the attention of the EU legislature. It is especially sensitive in cases like *Watts*, *Bosman* and *Viking Line* where the issue is not that the Court chooses to bite before the legislature, but where in fact the legislature is not able to bite because of constitutional and/or political blockages.

The deregulatory dynamic in internal market law is visible in the string of decisions in which – unjustified and often absurd – national measures have been squashed by the impetus towards an integrated market. Most cases are decided in favour of cross-border trade, but since the development of the internal market confronts the deadwood of centuries of regulatory tradition in all the Member States, combined with occasional bouts of devious or sometimes blatant protectionism, this is no surprise. The whole point of the exercise is regulatory renovation. Often, the Court is engaged in weeding out unrepresentative and outdated manifestations of national-level decision-making that are hostile to, and inappropriate in, an integrating European market of the type to which the Member States have committed themselves. But the Court's insistence, in line with the TFEU, that cross-border trading freedom is not absolute, is matched by its readiness in appropriate cases to take seriously the

---

[17] Directive 98/34, OJ 1998 L 204/37 as amended, now codified in Directive 2015/1535, OJ 2015 L 241/1; Regulation 764/2008, OJ 2008 L 218/21. For an approach to improving market management which is excellent on paper see *Mutual Evaluation* under Art. 39 of Directive 2006/123, OJ 2006 L 376/36: the true test will be the practice.

[18] The landmark case is Case C-194/94, *CIA Security International SA* v. *Signalson SA and Securitel Sprl*, [1996] ECR I-2201 (ECLI:EU:C:1996:172). See P. Oliver (ed.), *Oliver on Free Movement of Goods in the European Union* (5th ed., 2010), at paras 13.100–13.120.

[19] Case C-184/96, *Commission* v. *France*, [1998] ECR I-6197 (ECLI:EU:C:1998:495). This cannot exclude room in principle for a state to justify refusal to accept non-conforming products, as the Court made plain subsequently in Case C-24/00, *Commission* v. *France*, [2004] ECR I-1277 (ECLI:EU:C:2004:70).

[20] Cf. Regulation 1024/2012 on administrative co-operation ('the IMI Regulation'), OJ 2012 L 316/1. See also C. Janssens, *The Principle of Mutual Recognition in EU Law* (2013), Ch. 4, 'The Workability of the Principle of Mutual Recognition in the Internal Market'; Pelkmans, 'What Strategy for a Genuine Single Market?' CEPS (Centre for European Policy Studies) Special Report No. 126 (2016).

defence put up by national regulators. This has been explored in relation to public health, environmental protection and consumer protection and it is visible too in the cases associated with fundamental rights and national identity, where the Court normally loads an extra device designed to preserve national autonomy: the margin of discretion (or appreciation).

So the argument of this volume is that the Court does a generally respectful job in balancing the interest in market regulation expressed through (sincere and targeted) national rules against the interest in market deregulation achieved by holding obstructive national rules to be unjustified. Is this complacent? Scharpf has claimed there is a 'legitimate diversity' of socio-economic institutions and policies across the Member States, 'shaped by intense political conflicts and historical compromises'. They are highly politically contested and 'they need to be defended in public debates by governments facing the sanctions of political accountability. Instead, the supremacy of European law allows for judicial interventions that may short-circuit these political processes'.[21] He is clearly correct – they *may* do this. And sometimes they do – *Viking Line* is the most egregious example. It shows how, in short, economic constitutionalism may imperil social constitutionalism.[22]

But the full sweep of the case law demands attention. Many rules stripped away by the deregulatory flood of free movement law had no defensible purpose, exposed as protectionist or, at best, as anachronistic – border checks, rent-seeking subsidies and heaps of narrowly detailed technical standards. In other cases – though not *Viking Line* – the Court is actively receptive to sincere justification of rules that target particular problems – for consumers, for the environment, in sport, for rights of political protest and protection of human dignity, and so on. Unquestionably, the Court enjoys a hugely influential power to determine the shape of the internal market, which, in part because of the Treaty system but also because of its own interpretative choices, allows it to require the setting aside of national choices (the vertical issue) and sometimes in circumstances where its own rulings may not be displaced by political action at EU level (the horizontal issue), but the story of its adjudicative track record is far more complex and nuanced than relentless deregulation and disrespect for local social, moral and ethical choices that touch the market.[23]

---

[21] Scharpf, 'The Asymmetry of European Integration, or Why the EU Cannot Be a Social Market Economy', 8 *Socio-Economic Review* (2010) 211, 241.

[22] See Chapter 9.B; also D. Schiek, U. Liebert and H. Schneider (eds), *European Economic and Social Constitutionalism after the Treaty of Lisbon* (2011).

[23] Qualitative assessment certainly varies. Cf. Damjanovic, 'The EU Market Rules as Social Market Rules: Why the EU Can Be a Social Market Economy', 50 *Common Market Law Review* (2013) 1685; Schwarze, 'Die Abwägung von Zielen der europäischen Integration und mitgliedstaatlichen Interessen in der Rechtsprechung des EuGH', *Europarecht* (2013) 253: De Witte, 'Sex, Drugs and EU Law: the Recognition of Moral and Ethical Diversity in EU Law', 50 *Common Market Law Review* (2013) 1545; Gerstenberg, 'The Justiciability of Socio-Economic Rights, European Solidarity and the Role of the Court of Justice of the EU', 33 *Yearbook of European Law* (2014) 245; Nic Shuibhne, 'Margins of Appreciation: National Values, Fundamental Rights and EC Free Movement Law', 34 *European Law Review* (2009) 230; Semmelmann, 'The European Union's Economic Constitution Under the Lisbon Treaty: Soul-Searching Shifts the Focus to Procedure', 35 *European Law Review* (2010) 516; Schiek, 'The EU Constitution of Social Governance in an Economic Crisis: In Defence of a Transnational Dimension to Social Europe', 20 *Maastricht Journal* (2013) 185; Hojnik, 'The EU Internal Market and National Tradition and Culture: Any Room for Market Decentralisation?', 8 *Croatian Yearbook of*

The findings of this volume admit that EU law is not good at offering insulation *in principle* from the pressures of market-making, but emphasize that free movement law is not only about free movement. There is much receptivity to values other than the market visible and taken seriously in the Court's case law dealing with justification. So the internal market is and should be a site of diversity – in part because of the diversity of products and services that prevails in cross-border trade where the Court rules that an obstructive national measure may not be applied to restrain importation because it is not justified, but also because of the diversity of national rules that prevails when the Court rules that a national measure is beyond the reach of free movement law or where an obstructive national measure is treated as justified. The scope allowed for justification and the sensitivity to local preference embedded in the margin of discretion (or appreciation) is central to the Court's role in mediating the tensions between trade integration and local regulatory autonomy.

European Law and Policy (2012) 117; Gerstenberg, 'The Justiciability of Socio-economic rights, European Solidarity, and the Role of the Court of Justice of the EU', 33 *Yearbook of European Law* (2014) 245; Davies, 'Democracy and Legitimacy in the Shadow of Purposive Competence', 21 *European Law Journal* (2015) 2; Weatherill, 'Economic Rights and Fundamental Rights', in S. De Vries, U. Bernitz and S. Weatherill (eds), *The Protection of Fundamental Rights in the EU after Lisbon* (2013).

13

The Legislative Dimension

Harmonization

The Treaty on the Functioning of the European Union (TFEU) provisions on free movement and competition law sweep away a host of public and private practices that are incompatible with the aim of creating an internal market. As explained, their deregulatory momentum, though vigorous, is not absolute. One way or another there is room to justify practices that leave the market fragmented along national lines. The building of an internal market therefore also demands a supplementary role to be played by EU legislation. This entails the adoption of common EU rules, which may replace diverse but justified practices pursued at national level in order to level the regulatory playing field in order to open up a common trading area. This is known as 'harmonization'.

A. The Nature and Purpose of Harmonization

National measures that restrict trade yet remain lawful may be the subject of harmonized rules adopted by EU legislative act. In this way, the two routes to eliminating barriers to trade in goods and services may be seen as complementary: once the judicial route, which requires the setting aside of restrictive rules that are not capable of being justified, is exhausted as a result of the presence of justification, attention turns to the political process and the adoption of EU standards that apply in common in preference to diverse national rules. And so in this fashion the regulatory playing field of the internal market is levelled in order to promote unrestricted trade.

When the Court of Justice of the European Union ('the Court') rules that a state measure that restricts trade is incompatible with the TFEU, that measure may no longer be applied to impede cross-border trade. The relevant market is *de-regulated* – the national law is, in effect, sacrificed to the higher demands of market integration. Where the EU legislature decides to replace diverse state measures that hinder integration by an initiative of harmonization, here too the relevant market is *de-regulated*, in the sense that (on the simplest model) 28 different regimes are reduced to one common regime. But the market is also *re-regulated* – the EU rule becomes the (common) basis for the internal market's regulation of the sector in question. So the Court's application of the TFEU provisions on free movement is an exercise in removing state regulation and replacing it with market freedom; the legislature, in

The Internal Market as a Legal Concept. First Edition. Stephen Weatherill.
© Stephen Weatherill 2017. Published 2017 by Oxford University Press.

acting to harmonize laws, acts to remove, or at least reduce, state regulation, but it must make a choice as to the type and quality of (re-)regulatory regime it will introduce at EU level.

That free movement, promoting deregulation, must be joined by legislative action at EU level, promoting deregulation and re-regulation, in order to achieve an integrated market has *always* been perfectly clear. But where one stops and the other starts is not set in stone in the Treaties. The wider the reach of the free movement provisions in suppressing state regulatory autonomy, the greater the role claimed by the Court and its national judicial allies in directing the shape of the law of free movement at the expense of the EU's political institutions. This means that the Court's interpretation of the TFEU provisions on free movement is not simply directed at determining how deeply state regulatory autonomy is sliced away by the demands of EU law (the vertical issue). It also affects the location of the margin between judicially driven and legislature-driven approaches to advancing market integration in the EU (the horizontal issue). This has been made very clear in the explanation culminating in Chapter 12. It is exactly this theme which animates the significance of the choice made by the Court in *Cassis de Dijon* and other landmark cases including *Centros*, and which informs the way that the European Commission ('the Commission') immediately seized on the ruling in *Cassis* as a basis for re-focusing the harmonization programme on the range of national measures that survive testing under the Court's renovated and widened understanding of the scope of free movement law's control over national regulatory practice.

Despite its celebratory treatment of the (non-absolute) principle of mutual recognition derived from the Court's case law, the Commission recognizes that harmonization remains an indispensable element in the strategy for the maintenance of the EU's internal market. The foundationally important 1985 White Paper on *Completing the Internal Market* embraced 'a strategy that combines the best of' both conditional mutual recognition and harmonization.[1] Subsequently, it has admitted that '[m]utual recognition [sic] is not always a miracle solution for ensuring the free movement of goods in the single market, and that '[h]armonisation or further harmonisation remains without doubt one of the most effective instruments, both for economic operators and for the national administrations'.[2] And it is not only where national measures that act as obstacles to inter-state trade have been or are likely to be definitively found to be justified that a momentum builds for their harmonization. It is plausible too that release of (conditional) mutual recognition as a motor of integration will generate a sufficiently high level of uncertainty about what is allowed and what is not that pressure in favour of harmonization will in fact increase.[3]

---

[1] COM (85) 310, para. 64.

[2] *Second Biennial Report on the Application of the Principle of Mutual Recognition in the Single Market*, COM (2002) 419, para. 3.

[3] See, e.g., Davies, 'Is Mutual Recognition an Alternative to Harmonization? Lessons on Trade and Tolerance of Diversity from the EU', in L. Bartels and F. Ortino, *Regional Trade Agreements and the WTO Legal System* (2006); Kerber and Van den Bergh, 'Mutual Recognition Revisited: Misunderstandings, Inconsistencies, and a Suggested Re-interpretation', 61 *Kyklos* (2008) 447.

The question is: how much harmonization? And of what type? These are significant policy choices, laced with a constitutional flavour sourced ultimately in Article 5 TEU's principle of conferral. Here is another testing ground for the internal market as a legal concept.

B. Article 114 – an Instrument of Re-regulation

The Treaty has always conferred a competence to harmonize laws in the service of market-making. For goods, the relevant provision in the Treaty of Rome was Article 100 EEC, which is now (in amended form) Article 115 TFEU. For the self-employed, Article 57 EEC was the key provision, which is now (in amended form) Article 53 TFEU, and this is extended also to the market for services by Article 66 EEC, which is now (in amended form) Article 62 TFEU. These provisions were used to establish harmonized EU rules in a clutch of areas such as consumer protection,[4] labour market regulation[5] and environmental protection.[6] Most of these measures date from the 1970s and 1980s and although they typically expressed a logic based on the need to cure an appreciable distortion of competition in the internal market consequent on the existence of diverse national rules, they were also in part a consequence of the political initiatives taken (in particular) at the Paris Summit in 1972 to place a greater emphasis on social objectives rather than simply economic liberalization within the EU. So, for example, Directive 85/577, the 'Doorstep Selling' Directive, declared in its Preamble that disparities between national rules governing conclusion of a contract between a trader and consumer made away from business premises may directly affect the functioning of the market, but added that the consequent need for harmonization was also inspired by the preliminary programme of the Community for a consumer protection and information policy, which had been adopted in 1975. Harmonization is a means to improve the functioning of the internal market, but where what is harmonized is diverse measures of (say) social policy taken at national level, the consequence of harmonization is an EU choice about social policy. Harmonization in this sense serves a *dual function* in the internal market.

Article 100 EEC required unanimity in the Council of Ministers ('the Council') and was confined to the adoption of Directives: the same remains true of its current incarnation, Article 115 TFEU. But this Article has fallen into disuse. The key Treaty provision today is Article 114 TFEU, which was inserted into the Treaty by the Single European Act, with effect from 1987. Since Article 114 TFEU (which used to be Article 95 EC, and before that Article 100a) employs the ordinary legislative procedure it requires only a qualified majority vote in Council. It also permits the

---

[4] E.g., Directive 85/374 on product liability, OJ 1985 L 210/29; Directive 85/577 to protect the consumer in respect of contracts negotiated away from business premises ('Doorstep Selling'), OJ 1985 L 372/31, now replaced by Directive 2011/83, OJ 2011 L 304/64.

[5] E.g., Directive 75/117 on equal pay for equal work, OJ 1975 L 45/19; Directive 77/187 on safeguarding of employees' rights in the event of transfers of undertakings, OJ 1977 L 61/26. Both are now replaced by subsequent measures.

[6] E.g., Directive 73/404 on the bio-degradability of detergents, OJ 1973 L 347/51.

adoption of 'measures', rather than Directives alone. In practice, it has become by far the most important Treaty provision, equipping the EU with a legislative competence to adopt measures of harmonization in order to improve the functioning of the internal market. In recognition of its elevation, the Treaty of Lisbon inverted the running order in the TFEU of the two provisions: what is now Article 114 TFEU used to come immediately *after* what is now Article 115 TFEU, but the reverse is now true. Article 114 TFEU is *much* the more significant provision (and a bolder move would have been to delete Article 115 TFEU entirely).

Article 114 follows precisely the same logic as Article 115. It has the same rhythm of a *dual function*. It provides in its first paragraph that:

Save where otherwise provided in the Treaties, the following provisions shall apply for the achievement of the objectives set out in Article 26. The European Parliament and the Council shall, acting in accordance with the ordinary legislative procedure and after consulting the Economic and Social Committee, adopt the measures for the approximation of the provisions laid down by law, regulation or administrative action in Member States which have as their object the establishment and functioning of the internal market.

The legislative competence is accordingly driven explicitly by the internal market.

'Approximation' is the word used in Article 114, but 'harmonization' is more commonly used and for these purposes counts as a synonym. And there must *be* harmonization: creating something entirely new at EU level, leaving intact existing and diverse national forms, cannot be achieved by reliance on Article 114.[7]

The most striking feature of Article 114 is that it is functionally driven. *Any* national laws may be subjected to the discipline of harmonization provided only that the establishment and functioning of the internal market is promoted thereby. There is no limit to the subject matter of laws that may be harmonized by the intervention of the EU legislature, excepting only fiscal provisions, provisions relating to the free movement of persons, and provisions relating to the rights and interests of employed persons, which are cut out of the scope of Article 114 by its second paragraph. This does not at all deny the relevance of these matters to the construction of the internal market. It is simply a political refusal to open up their sensitivities to intervention pursuant to a qualified majority vote in Council. Article 115 is capable of being used to harmonize some such rules, but it would require unanimity in Council, which is very hard to assemble in such sensitive areas in an EU of 28 Member States. Unanimity in Council is also the rule for Article 113 on tax harmonization, while other sector-specific legal bases which normally attract the ordinary legislative procedure make special provision for Council unanimity where measures of a fiscal nature come into play.[8]

Article 114's reliance on the ordinary legislative procedure means that no state has a veto in Council over proposed measures of harmonization advanced pursuant to

---

[7] But Art. 352 TFEU may be used: Case C-436/03, *Parliament* v. *Council*, [2006] ECR I-3733 (ECLI:EU:C:2006:277).

[8] E.g., Arts 192(2)(a) TFEU (environmental protection), 194(3) TFEU (energy).

Article 114. The acceptance of the use of qualified majority voting (QMV) at the time of the adoption of the Single European Act in 1987 was the political adjustment required to make real the possibility of piloting through the EU system the large number of legislative measures that were deemed necessary to drive forward the internal market project.[9] Member States were willing to release the lock of unanimity in Council because in return they acquired the key to unlock every other state's veto.

C. Constitutional Commitments to Re-regulation

Were one designing an internal market in the abstract, one could feasibly ignore questions about the *quality* of the re-regulatory environment. The creation of a unified economic area requires only that rules apply in common, and it does not matter whether the rules are aggressively interventionist or light touch in nature. One could even in principle adopt a model whereby the governing rule is 'no rule': that a state must accept on to its territory any product or service which has been lawfully made or marketed in another state according to the standards (if any) that apply on that state's territory. However, public regulation of the market in Europe has developed incrementally for many centuries now, under a rich variety of motivating forces, and it would be surprising were states to allow the EU's market-making project simply to roll back the accumulated patterns of rule-making designed to protect groups such as consumers and workers from the imperfections and inequities of unregulated markets. That is not the choice made in the provisions on free movement, where room to justify national measures is permitted even where a trade-restrictive effect is found, and it is not a choice that is found anywhere in the legislative *acquis* either. This is, in part, simply the result of political practice: the adoption of harmonized standards in replacement for diverse national ones always involves some degree of commitment in common to set standards that regulate the market EU-wide. But it is also driven by the Treaty on the Functioning of the European Union (TFEU) itself. The EU, in adopting harmonized rules, does *not* simply pursue common rule-making. It is also constitutionally bound to pay attention to the content and quality of the rules which are being set at EU level in partial or total replacement for national rules.

This is mandated by Article 114, which in its third paragraph provides that '[t]he Commission, in its proposals envisaged in paragraph 1 concerning health, safety, environmental protection and consumer protection, will take as a base a high level of protection, taking account in particular of any new development based on scientific facts' and that in addition 'the European Parliament and the Council will also seek to achieve this objective'. The commitment to connect (inter alia) the internal market project to the protection of affected interests is strengthened by a host of what may be called 'horizontal' or cross-cutting clauses in the TFEU. Article 3(3)

---

[9] See Chapter 3.B.

TEU provides that the EU 'shall work for . . . a high level of protection and improvement of the quality of the environment' and Article 11 TFEU directs that environmental protection requirements 'must be integrated into the definition and implementation of the Union's policies and activities, in particular with a view to promoting sustainable development'. Article 12 TFEU does something similar for consumer protection requirements, which 'shall be taken into account in defining and implementing other Union policies and activities'. Article 168(1) TFEU provides that '[a] high level of human health protection shall be ensured in the definition and implementation of all Union policies and activities'.

The Charter of Fundamental Rights ('the Charter) also mandates that the general sweep of EU policy-making, of which the construction of the internal market forms an important part, must be conducted with due respect for a series of regulatory values. Article 35 on *Health Care* provides that '[a] high level of human health protection shall be ensured in the definition and implementation of all the Union's policies and activities'; Article 37 on *Environmental Protection* directs that '[a] high level of environmental protection and the improvement of the quality of the environment must be integrated into the policies of the Union and ensured in accordance with the principle of sustainable development'; Article 38 on *Consumer Protection* similarly instructs that 'Union policies shall ensure a high level of consumer protection'. Since '[t]he applicability of EU law entails applicability of the fundamental rights guaranteed by the Charter'[10] it follows that the shaping of internal market law is inextricably tied up with respect for fundamental rights expressed in and by the Charter.

Legislative harmonization under these influences provides a case study in the endemic tendency of trade integration to 'spill over' to confront and infuse ever more complex areas of public policy. Re-regulation in and of the internal market pushes the project far beyond an a-political technocratic exercise.[11]

D. Judicial Review and Re-regulation

The significance of the commitments discussed in the previous Section is both political and legal. They shape the political negotiation that occurs within the legislative process, while also asserting in a specifically legal context a requirement that the making of the internal market must accommodate concerns that go beyond simple deregulation.

1. Judicial Review of Inadequate Standards

It would be possible, in principle, to attack the validity of a measure of harmonization for failure to meet standards of protection set out in these several provisions of

---

[10] Case C-617/10, *Fransson*, judgment of 26 February 2013, not yet reported (ECLI:EU:C: 2013:280), at para. 21.

[11] E.g., M. Egan, *Constructing a European Market* (2001); K. Armstrong and S. Bulmer, *The Governance of the Single European Market* (1998).

the TFEU and the Charter. It is, however, improbable that a measure would be held invalid for failure to set sufficiently high standards provided that the legislative process has demonstrably addressed questions pertaining to choice among regulatory techniques. The Court has made plain that it is not required that the finally agreed harmonized norm must comply with the highest standard found among the Member States. The mere fact that a measure of harmonization may require a diminution in national standards in some Member States is not a basis for annulment of the measure.[12] The Court is anxious to preserve space for political compromise in the negotiation of a harmonized standard. The TFEU and Charter norms are 'soft': they do not stipulate a concrete level of protection below which a finding of invalidity follows. They direct the political institutions to take seriously the protections at stake when they shape the relevant rules. It follows from this that a manifest neglect to address the protective quality of the harmonized rule or a manifest error of appraisal regarding the applicable conditions would provide a reason for the Court to annul an adopted act.[13] But this will be rare. Assuming that the EU legislature is sufficiently conscientious to ensure citation of the relevant Treaty and Charter provisions in the Preamble to adopted legislation, it seems unlikely that the Court would declare any such measure invalid. Where such essentially procedural concerns are met the Court typically concedes a broad discretion to the EU legislature in the selection of the appropriate form of EU measure in areas involving political, economic and social choices in which it is called upon to undertake complex assessments and evaluations.[14] It is to political reform of the EU measure that disgruntled states (or other parties) should turn their attention.

2. Judicial Review of Over-regulation

That the quality of harmonized standards is constitutionally significant is also relevant in connection with a challenge coming from the other direction, to the effect that a measure of harmonization *over*-regulates the internal market to the detriment of property rights and the freedom to pursue a business, protected by Articles 15, 16 and 17 of the Charter. It is open to commercial operators to press in this way for a *constitutionalized* protection of private economic interests from public regulation. But here, too, the Court typically concedes a broad discretion to the EU legislature in areas involving political, economic and social choices in which it is called upon to undertake complex assessments and evaluations. The Court has long recognized the right to property under EU law, but has treated it not as an absolute right but, rather, as one that must be viewed in relation to its social function. The Court has no objection to legislative restriction on its exercise 'provided that those restrictions in fact

---

[12] Case C-233/94, *Germany* v. *Parliament and Council*, [1997] ECR I-2405 (ECLI:EU:C:1997:231).

[13] Case C-284/95, *Safety Hi-Tech* v. *S & T*, [1998] ECR I-4301 (ECLI:EU:C:1998:352), at para. 37; Case C-341/95, *Gianni Bettati* v. *Safety Hi-Tech*, [1998] ECR I-4355 (ECLI:EU:C:1998:353), at para. 35.

[14] E.g., Case C-66/04, *United Kingdom* v. *Parliament and Council*, [2005] ECR I-10553 (ECLI:EU:C:2005:743); Case C-270/12, *United Kingdom* v. *Council and Parliament*, judgment of 22 January 2014, not yet reported (ECLI:EU:C:2014:18); Case C-58/08, *Vodafone, O2 et al.* v. *Secretary of State*, [2010] ECR I-4999 (ECLI:EU:C:2010:321).

correspond to objectives of general interest... and do not constitute a disproportionate and intolerable interference, impairing the very substance of the rights
guaranteed'.[15] *Alliance for Natural Health* offers a neat and typical illustration of the
Court's reluctance to allow legislative intervention in the market to be overturned.[16]
The argument that it was disproportionately restrictive to allow the marketing only
of nutrients that had received a favourable opinion from the competent scientific authorities was pressed on the Court. Instead, it was argued, nutrients that had
not been shown to represent a risk to human health should also be allowed. This was,
in essence, an attempt to set aside harmonization because the chosen standards
were over-regulatory. The Court declined to intervene. It found the measures
'appropriate for achieving the objective which they pursue and that, given the obligation of the... legislature to ensure a high level of protection of human health, they
do not go beyond what is necessary to attain that objective'.[17] While accepting that
the 'positive list' system was a more burdensome means of regulating the market
than a 'negative list', the Court ruled that it was not a disproportionate burden.
It also found that the EU itself had not violated (what is now) Article 34 TFEU by
adopting the measure.

The Court ensures that EU internal market law allows space for political choices
about market (re-)regulation as well as market deregulation. It did something similar
in *Deutsches Weintor eG* v. *Land Rheinland-Pfalz*, a post-Charter case which concerns
Regulation 1924/2006 harmonizing rules governing nutrition and health claims
made about food.[18] Pursuant to the Regulation, a German public authority prohibited use of the phrase 'easily digestible' in connection with wines. This was challenged by a wine growers' co-operative, relying on Article 15(1) of the Charter which
grants the right to engage in work and to pursue a freely chosen or accepted occupation and on Article 16 of the Charter which guarantees the freedom to conduct a
business. However, Article 35 of the Charter, mentioned earlier, requires that a high
level of human health protection be ensured in the definition and implementation
of EU policies and activities. And alcoholic beverages are typically subject to particularly strict regulation also at *national* level: the Court was able to draw on its own
existing case law in which restrictions on advertising such products applied by Member
States had been held to be justified in the name of public health despite their restrictive
effect on inter-state trade.[19] This brought the Court to the conclusion that the legislative
regime was based on a reconciliation of the several fundamental rights at stake,
striking a fair balance between them. It was compatible with EU law.

---

[15] E.g., Case C-491/01, *R* v. *Secretary of State ex parte BAT and Imperial Tobacco*, [2002] ECR I-11543 (ECLI:EU:C:2002:741); Case C-200/96, *Metronome Musik GmbH*, [1998] ECR I-1953 (ECLI:EU:C:1998:172).

[16] Cases C-154/04 and C-155/04, *Alliance for Natural Health*, [2005] ECR I-6451 (ECLI:EU:C:2005:449).

[17] *Ibid.*, para. 111.

[18] Case C-544/10, *Deutsches Weintor eG* v. *Land Rheinland-Pfalz*, judgment of 6 September 2012, not yet reported (ECLI:EU:C:2012:526).

[19] E.g., Joined Cases C-1/90 and C-176/90, *Aragonesa de Publicidad Exterior*, [1991] ECR I-4151 (ECLI:EU:C:1991:327); Case C-262/02, *Commission* v. *France*, [2004] ECR I-6569 (ECLI:EU:C:2004:431). See Chapter 8.D.

This 'balancing' is structurally nothing new compared with the practice of the Court before the grant of binding status to the Charter with effect from 2009. This is underlined by the ruling in *Denise McDonough* v. *Ryanair Ltd* in which the Court upheld provisions on compensation for air passengers in Regulation 261/2004 as striking a 'fair balance' between, on the one hand, Articles 16 and 17 of the Charter and, on the other, Article 38 on consumer protection.[20] The ruling cites both *Promusicae*,[21] a pre-Lisbon ruling, and *Deutsches Weintor*, post-Lisbon, without any hint that they carry any difference in their substantive significance.

The Court has typically approved the 'balancing' performed by the legislature in setting the regulated terms of market integration.[22] This does not mean that the Court is *wholly* deferential to the exercise of legislative discretion. *Digital Rights Ireland* concerned Directive 2006/24 on data retention, adopted as a measure of harmonization under what is now Article 114 TFEU.[23] It is a measure which highlights the breathtaking scope of the harmonization programme: the measure represents the EU's choice about how best to regulate the retention of data by service providers in order to address the risk of criminal activity, and it reaches that sensitive domain simply by asserting that national provisions in the field vary considerably (on the types of data to be retained as well as the conditions and periods of retention), and so present obstacles to the internal market.[24] The Court had no objection to this: in fact it had previously found the Directive to constitute a valid exercise of the legislative competence to harmonize conferred by the Treaty.[25] But in *Digital Rights* the Court found it invalid for want of compliance with the Charter. The Court found that the since the Directive failed to lay down clear and precise rules governing the extent of the interference with the Articles 7 and 8 Charter rights on privacy and data protection, it entailed 'a wide-ranging and particularly serious interference with those fundamental rights in the legal order of the EU, without such an interference being precisely circumscribed by provisions to ensure that it is actually limited to what is strictly necessary'.[26] Given its sweeping breadth, unsupported by adequate safeguards, the measure could not stand. However, the lesson of the case law is that where the matter concerns general issues of market regulation, distinct from the particular and detailed context of a decision like *Digital Rights*, the Court is unlikely to intervene when invited to do so by traders arguing that harmonization represents *over*-regulation of the internal market.

---

[20] Case C-12/11, *Denise McDonough* v. *Ryanair Ltd*, judgment of 31 January 2013, not yet reported (ECLI:EU:C:2013:43).

[21] Case C-275/06, *Promusicae*, [2008] ECR I-271 (ECLI:EU:C:2008:54).

[22] See also, e.g., since 2009, Case C-283/11, *Sky Österreich GmbH*, judgment of 22 January 2013, not yet reported (ECLI:EU:C:2013:28); Case C-101/12, *Herbert Schaible*, judgment of 17 October 2013, not yet reported (ECLI:EU:C:2013:661).

[23] Joined Cases C-293/12 and C-594/12, *Digital Rights Ireland et al.*, judgment of 8 April 2014, not yet reported (ECLI:EU:C:2014:238).

[24] OJ 2006 L 105/54, Recitals 5 and 6.

[25] Case C-301/06, *Ireland* v. *Parliament and Council*, [2009] ECR I-593 (ECLI:EU:C:2009:68). Ireland's unsuccessful application was largely motivated by a concern to show that the 'third pillar' – now eliminated by the Lisbon Treaty – should have been used.

[26] *Ibid.*, at para. 65.

3. Judicial Interpretation of the Harmonized Legislative Acquis

A different story applies to interpretation of legislative texts, rather than their validity. Harmonization establishes common standards in order to promote trade that is unobstructed by regulatory diversity among the Member States, but the quality of those standards is constitutionally significant too. The commitment to a high level of protection has played a prominent role in the Court's interpretation of relevant legislative texts, sometimes in a remarkably ambitious manner. Consumer protection is one of several vividly illustrative areas.

Directive 93/13 harmonizes rules governing unfair terms in consumer contracts: in short, it requires that they be forbidden.[27] The system of protection intended by the Directive has been described by the Court as 'based on the idea that the consumer is in a weak position vis-à-vis the seller or supplier, as regards both his bargaining power and his level of knowledge'; and that this 'leads to the consumer agreeing to terms drawn up in advance by the seller or supplier without being able to influence the content of those terms'.[28] Article 6(1) of the Directive requires the Member States to provide that unfair terms will not bind the consumer, which the Court has described as a mandatory provision which aims to replace the formal balance which the contract establishes between the rights and obligations of the parties with an effective balance which re-establishes equality between them.[29] This is a harmonized regime constitutionally tied to the internal market but *also* motivated by concern to tackle the imbalance that flows from permitting contractual freedom free rein in the relationship between the trader and the consumer. Intervening in freedom of contract is readily rationalized in national law on the basis that preserving freedom of contract in imbalanced relationships is not freedom at all but, rather, licence for the powerful to impose on the weak, and harmonization transplants this protective concern to EU level. And this policy orientation has concrete consequences when the Court is invited to interpret the Directive. It does not adopt a neutral approach: it draws on the consumer protection rationale promised by EU law. For example, *Árpád Kásler* concerned the interpretation of Directive 93/13 in the context of a challenge to a term dealing with the exchange rate applicable to repayment of a loan denominated in a foreign currency.[30] Article 4(2) of the Directive directs that assessment of the unfair nature of terms will relate neither to the definition of the main subject matter of the contract nor to the adequacy of the price 'in so far as these terms are in plain intelligible language'. This, the Court reasoned, imposes a 'requirement

---

[27] OJ 1993 L 95/29.

[28] E.g., C-472/11, *Banif Plus Bank*, judgment of 21 February 2013, not yet reported (ECLI:EU: C:2013:88), at para. 19; Case C-537/13, *Birute Šiba*, judgment of 15 January 2015, not yet reported (ECLI:EU:C:2015:14), at para. 22; Case C-96/14, *Jean-Claude Van Hove*, judgment of 23 April 2015, not yet reported (ECLI:EU:C:2015:262), at paras 26–27.

[29] E.g., Case C-168/05, *Mostaza Claro* v. *Centro Móvil Milenium*, [2006] ECR I-10421 (ECLI:EU: C:2006:675), at para. 36; Case C-618/10, *Banco Español de Crédito* v. *Joaquín Calderón Camino*, judgment of 14 June 2012, not yet reported (ECLI:EU:C:2012:349), at paras 40, 63; Case C-472/11, *supra* note 28, at para. 20; Case C-415/11, *Aziz*, judgment of 14 March 2013, not yet reported (ECLI: EU:C:2013:164), at para. 45; Case C-470/12, *Pohotovost'*, judgment of 27 February 2014, not yet reported (ECLI:EU:C:2014:101), at paras 39–41.

[30] Case C-26/13, judgment of 30 April 2014, not yet reported (ECLI:EU:C:2014:282).

of transparency' which, given the consumer's 'position of weakness', must be interpreted broadly.[31] Therefore the requirement that a contractual term must be drafted in plain intelligible language covers not only formal grammatical intelligibility but also a transparent explanation of how the term shall operate, as a means to ensure the consumer is in a position to evaluate on the basis of clear criteria the economic consequences.[32] So, in the particular circumstances, the contract should set out transparently exactly how the mechanism of conversion for the foreign currency shall operate. If it does not, the relevant term does not escape review by a court pursuant to Article 4(2) of the Directive.

Directive 99/44 on consumer sales and guarantees, another measure of legislative harmonization,[33] formed the background to *Froujke Faber*.[34] The Court held that a national court must determine whether an individual counts as a 'consumer' even if the buyer has not relied on that status in the proceedings, for otherwise the rights intended to be conferred by the Directive would be jeopardized. The Court explicitly cited case law dealing with Directive 93/13, and stressed the common rationale of using EU measures of harmonization to address the consumer's relatively weak position while also seeking to advance the internal market. The *quality* of the harmonized landscape is constitutionally significant.

Directive 2005/29 which harmonizes rules governing unfair business-to-consumer commercial practices by prohibiting them carries a similar message about the Court's adventurous and consumer-friendly interpretative bias.[35] The Court has consistently treated pursuit of a high level of consumer protection as a reason to prefer a wide interpretation of the material scope of the Directive.[36] So, for example, in *Nemzeti Fogyasztóvédelmi Hatóság* the Court, making exactly this connection between the quest for a high level of consumer protection and the proper interpretation of the Directive, made clear that this precluded the imposition of restrictions on its material scope which were not explicitly foreseen by the Directive.[37] The consumer, it noted, is 'economically weaker and less experienced in legal matters' than the trader.[38]

The body of case law is huge and cannot be addressed here in any remotely systematic manner.[39] Article 12 TFEU and Article 38 of the Charter may be expected to act as an increasingly prominent frame for this pro-consumer interpretative approach, but they exert no transformative effect, for the Court's anxiety to treat the

---

[31] *Ibid.*, at paras 71–72.   [32] *Ibid.*, at para. 75.   [33] OJ 1999 L 171/12.
[34] Case C-497/13, judgment of 4 June 2015, not yet reported (ECLI:EU:C:2015:357).
[35] OJ 2005 L 149/22.
[36] E.g., Case C-122/10, *Ving Sverige AB*, [2011] ECR I-3903 (ECLI:EU:C:2011:299); Case C-428/11, *Purely Creative Ltd. and others v. OFT*, judgment of 18 October 2012, not yet reported (ECLI:EU:C:2012:651); Case C-435/11, *CHS Tour Services*, judgment of 19 September 2013, not yet reported (ECLI:EU:C:2013:574).
[37] Case C-388/13, *Nemzeti Fogyasztóvédelmi Hatóság*, judgment of 16 April 2015, not yet reported (ECLI:EU:C:2015:225).
[38] *Ibid.*, at para. 53.
[39] On Directive 93/13, see Micklitz and Reich, 'The Court and Sleeping Beauty: The Revival of the Unfair Contract Terms Directive', 51 *Common Market Law Review* (2014) 771; on Directive 2005/29, see Stuyck, 'The Court of Justice and the Unfair Commercial Practices Directive', 52 *Common Market Law Review* (2015) 721.

legislative *acquis* as infused with sensitivity to the needs of consumer protection is demonstrably long-standing.[40] The key message is that the internal market is no neutral legal concept: it implicates choices about the quality of the re-regulatory environment which are conducive to protection of weaker parties.

E. The Permissibility of Prohibition

Harmonization deregulates the market. On the simplest model, the diverse regimes of all the EU Member States become one. But it also regulates the market, because, in contrast to the effect of applying free movement law to an unjustified trade barrier, it does not lead to a regulatory void but, rather, it establishes a single standard of EU regulation: or, better and as already suggested earlier, of *re*-regulation, given that the EU, acting to harmonize, is reacting to pre-existing legislative choices at national level and superseding them with its own choice of technique. So where the measure promotes the functioning of the internal market and absorbs the dictates of a high level of protection in its chosen standard, it is no bar to recourse to Article 114 TFEU that the 'decisive factor' in the choice made by the EU legislator is some particular type of regulatory aim, such as public health[41] or animal welfare.[42] The point is that if national public health laws are being harmonized then an EU public health law emerges – albeit that it is also a measure designed to promote the good functioning of the internal market.

This means that it perfectly logical that the EU may harmonize rules in the service of the internal market by *prohibiting* particular goods or practices, provided only that the generally applicable criteria for reliance on Article 114 TFEU are met, which will typically mean that the ban must form part of a regime dealing with a wider category of products than simply those subjected to the harmonized ban. So a harmonized rule may consist in requiring all the Member States to authorize the marketing of the product or products concerned, subjecting such an obligation of authorization to certain conditions, or even provisionally or definitively prohibiting the marketing of a product or products, a wide vista which the Court has explicitly treated as connected to the (re-)regulatory values expressed in what were Articles 152(1) and 95(3) EC (now Articles 168(1) and Article 114(3) TFEU), buttressed by Articles 35 and 38 of the Charter.[43]

To take a simple example from legislative practice, a harmonized ban on unsafe products opens up the market for safe products, and the matter therefore falls within the permitted scope of legislative harmonization.[44] Directive 2005/29 on unfair

---

[40] Weatherill, 'Article 38 – Consumer Protection', in S. Peers, T. Hervey, J. Kenner and A. Ward (eds), *The EU Charter of Fundamental Rights: A Commentary* (2014).

[41] E.g., Case C-210/03, *Swedish Match*, [2004] ECR I-11893 (ECLI:EU:C:2004:802).

[42] E.g., Case T-526/10, *Inuit Tapiriit Kanatami et al. v. Commission*, judgment of 25 April 2013, not yet reported (ECLI:EU:T:2013:215).

[43] E.g., Case C-210/03, *supra* note 41, at para. 32; Joined Cases C-154/04 and 155/04, *supra* note 16, at para. 33.

[44] Directive 2001/95, OJ 2002 L 11/4.

commercial practices was mentioned earlier:[45] it follows the same logic, requiring the suppression of unfair practices in order to create an internal market featuring (only) fair practices. Harmonization of national laws is an exercise in vertical allocation of regulatory responsibility. It locates at EU level the need for an EU understanding of the nature and purpose of whatever is harmonized. This inevitably involves a sensitive choice between a range of possible approaches and techniques, and sometimes a prohibition is appropriate. The internal market as a legal concept is not exclusively a force for deregulation.

F. Legislative Practice and Re-regulation

Harmonization has a prodigious functional potential. Driven by a logic which treats regulatory divergence among the Member States as the propulsion to introduce replacement EU rules and standards, legislative harmonization has swept broad and deep across the regulatory landscape of the EU's internal market. This is of the highest significance to the shape and density of the internal market's legal architecture but, at more constitutional level, it also brings into question how realistic it is *in practice* to talk *in principle* about the limits of the EU's conferred competences. The 'internal market' is profoundly an empowering concept.

The inevitability that harmonization carries a re-regulatory dynamic combines with the functional breadth of harmonization envisaged by reliance on Article 114 TFEU to entail that the EU may become, and has become, intricately involved with a wide range of areas of regulatory activity. The foundation stone is the project of making an internal market. The initial focus of lawmaking under (what is now) Article 114 was on 'deadline 1992', the adoption of close to 300 measures that the Commission presented in its 1985 White Paper as essential for the completion of the internal market. But that did not exhaust the energy of the programme of harmonization. It is broad, and it percolates down into a vast range of areas of national rule-making. Not much is immune from EU internal market law: not much examination of *any* area of national law can today exclude the EU entirely, even if sometimes the EU's influence may be concealed, misperceived or exaggerated.

Consumer law has been discussed above, and it is a fine example of how legislative harmonization has pushed the EU into making choices about the style and manner of protection in both private and public law contexts. This is in formal terms internal market law: the legal base for the consumer law *acquis* is almost without exception Article 114 TFEU (or its predecessors). But it is also consumer protection law, delivered and shaped by the EU legislative process which is forced to become engaged with techniques and intensity of market regulation, and interpreted by the Court, frequently in the adventurous manner tracked above. Mandatory pre-contractual disclosure supplemented by a post-agreement 'cooling-off' period is a commonly employed EU regulatory technique, and it suggests an emphasis on transparency and the perfecting effect on the competitive market of the attentive consumer.[46]

---

[45] *Supra* note 35.   [46] See S. Weatherill, *EU Consumer Law and Policy* (2nd ed., 2012), Ch. 4.

But the legislative *acquis* is not confined to an informational model, as is demonstrated by Directive 93/13, which prohibits unfair terms in consumer contracts, and Directive 99/44 on certain aspects of the sale of consumer goods and associated guarantees, which imports certain standards of required quality into consumer contracts. This is an emergent – though certainly unsystematic – EU contract law. In administrative law, rules on advertising, suppressing misleading forms and liberalizing comparative practices, have all been harmonized in the name of the completion of the internal market.[47] Unfair commercial practices in business-to-consumer transactions are, as already mentioned, the subject of harmonized control pursuant to Directive 2005/29.[48] Directive 2010/13 on audiovisual media services establishes harmonized rules in the field in order to promote an integrated EU market for such services, but these rules, as responses to the diverse choices made at national level to protect consumers of broadcasting and related services from particular harms, represent the EU's own choices about the proper limits of the (internal) market.[49] So the Directive explicitly addresses minors and the promotion of tobacco and alcohol. This is the EU, acting to improve the functioning of the internal market by intervening to harmonize national laws, as a protector of children and as a lifestyle regulator. The Directive also contains provisions protecting the consumer from excessive advertising, which the Court has described as an essential aspect of the regime, while also going out of its way to make clear that this aim of protecting the consumer is justified despite the restrictive effect on provision of services across the EU.[50] Again: the internal market is much more than a liberalizing legal concept. Directive 2009/73 on common rules for the internal market in natural gas deals explicitly with security of supply, including the position of vulnerable consumers, showing the rise of targeted and detailed regulatory patterns at EU level.[51]

Out of this develops an understanding of EU consumer policy which has its roots in the internal market but which at the same time, under the inevitable influence of the re-regulatory dynamic which is harmonization's lifeblood, requires that choices be made at EU level about the nature, purpose and intensity of consumer protection. The result of this legislative programme is to create a pattern of 'regulated autonomy' within the internal market.[52]

Consumer protection is no more than an illustration of the functionally broad and deep re-regulatory capacity of harmonization in the internal market. There are hundreds more: several have been tracked in this volume, including the rise of the

---

[47] Directive 2006/114 concerning misleading and comparative advertising, OJ 2006 L 376/21.
[48] *Supra* note 35.   [49] OJ 2011 L 95/1.
[50] Case C-234/12, *Sky Italia*, judgment of 18 July 2013, not yet reported (ECLI:EU:C:2013:496).
[51] OJ 2009 L 211/94. Cf. generally Friant-Perrot, 'Le consommateur vulnérable à la lumière du droit de la consommation de 'Union européenne', 49 *Revue trimestrielle de droit europeen* (2013) 483; Waddington, 'Vulnerable and Confused: The Protection of Vulnerable Consumers under EU Law', 38 *European Law Review* (2013) 757; and more broadly D. Leczykiewicz and S. Weatherill (eds), *The Images of the Consumer in EU Law* (2016).
[52] Comparato and Micklitz, 'Regulated Autonomy between Market Freedoms and Fundamental Rights in the Case Law of the CJEU', in U. Bernitz, X. Groussot and F. Schulyok (eds), *General Principles of EU Law and European Private Law* (2013) Ch. 4.

EU as a regulator of public health with particular reference to tobacco products.[53] A small number of further illustrations must suffice.

Inquiry into the law relating to disability might not bring the EU quickly to mind, and certainly the matter is largely addressed as a matter of national law. But the soft edges of the principle of conferral are relevant here too. Directive 2001/85 on special provisions for vehicles used for the carriage of passengers comprising more than eight seats in addition to the driver's seat – buses and coaches, in short – is a measure of harmonization introduced to facilitate the proper functioning of the internal market for such vehicles.[54] The majority of the harmonized rules deal with the establishment of common safety specifications, but since national laws showed diversity in treatment of technical prescriptions to allow accessibility for persons of reduced mobility to the vehicles, the EU measure responds by itself (re-)addressing that issue. So disability law acquires an EU component. It is not at all a *major* component, but the message is that Member States enjoy no *exclusive* competence in the matter. Harmonization has this 'spillover' effect.

Directive 98/44 on biotechnology, which is based on Article 114, reduces regulatory diversity by establishing a common approach to the patenting of human biological material, but this plainly has both an economic and an ethical dimension which, as an exercise in selecting a European norm against background contested diversity in Europe, is conspicuously sensitive.[55] The internal market as a legal concept brings the EU legislature into the area and the adoption of legislation brings in the Court. *International Stem Cell Corporation* concerned a refusal to register national patents on the ground that the two applications related to parthenogenetic activation of oocytes concerning the use of human embryos.[56] This was excluded from patentability according to the scheme envisaged by Directive 98/44 on the legal protection of biotechnological inventions. What, the Court was asked, was the correct interpretation of 'human embryos', and, specifically, was an unfertilized human ovum whose division and development to a certain stage had been stimulated by parthenogenesis a 'human embryo' for these purposes? The Court insisted on the need for a uniform interpretation across the entire territory of the EU and added that, in pursuit of protection of human dignity, a wide approach to the scope of the exclusion should be taken. It then provided a careful analysis of when a non-fertilized human ovum should be treated as a human embryo, basing the threshold on whether it has the inherent capacity of developing into a human being. So the Court becomes a tribunal engaged in identifying the limits dictated by human dignity to the rise of biotechnology and genetic engineering. It is the internal market as a legal concept that takes it there.

---

[53] E.g., Directives 2003/33, 2001/37, 2014/40.   [54] OJ 2002 L 42/1.

[55] OJ 1998 L 213/13. Cf. Varju and Sándor, 'Patenting Stem Cells in Europe: the Challenge of Multiplicity in European Union Law', 49 *Common Market Law Review* (2012) 1007; Brownsword, 'Regulatory Coherence – A European Challenge', in K. Purnhagen and P. Rott, *Varieties of European Economic Law and Regulation* (2014).

[56] Case C-364/13, *International Stem Cell Corporation*, judgment of 18 December 2014, not yet reported (ECLI:EU:C:2014:2451). See Faeh, 'Judicial Activism, the Biotech Directive and its Institutional Implications', 40 *European Law Review* (2015) 613.

Article 114 TFEU enjoys a functional breadth which leads to the EU legislature being required to develop a stance on matters for which the TFEU provides little or no explicit policy direction – rather, as the Court sometimes (see Chapter 8) operates across territory uncharted by the TFEU, it shapes an understanding of when barriers to inter-state trade deserve to be treated as justified. Harmonization is another major source of this rising tide of EU law and the consequent reduction in the zone of national regulatory autonomy.

Perhaps there is something politically opportunistic about such exploitation of the functionally broad competence to harmonize which is founded on the internal market as a legal concept. Perhaps it leads to an over-regulation of the market that is anti-competitive and harmful to Europe's economic prospects. For sure, there are a whole host of interesting stories to tell about the incentives and the lobbying that leads to EU rules being adopted (or not) and of what kind. But there is no *constitutional* objection to this: the internal market as a legal concept drives a wide understanding of the *potential* allowed for re-regulatory activity. The 'internal market' as a legal concept leaves space for a political and economic debate about the intensity of the regulation of its space. This is the empowering function of the internal market.

G. The Limits of Harmonization

The Treaty-conferred competence to harmonize laws is functionally broad and has been exploited to create a remarkably wide-ranging programme of market re-regulation in the EU. But the competence is not unlimited. It cannot be unlimited, as that would violate the constitutionally fundamental principle of conferral found in Article 5 TEU. Simple diversity among national practices is not enough to justify EU intervention. There must also be a contribution to the functioning of the internal market. The empowering and the limiting concept is therefore the 'internal market' – and that is precisely the problem.

1. The Slow Road to Emergence of 'Competence Sensitivity'

For a long time the stretching of legislative competence at EU level attracted relatively little critical comment. The primary reason for this was that in its first 30 years the EU legislated, as a general, rule only where the unanimity of all its Member States, expressed in Council, was available to back up the initiatives proposed by the Commission. At one level unanimity is a stifling requirement, for it allows every Member State a veto power. But the more striking feature of the early years, when the EU was home to relatively few Member States and a sphere of action that was far narrower than is visible today, was that, provided unanimity could be assembled, there was an empowering force of political consensus which tended to lead to sidelining of rigorous constitutional inspection of the validity of proposed action. Put simply, there was unlikely to be a dissenting voice with any practical braking power provided that unanimity existed among the Member States. And, in particular, once the Paris Summit in 1972 had demonstrated that there was a unanimous support for

a more 'human' face, that began to be granted legislative shape in areas such as consumer and environmental law where the EU had no explicit competence under its
Treaty. So Article 100 EEC (today Article 115 TFEU) was employed. In matters of
social policy Article 100 supplemented the narrowly drawn competences found in
the original Treaty of Rome.

The matter rarely reached the attention of the Court of Justice of the European
Union ('the Court'): Why would it, given that applicants with ready access to the
Court would inevitably be directly implicated in the decision to agree to the rules?
Governments change but direct actions would be quickly out of time pursuant
to what is now Article 263(6) TFEU; private parties would struggle to meet the
restrictive standing rules contained today in Article 263(4) TFEU; while an action
before a national court triggering a preliminary ruling questioning validity, though
feasible, did not happen. Just occasionally the matter of 'competence sensitivity'
raised its head before the Court, but when it did the Court showed no inclination
to curtail legislative consensus about the breadth of the competence to harmonize.
The Court confirmed that environmental measures might be based on what was
Article 100 EEC (now Article 115 TFEU), in *Commission* v. *Italy*.[57] The case was
an infringement action brought by the Commission seeking a declaration that
Italy had failed to implement harmonizing Directive 73/404 relating to detergents.
The Directive's aim was to eliminate disparities between national rules governing
the biodegradability of detergents while also, in its content, restricting the use of
non-biodegradable detergents in order to reduce pollution of the natural environment. The Italian government stated before the Court that it did not intend to raise
the question of whether the Directive was valid in the light of the fact that combating pollution was not a task entrusted to the Community by the Treaty, but it
observed that in its view the matter lay 'on the fringe' of Community powers.[58]
The Court could probably have simply ignored this rather loose submission, but it
chose to express itself in a way that supported the validity of the legislative action.
It pointed out that the Directive had been 'adopted not only within the Programme
of Action of the Communities on the Environment... [but also] the General
Programme for the elimination of technical barriers to trade which result from disparities between the provisions laid down by law, regulation or administrative action
in Member States'.[59] Diverse national rules governing the environment and health
impose costs on undertakings to which they apply and, absent harmonization, the
Court agreed that 'competition may be appreciably distorted'. The measure had a
dual aim, and for the Court it was in this sense a valid measure of market-making
harmonization. Occasionally, sceptical examination of the legitimate reach of the
programme of legislative harmonization surfaced in the academic literature, but
critical analysis of this type was exceptional and appeared to attract little attention
and still less support.[60]

---

[57] Case 91/79, *Commission* v. *Italy*, [1980] ECR 1099 (ECLI:EU:C:1980:85).
[58] *Ibid.*, at 1103.   [59] *Ibid.*, para. 8 of the judgment.
[60] For a rare example, see Close, 'The Legal Basis for the Consumer Protection Programme of the
EEC and Priorities for Action', 8 *European Law Review* (1983) 8.

2. The Single European Act and *Tobacco Advertising I*

A practical edge was introduced once the Single European Act came into force in 1987. The introduction of what is now Article 114 TFEU, and the availability of qualified majority voting in Council for measures of harmonization in the service of the internal market, ensured that it was possible to adopt a measure despite the opposition of a minority of Member States. The consequence was that a *constitutional* dimension to determining the permitted scope of legislative harmonization emerged from the previous purely *political* reading. The character of the internal market as a legal concept *mattered*. And eventually a state that had lost the political battle in Council chose to bring before the Court the question whether the measure was even within the scope of the Treaty at all.

This was the first *Tobacco Advertising* case: *Germany* v. *Parliament and Council*.[61] Directive 98/43 on the advertising of tobacco products was annulled as being invalidly based on Article 100a EC (now Article 114 TFEU), and also Articles 57(2) and 66 EC (now Articles 53(2) and 62 TFEU), governing the services sector.

Germany had opposed the Directive in Council, but had been outvoted. It then brought the matter before the Court, arguing that the Directive, which imposed heavy (harmonized) restrictions on tobacco advertising, lacked a valid legal basis. Upholding this argument, the Court examined the Directive under two separate heads. First, it inquired whether it eliminated obstacles to the free movement of goods and services. The Court was persuaded that it did with respect to tobacco advertising in periodicals, magazines and newspapers, where a harmonized rule on advertising would facilitate cross-border trade in such goods. However, the Court did not think the same could be said of the prohibition of such advertising on posters, parasols, ashtrays and other articles used in hotels, restaurants, cafés and cinemas, since, it concluded, these prohibitions 'in no way help facilitate trade in the products concerned'.[62] Secondly, the Court asked whether the Directive eliminated distortions of competition. It insisted that only 'appreciable' distortions would suffice.[63] Were it otherwise, 'the powers of the Community legislature would be practically unlimited'.[64] This is (what we now know as) the principle of conferral in action. The requirement was, in the Court's view, not fulfilled, since no appreciable distortion of competition was involved – except as regards sponsorship of certain sports events, which were in danger of being relocated 'with considerable repercussions on the conditions of competition for undertakings associated with such undertakings'.[65]

The Court annulled the Directive in its entirety. It went too far: it went beyond the process of building an internal market. The thematic core of the judgment is a faithful embrace of the principle of conferral contained today in Article 5 TEU. The constitutional sensitivity of the matter is made explicit in the Opinion of Advocate General Fennelly:

The legal basis invoked by the Advertising Directive relates to the internal market. The Community's internal market competence is not limited, a priori, by any reserved domain

---

[61] Case C-376/98, *Germany* v. *Parliament and Council*, [2000] ECR I-8419 (ECLI:EU:C:2000:544).
[62] *Ibid.*, at para. 99.   [63] *Ibid.*, at para. 106.
[64] *Ibid.*, at para. 107.   [65] *Ibid.*, at para. 110.

of Member State power. It is a horizontal competence, whose exercise displaces national regulatory competence in the field addressed. Judicial review of the exercise of such a competence is a delicate and complex matter. On the one hand, unduly restrained judicial review might permit the Community institutions to enjoy, in effect, general or unlimited legislative power, contrary to the principle that the Community only enjoys those limited competences, however extensive, which have been conferred on it by the Treaty with a view to the attainment of specified objectives. This could permit the Community to encroach impermissibly on the powers of the Member States. On the other hand, the Court cannot, in principle, restrict the legitimate performance by the Community legislator of its task of removing barriers and distortions to trade in goods and services. It is the task of the Court, as the repository of the trust and confidence of the Community institutions, the Member States and the citizens of the Union, to perform this difficult function of upholding the constitutional division of powers between the Community and the Member States on the basis of objective criteria.[66]

The Court was not quite as candid about this wider context to the case. One would not expect it to be. But it comes close:

... the measures referred to in Article 100a(1) [now Art 114 TFEU] of the Treaty are intended to improve the conditions for the establishment and functioning of the internal market. To construe that article as meaning that it vests in the Community legislature a general power to regulate the internal market would not only be contrary to the express wording of the provisions cited above but would also be incompatible with the principle embodied in Article 3b of the EC Treaty (now Art 5 TEU) that the powers of the Community are limited to those specifically conferred on it.[67]

The Court duly showed itself willing and able to police what we would today describe as the principle of conferral: the internal market as a legal concept did not permit the adoption of a such a wide-ranging measure.

The implication of the ruling is that the Court thought most of the provisions of the Directive were not aimed at the construction of the internal market, but rather that they were in truth instruments of public health policy. The Union possesses a conferred competence in the field of public health, found in Article 168 TFEU (formerly Article 152 EC), but this explicitly excludes harmonization of laws. It was too fragile and limited a legal base to bear the Directive, which is why the Commission had never attempted to take that route in proposing legislation in the field through the 1990s.[68] But (what is today) Article 114, on which the Commission had pinned its hopes and with which the Council (acting by qualified majority) and the Parliament had agreed, could not bear it either, because in the Court's view the necessary market-making element was missing. It is important to be clear that the Court's objection was *not* that concerns to promote public health were so obviously prominent in the

---

[66] *Ibid.*, at para. of his Opinion.   [67] *Ibid.*, at para. 83; see also at paras 106–107.
[68] The proposal only finally bore fruit once a change of government in the UK in 1997 created a qualified majority in Council willing to support it. On the background see Khanna, 'The Defeat of the European Tobacco Advertising Directive: a Blow for Health', 20 *Yearbook of European Law* (2001) 113; Hervey, 'Up in Smoke? Community (Anti) Tobacco Law and Policy', 26 *European Law Review* (2001) 101.

legislative choice made, still less that the core of the harmonized regime was a *ban* on advertising. In fact the Court went out of its way to accept explicitly that the EU legislature may validly adopt harmonized rules even where 'public health protection is a decisive factor in the choices to be made'.[69] This, once again, underlines the unavoidable 'dual function' of harmonization: since the national laws subjected to the discipline of harmonization were 'inspired by public health policy objectives',[70] it is natural that the harmonized rules represent a choice about the proper shape of the EU's contribution to public health. What is more, this is recognized by both the TFEU and Charter (see Section C). And, as discussed earlier (see Section E), a ban is perfectly possible as a harmonized norm provided it forms part of a wider scheme governing on a common basis the sector in question (here, tobacco products). But the threshold for reliance on (what is now) Article 114 TFEU must be crossed. The flaw on which the Court relied was the inadequate contribution to the functioning of the internal market, not the vigorous commitment to protection of public health.

A measure of harmonization must actually contribute to eliminating obstacles to the free movement of goods or to the freedom to provide services or to removing appreciable distortions of competition. This is the threshold. This is Article 5 TEU's principle of conferral applied in the particular context of legislative harmonization. These are the limits imposed by the internal market as a legal concept on the reach of Article 114 TFEU. The Court's ruling counts as an assertion of competence as a constitutionalized value within the EU legal order at the expense of majoritarian political preference.

3. The Subsequent Case Law

So far, so heroic. But, as so often in the inspection of the internal market as a limiting legal concept, the reality is rather different. The Court's ruling needs to be assessed with an appreciation of the practice of 15 years since *Tobacco Advertising*. By far the most striking feature of the case law over the period since the landmark annulment of the Directive in that case is the almost complete failure of other attempts to persuade the Court that the EU legislature has failed to respect the limits of conferred competence. And this – again – eases the analysis towards an understanding of the internal market as more an empowering than a limiting legal concept.

In *Tobacco Advertising* the Court had openly explained that a Directive prohibiting the advertising of tobacco products in periodicals, magazines and newspapers could be adopted as a harmonized measure with a view to ensuring the free movement of press products. So after Directive 98/43 was annulled in *Tobacco Advertising* the EU legislature responded by adopting the similar but narrower Directive 2003/33 on the harmonization of laws relating to advertising and sponsorship of tobacco products, which did exactly that![71] Its validity was also challenged, but without success. This is *Tobacco Advertising II*.[72] The Court went out of its way to underline

---

[69] Case C-376/98, *supra* note 61, at para. 88.
[70] *Ibid.*, at para. 76.   [71] OJ 2003 L 152/16.
[72] Case C-380/03, *Germany* v. *Parliament and Council*, [2006] ECR I-11573 (ECLI:EU:C:2006:772).

that provided the necessary market-making dimension was present, there was no constitutional bar to public health protection serving as 'a decisive factor in the choices' made.[73] This means that the internal market's breadth as a legal concept radically subverts the restrictions on public health policy conducted by the EU which are carefully written into Article 168 TFEU. And in this case, unlike in the first *Tobacco Advertising* case, that was exactly the consequence. Directive 2003/33 passed the Court's test. Given the concrete advice the Court had provided to the legislature in the earlier case, which had been dutifully followed, no other outcome could have been anticipated.

It was demonstrated in Section C that the fundamental freedoms are read in a way that causes a significant curtailment of national autonomy in circumstances where the EU's sector-specific *legislative* competence could not extend so far. This empowers the Court. But, then, it also empowers the legislature under the functionally driven, not sector-specific, legal bases, of which Article 114 TFEU is the most high profile. It is an odd design. The EU's sector-specific legislative competences are in many cases *very* weak, and often include explicit or implied exclusions of harmonization. Article 168 TFEU on public health is of this type: so too are, for example, Article 167 TFEU on culture and Article 169 TFEU on consumer protection. Article 352 TFEU is calculatedly chained to these restraints: its third paragraph, an innovation of the Treaty of Lisbon, directs that measures based upon it 'shall not entail harmonisation of Member States' laws or regulations in cases where the Treaties exclude such harmonisation'. Article 114 is barren of any such fetter. So, by contrast, to the sector-specific legal bases Article 114 is *very* strong and broad, and therefore it is typically the EU legislature's weapon of choice. In fact, Article 114 makes a mockery of the carefully drawn restrictions in provisions such as Article 168. Once again, the impact of the concept of the internal market is revealed as both broad and operationally imprecise.

The Court's description of the threshold that must be crossed before reliance on Article 114 is valid has been conscientiously copied by the EU legislature in order to protect itself from the penalty of invalidation. The threshold, crafted from the internal market as a legal concept, is low and, most of all, it is extremely hard to refute claims that it has been crossed. This reveals much about the *practice* associated with the *principle* of conferral.

So, for example, *R* v. *Secretary of State ex parte BAT and Imperial Tobacco* involved a challenge to the validity of another of the EU's harmonized instruments dealing with tobacco products, Directive 2001/37 which dealt primarily with provisions on labelling (including the – increasingly grotesque – warnings) and also maximum tar and nicotine yield.[74] The Court considered that trade between Member States represented a relatively large part of the market for tobacco products in the Community. Rules relating to such products' designation, composition or packaging are liable to constitute obstacles to the free movement of goods. The Court was satisfied that it was likely that obstacles to the free movement of those products

---

[73] *Ibid.*, at para. 39. See also Section C.   [74] Case C-491/01, *supra* note 15.

would arise by reason of the adoption by the Member States of new rules' imposing requirements to print warnings on packets and to govern tar content. *Likelihood* is therefore a constitutionally significant criterion. The Court added that the public's increasing consciousness of the dangers to health posed by tobacco products was a factor prompting national rule-making.[75] This entails that a competence to harmonize which did not exist in the past may come into being where public pressure for national regulation increases and so pushes the prospect of such regulation beyond the constitutionally crucial threshold of 'likelihood'. In this sense, competence to legislate is a moving target. The Court concluded that the Directive was a valid measure of harmonization, since it 'genuinely has as its object the improvement of the conditions for the functioning of the internal market'.[76]

In *Alliance for Natural Health* the Court tamely approved the harmonization of laws governing food supplements, referring to cases brought before the Court concerning situations in which traders had encountered obstacles in target Member States when marketing food supplements lawfully marketed in their home state.[77] It relied too on the Explanatory Memorandum to the proposal for a Directive which stated the Commission services had received 'a substantial number of complaints from economic operators' on account of the differences between national rules which 'the application of the principle of mutual recognition [sic] did not succeed in overcoming'.[78] This makes it remarkably easy to legislate and, by way of corollary, very hard to assemble constitutionally (rather than politically) durable objections to valid reliance on Article 114 TFEU. Regulatory fragmentation is admittedly common in a landscape as varied as that found across the 28 Member States of the EU. The basic constitutional threshold, which is association with the internal market project, is therefore readily found to be crossed.

That *preventive* harmonization is permitted is confirmed and illustrated by *Vodafone, O2 et al.* v. *Secretary of State*.[79] An attack on the validity of the so-called 'Roaming Regulation' (Regulation 717/2007) failed. The Regulation capped the wholesale and retail prices which terrestrial mobile operators may charge for the provision of roaming services on public mobile networks for voice calls between Member States. Its legal base was Article 95 EC (now Article 114 TFEU). Advocate General Maduro did *not* think the Court's criteria for valid 'preventive harmonisation' were satisfied in the case. The Court, however, did not agree and it held the measure valid. It declared that the Regulation had been adopted in response to the likelihood that national price control measures of divergent type would be adopted aiming to address the problem of the high level of retail charges for EU-wide roaming services. So the Court was prepared to treat this as an instance of preventive harmonization aimed at improving the conditions for the functioning of the internal market, even though the evidence was thin, had not impressed its own Advocate General and even though there was a degree of implausibility in the assumption that national regulators really

---

[75] *Ibid.*, at para. 67.   [76] *Ibid.*, at para. 75.
[77] Cases C-154/04 and C-155/04, *supra* note 16.   [78] *Ibid.*, at para. 36, 37.
[79] Case C-58/08, *supra* note 14. E.g., also Case C-377/98, *Netherlands* v. *Parliament and Council*, [2001] ECR I-7079 (ECLI:EU:C:2001:523); Case C-491/01, *supra* note 15.

would act in such a way as to disadvantage suppliers based on their territory.[80] The Court conspicuously reached its conclusions in *Vodafone* by reference only to the observations presented by the EU's own institutions and those found in the recitals attached to the measure. It drew on both the explanatory memorandum to the proposal and the impact assessment to substantiate the finding that there was a likelihood of divergent development of national laws. The recital stated there was pressure for Member States to take measures to address the problem of the high level of retail charges for roaming services, and the Court adds that this was moreover confirmed by the Commission at the hearing.[81] So the institution that had proposed the measure was allowed a powerful voice in protecting it from invalidation. The internal market is here vividly revealed as an empowering legal concept.

One final example of this empowering dynamic. It might seem obvious that, where a matter is subject to national measures which exert an effect that is purely internal to a Member State, then there is no scope to subject the matter to harmonization. Article 114 and the project of creating an internal market is aimed at crossborder activity and effects. However, the border line between the purely internal matter and the matter with cross-border effects will frequently be hard to identify, and it is clear that the EU enjoys a competence to legislate even where there is doubt whether cross-border repercussions are in all circumstances at stake. Reliance on Article 114 does not 'presuppose the existence of an actual link with free movement between Member States in every situation referred to by the measure founded on that basis'.[82] The aim is certainty and predictability in application: were a measure of harmonization to be held applicable only to a specific situation which is demonstrated to have a cross-border dimension and to be, in effect, disabled in the absence of that dimension, then the result would be to create an uncertainty that would damage the basic aim of harmonization as a means to eliminate obstacles to the functioning of the internal market. But the result is legislative empowerment: a measure adopted pursuant to Article 114 may properly exert an impact in some instances on situations internal to a Member State.

4. Limits, What Limits?

If divergent national measures cause an *appreciable* distortion of competition, the matter falls in principle within the scope of Article 114 TFEU and legislative harmonization by the EU is permitted. If the distortion of competition is not appreciable, the matter escapes the scope of application of Article 114. The EU may not intervene to harmonize: the matter remains to be dealt with (in diverse ways) at national level. The adjective 'appreciable' carries heavy constitutional weight. It draws the line. Equally, provided that the emergence of obstacles is *likely* and that the measure in question is designed to prevent them, 'preventive harmonization' is

---

[80] See, in particular, Brennke, 'Annotation', 47 *Common Market Law Review* (2010) 1793.
[81] Case C-58/08, *supra* note 14, at para. 44.
[82] Joined Cases C-465/00, C-138/01 and C-139/01, *Rechnungshof* v. *Österreichischer Rundfunk*, [2003] ECR I-4989 (ECLI:EU:C:2003:294), at para. 41.

permitted pursuant to Article 114 TFEU. So if such emergence is not likely, the matter escapes the scope of application of Article 114. The EU may not intervene to harmonize. The word 'likely' carries significant constitutional weight, for it serves to define the limits of Article 114. It draws the line.

Whether these lines are crossed is hard to measure, and so hard to police. This exercise in drawing a line to separate the application of EU law and the autonomy of the Member States is familiar territory. Defining EU free movement law finds a parallel in defining EU harmonization law. Just as the EU reviews national measures but only where they are sufficiently damaging to the functioning of the internal market, so too the EU may harmonize national laws but only where the differences are sufficiently damaging to the functioning of the internal market. In *Åklagaren* v. *Mickelsson, Roos* the Court's attached the adjective 'considerable' to its test based on a rule's influence on consumer behaviour in shaping its location of the reach of Article 34.[83] In *Sayn-Wittgenstein*, dealing with Article 21 TFEU, it relied on the threshold that an inconvenience must be 'serious'.[84] This technique has much in common with its use of words such as 'appreciable' and 'likely' in the case law fixing the reach of Article 114. In all instances the aim is to capture the notion that just because national laws vary does not of itself mean there is (in short) 'an internal market problem' of a type that triggers EU law, whether Articles 21, 34, 56 or Article 114 TFEU are at stake. Simple diversity among national practices is not enough to justify EU intervention. But those lines are based on imprecise and unpredictable foundations. State aid law offers further examples: its reach into national autonomy rests on tricky notions such as distortion and selectivity (see Section E).

The deep question asks what allocation of competence to the EU is required to ensure the effective functioning of the internal market foreseen by Articles 3(3) TEU and 26 TFEU. The TFEU is deeply unhelpful.

The Court places enormous weight on slippery adjectives and adverbs in its attempt to define the limits of internal market law in a more sophisticated manner than does the TFEU. The objection is that the Court has created a litter of tests which simply describe the problem – that internal market law's incursion into national regulatory autonomy has a limit, which necessarily flows ultimately from Article 5 TEU – rather than providing a *workable* test for determining when those limits are in fact reached. More than that: if the ambiguity of the TFEU, in particular the ambiguity of the internal market as a legal concept, delegates considerable interpretative autonomy to the Court, what the Court has in fact done is to transfer that autonomy into the hands of the legislative institutions of the EU. It is easy for the legislature simply to copy-and-paste the Court's formula and very hard for such claims to be falsified in a constitutional challenge. And this is what has happened. In fact, if one reviews the text of the Directive annulled in the first *Tobacco Advertising* case and compares it with measures that have subsequently escaped invalidation, the striking

---

[83] Case C-142/05, *Åklagaren* v. *Mickelsson, Roos*, [2009] ECR I-4273 (ECLI:EU:C:2009:336): see Chapter 6.C.5.

[84] Case C-208/09, *Ilonka Sayn-Wittgenstein* v. *Landeshauptmann von Wien*, [2010] ECR I-13693 (ECLI:EU:C:2010:806): see Chapter 6.D.2.

feature is the sheer laziness of the legislative drafting. The original Directive was just four pages long and garlanded with only 12 Recitals: its successor, Directive 2003/33, though narrower in scope as a result of the Court's ruling, runs to 18 Recitals, while the 'Roaming Regulation' reviewed by the Court in *Vodafone* runs to nine pages and is larded with 39 Recitals, four of which ostentatiously brandish the need to ensure the functioning of the internal market as the measure's aim.[85] It is at least arguable that the change of style is more attributable to strategic legislative adoption of the Court's vocabulary rather than conscientious engagement with the question of what kind of regulatory platform the internal market truly needs.

That is speculation: what is clear is how hard it is to contest a claim to legislate on the basis of Article 114 TFEU. It is easy to assert actual or likely divergence between national laws which might conceivably cause interruption to the internal market. One might counter that such divergence is the very lifeblood of a healthy economy, but that is in EU law a political argument against exercising the legislative competence, not an argument against its existence as a matter of constitutional law. In practice, legislation is readily 'Court proofed', thanks to the ready adoption of the Court's own vague tests. The case law subsequent to the first *Tobacco Advertising* case is in consequence almost entirely marked by judicial green lights for legislative harmonization. The Court, in striving to provide a more concrete shape to the limits of Article 114 TFEU than does the terms of the Treaty, has simply offered up an invitation to the legislature to enjoy the protection of its slipstream. The EU's legislature is able to exploit the broad and ambiguously fuzzy contours of Article 114 TFEU to convert compliance with the principle of conferral into little more than a drafting exercise.[86] The consequence is that a line of case law that began with the impression of an exercise in legislative restriction has been converted into a theme of legislative empowerment. [87]

H. Subsidiarity and Proportionality

The EU must act within the bounds set not only by the principle of conferral but also the principles of subsidiarity and proportionality. This is clear from Article 5 TEU and it entails that even where a legislative competence *exists* – the domain of conferral – its *exercise* will be invalid if it trespasses beyond the restraint imposed on legislative action by the principles of subsidiarity and proportionality.

It is therefore a condition of validity of a measure of legislative harmonization that it shall comply with the principles of subsidiarity and proportionality.

The problem, however, is a familiar one. It is that the restraint imposed is in principle a good deal more impressive than its significance in practice. The problem, in

---

[85] Recitals 3, 4, 11 and 39.

[86] Cf. Weatherill, 'The Limits of Legislative Harmonisation Ten Years after *Tobacco Advertising*: How the Court's Case Law Has Become a "Drafting Guide"', 12 *German Law Journal* (2011) 827.

[87] Wyatt, 'Community Competence to Regulate the Internal Market', in M. Dougan and S. Currie, *Fifty Years of the European Treaties: Looking Back and Thinking Forward* (2009).

short, lies in the remarkably ambiguous character of these principles, which tends to mean that if there is adequate political support for legislative action it is improbable that the Court will be persuaded to intervene. So although conferral is a logically distinct (and a *priori*) matter from subsidiarity and proportionality, the rhythms are thematically similar: ambiguity in legal concept shields political choices from being set aside by judges.

1. Subsidiarity

Article 5(3) TEU contains the principle of subsidiarity. It applies in areas which do not fall within the EU's exclusive competence, so it applies to all areas pertaining to the internal market, save only for the establishment of the competition rules necessary for the functioning of the internal market.[88] It provides that 'the Union shall act only if and in so far as the objectives of the proposed action cannot be sufficiently achieved by the Member States, either at central level or at regional and local level, but can rather, by reason of the scale or effects of the proposed action, be better achieved at Union level'.

Legislative practice reveals faithful readiness to assert compliance with the principle of subsidiarity. It is normal to find the Preamble of a measure of harmonization include reference to subsidiarity. So, to take an entirely typical example, Regulation 1924/2006 on nutrition and health claims states that:

Since the objective of this Regulation, namely to ensure the effective functioning of the internal market as regards nutrition and health claims whilst providing a high level of consumer protection, cannot be sufficiently achieved by the Member States and can therefore be better achieved at Community level, the Community may adopt measures, in accordance with the principle of subsidiarity...[89]

Not a word more is offered about subsidiarity in the text of the measure. This is more assertion than explanation. But it is standard legislative practice. Routine recitation of subsidiarity is usually devoid of any substance and depth. Complying with subsidiarity is, in this sense, a question of ticking the box. If there is political will to act, the measure will be adorned with the shimmer of claimed compliance with subsidiarity. But subsidiarity plays no concrete role in guiding the EU towards the choice between action or inaction.

Subsidiarity *could* act as an invitation to pursue engagement with the debate about how to weigh up the competing merits of centralized rule-making and uniformity, on the one hand, and local autonomy, cultural particularity, diversity and room for experimentation, on the other.[90] But it does not. This general problem was helpfully illuminated by Jean-Claude Piris, at the time Director General of the Council's Legal Service, in evidence presented to the Subsidiarity Working Group of

---

[88] Article 3(b) TFEU.   [89] OJ 2006 L 404/9, Recital 34.
[90] E.g. Carbonara, Luppi and Parisi, 'Self-Defeating Subsidiarity', 5 *Review of Law and Economics* (2009) 742; G. Gelauff, I. Grilo and A. Lejour (eds), *Subsidiarity and Economic Reform in Europe* (2008).

the Convention on the Future of Europe.[91] He confessed that the Legal Service itself had rarely expressed doubts about compliance with the principle of subsidiarity, but he was determined to cast the net of (ir)responsibility more broadly. He explained that once it is decided to introduce rules at EU level, the process of political negotiation is typically characterized by Member States aiming to secure a result as close as possible to their own pre-existing systems. The outcome is typically cumulative: a package deal which crams into the harmonized standard aspects of many pre-existing national standards. In this sense it is the trade-restricting diversity of national regulatory practice which provides incentives to Member States to abandon purely national rule-making in favour of EU-level standards, but then the desire to minimize the costs of adaptation affects the way that the EU standard becomes shaped. Subsidiarity might usefully be relied on in making a case for *less dense* EU-level regulation, but in such circumstances it has lost any power to speak in support of preservation of national regulatory competence through *no* EU-level regulation. The nature of EU political bargaining tends to generate an intensification of rule-making damaging to expression of local autonomy. The subsidiarity principle, as a potential restraining influence, stands meekly on the sidelines.

In principle, the Court should intervene where the subsidiarity principle is violated. In practice, it does not – in practice, to a large extent, it cannot.

The Court's first engagement with the principle of subsidiarity as a basis to review the validity of adopted harmonization legislation arrived in *R* v. *Secretary of State ex parte BAT and Imperial Tobacco*.[92] This case, met earlier (see Section G.3), involved an unsuccessful challenge to the reliance on (what is today) Article 114 TFEU as the basis for a Directive harmonizing rules on labelling on tobacco products and tar and nicotine yields. The Directive was found to make an adequate contribution to the internal market. It complied with the principle of conferral. It was, accordingly, in principle open to review for compliance with the principle of subsidiarity, but the Court adopted an approach which makes it difficult to imagine circumstances in which a harmonization measure, or indeed any EU measure setting common rules, will be found to violate the demands of subsidiarity. Its formula deserves recitation in full:

... the Directive's objective is to eliminate the barriers raised by the differences which still exist between the Member States' laws, regulations and administrative provisions on the manufacture, presentation and sale of tobacco products, while ensuring a high level of health protection, in accordance with Article 95(3) EC [now 114(3) TFEU]. Such an objective cannot be sufficiently achieved by the Member States individually and calls for action at Community level, as demonstrated by the multifarious development of national laws in this case... It follows that, in the case of the Directive, the objective of the proposed action could be better achieved at Community level.[93]

This is deft or it is evasive, according to taste: the Court has deftly sustained subsidiarity as a legal principle on paper, while evasively conceding much in practice to

[91] WD-004 WG I 13 July 2002.
[92] Case C-491/01, *supra* note 15.   [93] *Ibid.*, at paras 181–183.

legislative discretion. Once it is determined that a competence to establish common rules exists, which is the nature of harmonization pursuant to Article 114 TFEU, the political decision to exercise that competence seems *in practice* immune from judicial subversion. This was not at all a one-off act of deft evasion. It has quickly become established as the Court's standard approach.[94]

It is not difficult to gain the impression that the Court has adopted a narrow approach to subsidiarity as a legal concept according to an assumption that it is in the political sphere in which subsidiarity concerns are most apt to be aired. And there is reason to be sympathetic to this approach. Subsidiarity is a statement of evident good sense as a general principle of governance, but it lacks the precision characteristic of a justiciable norm. Its aggressive application to upset political compromises would expose the Court to allegations that it trespasses beyond the proper role of judges. It is, moreover, another manifestation of the judicial concern to leave space for political decision-making which also animates the Court's review of enhanced co-operation[95] and of re-regulatory compromises struck in legislative harmonization.[96]

2. Proportionality

Article 5(4) TEU stipulates that under the principle of proportionality 'the content and form of Union action shall not exceed what is necessary to achieve the objectives of the Treaty'. As with subsidiarity, so too with proportionality: in the abstract this makes perfect sense and, indeed, proportionality was devised by the Court as a principle apt to control legislative excess long before it was embraced in the text of the Treaties, but plenty of questions remain open about how in practice to monitor the application of the principle when the EU exercises its legislative competence.[97] And here too, as is true of subsidiarity, the Court shows a high degree of caution when invited to condemn legislative measures as incompatible with the demands of proportionality.

The Court has long embraced respect for the broad discretion which it thinks proper to grant to the EU legislative institutions where political, economic and social choices are at stake and where complex assessment is demanded. This is commonly true of legislative harmonization. The Court tends to accept that only where such a measure is manifestly inappropriate in relation to the objective which it seeks will validity be called into question. Such a relatively light degree of scrutiny reflects the Court's general anxiety to keep separate judicial and legislative functions.

Alliance for Natural Health offers a typical illustration.[98] The Court ruled that a Directive which permitted the marketing of nutrients only where they had received a favourable opinion from the competent scientific authorities (a 'positive list' system) was more intrusive than a plausible alternative system permitting use of nutri-

---

[94] See similarly e.g. Case C-103/01, *Commission* v. *Germany*, [2003] ECR I-5369 (ECLI:EU:C:2003:301); Cases C-154/04 and C-155/04, *supra* note 16; Case C-58/08, *supra* note 14.

[95] Joined Cases C-274/11 and C-295/11, *Spain and Italy* v. *Council*, judgment of 16 April 2013, not yet reported (ECLI:EU:C:2013:240): see Chapter 2.B.

[96] See Section D.

[97] See generally T. Tridimas, *The General Principles of EU Law* (2nd ed., 2006), Chs 3 and 4.

[98] Cases C-154/04 and C-155/04, *supra* note 16.

ents provided they had not been shown to present a risk to human health ('negative list'), but that it was nonetheless not in violation of the principle of proportionality. Citing the obligation of the EU legislature to ensure a high level of protection of human health (see Section C), it believed the measures were appropriate for achieving that objective and that they did not go beyond what is necessary to attain it.[99] There was nothing inevitable about the Court's conclusion. In his Opinion in the case, Advocate General Geelhoed protested bitterly that the 'positive list' system needed to be designed 'with prudence and precision' in order to meet the expectations of traders but that in fact the legislated administrative procedure had 'the transparency of a black box'.[100] But his plea to condemn the measure for violation of the principle of proportionality did not persuade the Court which, adopting a much milder level of scrutiny, remarked that it 'would, no doubt, have been desirable' for the Directive to have included provisions governing transparency and time limits, but was content to rely on 'the responsibility of the Commission' to operate the procedure in accordance with standards of sound administration.[101] In similar vein, in *Vodafone, O2 et al.* v. *Secretary of State* the applicants complained that the 'Roaming Regulation' capped prices for not only wholesale charges but also for retail charges.[102] The Court, emphasizing the legislature's broad discretion and inspecting its explanations for this choice, found it had taken a legitimate view that regulation of the wholesale market alone would not have done the job intended by the measure. The Regulation was not 'manifestly inappropriate having regard to the objective which the competent institution is seeking to pursue'.[103]

Davies, writing one of the most bracing critiques of the EU's legislative practice, demolishes the pretensions of subsidiarity as a restraint on excess and instead places strong reliance on a more assertive application of the principle of proportionality.[104] The motivation and good sense behind his anxiety to install an operationally useful restraining influence is hard to resist, but reliance on 'judicial proportionality' is harder to embrace. After all, proportionality shares with subsidiarity an aptitude for generating demanding and politically charged questions about the proper intensity of regulation which are not familiar or comfortable material to use in judicial review of acts which are, by definition, supported by the Commission, Parliament and a majority of Member States.

3. Political Controls

If the Court's cautious attitude to the supervision of legislative choices in the name of subsidiarity and proportionality is correctly diagnosed as driven by disinclination to use open textured standards to undermine political judgement, then the key to strengthening oversight of perceived legislative over-ambition at EU level should be

---

[99] *Ibid.*, at para. 111.   [100] *Ibid.*, at paras 66, 85 of his Opinion.
[101] *Ibid.*, at paras 81–82 of the judgment.   [102] Case C-58/08, *supra* note 14.
[103] *Ibid.*, at para. 52.
[104] Davies, 'Subsidiarity: The Wrong Idea, in the Wrong Place, at the Wrong Time', 43 *Common Market Law Review* (2006) 63. See also Hofmann, 'Which Limits? Control of Powers in an Integrated Legal System', in C. Barnard and O. Odudu (eds), *The Outer Limits of European Union Law* (2009) Ch. 4.

found in the political environment. That, indeed, has been one of the most prominent preoccupations of the process of re-thinking initiated by the Laeken Declaration of 2001 which ran through the Convention on the Future of Europe and the failed Treaty establishing a Constitution to the entry into force of the Lisbon Treaty in 2009, but which was certainly not cleanly or satisfactorily consummated in that reform text. The internal market in general, and harmonization in particular, are just part of this debate, but they are a *major* part because of their associated conceptual breadth and ambiguity.

At the Convention on the Future of the Europe attention to the matter of competence control occupied much time and energy.[105] The greater one perceived the problem – of ever expanding EU competence and activity more generally – to be, the more radical the plans for reform. Conversely those less alarmed, or at least more anxious to preserve the EU's flexible powers even if the price to be paid for that was to leave the door open to unforeseen expansion, were more conservative and content to retain the essence of the pre-existing system. The latter – the conservatives – were broadly in the majority, and this set the path to what would ultimately emerge in the Treaty of Lisbon, entering into force in 2009.

In particular, no headway was made in persuading the majority at the Convention to accept 'hard lists', involving for example exhaustive and tightly defined lists of the areas in which the EU is competent to act, or identification of areas off-limits to the EU and therefore remaining within the exclusive competence of the Member States; nor did the creation of a new tribunal of 'competence review', separate from the Court, win much support. Of particular relevance to the internal market, the deletion of (what are now) Articles 114 TFEU and/or 352 TFEU had its advocates, but not enough of them. The case against was that they constitute the principal problem cases in the corrosion of what is commonly called 'competence creep' in favour of the EU, and indeed the Laeken Declaration had picked out these two Treaty provisions – and only these two – as requiring special scrutiny. But the damaging loss of flexibility that would follow from deletion of these two functionally driven legal bases was enough to limit the abolitionists to minority status. This is to highlight an abiding background tension: alleged 'competence creep' opens the EU to criticisms rooted in want of formal legitimacy, and yet the more restrictive the rules and procedures under which it is forced to labour, the more it risks becoming unresponsive and ineffective, to the detriment of its ability to gather legitimacy through effective problem-solving on behalf of its Member States.

What was accepted, and what is today the renovated 'competence method' of the EU, involved solutions at the modest end of the scale. The clarification and re-organization of the Treaty rules governing competence which is now found in Articles 2–6 TFEU was designed to promote a more transparent and informed debate about what the EU does, how it does it, and why. That is supplemented by institutional

---

[105] See, e.g., Weatherill, 'Competence Creep and Competence Control', 23 *Yearbook of European Law* (2004) 1; Constantinesco, 'Les compétences et le principe de subsidiarité', 41 *Revue trimistrielle de droit europeen* (2005) 305; Swenden, 'Is the EU in Need of a Competence Catalogue? Insights from Comparative Federalism', 42 *Journal of Common Market Studies* (2004) 371.

reform. National parliaments had no explicit place in the EU lawmaking process until 2009: it was assumed that their views would be represented by ministers in Council. But, under the reforms instituted by the Treaty of Lisbon, the system for monitoring the existence and exercise of competence is enhanced and deepened by creating a role for national Parliaments. This is based on an *ex ante* monitoring system: the 'early warning system'. Plainly, the assumption holds that the Council is in practice too remote from everyday national parliamentary practice to constitute a genuinely reliable voice of national and local particularity, and so national Parliaments are granted their own distinct institutional identity at EU level. They are, after all, the bodies most obviously and directly prejudiced by over-hasty and over-intrusive legislative activity at EU level, and they are therefore the bodies most likely to hold an incentive to interject a critical voice.

The role allocated to national Parliaments is in its detail carefully defined. The Protocol on the role of national Parliaments addresses a formal process of ensuring the distribution of information to national Parliaments. It then provides for the submission of a *reasoned opinion* in cases of suspected violation of the subsidiarity principle, followed by an eight-week legislative 'standstill' period designed to give national Parliaments a real practical opportunity to intervene, applicable in all but urgent cases. The Protocol on the application of the principles of subsidiarity and proportionality absorbs this procedure in its Article 6 (although it is only subsidiarity, not proportionality, over which national Parliaments are formally granted a monitoring role). Then in Article 7 it puts flesh on the bones. Where reasoned opinions on non-compliance with subsidiarity represent at least one third of all the votes allocated to national Parliaments, the draft must be reviewed. The Commission may then maintain, amend or withdraw the draft, giving reasons for this. This is known as the *yellow* card. Where reasoned opinions on non-compliance with subsidiarity represent a simple majority of votes cast by national Parliaments, then the Commission must review the proposal and, if it decides to maintain it, it must itself present a reasoned opinion dealing with its view why the proposal complies with the subsidiarity principle. These opinions are then made available to the legislator. They shall be considered in the manner set out in Article 7(3) of the Protocol. This more interventionist version of the procedure is known as the *orange* card.

What is blatantly missing is a *red* card. There is no veto. This is fully in line with the relatively cautious pattern of reform shaped at the Convention on the Future of Europe and taken over in adapted form by the Treaty of Lisbon with effect from 2009: a veto power was rejected as too interventionist and liable to damage the flexibility of action entrusted to the EU lawmaking process. The collective intervention of national Parliaments, focused on the yellow and orange card procedures applicable to compliance with the subsidiarity principle, is therefore best understood as an attempt to promote *dialogue* 'from below' about whether particular EU proposals are valid or well-intentioned. The basic structure of the EU's lawmaking process is left untouched, but a new and probably critically minded voice is added to the pattern of negotiation.

The conscious emphasis is on subsidiarity as a predominantly *political* principle. The involvement of national Parliaments does not at all remove the *legal* requirement that EU acts shall comply with the principle of subsidiarity. The monitoring role allocated to national Parliaments was, and is, designed to supplement, not to replace, judicial control. But, as considered earlier, the key insight is that the Court has, in practice, placed subsidiarity largely beyond the reach of judicially based control. And it probably did so according to a sense that it was a dangerous lure which would have hooked courts into addressing fiercely contested political questions about the virtues and vices of centralized rule-making *versus* expression of divergent local preference. If judges will not do it, and if judges likely should not do it, national Parliaments might: the reasoned opinion procedure represents an attempt to enrich *political* debate about centralizing bias, albeit that the yellow and orange cards are 'soft' rather than 'hard' safeguards for state autonomy.

This is not to dismiss the value of the Court's role. It could, in fact, help to enliven this political debate. It would not be incompatible with its reticence to use subsidiarity as a basis for *substantive* review to place firm *procedural* obligations on the legislature when they are in receipt of objections raised by national Parliaments.[106] So, without touching debate on an act's political merits, the Court could hold unlawful an act adopted which fails adequately to engage with objections voiced through reasoned opinions, which would in turn force the EU's political institutions to take seriously the channel of dialogue envisaged under the procedure, and also induce national Parliaments, encouraged that their views are taken seriously, actively to participate in critical intervention. The Court's willingness to take heed of impact assessment and explanatory memoranda in checking the validity of EU acts was criticized earlier (see Section G.3) on the basis that this is simply to allow the political institutions to rely on their own preparatory material to defend choices that should be reviewed more objectively, but no such scorn is deserved where the independent protests of national Parliaments are at stake. The Court in this way would encourage improved and widened political deliberation about the relative virtues and vice of EU rule-making, inter alia in the construction of the internal market.

To focus on its relevance to the concerns pursued in this volume, the aspiration of the reasoned opinion procedure involving national Parliaments is best summarized as an attempt to deepen appreciation of the internal market as a *political* concept. This is where subsidiarity, though in itself bereft of operational precision, can help to frame a much-needed inquiry into how much local preference and identity participants in the EU project are willing to surrender in order to generate economic benefits.

The Commission, reviewing practice so far, has strained to maintain an optimistic tone: national Parliaments have 'further enriched the discussions'.[107] True, it would be an error to exaggerate the potential dynamic. Pre-existing problems, such as sheer lack of time to turn the gaze away from domestic politics to 'Brussels', cannot be solved by creating a procedure on paper. And national executives dominate Parliaments most of the time in most of the Member States, so one needs to be cautious in identifying what fresh critical thinking national Parliaments may be able realistically

---

[106] Cf. Groussot and Bogojević, 'Subsidiarity as a Procedural Safeguard of Federalism', in L. Azoulai, *The Question of Competence in the EU* (2014).
[107] COM (2011) 344, at 10.

to contribute, and what they may not. Even as it was under construction there was legitimate doubt about how much the new arrangements could feasibly change *in practice*.[108] But the aim to raise the profile of *national*-level political processes and controls, and to make thinner the apparent divide between 'Brussels' and national political life, is thoroughly well-intentioned.

In 2011 64 reasoned opinions from national Parliaments were received by the Commission, relating to 28 different proposals.[109] In 2012 there were 70 reasoned opinions on 23 different proposals[110] and in 2013 this rose to 88 reasoned opinions on 36 different proposals.[111] In 2014 the number of reasoned opinions submitted by national Parliaments dropped to only 21, on 15 different proposals.[112] The decrease is attributed by the Commission to the reduction in the number of legislative proposals it had made, as it approached the end of its term of office, not to any diminished desire on the part of national Parliaments to make use of the procedure.[113]

The threshold for the yellow card has been crossed just twice, while that required for an orange card has not been crossed in any case. The first yellow card was aimed at the Commission Proposal for a Regulation on the exercise of the right to take collective action within the context of the freedom of establishment and the freedom to provide services.[114] This, the so-called 'Monti II' legislative proposal of the Commission, was, in summary, an attempt to provide a modest legislative clarification of the consequences of the Court's rulings on labour law and free movement of companies in *Viking Line* and *Laval*, which were examined at length in Chapter 9.B. The proposal was fiercely opposed by some Member States and by the Parliament too, and the criticisms of national Parliaments added to the ferment. The Commission withdrew the proposal. However, it adamantly refused to accept that it violated the subsidiarity principle, and preferred simply to cite an absence of adequate political support. The proposal has not been resuscitated. One might choose to treat this as evidence of the limited formal role played and playable by the subsidiarity principle and, instead, an insight into the overriding importance of the political debate about how best to manage the process of economic liberalization in the internal market – but in fact it is probably better to treat the episode as evidence of the absence of any viable divide between 'formal' subsidiarity and wider political contestation.

The second yellow card dates from Autumn 2013, and it is remote from the internal market. It concerns a Proposal for a Council Regulation on the establishment of the European Public Prosecutor's Office, and on this occasion the Commission duly reviewed the proposal, as required after receipt of the yellow card, but determined to maintain it.[115] It has not yet been adopted.

It is plain from inspection of the reasoned opinions[116] that there is considerable variety in the way in which national Parliaments across the Union have interpreted

---

[108] See, e.g., Auel, 'Democratic Accountability and National Parliaments: Redefining the Impact of Parliamentary Scrutiny in EU Affairs', 13 *European Law Journal* (2007) 487; P. Kiiver, *The National Parliaments in the European Union – a Critical View on EU Constitution-Building* (2006).
[109] COM (2012) 373.   [110] COM (2013) 566.   [111] COM (2014) 506.
[112] COM (2015) 315.   [113] *Ibid.*, at 2.2, 4.   [114] COM (2012) 130.
[115] COM (2014) 506, at 8–10.
[116] They are collected at the IPEX website (http://www.ipex.eu/IPEXL-WEB/home/home.do).

the reach of their designated role. Some have been careful to remain within a more-or-less convincing understanding of the principle of subsidiarity, whereas others have plainly used the procedure as a means to express much broader political anxieties about the content of intended legislative proposals. In one specifically legal sense this seepage is inevitable. The reasoned opinion procedure is attached to the principle of subsidiarity and not to the principle of proportionality, but this is an artificial and frankly unsustainable separation. There is a clear overlap between the two. So, for example, in *ex parte BAT* the Court found that 'the intensity of the action undertaken' was 'in keeping with the requirements of the principle of subsidiarity in that..., as paragraphs 122 to 141 above make clear, it did not go beyond what was necessary to achieve the objective pursued'.[117] The cited paragraphs, the analysis of which was recycled, were concerned with proportionality. So to pretend that the reasoned opinion is only about subsidiarity and not about proportionality makes a false assumption about the character of these two associated legal principles. More broadly, however, there is much to be said in favour of treating the review of subsidiarity which is promised by the reasoned opinion procedure as properly receptive to dialogue about the political merits of a proposal. If subsidiarity is to frame and promote a useful debate about (in short) centralization *versus* local autonomy as a general tension and as a means to frame discussion about sector-specific regulatory initiatives, then it should not be interpreted in a narrow way that rebuffs national Parliaments eager to enrich the debate. Put another way, the self-consciously minimalist attitude to judicial review on the basis of subsidiarity adopted by the Court (see Section H.1) should certainly not be the model for the development of the reasoned opinion procedure, or else it will prove simply useless. There is *legal* subsidiarity, but there must be – bigger, wider, more ambitious and more inquisitive – *political* subsidiarity too.

Gratifyingly, the Commission seems alert to this. It is plain from the Commission's annual reports[118] and from inspection of the reasoned opinions themselves[119] that, in practice, national Parliaments have engaged with the debates in a manner that stretches far beyond subsidiarity understood in a formal and narrow sense. They frequently engage with the political merits of legislative proposals. This is a good thing, in so far as it promises a richer debate about the relative virtues and vices of EU intervention. In this spirit the Commission itself appears to be content to take a flexible approach to the scope of the procedure. It has been encouraged to do so by COSAC, the (admittedly self-interested) Conference of Parliamentary Committees for Union Affairs of Parliaments of the European Union.[120] This should form part of the Commission's much broader programme of 'Better Regulation' within the EU,[121] although its May 2015 document entitled *Better Regulation for Better Results – An*

---

[117] Case C-491/01, *supra* note 15, at para. 184.
[118] Available via the European Commission's website (http://ec.europa.eu/smart-regulation/better_regulation/reports_en.htm).
[119] *Supra* note 116.   [120] E.g., Contribution of the LII COSAC, OJ 2015 C 181/1, section 2.
[121] See http://ec.europa.eu/smart-regulation/index_en.htm.

EU Agenda in fact contains only two references to subsidiarity in its 13 pages, both of them perfunctory.[122]

Commentators have expressed general approval of the intentions behind the reasoned opinion scheme and its early practical elaboration.[123] In fact, commonly the cry has been for more of it. The role allocated to national Parliaments has been criticized as too narrow, too cramped in the time allowed to act and, generally, too weak. One of the issues pursued by the UK government after its election in May 2015 has been an increase in the profile and power of national Parliaments, and an element in the agreed February 2016 're-negotiation' package was to create a 'red card', albeit with rather strict pre-conditions attached to its deployment.[124] Even if it is hard to take any of the British interventions as remotely concerned to offer balm to the functioning of the EU rather than the tortured soul of the Conservative party, there is genuine value in keeping under close scrutiny the proper balancing of political power between national institutions and those of the EU.

There is an unseen purpose to the reasoned opinion procedure. The point of equipping national Parliaments with yellow and orange cards is to grant them a voice at EU level. However, even though the creation of the procedure was largely motivated precisely by the failures of domestic political oversight of action taken by national ministers in Council, one may expect or at least aspire to greater activity in future by national Parliamentarians *within those domestic political processes themselves*. Denmark has famously been the state which has placed strict limits on the mandate granted to its ministers when they participate in Council deliberations, but it need not be alone. The *Bundesverfassungsgericht*'s Lisbon ruling extracted changes in domestic political oversight as a pre-condition to German ratification of the Lisbon Treaty.[125] Neither the requirement of unanimity in Council nor the relatively 'soft' yellow card granted to national Parliaments could meet the BVerfG's objection that state legislative bodies could be sidestepped by executive action taken pursuant to Article 352 TFEU, and so the closer involvement of the Bundestag and Bundesrat in the exercise of that competence was required. Before ratification of the Lisbon Treaty, German law was duly changed to accommodate this. In this sense, the Treaty of Lisbon not only created new rights for national Parliaments at EU level, it also provoked adjustment in scrutiny of EU activities carried out by national Parliaments *at national level*. It is, however, most peculiar that such emphasis was placed by the BVerfG on Article 352 TFEU and none at all on Article 114 TFEU.

---

[122] COM (2015) 215, both at 4.

[123] E.g., Cygan, 'The Parliamentarisation of EU Decision-Making? The Impact of the Treaty of Lisbon on National Parliaments', 36 *European Law Review* (2011) 480; Cooper, 'Bicameral or Tricameral? National Parliaments and Representative Democracy in the European Union', 35 *Journal of European Integration* (2013) 531; Bickenbach, 'Das Subsidiaritätsprinzip in Art. 5 EUV und seine Kontrolle', *Europarecht* (2013) 523; Guastaferro, 'Coupling National Identity with Subsidiarity Concerns in National Parliaments' Reasoned Opinions', 21 *Maastricht Journal* (2014) 320; Jančić, 'The Game of Cards: National Parliaments in the EU and the Future of the Early Warning Mechanism and the Political Dialogue', 52 *Common Market Law Review* (2015) 939.

[124] OJ 2016 CI 69/1. Implementation is contingent on the UK voting to remain in the EU in its June 2016 referendum.

[125] See http://www.bundesverfassungsgericht.de/entscheidungen/es20090630_2bve000208en.html.

In conclusion, for all the virtuous institutional reform focused in particular on national Parliaments designed to promote political reflection, neither subsidiarity nor proportionality serves as a *constitutionally durable* basis for opposing the adoption of EU rules in the name of the making of the internal market. They are too soft in character for that. That connects subsidiarity and proportionality readily to much of the wider discussion of line-drawing and competence-demarcation in this volume.

14

Legislative Competence More Broadly

The Treaty on the Functioning of the European Union (TFEU) contains a number of bases for the adoption of legislation in particular areas that are either explicitly or by (sometimes ambiguous) implication associated with the internal market. Section A looks relatively briefly at the wide sweep of these provisions. Section B takes one set in particular as a case study deserving deeper examination, both because of its substantive importance and also its capacity to provide insight into the contested and ambiguous character of the internal market. This is social policy and labour market regulation.

A. The Wide Sweep

Article 81 TFEU grants the EU a competence to develop *judicial co-operation in civil matters* having cross-border implications, which is available particularly – though not exclusively – when necessary for the proper functioning of the internal market. Article 113 TFEU provides for *harmonization of indirect taxation* to ensure the establishment and functioning of the internal market. Article 118 TFEU provides that in the context of the establishment and functioning of the internal market measures may be adopted to create *European intellectual property rights*. Article 168 TFEU provides for EU action relating to *public health*, which includes an explicit exclusion of power to harmonize national laws, although, as the case law discussed at Chapter 13.G.3 confirms, this has no restraining effect on recourse to Article 114 TFEU as a basis to harmonize national laws affecting public health where this makes an adequate contribution to the functioning of the internal market. Article 169 TFEU provides for EU action relating to *consumer protection*, which is confined to measures which support, supplement and monitor the policy pursued by the Member States and, not least for this reason, has been little used and is far out-stripped in importance as a source of EU rules on consumer protection by Article 114 TFEU. Article 194 TFEU provides for EU action on *energy* in the context of the establishment and functioning of the internal market. Other EU policies that do not immediately suggest an intimate connection with the internal market project are in some instances nevertheless politically part of the package. The Structural Funds and the Cohesion Fund, addressed in Articles 174–178 TFEU, which comprise Title XVIII on *Economic, Social and Territorial Cohesion* in the TFEU's immense Part Three, constitute in short the EU's regional policy. They were added to the

Treaty system in 1987 by the Single European Act as part of an understanding that although the internal market project was intended to create growth for all, the benefits would doubtless be unevenly spread and that accordingly a political commitment to effect a degree of distribution in favour of less advantaged regions was required.[1]

This is a breathless summary of a mixed bag. Some of these legal bases, such as Article 81 TFEU, have generated a modest stream of legislative activity, while others, such as Article 113 TFEU because of its requirement of unanimity in Council and Article 169 TFEU because of its extraordinarily narrowly drawn terms, have been of negligible significance. One of the thematic reasons that provokes the European Commission ('the Commission') to exploit Article 114 TFEU as a legal base as widely and regularly as it does, is the relatively narrow drawing of these sector-specific legal bases. The Court of Justice of the European Union ('the Court') has a generous understanding of the scope of Article 114, in particular in its permissive understanding of the internal market as a legal concept which is in principle limiting but in practice empowering of EU legislative action. This causes the subversion of the restraints which were laboriously written into the sector-specific legal bases at times of periodic Treaty revision, beginning in 1987 under the Single European Act and continuing to the most recent episode, the Lisbon Treaty, which inserted (inter alia) the title on *Energy* into the TFEU. All this occurred in line with the assembly of a political consensus that the Member States would benefit from some degree of co-ordinated action to tackle problems in the sectors concerned.

Articles 191 and 192 TFEU providing for EU action relating to the *environment* are versions of provisions originally introduced into the Treaties in 1987 on the entry into force of the Single European Act. They have generated a thicker pattern of secondary legislation than any of the provisions mentioned above, most of which are of more recent vintage. Environmental legislation is normally made according to the EU's ordinary legislative procedure, and so requires only a Commission proposal able to secure qualified majority in Council and the support of the Parliament, but exceptionally recourse to unanimity in Council in particular areas is mandated by Article 192(2).

It is easy to see the connection between environmental protection and the internal market. In the first instance national measures motivated by the protection of the environment are capable of acting as barriers to trade. It has already been explored in Chapter 8.E how cases have reached the Court in which national measures governing, for example, the recycling of products,[2] transport of waste[3] and obligatory use of sustainable forms of energy[4] have been found to impede cross-border trade and have therefore been subject to inspection to determine whether they are justified. Coherent schemes have been found to be justified. The presence of such justified inter-state regulatory divergence, which is capable of being viewed not only as a barrier

---

[1] On this bargain, see S. Bulmer and K. Armstrong, *The Governance of the Single European Market* (1998), at 28.

[2] E.g., Case 302/86, *Commission v. Denmark*, [1988] ECR 4607 (ECLI:EU:C:1988:421).

[3] E.g., Case C-2/90, *Commission v. Belgium*, [1992] ECR I-4431 (ECLI:EU:C:1992:310).

[4] E.g., Case C-379/98, *PreussenElektra AG v. Schleswag AG*, [2001] ECR I-2099 (ECLI:EU:C:2001:160).

to cross-border trade in goods and services but also as a distortion of competition as a result of the different costs imposed on traders in different Member States, readily provides a basis for the adoption of common EU rules as a means to promote the integration of markets. In particular, Member States with tough laws have strong incentives to promote EU level rules in order to avoid competitive disadvantage while also seeking to improve the quality of the environment. Germany has been an especially powerful motor. Accordingly, the earliest measures adopted in the field of environmental protection by the EU were adopted explicitly in the name of market-making, based on what was Article 100 EC (now Article 115 TFEU) sometimes coupled to Article 235 EC (now Article 352 TFEU).[5] In 1987, on the entry into force of the Single European Act, the EU acquired its own competence to legislate to promote environmental protection in its own right, and this has been made more elaborate and extensive over time, on periodic Treaty revision. The currently applicable provisions (Articles 191–193 TFEU) are barren of explicit reference to the internal market. They direct that EU policy on the environment shall contribute to the preservation, protection and improvement of the quality of the environment, the protection of human health, the prudent and rational utilization of natural resources, and the promotion of relevant measures at international level, to deal with inter alia climate change. This may readily be understood as a basis for action to deal with the environmental consequences of the economic growth released by the internal market project.[6] *Sustainable* development is the strongly emphasized policy paradigm.[7]

B. Labour Market Regulation and Social Policy

The pattern whereby environmental protection at EU level grew from an initial focus on the functioning of the market to achieve a much broader and, to some (imperfectly defined) extent, independent status has an echo in the story of the rise of EU labour market regulation and social policy. The matter is, however, more fiercely contested: still today – perhaps especially today – there is plenty of political division associated with questions about the extent to which, if at all, the internal market requires a degree of supporting activity designed to put in place common regulation of the labour market and of social policy more generally. This is to some extent reflected in the erratic pattern of Treaty revision in the area, which admittedly makes the story hard to digest in detail. The broad picture, however, serves as another case study apt to reveal the internal market as an ambiguous legal and also political concept. That is how the following narrative is structured: it is not written as an exhaustive account of EU social policy but rather as an interrogation of what EU social policy tells us about the internal market as a legal concept.

---

[5] The Court confirmed that environmental measures might be based on what was Article 100 EC (now Article 115 TFEU), in Case 91/79, *Commission* v. *Italy*, [1980] ECR 1099 (ECLI:EU:C:1980:85).
[6] See, generally, J. Jans and H. Vedder, *European Environmental Law* (4th ed., 2012); M. Lee, *EU Environmental Law Governance and Decision-Making* (2nd ed., 2014); N. De Sadeleer, *EU Environmental Law and the Internal Market* (2014).
[7] Arts 2(3), 395), 21(2)(d), 21(20(f) TEU; Arts 11 TFEU; Art. 37 Charter.

1. *Defrenne*

In the original Treaty of Rome, crafted in the 1950s, Article 119 EEC provided that '[e]ach Member State shall during the first stage ensure and subsequently maintain the application of the principle that men and women should receive equal pay for equal work'. Its modern form, stripped of reference to the first stage (which ended in 1962), is unchanged in substance: it is Article 157 TFEU, which provides that '[e]ach Member State shall ensure that the principle of equal pay for male and female workers for equal work or work of equal value is applied'. The motivation behind this was anxiety that a Member State with relatively strong legal regulation designed to secure gender equality would suffer as a result of undercutting pursued by Member States with less interventionist (or no) regimes, although here, in contrast to environmental protection, it was France that was the relatively progressive state that pushed successfully for an EU commitment to gender equality in matters of pay.[8] That commitment was strengthened by the Court's landmark ruling in *Defrenne v. SABENA*.[9] This was litigation brought by a determined air hostess against the (today long defunct) Belgian airline, Sabena, claiming compensation for having been paid less than men doing the same work.[10] The Court found that the Treaty provision was of itself directly effective, and so it required no legislative amplification before it could be relied on before national courts. Moreover the Court held that this was true even in horizontal cases, that is, it could be relied on before national courts by an employee against a discriminating private employer. The Court was not deterred by the fact that the Treaty provision was (and is) addressed to '[e]ach Member State': this did 'not prevent rights from being conferred at the same time on any individual who has an interest in the performance of the duties thus laid down'.[11] Moreover, the mandatory nature of the provision dictated that it applied not only to the action of public authorities, but also extends to collective agreements and to contracts between individuals. The Court also took the opportunity in *Defrenne* to express its view on the purpose of the equal pay rule. It is not only designed to avoid a situation in which undertakings established in states which have implemented the principle of equal pay suffer a competitive disadvantage as compared with undertakings established in states which have not so legislated, but also it is aimed at the advance of the social objectives of the EU, which embrace social progress and the constant improvement of the living and working conditions of their peoples.[12] So the EU pursues 'a double aim, which is at once economic and social'.[13] The analogy to legislative harmonization's 'dual function' is immediately resonant.[14]

---

[8] For a fuller historical account see J. Kenner, *EU Employment Law: From Rome to Amsterdam and Beyond* (2003), esp. Ch. 1; C. Barnard, *EU Employment Law* (4th ed., 2012), Ch. 1; also C. Hoskyns, *Integrating Gender: Women, Law and Politics in the European Union* (1996), Ch. 3.

[9] Case C-43/75, *Defrenne v. SABENA*, [1976] ECR 455 (ECLI:EU:C:1976:56).

[10] The background story is told in Ch. 4 of Hoskyns, *supra* note 8.

[11] Case 43/75, *supra* note 9, at para. 31.   [12] *Ibid.*, paras 8–10.   [13] *Ibid.*, para. 12.

[14] See Chapter 13.B. That duality appears in far less happy context in Case C-438/05, *Viking Line*, [2007] ECR I-10779 (ECLI:EU:C:2007:772), at para. 79 and Case C-341/05, *Laval*, [2007] ECR I-11767 (ECLI:EU:C:2007:809), at para. 105.

The Treaty's commitment to equal pay allowed the Court to make a clear and powerful choice expressing a strong normative preference for common rule-making motivated by both economic and social concerns. So the original settlement of the 1950s had, in one area, made a choice in favour of common and socially progressive EU standards and against a model of diversity in choice state by state. In *Defrenne* in April 1976 the Court had articulated that vision clearly. Labour market regulation was understood as part of an internal market project which required *both* a common set of rules applicable across the whole territory of the EU apt to curtail competitive distortion consequent on legislative diversity among the Member States *and* a wider social understanding of the role of the EU in setting common standards of protection. This is clearly of high significance to an understanding of the 'internal market' as a legal concept, and, in particular, it identifies the internal market as a project built not only on market freedoms but on the adoption of common rules of market regulation.

The Court's finding of a directly effective and horizontally applicable right in *Defrenne* propelled this particular vision, and took it out of the control of the autonomy of national systems and out of the gift of the (frequently unwilling) EU legislative process.[15] *Defrenne* empowered the Court itself, individuals and the Commission too. It has a thematic association with the momentum provided in control of technical standards by *Cassis de Dijon* (see Chapter 6.A.3), although, thanks to its horizontal application, the equal pay rule has even more vigour.

The pioneering approach adopted in *Defrenne* and developed since, sets the tone for what is today Article 3(3) TEU's embrace of the 'social market economy'. The Court has even gone so far on occasion to describe the economic aim of the Treaty's equal pay rule as 'secondary to the social aim pursued'.[16] But the long road from *Defrenne* in 1976 to the social market economy which supposedly exists 40 years later has been winding and there are competing route plans. In particular, the equal pay rule embedded in the Treaty (now Article 157 TFEU), is atypical. The deal struck in the 1950s left most matters concerning social policy untouched by concrete rules set by primary EU law. The realization of most of the EU's aspirations in the field of social policy depended on legislative amplification and so on the construction of political alliances. This was, and remains, hotly contested.

2. Policy Choices

The purpose(s) of EU labour market regulation, and social policy more generally, are illuminatingly contested. There is a diversity of choices found among the Member States. Two perceptions – polar opposites – offer themselves as extreme points on

---

[15] For a recent assessment of the academic reception of *Defrenne* at the time, see Sharpston, 'The Shock Troops Arrive in Force: Horizontal Direct Effect of a Treaty Provision and Temporal Limitation of Judgments Join the Armoury of EC Law', in M. Maduro and L. Azoulai (eds), *The Past and Future of EU Law* (2010).

[16] Cases C-270/97 and 271/97, *Deutsche Post AG* v. *Sievers, Schrage*, [2000] ECR I-929 (ECLI:EU:C:2000:76), at para. 57; Case C-50/96, *Deutsche Telekom AG* v. *Schröder*, [2000] ECR I-743 (ECLI:EU:C:2000:72), at para. 57.

a spectrum within which to assess the possible responses of the EU. One might argue that such diversity is the very lifeblood of competition. States choose different models according to local preference: some are willing to mandate high protective standards, others prefer less intervention. In so far as those choices lead to competition between jurisdictions, then firms as consumers of laws opt for the host jurisdiction that best suits their interest, and then that market will reveal which is the best solution. On this basis the EU should not disturb that diversity; on the contrary it should facilitate corporate mobility by allowing free movement unrestrained by reference to diverse patterns of market regulation. So, for example, a firm that chooses to re-locate to a low-cost jurisdiction should not for that reason face any impediment when it targets its economic activities at other jurisdictions, even where it uses its own workers to undercut rates in the target state. To provide otherwise would suppress the competitive advantage of low-cost states able to attract 'consumers of regulation' to their territory. This policy preference resonates with the Court's interpretative choices about the grip exercised by free movement law over the imposition of host-state regulations in landmark cases such as *Viking Line*[17] and *Centros*.[18] The contrasting vision – the polar opposite – would reject such diversity as both harmful to the competitive structure of the internal market, in that it distorts choices made by firms, and as inapt to achieve a common level of social progress. It would also emphasize the risk that without common rules states will be tempted to cut levels of social protection in order to attract corporate re-location, leading to a vicious circle as other states follow suit, leading to a race to the bottom. This will tend to suppress the economic virtue of a long-term approach to regulation aimed at improving education, training and job security. From this perspective common EU rules are necessary to sustain growth and to prevent economic and social harm. The Court's ruling in *Defrenne* conforms to this vision.

Both models make assumptions that can be subjected to some degree of empirical testing. The claim that opening up scope for competition between different legal regimes allows a market to reveal the 'best' solution deserves a sceptical inquiry: markets sometimes fail, and there is ample reason to suppose that informational asymmetry will taint this market. One may doubt that firms are truly sufficiently informed and/or mobile to make the demand side of this market work effectively. A different kind of failure would occur where firms are able to externalize the costs of underinvestment in matters such as training and research and development by relying on the state to step in. At the other extreme, the claim that absence of EU rules will unleash a race to the bottom is also open to doubt. Savage deregulation has a political cost. In the economic and political conditions prevailing in European countries, it is in most sectors highly improbable that a race to the bottom in regulatory protection is likely to occur. There is little evidence that electoral or economic advantage can be gained through such tactics and, in any event, in some jurisdictions there are entrenched constitutional impediments to such change. In the absence of evidence that it is politically attractive to pursue the magnitude

[17] Case C-438/05, *supra* note 14.
[18] Case C-212/97, *Centros*, [1999] ECR I-1459 (ECLI:EU:C:1999:126).

of the deregulation required to lure firms to be mobile, the supply-side of this market fails. Moreover, it is far from plain that cutting standards is a smart choice: a well-educated, well-motivated and high-skilled workforce may be attractive to producers.

Ultimately, much of this debate is fought on an ideological plane. And for several Member States, the economic crisis that was ignited in 2008 has burned away the luxury of a cool choice between these models. Pursuant to Treaty procedures designed to avoid excessive deficit and to strengthen budgetary discipline, EU measures have gone so far as to require the adoption of concrete measures at national level including adaptation of tax and pension systems, changes in statutory retirement age, and the downgrade of employment protection, including the facilitation of a greater use of temporary contracts.[19] Amid this horror, the internal market as a legal concept lacks any constitutionally firm steer and, in particular, it has no power to brake these trends.[20]

Defrenne counts as a signal that *one* understanding of the EU's 'internal market' is that it is not based on radical decentralization as a result of a choice in favour of unrestricted inter-jurisdictional competition. The EU – its Treaty, interpreted by its Court – did not simply leave it to the Member States to regulate (or not to regulate) the matter of equal pay. Instead, it treated diversity in national practice as a distortion of competition. This is a discourse that is familiar in legislative harmonization, where suppression of appreciable distortions of competition caused by inter-state regulatory diversity is a recognized competence-conferring objective,[21] and it spreads more widely too. For example, the General Court has explicitly observed that the harmonization of national fiscal legislation shares with the state aid rules the objective of combating distortions of competition as part of the project to promote the proper functioning of the internal market.[22] The concept of 'distortion' plays a constitutionally significant role here: it conveys the idea that sometimes diversity between national laws, which is normally of itself not enough to cause an 'internal market problem', crosses a threshold to become distortive as a result of the differences in costs shouldered by traders in different jurisdictions. But when exactly diversity becomes distortion does not seem to possess an objective definition. It is ambiguous.

How intense should be that pattern of common regulation, if any, is a matter of, first, identifying the scope of legislative competence conferred by the Treaty and,

---

[19] E.g., Council Decision 2010/320 OJ 2010 L 145/6, adopted pursuant to Arts 126(9) and 136 TFEU, and addressed to Greece. Much has happened, and continues to happen, since: the European Trade Union Institute's website is a helpful source of information (http://www.etui.org).

[20] The same is so far true of the Charter, though this may not endure: see, e.g., Barnard, 'The Silence of the Charter', in S. De Vries, U. Bernitz and S. Weatherill, *The Charter of Fundamental Rights: Five Years of Legally Binding Effect* (2015).

[21] E.g., Case C-380/03, *Germany* v. *Parliament and Council*, [2006] ECR I-11573 (ECLI:EU:C:2006:772), at paras 66, 85, 111.

[22] Case T-50/06, *Ireland* v. *Commission*, judgment of 21 March 2012, not yet reported (ECLI:EU:T:2012:134): the Court set aside the judgment in Case C-272/12 P, *Commission* v. *Ireland*, judgment of 10 December 2013, not yet reported (ECLI:EU:C:2013:812), on the basis that it disregarded the distinct roles of the Council and Commission in the two areas, but did not disagree with this point.

secondly, the assembly of the necessary political will to exploit those authorizations. Both landscapes have altered over time.

3. From the Treaty of Rome to the Single European Act

Although the original Treaties allowed little scope for legislation aimed explicitly at labour market regulation or at social policy, the political commitment to put a more 'human face' on the process – which was especially prominent at the transformative 'Paris Summit' in 1972 – led to legislative activity. The relevant legal bases chosen for this earliest wave were Articles 235 and 100 EEC (today, in amended form, Articles 352 and 115 TFEU). Neither had – has – any explicit connection to social policy, but by asserting that social policy counts among the EU's objectives and is part of the process of creating an integrated market the EU was able to begin to put legislative flesh on the bones of political aspiration.

Directive 76/207 on equal treatment for men and women as regards access to employment, vocational training and promotion, and working conditions was based on Article 235.[23] It is now replaced by the broader Directive 2006/54 on the implementation of the principle of equal opportunities and equal treatment of men and women in matters of employment and occupation, which takes as its basis the more specific Article 141(3) EC, now Article 157(3) TFEU.[24] This was labour market regulation rather than social policy more generally, but significant all the same in demonstrating the EU's unwillingness to leave regulation of such matters in state hands while also requiring, under the logic of the dual function, that the EU itself assume a responsibility to choose how best to regulate labour markets (in common). Directive 77/187 on safeguarding of employees' rights in the event of transfers of undertakings was adopted pursuant to Article 100 EC.[25] It has now been replaced by Directive 2001/23, which takes the same – albeit amended – legal base, Article 94 EC (now Article 115 TFEU).[26] Directive 75/129 and its successor Directive 98/59 on collective redundancies were both based on Article 100 EC.[27] Directive 80/987 on the protection of employees in the event of the insolvency of their employer was based on Article 100 EC[28] though its successor and the current version is Directive 2008/94, which takes Article 137(2) EC (now Article 153 TFEU), as its base, and its Preamble makes greater play of the protective element rather than simply the need to address regulatory divergence among the Member States.[29]

Some of these measures were accompanied by remarkable little explanation of why Article 100 EC was used. Doubtless this reveals that the presence of unanimity among the Member States eliminated any perceived need to explore the intricacies of constitutional legitimacy: political consensus meant no dissent; dissent meant no political consensus. But the measures openly complied with the vision of a double aim announced by the Court in *Defrenne*, and they showed a strong acceptance that market-making was inextricably linked with social protection, even if any careful

---

[23] OJ 1976 L 39/40. [24] OJ 2006 L 204/23. [25] OJ 1977 L 61/26.
[26] OJ 2001 L 82/16. [27] OJ 1975 L 48/29, OJ 1998 L 225/16.
[28] OJ 1980 L 283/23. [29] OJ 2008 L 283/36.

elucidation of just *why* was missing. Directive 77/187 explains – better, asserts – in its Preamble that differences between Member States' protection of employees can have a direct effect on the functioning of the common market, and that accordingly harmonization is required while maintaining the improvement in working conditions then described in Article 117 EEC (now found in Article 151(1) TFEU). Its replacement, Directive 2001/23, is a little more fully explained, and, in locating the measure's social objective alongside its economic, it relies also on the Charter of the Fundamental Social Rights of Workers ('the Charter') adopted on 9 December 1989. This non-binding document, today the subject of explicit embrace in Article 151(1) TFEU, states in its Article 7 that 'the completion of the internal market must lead to an improvement in the living and working conditions of workers in the European Community' and that '[t]his process must result from an approximation of these conditions while the improvement is being maintained'.

There is a ready parallel with the pattern of adoption pursuant to Article 100 EEC (now Article 115 TFEU), of measures in other areas. Consumer protection is one. Directive 85/577 (the 'Doorstep Selling' Directive met in Chapter 13.B) expresses a concern to put in place common EU rules *both* because disparities between national rules governing conclusion of a contract between a trader and consumer made away from business premises may directly affect the functioning of the market *and* because this will improve the protection of the consumer, as politically mandated by the consumer protection and information policy, which had been adopted in 1975 and which has its genesis in the Paris Summit of 1972. So too, as mentioned in Section A, environmental measures were based on what was Article 100 EC (now Article 115 TFEU), in advance of the addition of environmental protection to the Treaty as a dedicated legislative competence with effect from 1987. Here too, as in the case of labour market regulation, the initial political commitment to developing policies of market regulation was carried forward in the name of the building of an integrated market for the EU. In this sense, the market was a constitutionally useful load-bearer. But the EU market was, therefore, as a matter of descriptive observation, in the process of being built as more than an exercise in market freedom.

The Court itself typically employed the 'double aim' as a basis for interpretation of the legislative acquis. Directive 77/187 on the transfer of undertakings was at stake in *Commission v. United Kingdom*.[30] The Court's explanation of how *social* measures of this kind may be based on what was Article 100 EC (and is now Article 115 TFEU) offered a plain echo of *Defrenne*. It stated that '[b]y harmonising the rules applicable to the safeguarding of employees' rights in the event of transfers of undertakings, the Community legislature intended both to ensure comparable protection for employees' rights in the different Member States and to harmonise the costs which those protective rules entail for Community undertakings'.[31] So there are two purposes: both to develop a common regulatory strategy at EU level apt to protect employees and to put in place common rules apt to promote market integration. The protective or social as well as an economic rationale for harmonization

---

[30] Case C-382/92, *Commission v. United Kingdom*, [1994] ECR I-2435 (ECLI:EU:C:1994:233).
[31] *Ibid.*, at para. 15.

is readily traceable through the EU's legislative *acquis* and associated interpretative rulings of the Court stretching over several decades.[32]

On this approach, social policy is not something separate from the internal market. It is part of it. The internal market requires a degree of common policy-making in the field of social policy and labour market regulation for otherwise states will achieve an unfair advantage by reducing or eliminating the costs involved in complying with social protection regulation. And this brings with it the connected consequence of social progress.

4. From the Single European Act via Maastricht to the Treaty of Amsterdam

The Single European Act introduced into the existing Title on *Social Policy* a new provision, then Article 118a EC, which allowed legislative activity to address health and safety, particularly in respect of the working environment. This required only qualified majority vote in Council. It was by this time obvious that a unanimity requirement in Council was a severe hindrance to legislative progress, though in the Single European Act this was the only incursion made into the prevalence of reliance on unanimity as the voting rule in Council in matters associated with the rights of workers. What is now Article 114 TFEU was introduced by the Single European Act with a view to accelerating the adoption of harmonization legislation required for the completion of the internal market and it requires only a qualified majority, but its second paragraph excludes from its scope harmonization associated with the rights and interests of employed persons.

Directive 93/104 on working time was based on Article 118a EC. The Court took the opportunity, in an unsuccessful application for the Directive's annulment brought by the UK on the basis that the measure had been improperly classified as a measure of health and safety, to explain that the principal aim of the measure was the protection of the health and safety of workers, and so Article 118a was properly used (with the consequence that the UK had no veto), but it did not at all deny that the measure had ancillary effects on the establishment and functioning of the internal market.[33]

The Directive was later re-cast as Directive 2003/88,[34] adopted under Article 137(2) EC, which is today, in amended form, Article 153(2) TFEU. It has become something of a bête noire. It is the most commonly derided example of the lack of flexibility allowed to private autonomy and local variation by the EU. Even though much of this criticism may be driven by purely ideological distaste for any kind of worker protection enshrined in law and especially where its source is the EU, it is a

---

[32] E.g., on transfer of undertakings, Case C-164/00, *Katia Beckmann*, [2002] ECR I-4893 (ECLI:EU:C:2002:330), at para. 29; Case C-561/07, *Commission* v. *Italy*, [2009] ECR I-4959 (ECLI:EU:C:2009:363), at para. 30; on collective redundancies, regulated by Directive 98/59, also adopted under Art. 100 EEC, Case C-55/02, *Commission* v. *Portugal*, [2004] ECR I-9387 (ECLI:EU:C:2004:605), at para. 48; Case C-385/05, *CGT*, [2007] ECR I-611 (ECLI:EU:C:2007:37), at para. 43.

[33] Case C-84/94, *United Kingdom* v. *Council*, [1996] ECR I-5755 (ECLI:EU:C:1996:431).

[34] OJ 2003 L 299/9.

measure which is complex and rigid, not least because of the attempt to accommodate divergent traditions among the Member States on how working time is to be regulated, if at all, and by whom, whether by public act or private bargaining. Periodic rulings of the Court, usually favourable to the position of employees, have added to the impression that this regime is messier and more unpredictable than it needs to be.[35]

However it is thematically important that, in its interpretation of the Directive, the Court has openly embraced an understanding of the employee as 'the weaker party to the employment contract' and has identified the need 'to prevent the employer being in a position to disregard the intentions of the other party to the contract or to impose on that party a restriction of his rights'.[36] Here EU labour law makes a particular choice about its social orientation – one that it shares with trends in national labour law and one that it also shares with EU consumer law.[37]

The political criticism of the Directive holds that it diminishes national autonomy and that the EU would function better were it to permit Member States to make their own choices about how (and whether) to regulate working time. This supposed autonomy might be disciplined by regulatory competition and choice of mobile firms among competing and varied legal regimes, although it seems implausible that regulation of working time alone could be a deal-breaker in choice of corporate location. This, however, is simply a different political view of how the internal market should be shaped. It has no legal momentum behind it. The internal market as a legal concept is not in any constitutional sense wedded to a model of regulatory competition. Under the paradigm asserted by the Court in *Defrenne* as an interpretation of the Treaty, the reverse is true.

The so-called social dialogue, now found in Articles 154–155 TFEU, was also inserted by the Single European Act. This gave expression to a politically contested ambition to widen and deepen the involvement of both sides of industry in policy-making. Further adaption followed as a result of the Maastricht Treaty, which entered into force in 1993.[38] This widening of the scope of EU social policy came with a temporary price tag, because the UK's vehement refusal to ratify a Treaty that committed it to deeper commitments in the social policy field prompted the crafting of byzantine arrangements under a Protocol whereby the UK would not participate in the newly added competences.[39] This was symbolically important, in that it represented a plain unbridgeable divergence among the Member States about the virtue of common policy-making, but it was not *substantively* important, because precious little was in fact addressed under the new and wider legal bases: just four measures were adopted.[40] And legislation that was adopted under pre-existing legal bases

---

[35] In detail, see Barnard, *supra* note 8, Ch. 11; A.C.L. Davies, *EU Labour Law* (2012), Ch. 7.
[36] Joined Cases C-397/01 to C-403/01, *Pfeiffer and others* v. *Deutsches Rotes Kreuz*, [2004] ECR I-8835 (ECLI:EU:C:2004:584), at para. 82; Case C-429/09, *Günter Fuß v Stadt Halle*, [2010] ECR I-12167 (ECLI:EU:C:2010:717), at para. 80.
[37] See Chapters 13.D.3 and 13.F.
[38] See Waddington, 'Social Policy and the Maastricht Treaty: Much Ado about Nothing?', in M. De Visser and A.P. Van der Mei (eds), *The Treaty on European Union 1993–2013: Reflections from Maastricht* (2013).
[39] Kenner, *supra* note 8, Ch. 6.
[40] Directive 94/45 on European Works Councils, OJ 1994 L 254/64: Directive 96/34 on Parental leave, OJ 1996 L 145/4; Directive 97/80 on burden of proof in sex discrimination cases, OJ 1997 L 14/16; Directive 97/81 on part-time work, OJ 1998 L 14/9.

applied to the UK as to all the other Member States, and where qualified majority applied as the Council voting rule, the UK possessed no veto. So use was made of Article 118a on health and safety as the base for not only the Working Time Directive but also measures such as Directive 92/85 on the protection of pregnant workers[41] and Directive 94/33 on young people at work.[42]

But not all the output was conceived as a contribution to improving the working environment. The intimacy of the relationship between the economic and the social motivation for legislative activity was emphasized by the fact that Directive 96/71 on posted workers was based on Articles 57(2) and 66 EC, which are today in amended form Articles 53(2) and 62 TFEU.[43] The aim: 'laws of the Member States must be coordinated in order to lay down a nucleus of mandatory rules for minimum protection to be observed in the host country by employers who post workers to perform temporary work in the territory of a Member State where the services are provided'. [44] Free movement – for natural and legal persons – is itself part of the EU's social policy broadly understood and, accompanied by a raft of supporting measures of secondary legislation designed to induce migration by ensuring equal access to benefits, including for families, it is obviously intimately connected to the internal market project.[45]

Eighteen years of Conservative government came to an end in 1997 and, given the changed attitude of the incoming Labour administration, the UK's special but temporary position was brought to an end by the Amsterdam Treaty, which scrapped the Protocol and during the same period the few measures adopted pursuant to it were re-made to extend to the UK.[46] So EU social policy was re-unified but it was also extended by the Amsterdam Treaty.[47] The slender bases incrementally gathered at times of periodic Treaty revision were replaced by the considerably stronger legislative competence that was Article 137, and it was soon after strengthened further by the Treaty of Nice. It is now, in a further amended form, Article 153 TFEU.

5. The Lisbon Strategy and Europe 2020

Readiness to legislate in a way to create individual rights became increasingly accompanied by readiness on the part of the Member States to co-ordinate their wider policies in a more inclusive way. This was in part the consequence of the rise of the Eurozone, in which a common currency began to circulate from the beginning of 2002, which emphasized the unrealistic nature of the claim that social policy is capable of being understood as a purely or even mainly national matter. The European Employment Strategy (EES) was launched in the 1990s, as a process of policy co-ordination, and this was then affected by the rise of the Lisbon Strategy, agreed in March 2000, which was designed to convert the EU economy into the most competitive and dynamic in the world – or, perhaps more accurately, it was

---

[41] OJ 1992 L 348/1.   [42] OJ 1993 L 216/12.   [43] OJ 1997 L 18/1.
[44] Recital 13.   [45] Davies, *supra* note 35, Ch. 3.
[46] E.g., Directive 94/45 on Works Councils became Directive 97/74: it is now Directive 2009/38.
[47] Kenner, *supra* note 8, Ch. 8.

designed to promote the political appearance of engagement with this ambitious mission. The reality has proved far removed from the chosen goal, perhaps because it was in any event absurd to suppose that Europe could readily outperform every other area on the planet, but also perhaps because the EU was not able to act in the ways necessary to realize such an ambition. The 'Lisbon Strategy' had a defined goal and a deadline, which carries a clear echo of the management of the project to complete the internal market by the end of 1992 (see Chapter 3.B), but by contrast with that largely, though not completely, successful programme the Lisbon Strategy fell to be achieved through the use of a much wider and less concrete arsenal of techniques and instruments. The Lisbon Strategy 'relied on broader objectives, softer means, and weaker instruments'.[48] It embraced not only (and not mainly) the adoption of binding EU rules, but also 'benchmarking' and co-ordination rather than mandatory common action. The vision swept across social cohesion, education, research and development. These are areas where the EU's competence is limited and its resources and expertise scarce, and so it necessarily depended heavily on co-ordinated Member State action. There is appeal in this. The Lisbon Strategy and the Open Method of Co-ordination (OMC) generally suggest a sophisticated blend of co-ordinated EU *and* national action, and a move beyond the harsh dichotomies of EU *or* national action, binding *or* non-binding action. It is, however, not easily achieved and it can readily stall in practice, especially where issues become more politically contested or simply intractable, without the propulsion provided by classic EU-level action. The Lisbon Strategy was not a success.

The successor to the Lisbon Strategy, the Europe 2020 strategy, set out in a Commission Communication in 2010 fatuously entitled 'Europe 2020: A strategy for smart, sustainable and inclusive growth',[49] was presented through a set of guidelines. One of these guidelines was for the employment policies of the Member States.[50] This was adopted under Article 148 TFEU which is the Title on *Employment*, first introduced into the Treaties by the Treaty of Amsterdam with effect from 1999.[51] It shared with the Lisbon Strategy the aim of avoiding binding rules and instead promoting and provoking sharing of practice and expertise. It was here that Member States were encouraged to integrate the so-called 'flexicurity' principles endorsed by the European Council into their labour market policies: measures to enhance flexibility and security should be both balanced and mutually reinforcing. The aim was to promote labour mobility and labour market participation. 'Flexicurity' is yet another context in which to pursue the struggle between those who would treat EU action in this area as principally about promoting a competitive market and those more concerned to nurture the rules as measures of social protection and, deeper still, fundamental rights.[52]

---

[48] Bongardt and Torres, 'Lisbon Strategy', in E. Jones, A. Menon and S. Weatherill, *The Oxford Handbook of the European Union* (2012) Ch. 33, at 471.
[49] COM (2010) 2020.   [50] Decision 2010/707, OJ 2010 L 308/46.
[51] Kenner, *supra* note 8, Ch. 11.
[52] E.g., Bell, 'Between Flexicurity and Fundamental Social rights: The EU Directives on Atypical Work', 37 *European Law Review* (2012) 31.

The relative virtues and vices of the EU's evident engagement with innovative modes of governance are contested.[53] They doubtless demand and deserve careful sector-specific empirical investigation. So, for example, evidence that 'OMC' has pushed social inclusion on to the political and economic agenda for the first time in some Member States suggests an intriguing tale of the EU 'nudging' policy reform without any aspiration to stretch its competence and expertise by mandating particular processes or outcomes, but this must be set against the admission that evidence of concrete policy change in consequence is thin.[54] The anxiety, then, is that the EU may operate through OMC in a way that is superficial and ineffective, which is especially pressing where, as is true in times of austerity, eagerness to develop such policy concerns is battered by an antagonistic agenda focused on economic growth achieved through deregulation. Moreover, it is plain that strategies of co-ordination cannot and do not aspire to establishing common rules of the type presupposed by most forms of binding EU act, so pressures for reform triggered by such relatively 'soft' initiatives will generate highly divergent results across jurisdictions and over time.[55] Binding EU rules do not presuppose the delivery of identical patterns in all Member States; the Directive as a legal instrument in particular is intended to leave the manner and form of implementation to local decisions about what works best. But common action taken under the newer 'softer' forms of governance is a qualitative step still further away from common outcomes.

As a concluding observation, it is plain that the landscape of EU social policy and in particular its employment strategy is now occupied by a range of initiatives pitched at broader goals associated with improved competitiveness, and orthodox top-down binding legislation apt to generate individual rights to protection is a relatively small part of it.

C. EU Social Policy Today

The provisions that deal with social policy are today found in Title X of Part Three of the TFEU. They stretch from Article 151 to Article 161 TFEU. Article 157 TFEU's commitment to equal pay, the modern successor to the provision that provided the platform for *Defrenne*, is locked into the Treaty, but most of the relevant protective rules that apply in common across the territory of the EU are found in secondary legislation, mostly Directives. States that are politically opposed to the shaping of an EU social policy must seek to win that argument in the legislative

---

[53] In the employment context, see Barnard *supra* note 8, Ch. 3; Davies *supra* note 35, at 53–64. More broadly, emphasizing the heterogeneity of forms (and of critical evaluations), see Armstrong, 'The Character of EU law and Governance: From Community Method to New Modes of Governance', 64 *Current Legal Problems* (2011) 179.

[54] E.g., Dawson and De Witte, 'The EU Legal Framework of Social Inclusion and Social Protection: Between the Lisbon Strategy and the Lisbon Treaty', in B. Cantillon, H. Verschueren and P. Ploscar (eds), *Social Inclusion and Social Protection in the EU: Interactions between Law and Policy* (2012).

[55] E.g., in relation to labour market policies, Paetzold and Van Vliet, 'EU Co-ordination and the Convergence of Domestic Unemployment Protection Schemes', 52 *Journal of Common Market Studies* (2014) 1070.

process. The relevant provisions today almost all involve 'QMV' in Council, so a dissenting state normally needs allies to halt an initiative.

Article 151 TFEU directs that the Union and the Member States 'shall have as their objectives the promotion of employment, improved living and working conditions, so as to make possible their harmonisation while the improvement is being maintained, proper social protection, dialogue between management and labour, the development of human resources with a view to lasting high employment and the combating of exclusion'. It also states in its third paragraph that they 'believe that such a development will ensue not only from the functioning of the internal market, which will favour the harmonisation of social systems, but also from the procedures provided for in the Treaties and from the approximation of provisions laid down by law, regulation or administrative action'. This is the modern version of Article 117 EEC, which also set out these three routes: spontaneous alignment, the provisions of the Treaties (on social policy) and approximation.

1. Spontaneous Alignment

Spontaneous alignment suggests that the improvements in prosperity that should follow from economic integration should also manifest themselves in improved commitments to social protection expressed through national initiatives. This is plainly aspirational and programmatic, but such trends were visible in the early years as the EU enjoyed economic growth. By avoiding legally explicit commitment, this provision left room for political debate about how far social policy-making should accompany economic integration. In this sense there was in Article 117 EEC a precursor of Article 26 TFEU's own ambiguity about the *legal* meaning of the internal market, even though Article 26 and indeed the concept of the internal market (as distinct from the common market) itself appeared in the Treaties only with effect from 1987 (see Chapter 3.B). The hint in the original Treaty that co-ordination could occur without top-down EU rule-making is now capable of being read in the light of the – at the time certainly unforeseen – rise of soft forms of co-ordination among the Member States such as 'OMC'.

2. Legislation on Social Policy

Article 153(1) TFEU provides a list of areas in which the EU shall support and complement the activities of the Member States with a view to achieving the objectives of Article 151: (a) improvement in particular of the working environment to protect workers' health and safety; (b) working conditions; (c) social security and social protection of workers; (d) protection of workers where their employment contract is terminated; (e) the information and consultation of workers; (f) representation and collective defence of the interests of workers and employers, including co-determination; (g) conditions of employment for third-country nationals legally residing in Union territory; (h) the integration of persons excluded from the labour market, without prejudice to Article 166; (i) equality between men and women with regard to labour market opportunities and treatment at work; (j) the combating of social exclusion; (k) the modernization of social protection systems without prejudice to point (c).

According to Article 153(2)(a) TFEU the Parliament and the Council may adopt measures designed to encourage co-operation between Member States, excluding any harmonization (in a sense a formal embrace of 'OMC'); and, according to Article 153(2)(b), they may adopt Directives in the fields referred to in paragraph 1(a) to (i) which will establish minimum requirements for gradual implementation. The ordinary legislative procedure applies, except for fields referred to in paragraph 1(c), (d), (f) and (g), where the Council shall act unanimously in accordance with a special legislative procedure after consulting the Parliament. This is a bit messy. It is the product of the incremental growth of EU competence in the field over time. Article 153(5) cautions that these provisions shall not apply to pay, the right of association, the right to strike or the right to impose lock-outs. These, then, are areas so sensitive that the Member States have preferred to keep the EU out. But all is not as it seems: it is exactly here that functional reach of the free movement provisions as the basis for promoting market integration exceeds the reach of the EU's legislative competence, with consequent diminution in the protection granted to national autonomy. Article 153(5) keeps out the legislative institutions but it does not keep out the Court.[56]

Plenty of measures have been adopted under Article 153 TFEU, or its immediate predecessor Article 137 EC, including several measures that are renovation of earlier initiatives, such as the Working Time Directive 2003/88.[57] Other measures adopted under Article 137(2) EC include Directive 2002/14 establishing a general framework for informing and consulting employees.[58] It is, however, true that more recently legislative activity has slowed. Even given expanded competence and the widespread possibility of action by qualified majority in Council, there are political blockages to enhanced EU legislative activity in this field. In this sense, the patterns of co-ordination considered above, stretching across the Lisbon Strategy and now 'Europe 2020' might initially have been supplementary to legislative activity but they have now largely eclipsed it.

Article 156 TFEU, modern successor to the original Article 118 EEC, provides that in order to achieve the objectives of Article 151, the Commission shall encourage co-operation between the Member States and facilitate the co-ordination of their action in social policy. Article 157(3) makes separate provision for the Parliament and Council, acting in accordance with the ordinary legislative procedure, to adopt measures to ensure the application of the principle of equal opportunities and equal treatment of men and women in matters of employment and occupation, including the principle of equal pay for equal work or work of equal value.

The Treaty also provides for legislative activity aimed at broader equality rights beyond the working environment. Article 19 TFEU provides for a competence exercised according to a special legislative procedure involving unanimity in Council to take appropriate action to combat discrimination based on sex, racial or ethnic

---

[56] Case C-438/05, *supra* note 14, see Chapter 9.B.
[57] OJ 2003 L 299/9.　　[58] OJ 2000 L 80/29.

origin, religion or belief, disability, age or sexual orientation. This is the legal base for Directive 2000/43 on equal treatment between persons irrespective of racial or ethnic origin[59] and Directive 2000/78 establishing a general framework for equal treatment in employment and occupation.[60] It was explained above that the contention that labour market regulation and social policy should be about rights is opposed by those who prefer to emphasize the economic aim of making the market more competitive: by contrast discrimination and equality law is much more squarely and unarguably part of 'rights discourse'. The Charter of Fundamental Rights adds to this debate and even if its Chapter IV entitled *Solidarity* has been written with care to confine the justiciability of its provisions, in the limited circumstances in which it may be relied on to create individual rights for workers it is attractive because of its high constitutional status. In *Mangold* the Court found a general principle of EU law which prohibited discrimination on grounds of age which was applicable in proceedings involving two private parties, an employee and an employer.[61] The Charter of Fundamental Rights went unmentioned in *Mangold*, a decision which pre-dates its acquisition of binding force, but in the subsequent ruling in *Seda Kücükdeveci v Swedex GmbH & Co. KG* the Court added its Article 21, which prohibits discrimination based on age, to reasoning drawn from *Mangold*.[62] In *Association de médiation sociale* by contrast the Court was not willing to allow an individual to rely on Article 27 of the Charter on workers' rights to information and consultation, because it was not sufficiently textually precise.[63] Doubtless case law will clarify which Charter provisions are apt for direct application and which require legislative elaboration,[64] but it is plain that the Charter will not always help. In fact the Charter will not often help. Lawyers' natural tendency to pore over fizzily exciting rulings such as *Mangold* should not obscure the harsh reality that they have little to do with the experience of most workers in an EU of austerity.

3. Approximation/Harmonization

The third of the routes identified by Article 151 TFEU is legislative harmonization. Article 114 TFEU is not available to harmonize provisions relating to the free movement of persons nor to those relating to the rights and interests of employed persons, because they are excluded from its scope by Article 114(2). This is not a statement that such matters are unassociated with construction of the internal market. It simply reflects an absence of political consensus at times of Treaty revision to open them up to intervention pursuant to qualified majority vote under Article 114. Article 115 TFEU is capable of being used to harmonize such rules, but it requires unanimity in

---

[59] OJ 2000 L 180/22.   [60] OJ 2000 L 303/16.

[61] Case C-144/04, *Mangold*, [2005] ECR I-9981 (ECLI:EU:C:2005:709).

[62] Case C-555/07, *Seda Kücükdeveci v Swedex GmbH & Co. KG*, [2010] ECR I-365 (ECLI:EU:C:2010:21).

[63] Case C-176/12, *Association de médiation sociale*, judgment of 15 January 2014, not yet reported (ECLI:EU:C:2014:2).

[64] Cf. Lazzerini, 'Annotation', 51 *Common Market Law Review* (2014) 907. See also O. Cherednychenko and N. Reich, 'The Constitutionalization of European Private Law: Gateways, Constraints, and Challenges', 23 *European Review of Private Law* (2015) 797.

Council. As mentioned earlier (see Section B.3) it has in the past been used, but not recently. Assembling unanimity in Council in an EU of 28 is no small task.

D. Social Policy – the Current Debate

The Treaty super-structure captures the flavour of the EU's role in this field. Article 3(3) TEU provides that '[t]he Union shall establish an internal market' but also that it shall work for (inter alia) 'a highly competitive social market economy, aiming at full employment and social progress' and that it 'shall combat social exclusion and discrimination, and shall promote social justice and protection'. Article 9 TFEU is one of the 'horizontal' provisions: it directs that '[i]n defining and implementing its policies and activities, the Union shall take into account requirements linked to the promotion of a high level of employment, the guarantee of adequate social protection, the fight against social exclusion, and a high level of education, training and protection of human health'. The Charter too, especially its Title IV on *Solidarity*, addresses matters associated with the protection of workers and social policy more generally.

But there is nothing inevitable about the EU's delivery of social progress. In truth the 'social market' formula captures the ambiguity: how much is to be achieved by creating a competitive economy, how much is to be achieved by regulating it in common in the service of protection.

There is nothing systematic or comprehensive about EU social policy. It is rather fragmented; it is largely, though not exclusively, related to employment; it is ad hoc, often a product of moments of political opportunity. Much is missing – the core of the commitment to social welfare in the EU and, most obvious of all, the requirement of an attached budget, is not delivered by the EU. One can treat this as simply a reflection of the direction in Article 4(2)(b) TFEU that social policy is a competence shared between the EU and its Member States, so the full picture of social policy in (and not *of*) the EU must, as is true of all EU policies which are not exclusive in nature, be painted by national and EU measures entwined. But even so the edges will be and are rough. There is much talk about the 'European Social Model' but a good deal less clarity or consensus on what it entails. Across much of the EU, ravaged by the damage done by economic recession and pushed into labour market 'reforms' which have depressed levels of legislative protection, its supposed appeal is in any event fanciful.[65]

The internal market as a legal concept is ambiguously attached to this incrementally-shaped pattern of social policy. Plainly the deregulatory power of the free movement and competition law provisions exceeds that of the provisions that shape social policy. They are provisions that are complete in themselves and they are directly effective. Much – though not all, as *Defrenne* made clear – of EU social policy needs to find a legal base first of all, then be steered through legislative process

---

[65] Cf., e.g., Barnard, 'EU Employment Law and the European Social Model: The Past, the Present and the Future', 67 *Current Legal Problems* (2014) 199.

and then properly implemented at national level before it bites. There is a gap here. However, one of the understandings in favour of EU commitments to social protection is precisely that it serves as a complement to the perceived aggressive deregulation that is calculatedly part of the EU's endeavours to create an integrated trading space, and the legislative *acquis* sketched above is not negligible in scope or ambition, even if the momentum behind it has visibly stalled of late.

Accordingly, there is a strong descriptive argument that labour market regulation and social policy more generally has developed as an integral element of, not simply an optional supplement to, the internal market as a legal and political concept. This is predominantly the result of a combination of the Treaty platform, secondary legislation and judicial interpretation. There is a range of explanations – sometimes competing, sometimes fluctuating over time – for the EU's expedition into labour market regulation and social policy more generally.[66] There is room to argue that the EU has got it wrong. Neither Article 3 TEU nor Article 26 TFEU make a specific constitutionally enforceable choice about precisely what shall be the intensity of worker protection and social policy more generally in the EU. There is ambiguity. The relatively dense pattern of legislative activity could be reversed in different political times. And the precariousness of the place of judicial interpretation must also be reckoned with. The Court's decisions in *Viking Line*[67] and *Laval*[68] disrupt the conventional narrative whereby its interpretation of free movement law uses the device of justification to embed sensitivity to the virtue of social protection and labour rights when they come under pressure from the attempted exercise of cross-border trading freedom.[69] In the interpretation of the legislative acquis there is similarly one moment which sticks out like a sore thumb where the Court neglects its orthodox sensitivity to the function of EU rules as means to secure a high level of worker protection as well as a means to improve the functioning of the internal market. The awkward case here is *Alemo-Herron*.[70]

Alemo-Herron concerned employee protection on the transfer of undertakings, which has long been the subject of regulation at EU level. The legal base of the predecessor of the measure at stake in *Alemo-Herron*, Directive 77/187, was Article 100 EEC, while that of its successor, Directive 2001/23 which applied in *Alemo-Herron*,[71] was in turn the successor to Article 100 EC, that is, Article 94. The relevant provision today is Article 115 TFEU, the older but much less fashionable sibling of Article 114 TFEU. So its purpose is harmonization of laws in the service of the establishment and functioning of the internal market. A reference from the UK's Supreme Court asked whether a particular judicial approach to (national measures implementing) the EU's Directive 2001/23 was correct. That approach, which took a 'dynamic' view of the place of collective bargains in governing the rights of employees of transferred

---

[66] See, e.g., Davies, *supra* note 35, Ch. 1; Barnard, 'EU Social Policy: From Employment Law to Labour Market Reform', in P. Craig and G. De Búrca (eds), *The Evolution of EU Law* (2nd ed., 2011); P. Syrpis, *EU Intervention in Domestic Labour Law* (2007).

[67] Case C-438/05, *supra* note 14.

[68] Case C-341/05, *supra* note 14.

[69] Case C-438/05, *supra* note 14, Case C-341/05, *supra* note 14, see Chapter 9.B.

[70] Case C-426/11. *Alemo-Herron*, judgment of 18 July 2013, not yet reported (ECLI:EU:C:2013:521).

[71] *Supra* note 26.

undertakings, was noticeably more generous to the employee than the alternative competing ('static') interpretation. The Court approached the matter on the basis that the Directive called for a 'fair balance' between the employer and the employee, and it found that the managerial flexibility of the company to which the transfer is been made would be improperly confined were the dynamic interpretation to prevail. The Court relied on Article 16 of the Charter, which (it said) covers freedom of contract. It was then claimed in the judgment that were the English courts' interpretation to prevail, then the private firm, to which the business has been transferred, would find its contractual freedom seriously reduced to the point that there might be damage to the very essence of its freedom to conduct a business. So, in short, the more generous interpretation of the protective effect of the Directive was ruled out in favour of the less protective.

On the facts of the case, the Court's claim that damage to the company on such a scale would follow is extremely hard to believe. It is an exaggeration. However, the deeper objection to the ruling holds that the aggressive protection of the constitutional value of freedom of contract goes too far. The Court states that Article 16 of the Charter covers freedom of contract, but this is in fact not explicitly true and the Court in this case appears to have pushed understandings of contractual freedom beyond anything previously located within EU law.[72] The ruling is glaringly out of line with the scepticism about the reality of freedom of contract found in much of the EU's consumer legislation and case law (see Chapters 13.D.3 and 13.F) and in some of the older employee protection material as well.[73] And, shockingly, *Alemo-Herron*, asserting this powerful role to be played by Article 16 of the Charter, is written in a way that draws explicitly on the rulings in *Sky Österreich*[74] and *Deutsches Weintor*[75] as support for this interpretative slant, while failing utterly to confess that in those rulings, examined in Section D.2, the Court, carefully applying the Charter, authorized legislative *restrictions* on contractual and commercial freedom. They are not of the same hue as *Alemo-Herron* at all.

Such excessively and atypically heavy reliance on Article 16 of the Charter, unmediated by the *Solidarity* asserted by Chapter IV of the Charter or by the EU's track record in the field of labour market regulation and social policy more generally, would deliver a very different kind of 'internal market' from that developed, albeit unevenly, over the past 50 years. Appreciation of the dual function of harmonization – market-making *and* social protection – has gone missing in *Alemo-Herron*, where instead, under the discourse of a fair balance and sympathy for managerial flexibility, focus on the imbalance between employers and employees which is a motivating factor in the *acquis* and in the Court's past interpretation of it has been replaced by a vision which is blind to the particular concerns of a group – workers – who

[72] See Prassl, 'Freedom of Contract as a General Principle of EU Law', 42 *Industrial Law Journal* (2013) 434.

[73] See Weatherill, 'Use and Abuse of the EU's Charter of Fundamental Rights: On the Improper Veneration of Freedom of Contract', 10 *European Review of Contract Law* (2014) 157.

[74] Case C-283/11, *Sky Österreich GmbH*, judgment of 22 January 2013, not yet reported (ECLI:EU:C:2013:28).

[75] Case C-544/10, *Deutsches Weintor eG* v. *Land Rheinland-Pfalz*, judgment of 6 September 2012, not yet reported (ECLI:EU:C:2012:526).

lack the economic power to bargain effectively on an individual basis. *Alemo-Herron* shares with *Viking Line* exactly this blot. It, like *Viking Line*, should not become the norm.

E. Social Policy – the Continuing Debate

In so far as nothing *guarantees* the connection between the internal market as a legal concept and the delivery of a high level of worker and social protection, space is left for political debate. Perhaps this is no bad thing. One should not always hide behind the Court or even the Treaty. So is there a fuller and deeper normative case for arguing that the internal market is inextricably linked to social protection? Bland invocation of the notion of 'distorted' competition has carried the EU a long way, but it is unsatisfying. A deeper explanation of why diversity between national legal orders is prejudicial is needed; so, too, is a case for why the EU's common rules should aim at a high level of social protection are political not legal. There *are* other possible rationales for European harmonization. They lie, for example, in the advantages in global markets of competing 'upwards' in standards-setting in order to acquire a reputation for high quality;[76] in improving productivity and increasing inward investment by labour market regulation aimed at enhancing *quality*; in curtailing the 'race to the bottom' and 'social dumping', even if empirical support for such phenomena is relatively thin. Broader still, Sen's work is influential in promoting intervention to ensure citizens possess the resources they need to take advantage of opportunities.[77] So, for example, anti-discrimination laws can be seen as not simply prohibiting unjust practices but also as a means to facilitate genuine opportunity to participate – and thus as a means to correct the market failure caused by the lack of information that leads to discrimination in the first place.

There is room to propel the internal market as a site for social progress.[78] But, as a legal concept, it is in that vein ambiguous.

---

[76] A long influential starting-point is M. Porter, *The Competitive Advantage of Nations* (1998).

[77] A. Sen, *Development as Freedom* (1999); also M. Nussbaum, *Creating Capabilities: the Human Development Approach* (2011). Taken into the EU context, Deakin, 'The Capability Concept and the Evolution of European Social Policy', in M. Dougan and E. Spaventa (eds), *Social Welfare and EU Law* (2005).

[78] See, e.g., F. Vandenbroucke and B. Vanhercke, *European Social Union: Ten Tough Nuts to Crack* (2014); Barnard, *supra* note 65 (CLP 2014) 224 et seq. (arguing for a social compact to match the fiscal compact); N. Countouris and M. Freedland (eds), *Resocialising Europe in a Time of Crisis* (2013) (with, in its Epilogue, 10 principles for resocializing Europe); Syrpis, *supra* note 66; Schiek, 'The EU Constitution of Social Governance in an Economic Crisis: In Defence of a Transnational Dimension to Social Europe', 20 *Maastricht Journal* (2013) 185.

15

Pre-emption

The issue at stake here is the impact on residual national competence of the adoption of a legislative measure by the EU in a particular field. Clearly the Member States must comply with the EU measure, but to what extent, if at all, do they remain free to maintain or introduce stricter rules? This is another instance in which there is no straightforward answer. This is another instance where the internal market is an ambiguous legal concept.

A. The Directions Contained in the Treaty

Some provisions of the Treaty on the Functioning of the European Union (TFEU) make plain that legislative measures adopted pursuant to them do *not* exclude state competence to act in a more interventionist manner within the scope allowed by the Treaty. This is minimum rule-making and the permissive formula may be found in places such as Article 169(4) TFEU (consumer protection), Article 153(4) TFEU (social matters) and Article 193 TFEU (environmental protection). Article 114 TFEU, by contrast, contains no such *general* concession, but rather only the derogations contained in Articles 114(4)–(10) TFEU whereby states may be permitted to apply stricter standards than are envisaged by the agreed EU rule, but only under defined pre-conditions which are narrower than those available under Article 36 TFEU and which, moreover, are subject to supervision by and require the authorization of the European Commission ('the Commission'). That procedure was criticized at the time of its creation for having opened up scope for unilateral state action beyond the circumstances foreseen by Article 36,[1] but in practice it is relatively rarely invoked and still more rarely leads to approval of national measures.[2]

So whether Member States retain autonomy to act after the EU has itself acted depends on the particular subject matter. The fact that finding space for stricter national standards is treated differently depending on which legal base is chosen

---

[1] Pescatore, 'Some Critical Remarks on the Single European Act', 24 *Common Market Law Review* (1987) 8, 12.

[2] For the Court's control see, e.g., Joined Cases C-439/05 P and C-454/05 P, *Land Oberösterreich and Austria v. Commission*, [2007] ECR I-7141 (ECLI:EU:C:2007:510). See also P. Oliver (ed.), *Oliver on Free Movement of Goods in the European Union* (5th ed., 2010), at paras 13.30–13.42; I. Maletić, *The Law and Policy of Harmonisation in Europe's Internal Market* (2013).

The Internal Market as a Legal Concept. First Edition. Stephen Weatherill.
© Stephen Weatherill 2017. Published 2017 by Oxford University Press.

generates disputes. *Octapharma France* illustrates the point neatly.[3] The case concerned plasma products used in transfusions. There were two relevant Directives. One was adopted under Article 114 TFEU governing medicinal products, which the firm dealing in the products argued applied. The other was adopted under Article 168 TFEU governing blood and blood components, which the French public authorities argued was applicable. It *mattered* which Directive governed the matter at hand, for that in turn determined the scope of the possibility foreseen by the Treaty for the Member State to choose to apply stricter rules. This explains the strategies adopted by the litigants in the case. The firm had no principled desire to champion Article 114. The point was simply that if the Article 114 Directive applied, there would be no scope secured by the Treaty for the French authorities to adopt stricter rules curtailing its trading opportunities on French territory. The French authorities wanted the Article 168 Directive to prevail, for exactly the opposite strategic reason. In the event – though the detail of the outcome is of itself not of general interest – the Court of Justice of the European Union ('the Court') found that the Article 168 measure applied in the case of collecting and testing, and so stricter rules were allowed, whereas processing, storage and distribution fell within the scope of the Article 114 measure.

The question arises whether a measure of legislative harmonization adopted under Article 114 TFEU may itself provide that stricter national measures are permitted. That is, does the derogation foreseen by Articles 114(4) et seq. exhaust the scope for Member States to depart from the harmonized standard or is it open to the EU legislative process to grant derogations in the text of particular measures of secondary legislation? This asks questions about the shape of the internal market.

Two basic choices present themselves: minimum harmonization or maximum harmonization. A measure of *minimum harmonization* sets a common floor of regulation, which all Member States must respect, but it does not set a ceiling. The ceiling is set only by the broader legal rules of the internal market, most of all those governing non-discrimination and free movement. By contrast, a measure of *maximum harmonization* serves as both floor and ceiling. Member States must implement the rules that have been chosen as the EU regime – and they must apply *only* those rules. They are not permitted to apply stricter rules. The maximum model, in contrast to the minimum model, robs them of any space to argue that they are justified in choosing a higher ceiling of protection. Only the EU, by changing the harmonized standard, is able to provide a higher standard.

A minimum model allows more space for diversity and local autonomy; a maximum model seems to promise greater uniformity in the pattern of regulatory intervention chosen for the internal market. A minimum model preserves to a degree the independence of relevant institutions at state level; the maximum model transfers regulatory responsibility to the EU's legislative institutions – and, in the interpretation of both the material scope and the content of the measure, to its Court too. There are fierce debates about the appropriateness of these competing models for the structure

---

[3] Case C-512/12, *Octapharma France*, judgment of 13 March 2014, not yet reported (ECLI:EU:C:2014:149).

of the internal market, and there are varying legislative preferences too. At the heart of the debate, however, is a profound choice – one that concerns the distribution of regulatory authority in the EU.

B. Legislative Practice

Legislative practice is rich and it is instructively varied.

It is common to find measures of harmonization which establish rules on, and procedures to ensure the protection of, animal and human health which are treated as a complete system, apt to exclude any possibility for divergent national measures. So Member States are required to permit products that comply with the harmonized standards to be marketed without any restriction and they are also required to prohibit the marketing of products that do not so comply. Decisions of the Court have emphasized this structure, typically in circumstances where the Court interprets such measures as excluding any scope for Member States to have recourse to Article 36 TFEU to justify stricter measures.[4] The EU measure, usually a Directive, is, in the conventional jargon, taken to have occupied the field: it pre-empts Member State action. To upgrade the regime is the EU's job – in a sense, an area of exclusive EU competence has been *legislatively* created within the measure's material scope and on its terms. This means that the state dissatisfied with the standard of protection must try and prompt legislative reform at EU level. Unilateral departure is simply not allowed.

However, legislative practice reveals that much of the harmonized *acquis* pertaining to the protection of the economic interests of consumers is built on an assumption that minimum harmonization will be the norm. Take a case like *Buet*, considered earlier.[5] The Court ruled that although Directive 85/577 on 'doorstep selling' merely required that a consumer be allowed a right to cancel the contract concluded on the doorstep within a defined period, a total ban imposed by France on doorstep selling was compatible with the Directive which provided explicitly in Article 8 that the Directive 'shall not prevent Member States from adopting or maintaining more favourable provisions to protect consumers' and, given its contribution to consumer protection, it was also justified within the meaning of what is now Article 34 TFEU. Directive 93/13 on unfair terms in consumer contracts has an equivalent clause; so does Directive 99/44 on consumer sales and guarantees.[6] Minimum harmonization, involving EU standards but space for stricter national standards, is the political bargain that has characterized the growth of the harmonized legislative *acquis* affecting protection of the economic interests of consumers.[7]

---

[4] E.g., Case 35/76, *Simmenthal*, [1976] ECR 1871 (ECLI:EU:C:1976:180); Case 190/87, *Oberkreisdirektor* v. *Moormann*, [1988] ECR 4689 (ECLI:EU:C:1988:424); Case 60/86, *Commission* v. *United Kingdom*, [1988] ECR 3921 (ECLI:EU:C:1988:382); Case 148/78, *Ratti*, [1979] ECR 1629 (ECLI:EU:C:1979:110); Case C-374/05, *Gintec International*, [2007] ECR I-9517 (ECLI:EU:C:2007:654).

[5] Case 382/87, *Buet*, [1989] ECR 1235 (ECLI:EU:C:1989:198). See Chapter 8.F.

[6] Directive 85/577 has now been replaced by Directive 2011/83 which is a maximum, not minimum, measure: but Directives 93/13 and 99/44 retain their minimum character.

[7] See S. Weatherill, *EU Consumer Law and Policy* (2nd ed., 2012), Ch. 3.

This model shares with Article 114(4) et seq. the perception that harmonization need not involve the automatic subordination of national choices about market regulation to the dictates of trade liberalization, but minimum harmonization is more flexible in the leeway offered to states than the relatively tightly defined and Commission-managed provisions of Article 114(4) et seq. In fact it brings Article 114, as a basis for harmonized protection of consumers' economic interests, into functional alignment with Article 169(4) TFEU, which makes explicit that minimum rule-making is envisaged as far as supportive rules adopted as measures of consumer protection under Article 169(2)(b) are concerned. In this way, both the EU and the Member States retain competence to protect consumers even after the EU has intervened by way of secondary legislation. Minimum harmonization promotes the integration of markets, while also preserving regulatory diversity and it ensures space for expression for cultural particularity.

C. The Sources of Pressure on the Model of Minimum Harmonization

By leaving open space for national standards which reach above the harmonized EU standard, the model of minimum rule-making treats the internal market as a site of regulatory diversity. But there are two distinct sources of pressure on the model of minimum rule-making. The first is the Court of Justice of the European Union ('the Court'), the second is the European Commission ('the Commission').

1. The Court of Justice

In the first *Tobacco Advertising* case the Court criticized Directive 98/43 on the advertising of tobacco products because it 'contains no provision ensuring the free movement of products which conform to its provisions'.[8] This was certainly not the only reason which motivated the Court to find the Directive to be invalid, as has been explained (see Chapter 13.G.2), but it was certainly one of the relatively carefully elaborated constitutional objections recorded by the Court. Shortly afterwards, in the ruling in *ex parte BAT*, a plank in the Court's reasoning approving the validity of that measure of harmonization was the *presence* of a market access clause of this type.[9] Moreover, the measure annulled in *Tobacco Advertising I* was replaced by a more tightly drawn Directive (2003/33), which includes an explicit provision to the effect that products and services complying with its provisions shall be entitled free movement. The validity of that Directive as a sufficient contribution to the functioning of the internal market was confirmed in turn in *Tobacco Advertising II* and there too, as in *BAT*, the Court saw fit to express explicit approval of the presence of a free movement clause.[10]

---

[8] Case C-376/98, *Germany v. Parliament and Council*, [2000] ECR I-8419 (ECLI:EU:C:2000:544), at para. 104.
[9] Case C-491/01, *R v. Secretary of State ex parte BAT and Imperial Tobacco*, [2002] ECR I-11543 (ECLI:EU:C:2002:741).
[10] Case C-380/03, *Germany v. Parliament and Council*, [2006] ECR I-11573 (ECLI:EU:C:2006:772), at paras 73–74.

These decisions do not explicitly demolish the pretensions of minimum harmonization. But they are capable of being interpreted in such a way. It seems that in these rulings the Court has assumed that it is a condition of the validity of a measure of harmonization that it excludes the possibility of states making stricter demands of imports than are envisaged by the Directive itself. 'Minimum harmonization' would not seem to be constitutionally possible in so far as it is intended to refer to a standard which Member States must introduce but may also surpass, even if to do so is to create obstacles to cross-border trade. Stricter rules, it seems, could only be directed at a state's own producers operating domestically. On this approach, a state would be required to resort to the relatively narrow Commission-managed authorization procedure in Article 114(4) TFEU et seq. in order to secure a valid basis for such an impediment to inter-state trade going beyond the agreed EU harmonized standard.

However, the case law is not unequivocal. There are, in fact, two quite separate streams. In the second stream the Court has no objection in principle to 'minimum harmonization'. If it had, in *Buet*[11] it would not have assessed the justification for the ban on 'doorstep selling' advanced by France, because a ban, going beyond the EU Directive's scheme of providing a right of withdrawal from agreements concluded in such circumstances, would have been beyond the competence reserved to the Member State. Moreover, in a batch of judgments since *Tobacco Advertising I* the Court has dealt with measures of 'minimum harmonization', inter alia in the field of the protection of the economic interests of consumers, and has not showed any constitutional distaste for them.[12] The Court seems content to accept the assumption already rooted in *Buet*. It expressed no objection to the possibility that states may be able to justify rules above the harmonized norm provided the Directive expressly authorizes this possibility. Admittedly, in the cases in this divergent stream the Court does not mention *Tobacco Advertising I* at all, nor does it seem the issue was explicitly raised.

The argument in favour of minimum harmonization holds that, given its concession to the possibility of stricter national rules, it is admittedly imperfect as a means of *immediately* bringing about a fully integrated market in the relevant sector, but that the introduction of minimum rules brings the position closer to that which would prevail in a single market than that which obtained previously, under a completely unharmonized pattern, while also meeting regulatory objectives recognized by EU law at both EU level (in the minimum harmonized standards) and at state level (in any chosen stricter rules). It is, in short and once again, the dual function of harmonization! The best way to reconcile the two divergent streams of case law is to impose an explanation which admittedly the Court has not supplied, but which nevertheless does the job: *Tobacco Advertising I* was a case in which the Court thought

---

[11] Case 382/87, *supra* note 5.

[12] Case C-322/01, *DocMorris*, [2003] ECR I-14887 (ECLI:EU:C:2003:664); Case C-71/02, *Herbert Karner GmbH* v. *Troostwijk GmbH*, [2004] ECR I-3025 (ECLI:EU:C:2004:181); Case C-441/04, *A-Punkt Schmuckhandels GmbH* v. *Claudia Schmidt*, [2006] ECR I-2093 (ECLI:EU:C:2006:141); Case C-212/11, *Jyske Bank*, judgment of 25 April 2013, not yet reported (ECLI:EU:C:2013:270); Case C-235/14, *Safe Interenvios*, judgment of 10 March 2016, not yet reported (ECLI:EU:C:2016:154).

that a market access clause was required to make constitutional sense of *that* Directive, but it was not a case where the Court was insisting on a general *constitutional* rejection of the technique of 'minimum harmonization'.[13] The case law that tolerates minimum harmonization is therefore to be understood as rooted in the nature and purpose of the particular EU measures that formed the dispute's subject matter.

It is worth noting in addition that if the Court's case law is truly to be read as ruling out scope for the EU to harmonize while leaving room for stricter national standards applicable to imports, then some rather high-profile measures would crumble to dust. Directive 2006/123, the Services Directive, for example, was adopted only after tortuous negotiation.[14] Part of the deal involved agreeing that in some circumstances compliance with the common standards set at EU level governing the quality of services would not inevitably entitle a service provider access to target markets in other Member States. Specific provision was made to allow Member States to choose to set stricter rules, where justified within the parameters envisaged by the Directive.[15] The extreme and brutal understanding of *Tobacco Advertising I* would insist that such derogation is not permitted, but there is no sign of the Court taking such a (politically incendiary) approach. In fact, in *Rina Services* it explicitly contrasted the provisions of the Directive which do not allow Member States to justify stricter rules from those that do, without at all suggesting any constitutional objection to the validity of this species of minimum harmonization.[16]

A final point concerning the Court's views must be mentioned, albeit with reluctance. Might it be argued that the freedom to conduct a business guaranteed by Article 16 of the Charter militates against EU legislation which allows for stricter national provisions that will, on the territory of a regulating state, deprive a trader of the right to operate under the standards set by the EU measure? This is a preposterous suggestion: it pushes for an entirely absurd inflation in Article 16's vigour as a control of legislative discretion. It is, however, regrettably what the Court did in *Alemo-Herron*.[17] Article 8 of Directive 2001/23, the measure at stake in that case, provided that the Directive 'shall not affect the right of Member States to apply or introduce laws, regulations or administrative provisions which are more favourable to employees or to promote or permit collective agreements or agreements between social partners more favourable to employees'. This set the requirements of the Directive as a floor, not a ceiling, of regulatory protection, and so permitted Member States to adopt a more generous system of employee protection, should they so choose. The Court took the view that this proviso could not be interpreted 'as entitling the Member States to take measures which, while being more favourable to employees, are liable to adversely affect the very essence of the transferee's freedom

---

[13] Light may be cast on the Court's position in challenges pending to the validity of Directive 2014/40, OJ 2014 L 127/1, which replaces Directive 2001/37, OJ 2001 L 194/26 and which in its Arts 24(2) and (3) envisages scope for restrictions on imports which go beyond the harmonized norm (Case C-358/14, *Poland* v. *Council and Parliament*, Case C-477/14, *Pillbox 38*, and Case C-547/14, *Philip Morris*, pending).

[14] OJ 2006 L 376/36.   [15] In particular Arts 15(2), 16(3).

[16] Case C-593/13, *Rina Services*, judgment of 16 June 2015, not yet reported (ECLI:EU:C:2015:399).

[17] Case C-426/11, *Alemo-Herron*, judgment of 18 July 2013, not yet reported (ECLI:EU:C:2013:521).

to conduct a business'.[18] This is to write in a major limitation to the legislative grant of autonomy to Member States to adopt measures more favourable to employees. The Court's only explanation is provided in the same paragraph of the judgment: the reader is invited to 'see, by analogy, Case C–544/10 *Deutsches Weintor* [2012] ECR I-0000, paragraphs 54 and 58'. But those paragraphs and indeed the judgment in *Deutsches Weintor* generally have nothing to do with a 'minimum' provision of the type neutered by the Court in *Alemo-Herron*. The Court was therefore doing something entirely new and, in interpreting Article 16 of the Charter to attack a minimum rule, it was doing something entirely unwelcome, namely to assert a wholly unbalanced approach which privileges commercial freedom over regulatory protection. That, it should be noted, is the exact opposite of what the Court had done in *Deutsches Weintor!*[19] This aberrant ruling should not be relied on in future. Minimum rule-making by the EU should not be regarded as imperilled by Article 16 of the Charter.

In conclusion, the model of 'minimum harmonization' should be considered to be available to the EU legislature as one possible option in relying on Article 114 as a base for legislation. 'Minimum harmonization' might be rejected in particular cases for *political* or *economic* reasons but it cannot be rejected for clear and generally applicable *constitutional* reasons.

2. The Commission's Attack on 'Minimum Harmonization'

Beginning in a communication released in July 2001,[20] the Commission initiated a wide-ranging debate about the proper role of the EU in the field of contract law. It is here, most of all in the area of *consumer* contract law, that routine reliance on minimum harmonization as the preferred regulatory technique is readily visible. There are several themes and tensions evident in the progress of the debate, which is infused by a search for 'a significantly higher degree of coherence in European contract law', to borrow the apt words of one of the principal architects of the review within the Commission.[21] However, one of the most prominent is an increasing distaste on the side of the Commission for the long-established model of minimum harmonization. 'Coherence', it became evident, was to be promoted by working towards the abandonment of the model of minimum harmonization.

Milestones along the way advertised the Commission's thinking. Its Consumer Policy Programme for 2002–2006 advocated a 'move away from the present situation of different sets of rules in each Member State towards a more consistent environment for consumer protection across the EU'.[22] This meant maximum rather than minimum harmonization. The Commission's October 2004 document on contract law referred critically to perceived failings of a minimum model of rule-making.[23] Most of all it complained that minimum EU rules create unevenness in the legal

---

[18] *Ibid.*, at para. 36. The split infinitive will pain grammatical purists.
[19] As explained in Chapter 13.D.2.   [20] COM (2001) 398.
[21] Staudenmayer, 'The Place of Consumer Contract Law within the Process on European Contract Law', 27 *Journal of Consumer Policy* (2004) 269, 277.
[22] COM (2002) 208.   [23] COM (2004) 651.

regulation of the internal market in so far as Member States choose to apply stricter rules, which the Commission was able credibly to show that they do, in varying ways and to varying extents.[24] In February 2007, the Green Paper on the *Review of the Consumer Acquis* concluded what was described as the 'diagnostic phase' of the Commission's review, and set out the main options for reform.[25] The orthodox pre-existing model of minimum harmonization was not even allowed as a possible option for the future.

The Commission had a particular vision of the internal market in mind. The anxiety to suppress the scope for national variation which is the very nature of the minimum model of harmonization was inspired by a vision of maximum harmonization which would accelerate market integration by levelling the regulatory playing field. Uniformity rather than diversity was the guiding objective.

The Commission enjoyed some success in promoting its preferred design through the EU's legislative process. Directive 2005/29 concerning unfair business-to-consumer practices in the internal market adopts a maximum model of harmonization.[26] The Directive requires the suppression of such unfair practices. It prohibits practices which, contrary to 'professional diligence', 'materially distort the economic behaviour' of an average consumer. The notions of forbidden 'misleading' and 'aggressive' practice are elaborated in the body of the Directive, and its Annex contains a 'Black List' of practices considered unfair in all circumstances. But there is no scope for Member States to choose to establish stricter standards within the field occupied by the Directive. If a practice falling within the Directive's material scope is not 'unfair' within the meaning of the Directive, a Member State may not treat it as unfair. This is the stern message of several decisions of the Court on exactly this point.[27] So a Member State may not apply stricter standards: it has no room to seek to justify a tougher standard of 'unfairness' than is envisaged by the Directive because the whole point of maximum harmonization is to disable Member State competence to do anything other than apply the EU's harmonized rules. The point is that, from the perspective of cross-border trading freedom, the opportunities provided by the internal market have been increased. For the advocate of effective consumer protection, the anxiety is that, in contrast to the consequences that apply in a case of minimum harmonization, the nature and level of consumer protection is determined entirely and exclusively *by the EU*. Any dissatisfaction with the EU standard – on paper or as interpreted by the Court – must be expressed by attempting to provoke legislative reform *at EU level*. This type of internal market is not receptive to local regulatory variation at all.

The maximum model is based on a significant transfer of regulatory competence from the Member States to the EU.[28] However, the story of Directive 2011/83 on

---

[24] E.g., Commission Report on implementation of Directive 97/7 on distance contracts, COM (2006) 514; Commission Communication on the implementation of Directive 99/44, COM (2007) 210.

[25] COM (2006) 744.   [26] OJ 2005 L 149/22.

[27] E.g., Case C-261/07, *VTB-VAB NV*, [2009] ECR I-2949 (ECLI:EU:C:2009:244); Case C-122/10, *Ving Sverige AB*, [2011] ECR I-3903 (ECLI:EU:C:2011:299). See Stuyck, 'The Court of Justice and the Unfair Commercial Practices Directive', 52 *Common Market Law Review* (2015) 721.

[28] See also Directive 2007/64 on payment services in the internal market, OJ 2007 L 319/1; Directive 2008/48 on credit agreements for consumers, OJ 2008 L 133/66.

consumer rights reveals the politically contested nature of this shift in model of harmonization.[29] And it reveals the limits of the possible in the Commission's ambition to advance the internal market under an aggressively driven pattern of maximum harmonization.

The Commission's review of the 'consumer *acquis*' was focused on eight Directives that had been adopted over time in the incremental evolution of EU consumer law: Directive 85/577 on doorstep selling, Directive 90/314 on package travel, Directive 93/13 on unfair terms in consumer contracts, Directive 94/47 on timeshare, Directive 97/7 on distance contracts, Directive 98/6 on price indications, Directive 98/27 on injunctions and Directive 1999/44 on the sale of consumer goods and associated guarantees. This was an ambitious agenda which, had it yielded a comprehensive reform, could have done much to further the quest for greater 'coherence' to which the Commission review was wedded.[30]

But eight became four. In October 2008, as a result of its review of the consumer *acquis*, the Commission adopted a proposal for a Directive on Consumer Rights which would replace Directives 85/577, 97/7, 93/13 and 99/44 with a so-called 'horizontal instrument'.[31] This, it was argued, would provide a simplified and more consistent regulatory framework apt to realize the advantages of the internal market while also achieving a high level of consumer protection. The chosen legal base for this proposed measure was Article 95 EC, Article 114 TFEU's predecessor, and the explanation given fits perfectly comfortably into the notion that harmonization has a 'dual function': integration and protective (re-)regulation (see Chapter 13.B). But the key feature of the model of maximum harmonization, which is what was proposed by the Commission, is that the protective standard depends *exclusively* on what is delivered at EU level. The possibility to apply stricter state rules, the characteristic of minimum harmonization, would be switched off.

The 2008 proposal was greeted critically, even scornfully, in the academic literature, not least for its determined pursuit of the maximum model of harmonization which aimed to locate responsibility in the field *exclusively* at EU level.[32] In fact, it was hard to find any voices willing to side *with* the Commission.[33] Of more direct significance to the initiative's viability, there was sharp political opposition too. The Report of the Parliament's Committee on the Internal Market and Consumer Protection, published in February 2011, reveals the persisting *political* salience of choice of model.[34] Socialist and Green MEPs were typically antagonistic to maximum harmonization, treating it as a threat to established standards at national level. Representatives of the European People's Party and of the Alliance of Liberals and Democrats for Europe were much warmer about the value of broader maximum

---

[29] OJ 2011 L 304/64.   [30] *Supra* note 21.   [31] COM (2008) 614.

[32] Typical, though particularly powerful, was Micklitz and Reich, 'Crónica de una Muerte Anunciada: the Commission Proposal for a Directive on Consumer Rights', 46 *Common Market Law Review* (2009) 471. See also G. Howells and R. Schulze (eds), *Modernising and Harmonising Consumer Contract Law* (2009).

[33] But the Commission was not totally friendless: see Hondius, 'The Proposal for a European Directive on Consumer Rights: A Step Forward', 18 *Euro Rev Private Law* (2010) 103.

[34] A7-0038/2011, available online at http://www.europarl.europa.eu/sides/getDoc.do?type=REPORT &mode=XML&reference=A7-2011-0038&language=EN.

harmonization as a means to simplify business opportunities and ultimately to enhance choice and competition to the advantage of consumers. The sharply political context of harmonization and of the nature of the internal market more generally emerges with helpfully illustrative clarity from this disagreement.

In 2011 a compromise was struck. Pursuant to the complex operation of the EU's ordinary legislative procedure, the Parliament adopted a set of amendments to the Commission's original 2008 draft. The Council was satisfied, the formalities were completed in October 2011 and Directive 2011/83 on consumer rights was agreed. It is, however, a revealingly abridged compromise. Eight had become four in 2008 – now, in 2011, four had become two. The Commission had not surrendered its ambition to convert the regime into one of maximum harmonization: Directive 2011/83 is a measure of maximum harmonization which excludes stricter national initiatives in the area which it covers. But the price which the Commission was forced to pay for its ambitious venture into politically charged currents was measured in the material scope of the finally adopted Directive. Directive 2011/83 replaces and renovates only two Directives, Directives 85/577 and 97/7. This pair, it will readily be appreciated, are of significantly less vigour and general importance than the pair (93/13 on unfair terms, 99/44 on consumer sales) that were cut out in response to political disquiet which the Commission was unable to quell or circumvent.

The Commission's quest to widen and deepen the harmonized *acquis* in order to promote what it depicted eagerly as a 'coherent' regulatory environment for the development of the internal market had met a grudging and sceptical EU legislative process. The lesson: maximum harmonization represents a vertical transfer of authority from Member States to the EU and the more politically salient the subject matter at stake, the less likely that appeal to the economic virtues of the internal market will suffice to allay sensitivity about the constitutional and regulatory implications of what is intended.[35]

The Services Directive (i.e., Directive 2006/123[36]) offers a – considerably higher profile – example of such political constraints in the shaping of a harmonization programme apt to provide a foundation for the internal market. In Article 2 of the Directive several highly significant services sectors are excluded from the regime: including some that met a similar fate in the final negotiation of Directive 2011/83, such as financial services, services in the field of transport, healthcare services, gambling activities, and some social services. This, in line with the orthodox approach explained in Chapter 5.C, in no way sheltered those sectors from the cutting edge of free movement law, but at least it left space for Member States to have resort to the possibility there secured to justify restrictive rules. In assessing the sensitivities of the shift from primary to secondary law, this is not the only insight offered by inspection of the legislative 'pre-history' of Directive 2006/123. The so-called 'Bolkestein Draft', proposed by the Commission in 2004,[37] relied on a model of maximum

---

[35] Cf. Weatherill, 'The Consumer Rights Directive: How and Why a Quest for "Coherence" Has (Largely) Failed', 49 *Common Market Law Review* (2012) 1279.
[36] OJ 2006 L 376/36.   [37] COM (2004) 2.

harmonization that, under the orthodox logic explained above, would have converted the EU Directive into the exclusive source of regulation of the services sector. This would be a clean – but brutal – transfer of regulatory competence upwards, from Member States to the EU. This profound liberalizing initiative was opposed and ultimately defeated by energetic political resistance focusing on the planned release of, most strikingly, the 'Polish plumber' able to undercut local service providers.[38] Whether that would be a bad thing (for consumers, in particular) is a political, social and economic question of immense delicacy: from the purely legal perspective, it was certainly correct that the intended model of harmonization would have released opportunities for cross-border provisions of services falling within the material scope of the proposed Directive on condition that the EU standards contained in the Directive were met, but to the exclusion of national rules that purported to apply higher standards in the areas covered. This was politically too much to swallow. Concessions were made. The version which was finally agreed, Directive 2006/123, contains a model that instead leaves room for stricter national rules in some fields as well as asserting an abridged material scope, as mentioned above, although on both counts the final version, an awkward compromise, is laced with an illuminating level of imprecision.[39]

D. Normative Perspectives on the Choice between Models of Harmonization

Which model of harmonization *should* prevail?

The core question is about the *relative* costs and benefits. In the case of maximum harmonization the risk is that common rules will result in a depreciation in standards of protection from market failure and/or market inequities which cannot be corrected locally. To take the particularly vivid and topical case of consumer protection, the fear is that *some* groups of consumers in *some* Member States will lose out as a result of a priority for market-making to the exclusion of local regulatory autonomy. Maximum harmonization asserts a single notion and standard of consumer protection when in fact consumer preferences, tastes and capabilities differ in Europe.[40] Minimum harmonization has costs too. The Commission is correct to connect the technique of minimum harmonization to a persistently fragmented regulatory landscape in the internal market. That is the very nature of minimum harmonization and, for its adherents, this is its very appeal – it leaves space for diversity. For the Commission, however, the narrative in its contract law review was mainly about costs measured in the disruption to cross-border trade. The

---

[38] See, e.g., Loder, 'The Lisbon Strategy and the Politicization of EU Policy-Making: The Case of the Services Directive', (2011) 18 JEPP 566.

[39] Cf., e.g., Barnard, 'Unravelling the Services Directive', 45 *Common Market Law Review* (2008) 323; Hatzopoulos, 'Le Principe de Reconnaissance Mutuelle dans la Libre Prestation de Services', 46 *Cahiers de Droit Européen* (2010) 47; *Wyatt and Dashwood's European Union Law* (6th ed., 2011), Ch. 18.

[40] Cf., e.g., Wilhelmsson, 'The Abuse of the Confident Consumer as a Justification for EC Consumer Law', 27 *Journal of Consumer Policy* (2004) 317; Mak, 'Review of the Consumer Acquis: Towards Maximum Harmonisation?', 17 *European Review of Private Law* (2009) 55.

Commission, in advocating a shift to maximum harmonization, at no stage neglected a policy commitment to levelling that field at a high standard of consumer protection, but, plainly, it located delivery of protection as a task exclusively loaded on the EU. The issue is that what the quality of protection set at EU level involves evidently becomes a great deal more important to the advocate of effective consumer protection than under a minimum model where the safety valve of stricter rules adopted at national level remains open. Maximum harmonization locates at EU level the exclusive responsibility to achieve and maintain a workable system – that means the EU legislative process, which is asked to deliver a high level of protection and a sufficiently unambiguous text, but it also means the Court, which is asked to interpret what emerges from the legislative process.

Coherence is not a 'one way street'. The more 'coherent' the EU régime, the less coherent national systems may become. Maximum harmonization may make the EU rules look much 'cleaner' but, at national level, significant dismantling of established rules that are found to fall within the material scope of the EU measure may be required, to the detriment of accumulated local preferences. Minimum rule-making allows space for stricter rules which are not simply disallowed in a maximum regime: they must in fact be ruthlessly suppressed. The implementation costs at national level of a measure of maximum harmonization are notably higher than those attached to the minimum model.

This is not a technical matter. Emphasis on economic growth may subvert hard-fought adjustments in national law which have promoted the protection of groups such as consumers, workers and tenants under an assumption that such economically disadvantaged parties are deprived of a genuine right of self-determination in an unregulated market. Contract law's shaping is not apolitical.[41] Where the EU rules are maximum in character, thereby foreclosing national variation, the break with national autonomy is decisive. It is to the EU – exclusively – that one must look for such protection. Here, too, 'coherence' needs to be seen in its fullest dimensions. The Commission is open to the accusation that it is using the discourse of internal market-driven 'coherence' to disguise the sensitive political implications of its policy preferences. This is in many ways the lesson of the shrunken Consumer Rights Directive, 2011/83.

The shift from minimum to maximum harmonization goes to the very heart of deciding which institution(s) are responsible for delivering regulation of the European market A maximum model radically shifts the pattern of European law-making away from a co-operative model towards a more hierarchical pattern. Maximum harmonization is a centralizing, homogenizing approach. Moreover, it cleaves open national systems along lines of demarcation that may make some sort of sense at EU level, but frequently will not at national level. From this perspective there is a respectable case to be made *against* coherence at EU level – at least, one must appreciate that pursuit of coherence at EU level cannot possibly be cost free.

---

[41] E.g., Study Group on Social Justice in European Private Law, 'Social Justice in European Contract Law: A Manifesto', 10 *European Law Journal* (2004) 653; Hesselink, 'European Contract Law: A Matter of Consumer Protection, Citizenship, or Justice?', 15 *European Review of Private Law* (2007) 323; Hesselink, 'Democratic Contract Law', 11 *European Review of Contract Law* (2015) 81.

There are legal principles that support an interpretation in favour of the constitutional vitality of minimum harmonization, although it is freely conceded that they are of an ambiguous nature. Article 38 of the Charter on Fundamental Rights provides that 'Union policies shall ensure a high level of consumer protection'. Article 12 TFEU provides that '[c]onsumer protection requirements shall be taken into account in defining and implementing other Union policies and activities'. An argument may be constructed that these identified objectives are most effectively achieved by retaining a model of consumer protection built *not only* on EU rule-making *but also* on national level contributions above the EU minimum. Maximum harmonization suppresses one important – i.e., national – source of rule-making. That prescription is directed at the EU legislature but one could plausibly add that there should be a supplementary *judicial* presumption against finding that EU legislative acts pre-empt national competence in the field which they cover. *European Air Transport SA* is vividly illustrative of the competing questions about regulatory design.[42] The case turned on what are 'operating restrictions' which may be imposed (at Brussels airport) in conformity with Directive 2002/30, and then what scope is left for stricter national measures. Advocate General Villalón's Opinion contains a fascinating assembly of interpretative techniques *against* maximum harmonization relating to the need to balance transport policy and environmental protection. He also refers to fundamental rights associated with protection of the environment and he is wary of finding a 'paralysis of state action' to do anything beyond that mandated by the EU which would follow a finding that the measure is maximum in nature. The Court simply addressed the definitional question of whether there is an 'operating restriction' and went no further, but the Advocate General's analysis is hugely appealing, and easily transplanted to consumer policy, contract law and beyond. Under the maximum model of harmonization, the EU – its legislature and, sometimes unexpectedly, its Court too – always leads the way, to the exclusion of dialogue and learning. This is a model that deserves a sceptical reception if advanced as general prescription for the EU. There is a strong case to be made for regarding maximum harmonization as applicable only exceptionally, where its use has been carefully justified in prevailing sector-specific conditions, taking full account of the costs and the benefits.

Recognition that the adoption of a rigid, uniform and immutable EU norm is not the necessary and inevitable consequence of EU intervention in a particular field is highly significant. It is neither politically feasible nor economically desirable to expect all 28 Member States to advance as a single bloc in all the sectors of economic activity now affected by EU policy. Any trend away from the single rule carries the potential to cause the fragmentation of the internal market – as the Commission correctly highlighted in its contract law review – yet it may be seen as a realistic attempt to accommodate diverse national tradition and consumer expectation within the process of integration – a dimension underplayed by the Commission in its contract law review.

---

[42] Case C-120/10, *European Air Transport SA*, judgment of 8 September 2011, not yet reported (ECLI:EU:C:2011:556).

Ultimately, the internal market as a legal concept cannot resolve this debate. It depends on one's conception of the contested character of the internal market.[43] What is in fact thematically at stake here is the legislative version of a matter discussed in Chapter 12 in connection with questions of justification under free movement law: to what extent is the internal market to be a site of diversity. Pre-empting Member State action minimizes diversity but, on some accounts, is conducive to achieving the full economic benefits of the internal market by putting in place common rules from which Member States may not deviate. This is the levelling of the EU's regulatory playing field. The counterpoint to this does not at all deny that pre-empting Member State action may have attraction as a means to create and cultivate a single coherent EU regulatory landscape, but doubts that this advantage is strong enough to outweigh the serious consequential disadvantages which are measured in inflexibility, insensitivity to local preference and suppression of regulatory experimentation. On this approach diversity should be cherished, and it is preserved by a preference for an approach to EU pre-emption which leaves space for stricter national rules above the basic EU floor. There is no simple answer as to which is right. The internal market is ambiguous as a legal concept.

---

[43] Cf., e.g., Boeger, 'Minimum Harmonization, Free Movement and Proportionality', in P. Syrpis (ed), *The Judiciary, the Legislature and the EU Internal Market* (2012); Weatherill, 'Maximum versus Minimum Harmonization: Choosing between Unity and Diversity in the Search for the Soul of the Internal Market', in N. Nic Shuibhne and L. Gormley (eds), *From Single Market to Economic Union: Essays in Memory of John A Usher* (2012).

16

Conclusion

This volume's principal organizing theme holds that, in pursuit of the construction of the internal market, the Treaty has always left open both the precise nature of the vertical distribution of competences between the EU and the Member States and the horizontal allocation of powers between the EU's judicial and legislative institutions. By placing this zone of constitutional and institutional *ambiguity* at the heart of the law of the internal market the Treaty system delegated interpretative power to the Court of Justice of the European Union ('the Court'). Its choices – which have fluctuated – determine the relationship between deregulation and re-regulation in the internal market. That is the pattern examined in this volume.

A. Ambiguity and Limits

The vertical issue addresses the type of national measures which threaten the achievement of the internal market and which are therefore within its scope. Put another way, this asks where EU internal market law ends and Member State autonomy begins. The examination has been conducted around three main themes: the internal *market* (when is there an economic context: Chapter 5), the *internal* market (when is there a cross-border dimension: Chapter 6), and the personal scope of the provisions (Chapter 7). Each has its own ambiguous rhythm.

The Court treats discrimination against goods, labour or services as a sufficient but not necessary basis for invocation of EU law. In the case of technical rules, there is harm to the patterns of inter-state trade in so far as goods and services which comply with their home state rules are excluded from the market of the host state where rules are different. Even where rules are *not* different, a host state which regulates in a way that closes off access to its market may be taken to harm the internal market. Rules such as those governing product composition and qualifications required of service providers are more likely to fall foul of a test rooted in and inspired by the protection of the internal market than rules associated with the marketing of goods and services, but caution should be exercised lest the law descend into formalism blind to the economic context of the internal market. This is emphasized in Chapters 6.F and 12. The Court has not alleviated all the prevailing and painful ambiguity: open (descriptive and normative) questions surround convergence in interpretation across the freedoms (see Chapters 6.B and 6.F); EU citizenship's role as an amplifier of economic rights remains elusive (see Chapter 6.D.3); the personal

The Internal Market as a Legal Concept. First Edition. Stephen Weatherill.
© Stephen Weatherill 2017. Published 2017 by Oxford University Press.

scope of the provisions varies without clearly articulated explanation (see Chapter 7); and 'abuse' remains a nebulous control (see Chapter 10). However, a fair summary is that the Court has opted for an interpretation of free movement and competition law which leaves relatively little in the exclusive grip of national autonomy. The *vertical* cut is deep.

The scope allowed for justification of national measures that are treated as barriers to trade in the internal market, introduced in Chapter 8, shows that the Court has pushed the scope of permissible justification into ever broader realms and that even if a quantitative assessment would focus on the fierce deregulatory power of EU law, a more qualitative assessment would look beyond the mountain of regulatory absurdity obstinately defended by Member States and take account also of the – minority – of cases where sincere justifications are advanced and are treated with care by the Court. This will not satisfy the labour lawyer and no attempt can be made to satisfy the labour lawyer without change in that area of internal market law (see Chapter 9.B), but the cases on public health, environmental protection and consumer protection addressed in Chapter 8 and those on fundamental rights and national identity considered in Chapter 11 are more typical representations of the Court's usual priorities and technique in its elaboration of the law of the internal market.

The horizontal issue asks whether, in circumstances where Member State autonomy is subjected to review in the name of EU internal market law, the Court resolves the matter or instead the matter falls for legislative intervention. The Court's relatively eager application of free movement and competition law has the consequence that there is reduced need for legislative action. The *horizontal* reach is long. This is plainly a question of institutional power, but it also serves to determine the shape of the internal market and in particular it propels the balance in favour of deregulation achieved by judicial decision at the expense of re-regulation achieved by political intervention. It does not, however, eliminate the significance of legislative action in the construction of the internal market. Legislative harmonization has a role where free movement law's limits are reached, most obviously where national rules restrict inter-state trade but are justified. As Chapter 13 elucidates, its scope, once reached, is broad and deep. The 'dual function' of harmonization pushes this beyond market-making narrowly understood as a deregulatory project, with consequences for the intensity of the regulatory landscape in the EU. There is also a – certainly constitutionally ambiguous – inquiry about how much supporting regulatory intervention the internal market requires in fields such as labour market regulation and social policy more generally. This is examined in Chapter 14. The 'dual function' of EU rule-making is more overtly contested in this area: the limits of the EU's interventionist capacity are monitored more suspiciously. The Lisbon Treaty added rhetorical flourishes to the EU's role, but it did not add hard competences. A bewilderingly dense array of rules on doorstep selling, unfair commercial practices, biotechnology, minibuses and so on (see Chapter 13.F) does not a social market economy make. And the debate about minimum and maximum harmonization, explored in Chapter 15, brings another facet of ambiguity and contestation over the proper (vertical) relationship between Member State and EU competence once the EU has legislated.

B. Limits and Lines

The internal market is both a *limiting* and an *empowering* concept.

As a general observation, the Court's concern is to devise *not only* a set of limiting threshold tests which are apt to show fidelity to the promises made in Articles 4 and 5 TEU that the EU enjoys only the competences and powers conferred on it by its Treaties and that competences not conferred upon the EU in the Treaties remain with the Member States *but also* a set of empowering threshold tests that are apt to protect the internal market which is set as an aim by Article 3(3) TEU, defined by Article 26 TFEU and given momentum by a host of Treaty provisions, most prominent among them the negative law provisions on free movement and competition and the positive law provisions that equip the EU with legislative competence, in particular Article 114's authorization to harmomize laws.

The Court's case law is littered with detailed tests which are targeted at the need to make the necessary jurisdictional demarcation. They have been examined at length in this volume, so the job here is simply to collect the shards. There must be an economic dimension: this was the subject of exploration in Chapter 5. The cross-border requirement was expressed in *Dassonville*: the net catches only rules 'which are capable of hindering, directly or indirectly, actually or potentially, intra-Community trade' (see Chapter 6.A.2). Article 34's application to restrictions on use depends on the demonstration of a *considerable* influence on the behaviour of consumers or on identifying a measure *greatly* restricting the use of goods (see Chapter 6.C.5). Otherwise the matter rests with the local regulator. Where national practices affect commercial freedom but exert an effect on cross-border trade that is too uncertain or indirect or remote, they are not touched by free movement law (see Chapters 6.B and 6.D.1). In its Article 21 TFEU case law the Court has ruled that a national measure which causes inconvenience to an affected person is not caught: the inconvenience must be *serious* (see Chapter 6.D.2). The *purely internal* situation escapes the scope of application of internal market law (see Chapter 6.A): so too do measures which might *hypothetically* damage cross-border movement (see Chapter 6.A and 6.D.1). In competition law an effect on inter-state trade must be *appreciable*: if it is not, it is not within the scope of review claimed by Articles 101 or 102 TFEU (see Chapter 6.A.4). The application of the state aid rules is blocked where there is regulation which does not entail any direct or indirect transfer of state resources; so too the EU's supervision does not apply to schemes which lack the jurisdictionally required element of selectivity (see Chapter 6.E). Harmonization is not a general regulatory competence conferred on the EU legislature but rather requires the demonstration of an *appreciable* distortion of competition caused by diverse national rules or, in its preventive version, the *likelihood* that such Member State action will be taken (see Chapter 13.G). The protection of national autonomy promised by Article 5 TEU's principle of conferral is expressed in detailed form through the lines drawn by these tests.

In extra-judicial contributions the Court's judges sometimes openly acknowledge the proper limits of EU law and of their own expertise. Koen Lenaerts, now Vice-President of the Court, was a judge of the CFI when he questioned 'the legitimacy and the feasibility of making policy choices, of weighing the Community interest in having an internal market...and the Member States' interest in protecting what they see as fundamental local values' – though in the paper he then immediately proceeded to present a staunch (and convincing) defence of the Court's *Cassis de Dijon* jurisprudence.[1] Ole Due, writing shortly after the end of his term as President of the Court, explained *Keck* as a return to a proper understanding of *Dassonville*, and as motivated to avoid 'an unnecessary and almost impossible task: to evaluate national policy choices in areas which have very little to do with intra-Community trade or with Community law in general'.[2] Gil Carlos Rodriguez Iglesias was President of the Court when he summarized *Keck* as a correction of case law in which the Court had 'to take a position on the possible justification of measures which could be politically controversial, such as the question of Sunday trading, but in fact had nothing to do with the free movement of goods'.[3] And he also helped reveal judicial thinking about the application of the subsidiarity principle when he argued that 'subsidiarity is a principle of an essentially political nature' and asserted a concern to purge the Court's diet of 'political hot potatoes'.[4] This, as explained in Chapter 13.H.1, is in essence exactly what the Court has achieved.

All these tests – these nouns (*likelihood*), these adjectives (*considerable, serious, appreciable*), these adverbs (*greatly*) – carry heavy constitutional significance. They demarcate the zone of EU influence from that of Member State autonomy. The tension lies in the ease with which these lines are crossed and the difficulty in countermanding a claim by the EU's judicial and political institutions that they *have* been crossed.

The threshold tests are appallingly flexible. There must be an economic dimension: but there usually is. There must be a cross-border dimension: but there usually is. The Court needs minimal persuasion: its readiness to agree that it is 'far from inconceivable' that cross-border trade may be affected by a national practice, supported by no call for empirical evidence (see Chapter 6.B) is simply the most strikingly extreme version of a consistent trend favouring the empowerment of EU law. Tests rooted in the need to show a *considerable* influence on the behaviour of consumers, a *serious* inconvenience, an *appreciable* effect on inter-state trade, an *appreciable* distortion of competition, action by Member States that is *likely* all share the common feature that they are vague, hard to measure and so their alleged satisfaction is very hard to contradict. Free movement law, competition law and legislative harmonization all accordingly acquire unleashed vigour. In fact, *Keck* (see Chapter 6.C.2) and *Tobacco Advertising I* (see Chapter 13.G.2) go hand in hand:

---

[1] Lenaerts, 'Some Thoughts about the Interaction between Judges and Politicians in the European Community', 12 *Yearbook of European Law* (1992) 1, 12.

[2] Due, '*Dassonville* Revisited or No Cause for Alarm?', in A. Campbell and M. Voyatzi (eds), *Legal Reasoning and Judicial Interpretation of European Law: Essays in Honour of Lord Mackenzie Stuart* (1996) Ch. 2, at 27. Less convincingly, Due also seeks to deny there is 'any irritation' in *Keck*'s comment on traders' 'increasing tendency' to invoke Art. 34 TFEU, see Chapter 6.C.2.

[3] 'Drinks in Luxembourg: Alcoholic Beverages and the Case Law of the European Court of Justice', in D. O'Keeffe and A. Bavasso (eds), *Liber Amicorum in Honour of Lord Slynn of Hadley: Judicial Review in European Union Law* (2000) Ch. 33, at 527.

[4] 'The Court of Justice, Principles of EC Law, Court Reform and Constitutional Adjudication', 15 *European Business Law Review* (2004) 1115, at 1117.

both are concerned to place a restriction on the scope of EU incursion into national autonomy to regulate markets, but both have been revealed to have inconsequential effect in performing that mission. They are more symbol than substance.[5] The cases on state aid examined in Chapter 6.E are notable for the Court's preference to place awkward cases on the *limiting* side of the line and to show respect for the autonomy of states' general regulatory competences: but *empowerment* is the more common feature of line-drawing in internal market law.

Even if several of these tests are best understood as the Court trying to make sense of the thorny route between limiting and empowering which the ambiguity of the internal market as a legal concept forces it to try to find, there are some occasions where the Court itself has cut a new path. The *Sunday Trading* cases took the vertical cut *too* far: they threatened to re-conceptualize free movement law as a basis for review of measures that restricted commercial freedom with no demonstrated connection to inter-state trade patterns (see Chapter 6.C.1). *Keck* was an attempt, successful to an extent, to re-adjust the vertical distribution of competences onto a more stable footing (see Chapter 6.C.2). *Carpenter*, however, is a decision that is vulnerable to the criticism that it inflates free movement law too far, to the detriment of national autonomy to decide matters concerning the residence rights of third country nationals (see Chapters 6.B and 6.D.2). It was a case where in the particular circumstances that led to the litigation the harm to free movement seemed as remote as in other cases where the Court has refused to acknowledge the invocability of EU law. *Ruiz Zambrano* and *Dereci* are even more remarkable, for there the Court did not even claim there was any inter-state element (see Chapter 6.D.3). It drew a new line: Article 20 TFEU 'precludes national measures which have the effect of depriving citizens of the Union of the genuine enjoyment of the substance of the rights conferred by virtue of their status as citizens of the Union'. EU law's vertical intrusion was strengthened: matters of migration policy become gripped by internal market and citizenship law.

Here there is none of the sense of judicial restraint quoted above. There is, instead, a strong sense of a Court sorely tempted to promote itself as a human rights tribunal of general jurisdiction and a weaker sense that EU citizenship ('Citizenship of the Union') is to provide the animating theme. Empowerment prevails over limitation, and on the basis of thin reasoning and meagre appreciation that there are sources of fundamental rights protection in Europe other than the EU.

C. Lines and Choices

The lines which the Court has drawn represent its attempts to provide an operational limit to the internal market as a basis for intervention into national autonomy. But the lines also represent choices. The Treaty's lack of definitional precision in effect delegates line-drawing to the Court in circumstances where more than one option is

---

[5] See, especially, Barnard, 'What the *Keck*? Balancing the Needs of the Single Market with State Regulatory Autonomy in the EU (and the US)', *European Journal of Consumer Law* (2012) 201.

plausible. The choices made by the Court dictate the shape of the internal market and, most of all, the vertical and horizontal consequences.

According to Article 4(2)(a) TFEU the internal market as a legal concept is built on a competence to open up markets and to regulate them which is *shared* between the Union and the Member States. There are Member State laws and practices which are subject to judicial supervision (which does not necessarily entail that they be set aside) under EU free movement law and/or to (partial or total) replacement by legislative initiatives at EU level. Which route is preferred determines the shape of the internal market.

Cassis de Dijon is the unmissable landmark. The Court opted decisively to break with a discrimination-based focus for free movement law but it broke too with the miserly approach to justification promised by Article 36 TFEU. This was certainly a key moment in the judicial shaping of the internal market, which was, as argued in Chapter 6.A.3, not the only possible interpretation of the system mapped by the Treaty but one which was comfortably within the bounds of legitimate judicial interpretation. The consequence was to confine national regulatory autonomy (the vertical dimension), in that few practices escape free movement law entirely, and also to curtail the need for legislative action at EU level (the horizontal dimension), in that free movement law took the strain even where obstructive practices were not discriminatory. The Court has even nudged its role still further outwards, as it has – albeit ambiguously – brought free movement law to bear even on national measures that hinder access to the market (see Chapter 6.F). The net result is to place a heavy load on justification as the device for recognizing the permissible scope of national action even where that might be antagonistic to the process of market integration.

The model of conditional or non-absolute host state control involves a distribution of regulatory competences consequent on scrutiny of the merits of the competing claims. The host state regulates the matter – as long as it shows it has a sufficient reason to do so. In the absence of justification, there is scope for inter-jurisdictional competition, deregulation and choice and diversity as the hallmarks of the internal market. Justification is the safety valve. Finding justification preserves diversity among national rules and in particular a generous approach to the availability of justification tends to shift responsibility to the EU legislative process.

It is conventionally understood that the development of the EU, and of the internal market in particular, has broken down a divide between the EU as a guarantor of market freedom and the Member States as the source of social protection and welfare, including distributional, choices. Free movement and competition law and legislative harmonization all testify to this trend. The consequence of the Court's choices about the breadth of the relevant provisions is that in the shaping of the regulatory landscape of the internal market a huge weight rests on the determination of whether a practice is justified: it is here that national conceptions of (inter alia) social protection must survive inspection according to the standards of EU law. So too, for all the apparent restraint signalled by *Tobacco Advertising*, the Court interprets the scope and re-regulatory potential of legislative harmonization broadly (see Chapter 13.D and 13.G.3), and is reluctant to interfere with legislative choices when pressed to apply the principles of subsidiarity, proportionality and fundamental and other Charter rights (see Chapter 13.H). Chapter 13.F notes that objections to the EU's perceived heavy regulatory hand are part of a proper political and economic debate about the EU's agility in global markets, but they do not amount to sharp-edged *constitutional* objections.

Most of the Court's approach is in line with the structure of the Treaty itself. Any attempt to preserve a rigid divide between the EU as a guarantor of market freedom and the Member States as the source of social protection would have led to a very shallow process of market integration. And were one to accede to the case for exclusion of, say, health care from the reach of internal market law, one would have to reckon with the same appeal from sports federations, trade unions, and so on. The Treaty is structured in a broad, functionally driven manner: it refuses to place particular areas of Member State activity firmly off-limits. There is, as mentioned at Chapter 5.C, a category of competence calculatedly omitted from Articles 2–6 TFEU, that of exclusive Member State competences. Respect for the regulatory autonomy of the Member States is limited and unreliable. That is the nature of the Treaty system.

So EU law is not good at offering insulation *in principle* from the pressures of market-making, but there is much receptivity to values other than the market visible and taken seriously in the Court's case law dealing with justification, which is where distinctive sector-specific concerns come rushing back in. So the internal market is, and should be, a site of diversity, mainly because of the scope allowed for justification and the pluralist sensitivity to local preference embedded in the margin of discretion. This is especially salient where the Court is asked to operate in the gap between EU legislative competence and the (wider) reach of the law of the internal market. Here its assessment of challenged practices at national level should be sensitive *both* to the relative lack of developed policy guidance in the texts of EU law *and* to the limited or non-existent capacity of the EU to offer any legislative resolution of the matter. And usually the Court is sensitive. But not always. The core objection to *Viking Line* (see Chapter 9.B) is that the Court treated free movement law as if it operates in a vacuum, without awareness of the complexity of interests at stake in the justification advanced for trade-restrictive practices and without awareness of the unfeasibility of any *political* correction of its decision. A lot of the Court's work involves assessing the vertical and horizontal implications of its interpretation of internal market law. *Cassis de Dijon* has been presented as a deeply considered and supremely well-judged choice (see Chapter 6.A.3). *Viking Line* is not. As in *Carpenter* and especially as in *Ruiz Zambrano* and *Dereci* the friction flows from inadequate perception by the Court of its place alongside other (national and EU) institutions in the vertical distribution of competences and the horizontal distribution of powers. But such judicial aberration is atypical.

D. Choices and Empowerment

The internal market serves as a limiting concept in principle, but its empowering function is in practice highly significant. Free movement law and, in particular in the wake of *Wouters* (see Chapter 8.C.2), competition law both load so much weight on justification that EU law in general and the Court in particular are pushed to develop an understanding of the legitimate claims underpinning national practices which collide with trade integration. Free movement law is not only about free movement – but as a corollary national regulation of the market which collides with trade integration can no longer be treated exclusively as national regulation of the market. It must be justified in the light of its impact on the EU's internal market. Legislative harmonization carries the same dynamic. The values which underpin (diverse) national measures of market regulated are transmitted through the EU legislative process and in some form or other emerge as values embedded in the EU's regulatory technique and choices. It is, in short, the 'dual function' of harmonization. Article 114 TFEU, as explained in Chapter 13.G.3, is qualitatively different from the EU's sector-specific legislative competences and in fact its empowering functionally broad re-regulatory force goes a long way to rendering their carefully drawn limits entirely worthless.

The impact of the EU reaches across the wide expanse of competences mapped by Articles 2–6 TFEU and, still further, into areas touched by internal market ('negative') law in the absence of any authorized EU legislative competence. EU law and policy-making typically lacks the systematic character of national practice, because of the constitutional constraint of the principle of conferral, but in practice the EU legal order is structured to bring a very wide range of activities actually or potentially within its scope, and the internal market as a legal concept is a major force nurturing this growth. A collection of often skeletal Treaty provisions, patchwork secondary legislation, decisions of courts, and soft law infiltrates the zone of national regulatory competence. So across a wide range of fields of activity one might sensibly hesitate to refer to the laws *of* a Member State and instead think of laws *in* a Member State: national laws, EU laws (of various types) and more besides, reflecting economic interdependence and the cascade of multi-level governance. EU law and practice 'spills over' to provoke new *academic sub-disciplines* which are fully reflected in descriptive and normatively ambitious academic literature and in specialist legal practice. New niche journals abound, new career paths are forged. Sport has been used more than once in this volume as an intriguing case study in this vein.[6] EU consumer protection too has been shown to have acquired its own distinct shape and narratives.[7] But they are far from alone as instances of the empowering zeal of EU law. There is EU environmental law,[8] labour market regulation,[9] culture,[10] taxation,[11]

---

[6] See, e.g., S. Weatherill, *European Sports Law: Collected Papers* (2nd ed., 2014).

[7] E.g., S. Weatherill, *EU Consumer Law and Policy* (2nd ed., 2013); Micklitz, 'The Expulsion of the Concept of Protection from the Consumer Law and the Return of Social Elements in the Civil Law: A Bittersweet Polemic', 35 *Journal of Consumer Policy* (2012) 283; Basedow, 'Freedom of Contract in the European Union', 16 *European Review of Private Law* (2008) 901.

[8] E.g., J. Jans and H. Vedder, *European Environmental Law* (4th ed., 2012).

[9] E.g., C. Barnard, *EU Employment Law* (4th ed., 2012); A.C.L. Davies, *EU Labour Law* (2012).

[10] E.g., Psychogiopoulou, 'Cultural Mainstreaming: The European Union's Horizontal Cultural Diversity Agenda and its Evolution', 39 *European Law Review* (2014) 626.

[11] E.g., B. Terra and P. Wattel, *European Tax Law* (6th ed., 2012).

railways,[12] lifestyle policy,[13] minority protection,[14] health care[15] including specifically mental health[16] and new health technologies,[17] disability,[18] poverty and social exclusion,[19] family law,[20] parental rights,[21] the law of children's rights,[22] domestic violence,[23] civil procedure,[24] and even the law of succession,[25] property law[26] and, of especially fast rising significance, criminal law.[27] One might describe this as 'Europeanization' – a calculatedly imprecise term that suggests the plurality of influences exerted on national practice by EU law and policy as distinct from any exaggerated claim that these become areas subjected to direct or, still less, exclusive EU legislative mandate. It is, moreover, a pattern of extraordinary diversity and complexity: the 'internal market' is not at all a homogenous creation, either in law or by way of empirical economic observation. It is different, sector by sector. Competence is shared but the pattern of sharing is of many different colours. The push to maximum harmonization, addressed in Chapter 15, is relevant here as a threat to the shared model. Maximum rules are simpler, but may lack nuance and local sensitivity and, moreover, may rob the EU of space for regulatory experimentation.

This *bricolage* means that the law of the EU may exercise a far wider influence than a formal inspection of the text of the Treaty may lead one to expect, and in particular its true transformative potential would be missed by an inspection of only Article 5 TEU, containing the principle of conferral, and Articles 2–6 TFEU, the competence catalogue.

[12] H. Dyrhauge, *EU Railway Policy-Making: On Track?* (2013).

[13] E.g., Alemanno and Garde, 'The Emergence of an EU Lifestyle Policy: The Case of Alcohol, Tobacco and Unhealthy Diets', 50 *Common Market Law Review* (2013) 1745.

[14] E.g., Ahmed, 'The Treaty of Lisbon and Beyond: The Evolution of EU Minority Protection', 38 *European Law Review* (2013) 30.

[15] E.g., J. Van de Gronden, E. Szyszczak, U. Neegaard and M. Krajewski (eds), *Health Care and EU Law* (2011).

[16] E.g., McHale, 'Mental Health Law and the EU: The Next New Regulatory Frontier?', 19 *Medical Law Review* (2011) 606.

[17] E.g., M. Flear, A.-M. Farrel, T. Hervey and T. Murphy (eds), *European Law and New Health Technologies* (2013).

[18] E.g., L. Waddington, 'A Disabled Market: Free Movement of Goods and Services in the EU and Disability Accessibility', 15 *European Law Journal* (2009) 575.

[19] E.g., H. Verschueren, 'Free Movement of EU Citizens: Including for the Poor?', 22 *Maastricht Journal* (2015) 10.

[20] E.g., K. Boele-Woelki, J. Miles and J. Scherpe (eds), *The Future of Family Property in Europe* (2011).

[21] E.g., Caracciolo di Torella and Foubert, 'Surrogacy, Pregnancy and Maternity Rights: A Missed Opportunity for a More Coherent Regime of Parental Rights in the EU', 40 *European Law Review* (2015) 52.

[22] E.g., H. Stalford, *Children and the European Union: Rights, Welfare and Accountability* (2012); Grugel and Iusmen, 'The European Commission as Guardian Angel: The Challenges of Agenda-Setting for Children's Rights', 20 *Journal of European Public Policy* (2013) 77.

[23] E.g., Lamont, 'Beating Domestic Violence? Assessing the EU's Contribution to Tackling Violence against Women', 50 *Common Market Law Review* (2013) 1787.

[24] E.g., E. Storskrubb, *Civil Procedure and EU Law: A Policy Area Uncovered* (2008).

[25] E.g., Stumpf, 'EG-Rechtssetzungskompetenzen in Erbrecht', *Europarecht* (2007) 291.

[26] E.g., Simon Moreno, 'Towards a European System of Property Law', 19 *European Review of Private Law* (2011) 579; Ramaekers, 'The Development of EU Property Law', 23 *European Review of Private Law* (2015) 437.

[27] E.g., Mitsilegas, *EU Criminal Law* (2009); Herlin-Karnell, *The Constitutional Dimension of European Criminal Law* (2012).

In practice one could go so far as to say that the reality is that the EU does not have conferred powers, but in fact original powers.[28] This is to an extent a more provocative version of the well-known observation of Koen Lenaerts 'there simply is no nucleus of sovereignty that the Member States can invoke, as such, against the' EU.[29] There is truth in the claim that the EU system is structured in such a way as to grant a very strong influence to majority political preferences about the scope and exercise of competence. The retreat in *Keck* and the restraint of *Tobacco Advertising I* are exciting because, like the flash of the kingfisher along the riverbank, they are rarities. The principle of conferral is deficient, and the rise of national Parliaments is not yet at all sufficient compensation. Legality is 'leaking'; the risk is 'unpredictable and uncontrollable competence creep'.[30] This is the nature of the internal market. And that is the problem.

E. Empowerment and Ambiguity

Were the creation of the EU's internal market simply an exercise in deregulation, it would require a dense set of rules designed to suppress practices found in the Member States that obstruct commercial freedom. Markets need rules, especially in a Europe fragmented by centuries of difference. But the model of the EU's internal market is in any event a great deal more complex than an exercise in pure deregulation. Its rules are aimed at national practices which obstruct cross-border trade, not simply commercial freedom, and even those rules are not forbidden: rather, they are put to the test of justification. So there is space for national regulation within the internal market. And, far beyond deregulation pure and simple, the EU legislative process generates a heavy body of re-regulatory EU-level norms to underpin the internal market. Both the Treaty and the Charter confirm that this is not at all an exercise in deregulation alone, and the promotion of concerns such as consumer protection, environmental protection and, still more profound, fundamental rights is accordingly deeply embedded in both the law governing free movement and competition ('negative law') and the legislative *acquis* ('positive law'). Social policy's place in both dimensions of the internal market is more awkward (see Chapter 14), but in admittedly contested and fragmentary ways it too forms part of the EU's regulatory landscape. The result is an extraordinarily dense network of governance: deregulation and re-regulation in and of the internal market is, and has long been understood as, something that transcends a value-free exercise in improving competitiveness and economic performance.[31]

[28] E.g., A. Somek, *Individualism: An Essay on the Authority of the European Union* (2008).
[29] Lenaerts, 'Constitutionalism and the Many Faces of Federalism', 38 *American Journal of Comparative Law* (1990) 205, referred to already in Chapters 4 and 5.C.
[30] Prechal, De Vries and Van Eijken, 'The Principle of Attributed Powers and the Scope of EU Law', in L. Besselink, F. Pennings and S. Prechal, *The Eclipse of the Legality Principle in the European Union* (2011) Ch. 12, at 246.
[31] E.g., M. Egan, *Constructing a European Market* (2001); K. Armstrong and S. Bulmer, *The Governance of the Single European Market* (1998); Höpner and Schäfer, 'Embeddedness and Regional Integration: Waiting for Polanyi in a Hayekian Setting' 66 *International Organisation* (2012) 429; Hatje, 'The Economic Constitution within the Internal Market', in A. Von Bogdandy and J. Bast, *Principles of European Constitutional Law* (2nd ed., 2010) Ch. 16. See also Chapter 6.F.

There is no pre-determined constitutional model which directs precisely how the EU shall affect the relationship between public regulation and the market, nor does the development of the internal market 'fit' any particular philosophy. The pattern is mixed. So one could convincingly identify traces of Ordoliberalism – associated with constitutionalized protection of economic freedom and private autonomy in the market – and traces of *service public* – which makes powerful claims about the proper role of public intervention – in the evolution of the law of the internal market, but one would not find anything that amounts to a vindication of one over the other.[32] The Treaty would resist any such ideological priority: this is its governing ambiguity. The Court is normally sensitive to preservation of this 'agnosticism' about which model should prevail.[33] The result is to leave space for political process.

The 'internal market' became a formal part of the EU lexicon in 1987 on the entry into force of the Single European Act. It was both an economic and a political project, and the connection between the two lay its purpose as a re-energizing force for a sluggish European Union (see Chapter 3.B). But although it was granted a legal definition – the 'area without internal frontiers' now located in Article 26 TFEU – much of its intent was left constitutionally ambiguous as a result of absence of sharp consensus among the Member States and therefore in effect delegated for practical elaboration to the judicial and political institutions of the EU. Most of all – this volume's principal organizing theme, noted previously – the precise nature of the vertical distribution of competences between the EU and the Member States and the horizontal allocation of powers between the EU's judicial and legislative institutions was left ambiguous. The choices made govern the depth of deregulation in the internal market and the scope for re-regulation. The interpretation of legal rules dictates how much local autonomy can and should be preserved in an internal market and how much (re-)regulation should be delivered at EU level. The internal market as a *legal* concept is inextricably connected to the internal market as a political, economic and cultural concept. They are all ambiguous. This is why, as the Commission has repeatedly insisted, the internal market will never be 'completed';[34] it 'is evolving, it will never be finalised'.[35]

---

[32] See, e.g., W. Sauter and H. Schepel, *State and Market in the European Union: The Public and Private Spheres of the Internal Market before the EU Courts* (2009).

[33] Snell, 'Varieties of Capitalism and the Limits of European Economic Integration', 13 *Cambridge Yearbook of European Legal Studies* (2010–11) 415.

[34] Commission's Internal Market Scoreboard No. 11, 11 November 2002.

[35] *A Single Market for Citizens*, the interim report to the Spring 2007 European Council, COM (2007) 60, February 2007, at 3, 10. See further Chapter 4.

Index

abortion services 39–40
abusive practices 131–3
academic titles 62
administrative covenants 27
agricultural products 33
air navigation services 36
alcoholic drinks 5–6, 102, 109–10,
    111, 164
  beer 23, 115
  Cassis de Dijon 53–7, 66, 67, 99, 103,
    104, 105, 108, 109, 114, 115, 117,
    135, 144, 146, 147, 226, 228, 229
  wine 158, 215
ambiguities 4, 12, 18, 19, 20, 21, 28, 174,
    175, 232–3
  social policy 204, 207
  subsidiarity and proportionality 176
  vertical and horizontal issues 1–2, 29, 30, 57,
    204, 223–4, 227, 228
ambulance services 36–7
anti-competitive agreements 42
anti-doping rules 38, 45, 107, 125
approximation 203–4
art and culture 100, 104
Austria 77, 96–7, 113–14, 119, 136
  national identity 139–40
  Schmidberger 137–8, 139
autonomy of Member States 4, 6, 29, 30, 31,
    43, 47, 60, 93, 224, 226, 227
  Cassis de Dijon 53–7, 146, 228
  competition law 59
  harmonization and 174
    reasoned opinions on non-compliance
      with subsidiarity 181–5
  home/host state 54, 56, 70, 102, 106,
    132, 146
  national regulatory autonomy 63, 64, 65, 70,
    73, 76, 77, 79, 90, 148, 152
    restrictions on use 74–6
  national standards 209, 211, 213, 220,
    221, 224
  social policy 202
autonomy of private parties 98
Azoulai, Loïc 48

balanced progress 11
barriers to trade *see* trade barriers
beer 23, 115
Belgium 22, 70, 78, 112, 120
benefit tourism 41
biodegradable detergents 167
biotechnology 165
blood products 210

Canada 145
cannabis 40
case law *see* Court jurisprudence
certification services 38
Chalmers, Damian 29
Charter of Fundamental Rights 20, 105, 106,
    135, 140, 156, 203, 206
  see also fundamental rights
child protection 104, 106, 164
citizenship 6–7, 79, 81–4, 93, 227
closing hours 78
  see also Sunday trading rules
collective action 125–8
collective agreements 42, 43, 96, 205
Commission *see* European Commission
common agricultural policy 33
common market 18, 19
company law 132
competence control 180–1
  reasoned opinions on non-compliance with
    subsidiarity 181–5
competence sensitivity 166–7
competences
  catalogue of 4, 231
  conferral 3–5, 8, 11, 12, 43, 48, 49, 60, 93,
    123, 175, 176, 231, 232
  horizontal distribution 2, 29, 30, 57, 204,
    224, 228
  shared 4
  vertical distribution 1–2, 29, 30, 57, 223–4,
    227, 228
competition law 4, 5, 7, 9, 23–4, 31, 43
  Albany exception 42–3, 108
  De Minimis Notice 59
  distortion 85, 90, 173, 193
    see also state aid
  justification of trade barriers 106–9
  market sharing 116
  matters wholly internal to a Member State 50
  private parties 95
  relationship with free movement law 57–60
conferral 3–5, 8, 11, 12, 43, 48, 49, 60, 93,
    123, 175, 176, 231, 232
consumer choice 23, 57, 116
consumer protection 100, 103, 105, 115–21,
    123, 153, 156, 159
  doorstep selling 118–19, 211
  maximum harmonization and 219, 221
  minimum harmonization and 215–17,
    220, 221
  pre-contractual disclosure 163
  unfair commercial practices 161, 162–3, 164
  unfair terms 160–1, 164

contractual freedom 98
convergence 63, 90
 absence of 95
co-operation 27
corporate interests 125
corporate mobility 132–3
Council
 Legal Service 176–7
 qualified majority voting (QMV) 17, 19,
  153, 155, 168, 198, 201, 202, 203
 unanimity 153, 154, 185, 204
Court jurisprudence
 adjudicating between competing
  interests 123, 125, 128, 143, 148
 Alema-Herron 205–7, 214, 215
 barriers to trade *see* trade barriers
 Cassis de Dijon 53–7, 66, 67, 99, 103, 104,
  105, 108, 109, 114, 115, 117, 135, 144,
  146, 147, 226, 228, 229
 challenges to legitimacy 128–9
 competition law 23–4, 36, 37–8, 57–60, 106–9
  Albany exception 42–3, 108
 Dassonville 51–3, 64, 65, 67, 97, 104, 113,
  114, 144, 225, 226
 Defrenne 190–1, 192, 193, 204
 early rulings 33–4, 50–1, 136–7
  Van Gend en Loos 34, 50
 'economic activity' 35–7, 39, 40, 42, 46
 economic integration in conflict with national
  practices 43–4, 47
 'effectiveness' and 'equality' rationales 96, 98
 free movement of goods 33–4, 51, 65
  Keck 68–70, 71–3, 77, 78, 92, 100
  restrictions on use 74–6
  Sunday trading rules 66–8, 72
 free movement of persons 36, 41, 65
  citizenship 79, 81–4
  families 78–81
  remoteness test 76–8
 free movement of services 36, 39
 freedom to provide (and receive) services 34–5
 fundamental rights *see* fundamental rights
 harmonization *see* harmonization
 influence on shaping the internal market 31
 judicial review *see* judicial review
 jurisdictional demarcation 225
 justification of trade barriers *see* trade barriers
 lack of judicial restraint 225–8
 lack of precision 69, 91, 92, 98, 174, 175, 226
 legislative competence *see* legislative competence
 mobile telephone installations 70–1, 73
 objections to minimum
  harmonization 212–15
 personal scope of the Treaty 95–8
 scope of free movement provisions 144
 social objections 24–5
 social policy *see* social policy
 sporting practices 38, 44–6, 47, 61–2, 77,
  95–6, 101–2, 107–8, 124–5

 subsidiarity 177–8
 unpredictability 28, 31
 variety of terminology 91
 Viking Line 25, 47, 96, 125–9, 147, 148,
  183, 192, 205, 207, 229
cultural particularity 212
customs union 5

data retention 159
De Minimis Notice 59
Deadline 1992 27
Delors, Jacques 17
Denmark 112, 132, 185
deregulation 18, 28, 29, 99, 147, 148, 151,
 152, 162, 200, 232
 social policy and 204, 205
 see also harmonization
derogation 8
direct effect 34, 69, 144
direct taxation 70
disability legislation 165
discriminatory practices 49
 Cassis de Dijon 53–7, 66, 67, 99, 103–5, 108,
  109, 114, 115, 117, 135, 144, 146, 147,
  226, 228, 229
diversity 143–9, 229
 labour market regulation and social
  policy 191–4
 pre-emption and 222
doorstep selling 118–19, 211
doping offences 38, 45, 107, 125
Due, Ole 226

economic activity 35–7, 39, 40, 42, 46
economic context 21–4
economic integration 15, 16, 17, 19, 20, 21,
 24, 44
 associated gains 27
 in conflict with natural practice 43–4, 47
 spontaneous alignment 201
economic rights 135
education 35
electricity suppliers 87, 113
employment policy *see* labour market regulation
empowerment 229–32
enhanced co-operation 8–10
environmental protection 100, 104, 112–14,
 153, 156, 167
 legislative competence 188–9
 maximum harmonization and 221
equality rights 202–3
Eurocontrol 36
Europe 2020 199, 202
European Commission 144, 147, 152
 harmonization 152, 182
  reasoned opinions on non-compliance with
   subsidiarity 183, 184
 objections to minimum harmonization
  215–19, 220

European Economic Area (EEA) 24
European Economic Community (EEC) 15
European Employment Strategy (EES) 198
European unity 24–5
ever closer Union 20

families: free movement of persons 78–81
food supplements 158, 172, 178–9
football 45, 61–2, 77, 101–2, 124
France 111, 131
   Cassis de Dijon 53–7, 66, 67, 99, 103–5,
      108, 109, 114, 115, 117, 135, 144, 146,
      147, 226, 228, 229
   doorstep selling 118–19, 211
   Keck 68–70, 71–3, 77, 78, 92, 100, 226, 232
free movement of goods 33–4, 51, 65
   Keck 68–70, 71–3, 77, 78, 92, 100, 226, 232
   Sunday trading rules 66–8, 72, 227
free movement of persons 36, 41, 65, 76
   families 78–81
   remoteness test 76–8
free movement of services 6, 36, 39, 81, 101,
      102, 111, 138, 140
free movement provisions 3, 6–7, 15, 21, 27,
      28, 31, 43, 47, 49, 123
   competition law and 57–60
   convergence 63, 90
   fundamental rights and 135
   harmonization and 151, 152, 155
   justification of trade barriers 103–6
   margin of discretion 143
   private parties 95
   scope 144
freedom of expression 136
freedom to provide (and receive) services 34–5
fundamental rights 227
   Charter 20, 105, 106, 135, 140, 156,
      203, 206
   early rulings 136–7
   national identity 139–41
   Omega 138–9, 141
   Schmidberger 137–8, 139

gas sector 47, 121
General Agreement on Tariffs and Trade
   (GATT) 52
Germany 37, 49, 50, 60, 76, 106, 111,
   113, 158
   beer purity laws 23, 115
   Cassis de Dijon 53–7, 66, 67, 99, 103–5, 108,
      109, 114, 115, 117, 135, 144, 146, 147,
      226, 228, 229
   national identity 139–40
   Omega 138–9, 141
   ratification of the Lisbon Treaty 185
   state aid 86, 87
   Tobacco Advertising I 168–70, 174, 175, 212,
      213, 214, 226, 232
   wine growers 158, 215

harmonization 4, 11–12, 18, 19, 28, 31, 114,
   117, 145
   'appreciable' distortion of competition 173
   Article 114 153–5
   choice between models 219–20
   coherence 220
   Constitutional commitments to 155–6
   judicial review *see* judicial review
   legislative practice and re-regulation 163–6
   limits 166
      Alliance for National Health 172, 178–9
      BAT and Imperial Tobacco 171, 177,
         184, 212
      competence sensitivity 166–7
      political controls 179–86
      reasoned opinions on non-compliance with
         subsidiarity 181–5
      Tobacco Advertising I 168–70, 174, 175,
         212–14, 226, 232
      Tobacco Advertising II 170–1, 212
      Vodafone 172–3, 175, 179
   maximum 210, 216, 217, 218, 219,
      220, 221
      environmental protection and 221
      Services Direction 218–19
   minimum *see* minimum harmonization;
      pre-emption
   national fiscal legislation 193
   nature and purpose of 151–3, 224
   over-regulation 157–9, 166
   permissibility of prohibition 162–3
   preventive harmonization 172, 173–4
   proportionality 175, 178–9, 184
   regulatory diversity and 146, 151
   re-regulation 151–2, 155–6
   Single European Act 168
   social policy 203–4, 205
   subsidiarity 175, 176–8
      non-compliance with 181–5
health care 44, 156
   see also medical treatment
heroin 40
home/host state 54, 56, 70, 102, 106, 132,
   133, 146
horizontal distribution of powers 2, 29, 30, 57,
   204, 224, 228
human dignity 138–9
human rights law 141
Hungary 61, 71, 73

industrial action 47
insurance 120
integration 15, 16, 17, 19, 20, 21, 24, 44
   associated gains 27
   in conflict with national practices
      43–4, 47
   spontaneous alignment 201
intellectual property rights 12, 46–7
   patent protection 9–10

internal market
  ambiguous legal concept *see* ambiguities
  common market and 18, 19
  competition *see* competition law
  constitutional character 20, 21
  control over measures antagonistic to 5–10
  Court rulings *see* Court jurisprudence
  definition 1, 3, 10, 15
    lack of precision 13, 227
    see also Treaty provisions
  dynamic concept 27–8, 29, 93
  early instances of the concept 16, 19, 233
  economic context 21–4
  empowering function 229–32
  immunity
    Cassis de Dijon 53–7
    Dassonville 51–3, 64, 65
    matters wholly internal to a Member
      State 49–50, 60, 131
  inter-State divergence 55, 188, 191–4
    see also autonomy of Member States
  limits 2, 60–5, 90–3, 225–7
  market element *see* market-driven aims
  plurality of models 1
  required inter-state element 50, 51, 57, 58,
    61, 131
  scope of the law 4
  site of diversity 143–9, 222, 229
  spectrum of possible internal markets 30–1
  state aid *see* state aid
  variety of terminology 91
interventionism 58, 155, 181, 190,
  209, 224
Ireland 23, 39–40
Italy 33–4, 38, 50, 104, 118, 133, 146, 167

jet-skis 75
judicial review 156
  inadequate standards 156–7
  judicial interpretation of the harmonized
    acquis 160–2
  over-regulation 157–9
jurisdictional demarcation 225

labour market regulation 100, 153, 189
  Alemo-Herron 205–7, 214, 215
  Defrenne 190–1, 192, 193, 204
  deregulation and 204, 205
  Europe 2020 199, 202
  fragmentation 204
  inter-State diversity 191–4
  Lisbon Strategy 198, 199, 202
  Maastricht Treaty 197
  Open Method of Co-ordination (OMC) 199,
    200, 201
  Paris Summit 1972 194, 195
  Single European Act 196, 197
  transfer of undertakings 205
  Treaty of Rome 190, 191, 194
  Treaty provisions 200–1
    approximation/harmonization 203–4, 205
    legislation on social policy 201–3
    spontaneous alignment 201
  Viking Line 25, 47, 96, 125–9, 147, 148,
    183, 192, 205, 207, 229
  Working Time Directive 196, 197, 198, 202
  see also collective action; collective agreements;
    industrial action; trade unions; worker
    protection
Laeken Declaration 180
legal profession 107, 133
legislative action 10–13, 29
legislative competence 11, 43, 48, 146
  broad scope of EU action 187–8
  competence control 180–1
    reasoned opinions on non-compliance with
      subsidiarity 181–5
  competence sensitivity 166–7
  environmental protection 188–9
  home/host state 54, 56
  social policy *see* social policy
legislative harmonization *see* harmonization
legislative over-ambition 179
legitimacy 21
Lenaerts, Koen 29, 225, 232
Lisbon Strategy 198, 199, 202
Lisbon Treaty 19–21
  ratification by Germany 185
local regulatory autonomy *see* autonomy of
  Member States
lotteries 35–6

Mastricht Protocol 197, 198
Maastricht Treaty 197
margin of discretion 102, 143, 148, 149
marijuana 40
market distortion 85, 90, 193
  see also state aid
market-driven aims 20, 22, 33, 229
  breadth of the market as a legal market 33–9
  limits of the market 39–43
  public regulation and 233
  scope of positive law taken beyond that of
    negative law 43–8
market sharing 11
maximum harmonization 210, 216–21
  environmental protection and 221
  Services Directive 219
  see also pre-emption
**measures having equivalent effect to a
  quantitative restriction (MEQRs)** 51
medical aid organizations 37
medical practitioners 38
medical treatment 35, 43
migrants 41
migration policy 227
minimum harmonization 210, 212,
  219, 221

objections to
   Commission 215–19, 220
   Court of Justice 212–15
   see also pre-emption
mobile telephone installations 70–1, 73
mutual recognition 54, 55, 132, 152, 172

narcotic drugs 40
nation state 16
national autonomy *see* autonomy of Member
   States
national identity 139–41
national standards 209, 211, 213, 220, 221, 224
negative law 5–10, 28, 29, 43, 46, 47, 93, 128,
   135, 225, 230, 232
Netherlands 38, 40, 47, 58–9, 107, 110, 121
non-discrimination
   academic titles 62
   technical standards 55, 56, 57, 144
nutrients 158, 172, 178–9

Olympic Movement 38
Open Method of Co-ordination (OMC) 199,
   200, 201
ordinary legislative procedure 12, 19, 153,
   202, 218
over-regulation 157–9, 166

Paris Summit 1972 194, 195
patent protection 9–10, 46
pension funds 42
plasma products 210
plurality of models 30–1
policy-making 18
political boundaries 21
pollution 123, 167
positive law 10–13, 28, 43, 46, 47, 123, 129, 232
pre-emption
   choice between models of harmonization
     219–22
   legislative practice 211–12
   Treaty provisions 209–11
   see also maximum harmonization; minimum
     harmonization
private economic interests 157
private parties 95–8, 146
privatization 47, 121
professional services 106, 108
prohibited goods and practices 162–3
property ownership 47
proportionality 123, 175, 178–9, 184
protectionism 121, 147
public authorities 36, 37, 95, 97
public health 100, 101, 102, 109–12,
   165, 169–70
public interest 103, 105
public intervention 233
public order 44
public policy 100, 101

qualified majority voting (QMV) 17, 19, 153,
   155, 168, 198, 201, 202, 203
quantitative restriction/quotas 51

Reich, Norbert 29
regulatory policies 1
   Better Regulation 184–5
   harmonization *see* harmonization
   national regulatory autonomy 63, 64, 65, 70,
     73, 76, 77, 79, 90, 148, 152
   see also legislative competence
remuneration 35, 38
renewable energy 87, 113
re-regulation 151, 152, 155–6, 162
   judicial review *see* judicial review
   legislative practice 163–6
   see also harmonization
residence rights 41
restrictions on use 74–6
restrictive tax measures 8
retention of data 159
right of association 47
right to strike 47
restrictive practices 47
rule-making 10–13, 16
   see also legislative competence

Sarkozy, Nicolas 20
sector-specific controls 8, 31, 36, 229
self-determination 220
   see also autonomy of Member States
Sen, Amartya 207
Services Directive 218–19
Single European Act 16–17, 168
   labour market regulation and social
     policy 196, 197
slot machines 61, 71, 73
social benefits 41, 42
social market economy 20, 127, 128
social objectives 24–5, 29, 37, 38, 42
social policy 100, 190
   Alemo-Herron 205–7, 214, 215
   ambiguities 207
   Defrenne 190–1, 192, 193, 204
   deregulation and 204, 205
   Europe 2020 199, 202
   fragmentation 204
   inter-state diversity 191–4
   Lisbon Strategy 198, 199, 202
   Maastricht Treaty 197
   Open Method of Co-ordination (OMC) 199,
     200, 201
   Paris Summit 1972 194, 195
   Single European Act 196, 197
   transfer of undertakings 205
   Treaty of Rome 190, 191, 194
   Treaty provisions 200–1
     approximation/harmonization
      203–4, 205

social policy (*cont.*)
    legislation on social policy 201–3
    spontaneous alignment 201
    Viking Line 25, 47, 96, 125–9, 147, 148,
        183, 192, 205, 207, 229
    Working Time Directive 196, 197, 198, 202
social security systems 105
solidarity 38, 206
sovereign powers 29, 43, 44
spontaneous alignment 201
sporting practices 38, 44–6, 47, 61–2, 77,
    95–6, 101–2, 107–8, 124–5
state aid 7, 84–6, 93
    comparison with US and GATT law 89
    distortions of competition 85, 90
    'granted directly or indirectly through state
        resources' 86–8
    selectivity 88
state autonomy *see* autonomy of Member States
subsidiarity 47, 175, 176–8
    non-compliance with 181–5
Sunday trading rules 66–8, 72, 227
Sweden 74

tax measures 8, 70, 71
technical standards 53, 55, 56, 57, 144, 146,
    147, 223
tobacco products 164, 165, 168–71, 174, 175,
    177, 184, 212–14, 226, 232
trade barriers 8, 10, 18
    case law 22–3
        Cassis de Dijon 53–7, 66, 67, 99, 103–5,
            108, 109, 114, 115, 117, 135, 144,
            146, 147, 226, 228, 229
    home/host state 54, 56, 70, 102, 106, 132, 133
    justification 63, 64, 99–100
        abuses 131–3
        competing interests 123, 125, 128, 143, 148
        competition law 106–9
        consumer protection 100, 103, 105, 115–21
        environmental protection 100, 104, 112–14
        free movement law 103–6
        mandatory requirements 103
        margin of discretion 102, 143, 148, 149
        public health 100, 101, 102, 109–12
        Treaty provisions 100–3
trade unions 96

transfer of undertakings 205
Transatlantic Trade and Investment Partnership
    (TTIP) 145
Treaty of Lisbon 19–21
    ratification by Germany 185
Treaty of Maastricht 197
Treaty of Rome 15
    labour market regulation and social policy 190,
        191, 194
Treaty provisions
    conferral 3–5, 8, 11, 12
    control over measures adopted at national
        level 5–10, 229
    definition of internal market 1, 3, 10, 15, 227
        lack of precision 13
    free movement *see* free movement provisions
    harmonization and *see* harmonization
    justification of trade barriers 100–3
    legislative action: positive rule-making 10–13
    personal scope 95–8
    pre-emption 209–11
    social policy 200–1
        approximation/harmonization 203–4, 205
        legislation on social policy 201–3
    variety of terminology 91
Turkey 25

UK 18, 88
    company law 132
    Maastricht Protocol 197, 198
    re-negotiation package 185
    Sunday trading rules 66–8, 72
unfair commercial practices 161, 162–3, 164
unfair terms in consumer contracts
    160–1, 164

vertical distribution of competences 1–2, 29,
    30, 57, 223–4, 227, 228
veto 17, 18

waste disposal 34, 112–13, 114
wine growers 158, 215
worker protection 86, 104
workers 34
    see also labour market regulation
Working Time Directive 196, 197, 198, 202
World Trade Organization (WTO) 52